"I Do !"

Couples dancing in front of small frame residence, Amarillo, Texas (The Institute of Texan Cultures, San Antonio)

"I Do!"

Courtship, Love and Marriage on the American Frontier

A GLIMPSE AT
AMERICA'S
ROMANTIC PAST
THROUGH
PHOTOGRAPHS,
DIARIES AND
JOURNALS
1715–1915

Cathy Luchetti

CROWN TRADE PAPERBACKS
NEW YORK

HALF-TITLE PAGE: *"Marriage." Unidentified couple*
(California Museum of Photography, Keystone-Mast Collection)

TITLE PAGE: *Unidentified young woman and Joe Wells*
(Photos by Frank B. Fiske. State Historical Society of North Dakota)

Published by Crown Trade Paperbacks,
201 East 50th Street, New York, New York 10022.
Member of the Crown Publishing Group.

Random House, Inc. New York, Toronto, London,
Sydney, Auckland

CROWN TRADE PAPERBACKS and colophon are trademarks
of Crown Publishers, Inc.

Printed in the United States of America

Design by Nancy Kenmore

Library of Congress Cataloging-in Publication Data
Luchetti, Cathy, 1945–
"I do": courtship, love, and marriage on the American frontier/
Cathy Luchetti.—1st paperback ed.
1. Courtship—United States—History. 2. Marriage—United States—History.
3. Frontier and pioneer life—United States. 4. United States—Social life and customs.
I. Title.
HQ801.L828   1996
306.73'4'0973—dc20   96-15
                                              CIP

ISBN 0-517-88449-6

10 9 8 7 6 5 4 3 2 1

First Edition

"When Love Is Young" (Photo by E. W. Kelley. Library of Congress)

Unidentified couple (Library of Congress)

To those who look for love,
those who have lost it,
and those—most blessed—who
live each day
with love's immediacy.

Sergeant (3d U.S. Infantry) and friend, Fort Stanton, New Mexico, ca. 1886–90 (Museum of New Mexico)

Acknowledgments

WITHOUT THE PAINSTAKING JOURNAL-KEEPING OF the nineteenth century, few would know the deepest reflections of the men and women from the country's past. Free to confide their innermost thoughts on paper, they wove together past and future, inscribing a saga of fear, joy and often love, as their lives unfolded. "What should I do without my journal!" wondered Mollie Sanford. "They do not understand . . . the pleasure I take in transferring my thoughts to its pages."

Other pleasures are recalled in small, intimate discoveries, such as the wedding ring of golden braid found near River Creek in Poquoson, York County, New York, dated near 1650 and inscribed: "Time shall tell, I love thee well . . ." Past memories inform today's seekers: those who discover, in the words of Thomas Mann, that "love, not reason," is stronger than death.

Creating this book has also been a labor of the heart, made possible through the supportive efforts of curators, archivists and librarians throughout the country, including, among many, Gail Harris in the copyright department of the Library of Congress; Richard Pearce Morse at Arizona State Archives; and Leslie Masunaga, library archivist, San Jose, California. Also of great value: the contributions of Lillian Schlissel, director of American Studies at Brooklyn University, for her thought-provoking suggestions about pie socials, competition, repressed sexuality and particularly, the role of romantic love in women's growing autonomy.

To those who helped in the photographic search, my sincere appreciation: George Hobart, curator of documentary photographs at the Library of Congress; Elizabeth Jacok, librarian at the Idaho State Historical Society archives; Todd Strand of the North Dakota Heritage Center; and Lorna Mason.

Special thanks to Jacki Whitford for her invaluable research outpouring; to Dr. Richard Dillon and Bob Hawley, for continually keeping my research needs in mind; to individuals who have shared their stories—Pauline Graves, Murray Morgan, Lorelei Randazzo, Joyce L. Taylor, Virginia Turner, Peter Koch and my aunt, Grace Taylor; to folklorist and author Jim Garry for providing new ideas on the subject of marriage in the west; and to Vera Quang, for relating personal and family history concerning courtship practices.

I greatly appreciate the editorial suggestions of Eli Leon, Jim Solomon, and Susan Coerr, and the staff assistance of Zack Luchetti and Lindsay Firman. And special thanks to my intuitive and talented research assistant, Erin Williams.

Unidentified bride (Idaho State Historical Society)

Contents

Unidentified Victorian woman in period costume (Arizona State Historical Society)

Mary Hallock Foote (The Huntington Library)

*"Romance is not,
nor ever will be, dead.
Not in the heart of a
woman, anyway."*

—ANNE ELLIS

Kissing couple (California Museum of Photography, Keystone-Mast Collection)

Introduction

*"How strange the union of man and wife,
how much they are dependent on
each other for happiness."*
—Rev. Isaac Owen, 1851

HIGH HOPES AND RIGOROUS LIVING MARKED THE LIVES OF the men and women who flooded west during the peak years of the overland migration, 1830 to 1915. Bent on freedom, expansion and land ownership, countless emigrants eagerly set forth to survey what seemed theirs for the taking: a land rich in rippled grasslands and high promise and seemingly as vast as the ocean. Penniless or privileged, alone or with families, nearly all shared the same deep pangs of isolation that marked the inexorable, widening distance between themselves and home. As the miles mounted, some panicked, some prayed, and a number chose to bravely seek romance and follow their hearts through the timeless paces of courtship, love and, often, marriage.

Little wonder that when overloaded wagons were forced to "lighten up," last to go was the cedar-scented repository of many a marriageable young girl's dreams—the hope chest. Here, visions of veils superseded sunbonnets as westering young women sought out beaus with high morals, good sense, honest intentions and steady habits—lofty requirements that might have given pause to young men with dreams of their own, perhaps to wield a whip and drive a stagecoach, to hunt and trap or to pan for gold. The search for a proper mate on America's frontier seemed particularly poignant at this unsettled time, when old values and old loves were abandoned in the headlong rush west. Transience was the norm, flirtations were frequent, love letters flew back and forth and courtship keepsakes, from lockets and silver nutmegs to silver dimes inscribed with a lover's name, were forlornly exchanged. The most intimate token of remembrance, a lock of hair, was particularly suited to the pioneer budget. The most lavish gift on record was from storekeeper Rufus Klimpton to his wife, Celina—her entire hometown Anglican church, "stolen" upriver, disassembled, and transported by barge to "give her a treat." And why not? he reasoned. Didn't she deserve a surprise?

An upstart spirit was sweeping through the land, sparking social commotion in every arena, from nuptials to politics to prayer. Westward expansion had transformed the country both socially and emotionally, with little pause for rank or gender. Few escaped its heady effects, particularly young western couples, rudderless exiles from society's "tyranny of opinion," who were breaking free of parental discipline, church hegemony and the constraint of scrupulous etiquette to confront issues of suffrage, mid-Victorian moralism, women's growing independence, the new availability of contraceptive devices and an upsurge of cheap and easily won western divorces. And more: there was also the frontier phenomena of common-law marriage, interracial sex, Mormon polygamy, utopian free love, ascetic communes and brides by mail—much of which was brought to the fore by the dread "unshackling" of the American woman. "[No] nation [is] organized in the same manner as the Americans," French critic Alexis de Tocqueville reflected, struck by the spirit of civic irreverence and feminine independence that prevailed. The issue was simple to a lawmaker in Cheyenne, Wyoming, after women in the territory won the vote in 1896: "To the lovely ladies," he toasted. "Once our superiors, now our equals."

Arizona couple in swing, California, 1880s
(Arizona State University Libraries)

Kinship was still integral to the marriage process—yet parents drifted in and out of importance as the frontier courtship scene evolved. Autonomy blossomed, filial obedience declined and couples married for love, not property, in the freewheeling, free-choice style of the day, gambling that industry would overcome all obstacles, even poverty. "You must not repine," a penniless young John Coalter advised his fiancée, Marie Rind, when she questioned their financial future. "You must be chearful and happy [for my fate] is interwoven with your[s]. . . ."

Even religious values lapsed, as young couples used prenuptial pregnancy to force reluctant parental blessings. The same strict Calvinism that produced such impedimenta as the courting lamp—a small pewter burner with limited oil that flickered an ominous warning as tryst time was up—also led to the immodest Pennsylvania Dutch custom of bundling, when a suitor bedded down overnight with his sweetheart after an arduous day of "keeping company." What parent, after all, could send a young fellow out the door at night, when homesites were far-flung and winter nights so cold? Courting couples, often blessed with names such as "Praise God Barebones," "Consider Adams" and "Freelove Drummond," were bundled into the same bed as casually as if Calvinism had ceased to exist. Even the clergy approved of the practice as long as the girl was tightly swaddled with a long wrapping sheet, tied at the feet and separated from her suitor by a heavy dividing board festooned with sleigh bells, rigged to ring at the tiniest jostle. Bells, boards and bunting sheets proved wholly inadequate, and the thirty-year period in which rural couples "bundled" produced more arch commentary and early offspring than any time in American history, save perhaps the years of the "love feasts" of the Great Revival. Bundling was snidely dubbed the unofficial means of testing fertility before commitment, and commenced, wrote Washington Irving, "where [marriage] usually finished."

Such a laissez-faire attitude was common as long as the couples met under the parental roof, came from local families and happily accepted supervision. Yet the security of a stable community often proved false; "Thou Shalt Not" often led to "Oh, Why Not," as groups of local youth danced until dawn, strolled hand and hand in the moonlight and made merry at balls and barbecues without much ado. When Pamela Brown attended the Town Meeting Day dance in her tiny village, she "staid out until about day" and "danced until tired of it" and no one thought a thing of her behavior. Wasn't she with neighbors, after all? Curfews eventually grew stricter as activities accelerated and marriageable young girls clamored to leave their rural homes for the cities, where impropriety lurked and restless urban youth cruised the public streets, gallivanting their way to and from nickelodeons, theaters and dance halls.

Feminine independence brought further discord; a liberalization of the middle-class code of sexual conduct took place between 1870 and 1920, as freedom-seeking belles clamored to vote, voice opinions, open bank accounts and be paid a reasonable wage—hardly attractive attributes of a modest, traditional "angel of the hearth," whose virtue was presumed to uphold the safety and security of the social order.

Such contrariness sparked deep parental concern, raising doubts about daughters who embraced careers, left home or settled afar in guest hotels or boardinghouses. Who would take a parent's place and guide their romantic lives? Or caution a girl against loud talking, undue familiarity or laughing in the street? *The Boston American* warned against "cheap emotions and light flirtations," while the *Ladies' Home Companion* inveighed against "removing gloves during a formal call"—but had little to say about "spooning" and "sparking," the true parental concern. Furthermore, who would judge the social activities permissible for virtuous young girls? The answer: a chaperon, whose brood

Unidentified engaged couple
(Photo by Frank B. Fiske. State Historical Society of North Dakota)

Unidentified couple (University of Wisconsin–Lacrosse Murphy Library)

ing presence on the social scene had become a fixture by 1880, preventing well-brought-up youth from nestling too close in the dark or holding hands in public. A chaperon softened the reality of a youth's first breakaway from home, but was powerless in the case of a far more grave situation: the mismatch. As democratic youths demanded the freedom to choose their mates at will, the social impediments to prevent an error were no longer in place. A desirable spouse was still linked to lineage, parental approval and bankability, but in the west, who could be sure of who was what? The country teemed with footloose men, from European nobility, schoolteachers, artists, entrepreneurs and shysters to the ubiquitous cowboys, who swaggered and swore and dressed like gypsies, consorted with hussies and sought out saddles, not wives. Obviously, they were beneath consideration as husbands. Yet Nannie Alderson, a West Virginia socialite, was helpless to explain her attraction to Walt, the rogue son of the family friend whom she was visiting in Kansas. Decked out in a tall sombrero and chaps that squeaked at every step, Walt was every inch the dreaded cowboy, with twinkling eyes and bursting with energy, who had run away to Texas at the age of twelve and, for some reason, chosen just that day to return home. Nannie was spellbound. "He [is] tall . . . blue-eyed, and of fine appearance," she pointed out to her anxious parents, who were nearly speechless with fear that a man of such wild reputation and work-for-hire status would make a bid for their daughter. Walt's eventual decision to start a cattle ranch in Montana bespoke a brighter future, and, reluctantly, the Aldersons blessed what was surely inevitable. The couple commenced to wed.

Marriageable young women were more concerned about male suitability than availability; with record numbers of westering men and fewer women by far, the role of a debutante in western society was assigned to any available female—looks, age and dowry aside. Marriageable girls were few, and those who arrived west were free to pick and choose among dozens of eager suitors who jostled and argued for attention.

By 1865 record numbers of Civil War widows added to the staggering gender imbalance between east and west—as many as thirty thousand unattached women were recorded back east, while the western demand for brides was so great that a visitor to Texas in 1837 noted "no more than sixty or seventy females . . . in the whole population of Houston." In fact, he added, "the bushes were beaten along the Brazos . . . to make up the necessary complement." As a venture for profit, dozens of women were to be shipped "round the slope" from the east to Oregon and California by matchmaking entrepreneurs Asa Mercer and Eliza W. Farnham. The women were highly respectable—Farnham's girls were vouched for by the likes of Horace Greeley and Henry Ward Beecher, while a hundred Mercer girls, recruited as "school teachers and music teachers," were touted as women of "intelligence, modesty and virtue." They arrived in Puget Sound to a lively male welcoming committee and were wed within a year— even an older belle who accidentally lost her dentures overboard when seasick and then flashed a brave but toothless smile to the men waiting on the dock. No sooner had one shipload of "the girls" disembarked than a wistful observer voiced the hope that "Mrs. Farnham could send 10,000 more."

In fact, romance, and the concept of romantic love, was revolutionary for nineteenth-century women, more important, even, than suffrage. Men could leave home for land, adventure and opportunity, but women, historically, had been denied such freedom. With romantic love came the first unassailable way to strike out on their own, leaving behind dictatorial parents, family servitude and arranged marriages. Romantic love often drew women west to claim Oregon Donation Act acres, to homestead and to marry, turning the U.S. government into the equivalent of a marriage bureau.

Woman overlooking rural scene ("West" Collection, National Archives)

Bride and groom beside decorated carriage, probably in Lee County, Texas
(From Grace Walker, Seguin, Texas, The Institute of Texan Cultures, San Antonio)

Courting couple (Dresher Collection, Kansas State Historical Society)

Romantic love thus altered and affected the tide of history in the west, as whole populations shifted to fill gender voids. But other relationships also had their effect. Prostitution drew women west in unprecedented numbers, constituting the largest single employment opportunity for women outside the home, from one boomtown to another, and interracial unions sparked both racial hatred and racial mingling—and even influenced trading patterns between Native Americans and mountain men.

Romantic or arranged, the idea of marriage was foremost in the feminine mind, and young girls, no matter how far west they traveled, still hoped that personal beauty would lead to a better match, a notion that was generally encouraged by parents, peers and society at large. Careful mothers noted the effects of coarsen-

ing sunburn on their girls' delicate necks and noses and scoured their faces with lemon and vinegar, or cut cardboard strips from shoeboxes to stiffen drooping sunbonnet brims to block the burning sun. The girls, meanwhile, dabbed on vanilla for perfume, softened their hands nightly in gloves filled with chicken fat and rolled their hair in paper curlers. Yet despite the push toward pampering, a young girl's "coming out" ceremony on the frontier was often heralded by harsh sun, malnutrition, illness and fatigue rather than pomp and French millinery. The result: stronger, more opinionated women who, over time, claimed new rights for themselves, politically and emotionally, prompting French critic Alexis de Tocqueville to note his frequent "fright" at the "boldness with which women in America manage[d] their thoughts and language." Like many Europeans, he believed that such rampant equality would spawn "weak men and disorderly women"—a caution not without basis.

In the west, a dogged and determined cadre of women had shifted from the role of "sunbonnet saints" into one of sheer self-reliance; they were women to be reckoned with, who were less willing to settle for a second childhood just to please a man. Domestic patriarchy gave way, as had the British monarchy on American soil, to the new, democratic ideal, "companionate marriage," changing tyranny and servility into the "mutual forbearance" of partners who saw happiness as their standard, rather than compulsory obedience. Such matrimonial democracy worked best among the educated, urban elite rather than in makeshift backwoods shanties.

Perhaps one of the first advocates of such independence was Abigail Adams, who pleaded with her husband in 1776: "Do not put such unlimited power in the hands of the husbands. Remember all men would be tyrants if they could." Another woman, Malinda Jenkins, reacted so strongly to Jonah Small's "management" of her life—reading and hiding her mail—that she pitched his engagement ring into the bushes. "I never want to see your face again," she cried. Nor did she.

Such optimistic thinking suited the "new," post-Victorian female well: she had shaken loose from old restraints and now quested for a man modern enough to adjust to the emerging order, yet who retained sensitivity enough to employ the language of romance. Such a man was Hutchings Hapgood, whose stormy marriage to newswoman Neith Boyce was a war song of reprisals, long separations, extramarital affairs and tearful reunions, mutually presided over by both with surprising equanimity. Other men were less enlightened, viewing women as weaker vessels and lissome children. When one young man called his sweetheart, Emily Magill, "a child in many ways," saintly enough to "turn weeds into immortal flowers," his days of popular metaphor were numbered. In the west, the "vessels" were tougher, more resilient and more demanding than ever before—and many had the courage to divorce if a marriage turned sour. In San Joaquin County, California, alone, there were 210 divorces between 1852 and 1877—all initiated by women protesting fraud, cruelty, neglect, intemperance, desertion, adultery or a combination thereof. "It would appear as if there were some hidden law compelling ladies to obtain divorces from their first husbands and choose others," wrote Louise Palmer from Virginia City, Nevada, echoing an earlier thought by a backwoods woman who tried to explain local matrimonial mores to a fascinated British traveler: "My husband's got to . . . make himself agreeable to me if he can," she stated. "If he don't, there's plenty will."

On the frontier, courting men and women met, mingled and marked the passing days with familiar themes of music, dance and conviviality. British lawyer James Bryce found the west to be "the most American part of America," a convivial land in which frolics and festivities sprang to life overnight, along with bees and balls and taffy pulls, during which outmoded social rigidities were

Portrait of two couples, Las Cruces, New Mexico
(Rio Grande Historical Collections, New Mexico State University Library)

abandoned to the squeal of a wild violin and the rising excitement of a night-long fling.

Urban etiquette was cast aside as couples met, chatted, flirted and gaily took to the floor, swinging to the insistent music of polkas and the Scotch reel. Young girls were no longer tied to formal apparel in the buttoned-to-the-chin respectability of the earlier 1800s. Temporarily freed of fashion's dictates by several thousand miles of rough and lonely terrain, ladies tossed aside what remained of hats, feathers, bustles and dust-gathering trains and turned instead to simpler lawn and muslin gowns that doubled for dance-floor use or domestic duties—their own version of frontier dress reform. Circumstances lent style to rural events. Dancers who lined up for a quadrille in a hand-hewn barn "leaped" through the movements of the dance Prairie Queen in

Playing cards, 1909 (Museum of History and Industry, Seattle)

unforeseen ways: the hand-planed puncheon floor beneath their whirling feet was laced with huge cracks—an ankle-twisting threat to the unwary that caused them to leap and jump at odd moments. Celebrants also ignored the dictates of the proper waltz, whereby "toes must be turned out at an angle of 45 degrees" and, in typically democratic fashion, danced as they pleased in the style that suited best.

Other favorite frontier flings followed the calendar of the seasons, from apple-butter bees in fall to winter revelries of chestnuting, sledding and maple-sugar pulls. The traditional twelve days of Christmas were set aside for syllabub, wassail, eggnog, hot flip and lively, romantic conversation around a smoking yule log. Church life, too, provided flirtatious focus, from fund-raising fairs and choir concerts to the emotional "love feasts" held at revivals. In large gatherings, some etiquette prevailed, making "pairing off" an unsocial and unsporting act and an offense to the single men who often organized the affairs and transported the women to and from them. Gaiety prevailed, as a Minnesota schoolteacher recalled of a hayride she chaperoned one starlit night, after which the revelers were welcomed back by a lively hostess who "donned an apron, stirred up a fire . . . baked biscuits, fried salt pork, boiled potatoes, brewed barley coffee then added great, generous cucumber pickles and twisted doughnuts to the feast . . . " Spring brought husking bees and berry picking and jaunts along the riverbank, where a couple could share a picnic lunch or lose themselves in contemplation.

In contrast, city entertainment was never farther than a streetcar ride away; nightlife offered both the bon vivant and the working girl—newly employed outside the home in offices, department stores and factories—a tempting choice of high-strung diversions. Busy tearooms beckoned, dance halls glittered and vaudeville shows rang with shouts and tinkling tunes. Plush restaurants, often considered forbidden pleasure palaces, offered private booths where couples could discreetly meet and share an evening together. Such intimacy—actually the root of twentieth-century dating—was a radical departure from the banked-passion prudery of the Victorian era, when a man could not walk arm in arm with a girl unless engaged, and even then could expect to draw comments from her male relatives.

To some, the pleasures of courtship came too late, love failed to bloom or the sorrow of death intervened. The Civil War, Indian uprisings and general ill-health from dysentery, starvation and malaria had widowed vast numbers of women, while others—often those who had nursed siblings or elderly parents until they were past the marrying years—were spinsters. Both fulfilled an important societal role in the west, acting as teachers and chaperons, milliners, church worthies and seamstresses, though in earlier times they would have attracted the taunts of pesky children who mocked their solitary role as "spinners" of wool. But in the frontier west, widows were often in demand, not only for the properties they might own, but for their expertise in domestic economy; they often remarried quickly, perhaps on the theory that "once tried, better accustomed." Such was the allure of one widow, Betsey Hamlin, that by the age of ninety-four she had accrued four husbands—Mr. Culver, Hesekiah Dunham, Nathaniel Farrar and Adamson Bentley. Her motto, often repeated to nervous young girls seeking advice: "I would just as soon stand up and get married as not!"

The role of a bachelor in frontier society was equally well defined, embracing lone uncles, cranky argonauts defending their mines from claim jumpers, and hundreds of military men and ranchers in locales so remote they had nearly vanished from society. For the bachelor male, freedom failed to grant liberation from women, since he needed females to launder and mend clothes and prepare his meals. So prized was the feminine touch that on Luzena Wilson's first day in a California mining camp, a miner

Listening to recorded music, 1909 (Museum of History and Industry, Seattle)

Two young ladies and gentleman with bicycles (Photo by Wilcox. Museum of History and Industry, Seattle)

Picnic on S.S. Orion
(Museum of History and Industry, Seattle)

Dance under the canopy of a Magnolia Oil gasoline station
(The Amon Carter Museum)

repeatedly pestered her with the offer: "Ten dollars, ma'am, for bread baked by a woman."

Bachelors suffered only a partial loss of feminine companionship, since women often dined with them at lodges and boardinghouses, and might often act as the lady-in-residence presiding over the dinner table, much as a wife would. Family needs were satisfied by visits to married friends. "Bachelor neighbors brought laughter, news, excitement and music," recalled farm wife Barbara Levorson—a fair enough exchange for home-cooked food and the short-term company of women and children. In the cities, single men were eagerly demanded as escorts for matrons whose elderly or disinterested husbands eschewed the nightly rounds of frivolous merrymaking at balls, societies and parties. Usually practiced in the upper levels of society, such attention echoed the European chivalric code: a gentleman could pay court to another man's wife as long as the relationship remained platonic. Of the young gallants in her sway, a Nevada matron once exclaimed: "It is their allotted duty to escort ladies!" In her rural

site, such an "unnatural craving" was deemed indelicate, even scandalous, while in the cities, where values varied, secular nuptials took place and divorce continued to ruffle the calm waters of precedent, such a libertine impulse would spark only a few whispers.

Most European immigrants landing on the country's shores wanted no less than a home, land to cultivate, food and friendship and, ultimately, children to carry on. Weddings transpired with happy regularity, whether held amid a cluster of Conestogas, in a dirt-walled sod hut or in the church proper. Some nuptials were clergy-blessed, but the vast prairie stretches between settlements and a lack of ordained ministers often postponed official sanction. Numerous couples lived happily as common-law partners for years before seeking the offices of priest or preacher. When couples did wed, the ceremonies were highly heterogeneous, as befitting the tangled skein of race, religion and culture found throughout the west.

In rural America, wedding fare was seasonal and sporadic,

bowing to the exigencies of hunt and harvest. A nuptial feast might offer the finest almond-iced wedding cake, festooned with cupids and flowers, banners and fringe, and even sporting a pearl-studded trelliswork between tiers—or, more often, cake and cold water served with an entrée, perhaps, of roasted coon. One Idaho missionary recalled a wedding of which half-breeds, Indians and French mountain men were treated to a frugal fare of potatoes, turnips and bacon, served without dishes. The Indians "very readily" emptied the first course of potatoes into their blankets, and then scooped into the communal milk pan for the remaining turnips and bacon.

A more fortunate couple, employing an army of friends and relatives to help, might have financed a pony keg of beer, or lemonade brewed from cold well water or, with luck, a marzipan wedding cake of egg white and nut meats shaped into sections for all sixty of the church holy days. Walnut molds with carved confectionery designs, or "sugar bakers," stamped out a good-luck message to the bridal couple upon jelly cakes, flat breads and sugar-almond cookies.

Such mellifluous treats were steeped in more than sugar; each had symbolic consequence left over from earlier decades of European wedding customs, altered only in the mid-twentieth century with the decline of religiosity, the rise of secularism and continual cross-cultural matching.

The old saying "A bride weeps on her wedding day, or tears will fall later" might describe a pioneer bride, still clutching a handkerchief as rice showered on her, a sign of fertility and luck. Cake crumbs, in English tradition, drew down good fortune, while cake under the bridal pillow secured fidelity and, as one Norwegian emigrant discovered, tapped a wellspring of sorrowful nostalgia. At the sight of a crust of bridal cake in an old steamer trunk, she cried over the morsel until it "fell into a pudding," then angrily slammed the trunk lid down on her girlhood memories.

Unidentified couple
(Smith-Keene Studio, Mankato, Minnesota.
State Historical Society of North Dakota)

From Norwegian *lefse* to rambo apples—a yellow-white apple offered as a Dutch wedding treat—the most humble nuptial meals were served up with grace and gumption to appreciative wedding guests.

From England came the belief that if a girl finishes a patchwork quilt alone, she will never marry, just as the girl who begins a quilt will not marry until the last stitch is drawn. Further augury: If a quilt is shaken out the front door, the next person to enter through that doorway will be her husband. Quilts bore the strong folkloric influence of courting, with hearts stitched onto

Unidentified urban wedding (California Museum of Photography, Keystone-Mast Collection)

Unidentified urban wedding (California Museum of Photography, Keystone-Mast Collection)

George Defender
(Photo by Frank B. Fiske. State Historical Society of North Dakota)

love would play host at a nuptial banquet; that all were welcome, all should come. At a German wedding, couples danced the polka to the din of a Callithumpian Band, led by the noisy, keening wail of stringed instruments, the "Devil's Fiddle" and the "Bull Roar." A rural couple, too plain for a hired instrument, might have settled for the moan of a log bow drawn over a tightly stretched "string" of hemp rope, crudely made but able to carry a tune, often for some distance. Ubiquitous noisemakers shattered nearly every ceremony, from Chinese to Finnish, with the clack and clatter of cowbells, horns and shotguns. The Irish saluted with fireworks, and in the west, Presbyterians adapted the custom by peppering the nuptial retreat with a volley of musket fire. One bridal couple in 1830 was saluted by the misfire of a village cannon that blew the mortar chinking from the cabin walls and blackened the pair, head to toe.

At a typical rural wedding, the bride might marry in old shoes and a petticoat of flour sacks, since brand-new brogans were too expensive and might pinch, anyway. When Anne Ellis's mother wed on Easter Sunday, her barefoot past was cruelly revealed by feet so swollen she had to soak them in a stream, with her guests nearby. A Wyoming bride refused to be cast down by circumstances; she cheerfully decided that frills and finery might be desired but her "shoes were comfortable and the apron white and . . . it could have been worse."

Those blessed with a "bridal tour," or honeymoon, found that the American version was far removed from the traditional English junket called a "honey" moon, an agreeable diversion and month-long gentle getaway for the newlywed pair. A western bridal tour, although still a getaway, would be part migration, part celebration and almost all hard work—as discovered by a young couple traveling west from Philadelphia during the height of the Indian wars. Surprised from their nuptial bed by an early-morning attack near Fort Ridgely, Nebraska, the Moores cast

the cover as the insignia of true love. Unlucky the couple that broke custom and warmed the quilt before marriage. Such beliefs, fraught with symbolism, often transformed the quilts, or the workaday task of their completion, into a metaphor of married life.

Another folk practice, typically American, often involved an object being placed under or about a bed, a quilt or a pillow—anything from a thimbleful of salt to a beef bone, a slice of wedding cake, a mirror or pea pods—to induce a vision of the lover-to-be.

Music also set the tone for the wedding event, calling out an invitation to friends, strangers and passers-by, announcing that aside romance, grabbed guns and fought for their lives, surviving through the night by luck and by pluck until morning, when they were pleased, quite literally, to survive their first day of marriage. Fortunately, only horses, not humans, were lost in the brutal attack.

Ordinarily, a honeymoon sparked intense interest from friends and relatives, although few would breach etiquette enough to pry about the young couple's destination. "You must not give it away," honeymooner Charles Andrews instructed his mother, concerning the honeymoon plan, while his bride-to-be pondered the nagging details of contraception—withdrawal, douching with hot water, ice water, alcohol or sulfate of zinc, a male sheath, a rubber cap over the uterus, or in one case, the unexplained use of cocoa butter. Ovulation timing was most popular—a means of scheduling festivities during periods of "natural infertility." For women, marriage was either choice or destiny—who could tell which?

Discreetly described contraceptive nostrums made family planning a possibility, using "rubber goods," "French Female Pills" and abortifacient powders, not to mention the folk applications of tansy root, rue root, pulverized ergot, aloe and rusty-nail-water tea. By the 1860s, more than twenty-five different chemicals clamored for attention in newspapers, postal circulars and pharmacies, each promising to solve the sexual dilemma faced by young couples.

Another problem confronted American ethnics and Old World immigrants: how to keep alive native wedding costumes, foods, music and traditions in the face of criticism, cross-cultural mingling and the inevitable process of forgetting. Although ethnic wedding customs brightened every community, with Jewish canopies and money-pinned dresses to three-tiered Danish *kransekake* wedding cake, a "perfect triumph of the confectioner's art," as time passed and succeeding generations adapted to Amer-

"The Wedding Ceremony" (Library of Congress)

ican life, some traditions began to fade. Thus when Jewish merchant Isador Choynksi married his young Catholic housekeeper, San Francisco was divided in its response. Many were shocked at such scandalous backsliding and heaped blame upon him and the upstart rabbis who performed conversions without the proper formalities. But others viewed this union in the spirit of modern change, recognizing that for every courtship and wedding custom that passed away, another prevailed—while others sprang up for future generations to preserve through the passionate lineage of romance, story and song.

PART **I** ONE

Colonial

Courtin'

First Families

"Let every man have his own wife, and let every woman have her own husband . . . for it is better to marry than to burn."

—I Cor. 7:1–9

Unidentified women entering carriage
(Library of Congress)

THE PURITAN COLONISTS MET THE "HOWLING, BOUND-less" wilderness of America clustered together in unrelieved interdependence, finding in every defeat renewal and in every failure new resolve. They were God's chosen few, cast up in a promised new land, struggling free of class restraint and religious intolerance, able to mingle together without prejudice, work in collaboration and establish a new covenant on a new continent. As religious reformers, the colonists constructed a code of laws that called for perfection and demanded strict obedience to the will of God. Yet each day brought reminders of human frailty, and the notion that the Puritans were moral bigots and uncompromisingly straitlaced is countered by a history of prenuptial pregnancies and ribald sexuality that filled the records of the New England courts. The results of such demonstrated carnality fashioned a pragmatic people, able to balance faith with facts and to view situations realistically, particularly in the realm of courtship, love and marriage.

In the first years of Puritan settlement, large numbers of men sailed from England without their wives, neglecting to rejoin their families as proscribed by law and, instead, staying on in America—single, lonely and sexually anxious. Added to their unstable numbers was a high ratio of indentured servants, who were not allowed to marry. Together they formed a sizable uncommitted male body whose dalliances and sexual vicissitudes involved as many women as could be persuaded.

Although Puritan America was a rigidly moral society, the ratio of seven men to every woman often caused "wickedness [to] grow and break forth" in the new land, including "folly and lewdness" and sins "too fearful to name," namely sodomy, called buggery. Aberrant behavior was punishable in a number of ways. In Pennsylvania, bigamists drew lifetime jail sentences; in Connecticut, incest invoked forty lashes and a huge *I* sewn upon the offender's sleeve. In one case in 1642, a teenage boy confessed to consorting with animals, and all were executed together, including a "cow, two goats, five sheep, two calves, and a turkey." In all the settlements adultery invited death, while fornication was punished by flogging.

How to battle temptation? The Puritans prayed that marriage would forestall carnality, reduce sexual indiscretions, legitimize the continual stream of children born out of wedlock and form the cornerstone of the self-contained family clusters essential to the colony's success. So serious was the marriage bargain that in Massachusetts, suitors had to post bond to ensure their adherence to local marriage rules. Although weddings were civil rather than religious, a solemnized contract was as binding as a sacrament to reformist Protestants of New England. In addition, marriage should take place early, before mischief could occur. Virginity preserved for virtue's sake was a "Popish" concept, according to the Reverend John Cotton; and also, the maintenance of this youthful state was generally unhealthy and it should be quickly eliminated. Thus, matches were struck up in rural townships between youth, even children, in order to have them wed safely.

"Companionate marriage," on the other hand, was a makeshift union without benefit of clergy or judge, so commonly forged as to defy punishment, yet often prompting wry or imaginative solutions from both. One cohabiting Connecticut couple who boldly called themselves "servant and master" was finally confronted on the street by a civil official, asked loudly if they wished to marry and, before they could answer, was pronounced man and wife.

In early America, marital roles were strongly defined. A husband was the patriarch, expecting obedience of his virtuous handmaiden-wife. She, in turn, was bound by an archaic British common-law system into complete legal dependence—robbed by marriage of her rights to sign legal documents, own property or bequeath her goods without legal intervention. Plus, she had to submit to her husband's will and relinquish to him all personal property, which created a strong material dependency. Widowed women would quickly remarry, but usually in a "shift" union, where the second husband symbolically divorced himself from any responsibility toward any debts or claims against her past husband's estate. The woman was married barefoot, sometimes without clothing at all but more frequently in a loose shift—thus arriving at her second marriage unburdened. In "closet weddings," the nude bride, according to author Linda Lipsett, was hidden behind a makeshift blanket tent, or in a closet. Grasping hands through a flap in the blankets or through a partially open door, the couple wed and the bride then changed into her finery— which, in the world of Colonial plainness, was a simple dress devoid of ribbons or buckles or any impedimenta that bespoke social standing.

Because women were scarce, their labor essential and their lives at risk, Colonial lawmakers devised a means of offering greater protection to married women, primarily by placing limits on wife beating. According to the old English law of Virginia, the only limit on domestic violence was the size of the stick a man used for spousal discipline. If it was smaller than the husband's little finger, then he was not exercising cruelty, but simply "bringing her to terms."

"Without women there is no comfortable Living for man," mused the Reverend John Cotton, acknowledging the important role played by women in Colonial society. The colonists legislated new laws, one guaranteeing a woman bed and board at her husband's expense, another allowing her to inherit from a husband's estate, and a third, decreed in 1668 by the General Court of Massachusetts, ordered that any man begetting a "Bastard childe" would have to "bring up the same" by financially helping the compromised mother. Divorce was uncommon in the early years of the eighteenth century, when the plow prevailed and

spouses were economically interdependent. Divorce was not considered acceptable, but neither was sexual incapacity. In Pennsylvania, a 1785 law decreed that impotence was grounds for divorce, although it was more common for men to sue their wives for adultery.

Indeed, the Puritan ethic, "to live soberly . . . purely, discreetly, modestly, temperately and sagely" seemed, at times, more theory than practice in the light of their struggle to dissolve all differences between civic and prophetic, as rigid restraint gave way at times to wild abandon, and both became companions in evidence in the new land.

Although Colonial Americans were still straitlaced in their habits—music presaged evil and was always forbidden—there was an oddly casual, even freewheeling aspect to courtship that began in childhood, as both sexes grew up together in sprawling, mixed-gender communities, and lasted until marriage. The effortless camaraderie of childhood extended to early adulthood; those who had played together as children, shared sleeping quarters and furrowed one another's fields saw marriage as a logical and neighborly next step. Courtship was matter-of-fact and free of coquetry, subterfuge and, for the most part, close parental monitoring—an unconventional and lenient approach that deviated sharply from the British social norm. Ideally, youth's courting hours were spent in a cozy sitting room warmed by an open-hearth fire, free from the ungodly distractions of French novels and questionable theater; there they could easily conduct a "searching and tireless preoccupation" with self, or, perhaps, a willing companion.

In the kitchen, meals were shared, books read, guns cleaned and wool spun in the fireplace's cheerful reflected glow. Young sweethearts would pledge allegiance in rapt whispers, oblivious to the warning flicker of the courting lamp. Perhaps a "courting stick" was used—a long, hollow tube with mouth- and earpiece to carry confessions back and forth in utmost privacy. So attractive was the sprawling, efficient seventeenth-century household that female members often remained spinsters; they feared leaving the security of the family hearth and chose, according to colonist Hannah Edwards, "to make Religion & knowledge their chief end."

Not all sexual fires could be so easily banked. Although religious leaders admonished vigorously and civic law was studded with grim statutes against fornication, the unbounded privacy and freedom of the young led to frequent trysting and premarital sex. Also, couples typically considered sexual union as a sign of serious intent, and bundling—the sharing of a bed between a courting couple—as its forerunner. Even after the practice had ceased, courting couples conducted warm-weather trysts, or employed another instrument of compromise, the sofa. The stronger the prohibitions against intimacy became, the greater was the temptation.

Informality stopped short when it came to parental approval, at least in the early decades of the 1700s. Slack as parents might appear, there was still a fine of five pounds levied on any young man so bold as to propose without first seeking parental approval. "A young man courted the daughter [but] proposed marriage to her parents," wrote historians John D'Emilio and Estelle Freedman, noting the importance of family connections and the priority of compatibility over romance.

Yet courtship American-style forced parents to slacken their grip on the wedded destiny of their children. Traditionally, the threat of disinheritance had kept offspring uneasily homebound well into their adult years. But as homestead lands opened up farther west, there was little left to keep ambition shackled. Why wait a lifetime for a parcel of overworked paternal acreage when, farther west, there was land aplenty, free for the taking? A couple could easily begin anew with the same spirit of upstart democracy shown a generation earlier by their forebears.

For descendants of the Puritans, new immigration brought new angst; the strain of coping with a diverse society of Catholics, Anabaptists, Calvinists, Separatists and even some Jews drove many to seek a tranquil utopia in communal society. Here Rappites, Shakers, Owenites, Mormons, Zoar Separatists and Noyes Perfectionists channeled Scripture through a practice of mutual criticism, communal living, severe paternalism and, in some cases, spousal selection. Here they could safely ignore heresy in contemplative seclusion of the like-minded.

Although some of the groups were not established until well into the 1800s, they were spiritual descendants of the first protesters, the Quakers. Even in the New World, Quakers were mercilessly banned, branded, mutilated and hung, finally fleeing to Philadelphia from New England in the early 1700s to live out their dissent under the aegis of William Penn.

In Quaker society, young women viewed their spinster elders as leaders, and expected to be "called to task" for religious infractions, perhaps marrying outside the faith or, worse, engaging in worldly behavior or premarital sex—always a concern.

So abundant were these colonies that, according to historian Robert Handy, "well over a hundred communities in which property was held in common were inaugurated." Some of the groups were sacred, others secular, but all found means of religious expression that revolved, somehow, around sexuality. The Adamites worshiped while nude and were termed "heretiques" in the most decided terms by the Connecticut legislature in 1656.

Groups espousing celibacy included the Rappites—devout pietists who founded Harmony and Equality communities in Pennsylvania, and Zoar, Ohio—and the Shakers, ranked most prolific among the celibates and who enlivened the mid-1800s with a mysticism that often gripped them in wordless songs, ecstasy or joyful, trembling dances that were, in fact, physical preparation of the spirit for Christ's coming. The revelations of

Mother Ann Lee established a new order based on celibacy, peace, community and equality—claiming "equality of the sexes, virgin purity and unworldliness." Such notions angered many Christians, who were irked by the idea of gender equality and simply baffled by the idea of celibacy. Did not celibacy threaten the foundations of family structure? And wasn't the wild, uninhibited "dancing" of the sect lewd, even licentious in its abandon? Mother Ann was routinely accused of harlotry, drunkenness and witchcraft.

As the years flew by, Shaker "estacies" were channeled into a type of folk dance. By 1821, the seventeen Shaker societies, in eight states, had a total membership approaching five thousand; but without procreation, found their growth threatened. How to reproduce without sexual encounter? How to repopulate without bearing children? Orphans were regularly adopted, but at maturity, nine out of ten left the fold. Industrialization, shifting populations and the group penchant for celibacy further diminished this pious membership. "Go home," said Mother Ann to two believers, "set out apple trees, and rise calves . . . and gather something to do good with."

In the sects that allowed marriage, customs varied. Amish and Mennonite women wore caps during marriage as a visible sign of subjection, and unmarried women, as if to rehearse for their wedded future, would also don the same proper headgear, although of a slightly different size and design. To "depart the Gospel plainness," argued a petition of the German Baptist Brethren in 1886, would "destroy oneness" and invite the "popular fashions of a proud world." Interestingly, plain dress among the sects, used to promote human equality, also served as a sign of married women's inequality.

One group established in Oneida, New York, espoused a third marital option: complex marriage. The Noyes Perfectionists argued that true belief exonerated all sin, leaving the faithful free to participate in the Noyes system of complex marriage, whereby each woman wed every man and all lived accordingly in a roomy central house erected for their unique, syndicate activities. Perhaps to temper the intensity of so much conjugality, men were coached in the skill of *coitus reservatus*, and children were conceived only as a group decision. Other communitarian movements—Hopdale, Brook Farm, the socialist Rappites, Swedenborgians and Owenites—flowered, then folded, with only a memory to remain of the earliest, emigrating people. They marked America with their sense of mission, mingled spiritual uniqueness with civic affairs and cast the future of American love relationships in their own multifaceted images.

ABIGAIL BAILEY

Abigail and her husband, Asa, were married in Haverhill, New Hampshire, where she was a devout and longtime member of the Haverhill Congregational Church. Her faith sustained her through years of infidelity and illness, and gave her the strength to confront her husband about his acts of incest toward their middle daughter. When Abigail threatened divorce, Asa lured her west on the pretext of selling their property for mutual division; he actually planned to hold her captive three hundred miles from their home in a primitive cabin, while he returned to dispose of their home, property and children. Sick and weak, she struggled home on horseback and foiled his efforts. When he was in prison, she finally obtained the divorce so long overdue.

I, Abigail Bailey, do now undertake to record some of the dealings of the allwise God with me, in events which I am sure I ought someday to remember, as long as I live. . . .

APRIL 15, 1767

I was married to Asa Bailey, just after having entered the 22nd year of my age. I now left my dear parents—hoping to find in my husband a true hearted and constant friend. My desires and hopes were that we might live together in peace and friendship; seeking each other's true happiness till death . . .

It had been my hope to find a companion of a meek, peaceable temper; a lover of truth discreet and pleasant. I thought one of the opposite character would be my greatest disappointment and trial.

But the allwise God, who has made all things for himself, has a right, and knows how to govern all things for his own glory; and often to disappoint the purposes of his creatures . . .

Relative to my new companion, though I had found no evidence that he was a subject of true religion; yet I did hope and expect, from my acquaintance with him, that he would seek good regulation in his family, and would have its external order accord with the word of God. But I met with sore disappointment—I soon found that my new friend was naturally of a hard, uneven, rash temper; and was capable of being very unreasonable. My conviction of this was indeed grievous, and caused me many a sorrowful hour. For such were my feelings and habits, that I knew not how to endure a hard word, or a frowning look from any one; much less from a companion. I now began to learn, with trembling, that it was the sovereign pleasure of the allwise God to try me with afflictions in that relation, from which I had hoped to receive the greatest of my earthly comforts . . . Before one month, from my marriage day, had passed, I learned that I must expect hard and cruel treatment in my new habitation, and from my new friend . . .

I think God gave me a heart to resolve never to be obstinate, or disobedient to my husband; but to be always kind, obedient, and obliging in all things not contrary to the word of God. I thought if Mr. B. were sometimes unreasonable, I would be reasonable, and would rather suffer wrong than do wrong . . . I felt in a forgiving spirit towards him . . .

After three years—alas what shall I say? My heart was torn with grief and my eyes flowed with tears, while I learned, from time to time, the *inconstancy* of a husband! In September, 1770, we hired a young woman to live with us. She had been a stranger to me, I found her rude, and full of vanity. Her ways were to me disagreeable. But to my grief I saw they were pleasing to Mr. B. Their whole attention seemed to be toward each other, and their impertinent conduct very aggravating to me, and (I was sensible) provoking to God. I learned to my full satisfaction, that there was very improper conduct between them.

Now I felt as though my earthly joys were fled. . . . I kept my troubles to myself as much as I could. But I most earnestly pleaded with Mr. B. from time to time to consider the evil of his ways; and to forsake the foolish and live. But he turned a deaf ear to all my entreaties, and he regarded neither my sorrows, nor the ruin of his family, and of himself, for time and eternity.

Some vent to my private grief I found in writing it; but in such language as none but myself, or a guilty companion, could understand . . .

Soon after this, through the mercy of God, I prevailed to send away the vile young woman from our family. After this Mr. B. became again more regular, and seemed friendly. But alas, my confidence in him was destroyed in a great measure. But this I kept to myself. I labored to put these evils from my mind as much as possible . . .

JULY 1773

Alas, I must again resume my lonely pen, and write grievous things against the husband of my youth! Another young woman was living with us. And I was grieved and astonished to learn that the conduct of Mr. B. with her was unseemly. After my return home from an absence of several days visiting my friends, I was convinced that all had not been right at home. Mr. B. perceived my trouble upon the subject. In the afternoon . . . he fell into a passion with me. He was so overcome with anger, that he was unable to set up. He took to his bed and remained there till night. Just before evening he said to me, "I never saw such a woman as you. You can be so calm; while I feel so disturbed."

My mind was not in a state of insensibility. But I was blessed with a sweet composure. I felt a patient resignation to the will of

God. I thought I enjoyed a serene peace, which the world can neither give nor take away. . . .

When I came into the house, I found Mr. B. still on the bed. He groaned bitterly. I asked him if he was sick? or what was the matter? [He] told me, that as soon as I went out to milk, he rose from his bed, and looked out at a window after me; and thought that he would put an end to my life, before I should come into the house again. But he said that when he thought of committing such a crime, his own thoughts affrighted him, and his soul was filled with terror. Nor did he dare to stand and look out after me; but fell back again upon his bed. Then he said he had a most frightful view of himself. All his sins stared him in the face. All his wickedness, from his childhood to that hour, was presented to mind. . . .

Much time I had spent upon my knees, in my closet, pleading with God for him. I longed and wept for him in secret places. I had long been impressed with an idea, that Mr. B. would not lead a common life; that he would be uncommonly *bad*; or uncommonly *good* . . . I now lived in peace and comfort with my husband; willing to forgive all that was past, if he might but behave well in the future.

JOHN CONNELL

John Connell's first marriage, in 1791 to Mary Hedges, was recorded at West Liberty, Ohio County, Virginia. After her death, his desire for a second wife led him to many a last-minute substitute. His acquiescence and the girl's own unquestioning obedience in the matter reflect the contractual and economic aspects of marriage at the time, rather than the romantic. On March 14, 1812, John Connell was determined to wed—no matter to whom. His bride turned out to be Eleanor, the youngest daughter of John and Eleanor (Dawson) Swearingen of Brooke County.

Eleanor was born 28 June 1786. Her father, John, was a Revolutionary soldier. A man of determination and strong discipline, no doubt inherited from his Dutch ancestor, Garret Swearingen. He believed as many of that day, that marriages should be planned and contracted for, by the parents for their daughters. The marriage of one of his older daughters was arranged with the widower, John Connell, although the young lady was in love with her cousin and did not want to marry John, who was many years her senior.

On the day of the wedding, relatives and friends of both families gathered from far and near and sat at the Swearingen home. In pioneer fashion, food and strong drink were plentiful. The celebration of the occasion began early in the afternoon and extended through the night. That evening when the nuptial time drew near, John Swearingen left his guests, ascending the stairs, [and] only in minutes returned with a stern look on his face and ushered his prospective son-in-law through the front door to privacy without. Their departure was hardly noticed, though some showed signs of curiosity which was quickly dispelled upon the return of their host and the bridegroom.

John Swearingen returned to the second floor and John Connell took his place near the minister. The usual moments of tension and expectancy that captures a gathering on such occasions was prolonged into one of restlessness and wonder, but at last the father and the bride, beautifully dressed for the occasion, descended the stairs. Whispers and exclamations of surprise and excitement filled the air, for the pale and trembling bride who walked forth and married John Connell, was Eleanor, not her older sister, who shortly before had escaped through a window, descended a ladder and eloped by horseback with her cousin.

After finding that one of his "birds had flown the nest" and that Eleanor, a younger sister, had been of help in the escape, Swearingen angrily stated, "If John Connell was willing to marry a younger and prettier bride, there would be a wedding that night as planned." With no further ado, he left to consult with his prospective son-in-law. After being assured by Swearingen that if Eleanor too would agree to the match, John Connell declared his willingness and that, as Clerk of Court, he could adjust the necessary documents. Swearingen then returned to his weeping wife and daughter, who through fear and obedience, complied with his stern demands. With her mother's help, Eleanor put on the new dress, dried her tears and on her father's arm, became the bride in place of her sister . . .

John Swearingen's action on the occasion . . . brought expected criticism from very few; many admired his discipline, while others felt that he was doing the best thing for his family and for one of his daughters and at the same time, saving a good son-in-law. The majority, however, were entertained and delighted and felt the wedding a great success and thereafter gave it little thought.

PART **II** TWO

Courtin' by

the Mile

Trappers and Traders

RELIEF FROM THE CONSTANT ROUND OF GROG FEASTS and yarn spinning in the fur trade forts of the old northwest came in a particularly joyless fashion: womenless dances, where motley members of the fur trade, called *couriers des bois,* or free traders, would paddle down the Missouri River and stop at the military posts for day-long binges of hard drinking, reckless fighting, carousing and thievery. For dress, some wore rancid clothes of "well-greased" buckskin and stiff buffalo hide, while others, of a more formal mind, donned "blue capots, tasseled caps and woven red sashes" to spend the day firing musket rounds aimlessly in the air while downing "four or five glasses of Grog" and shouting to all, "Compliments of the Season," according to an 1839 record from Fort Simpson, Oregon.

Lacking fiddles or flutes, these bewhiskered, roughshod men, inebriated and usually spoiling for a fight, would hum and sing to accompany each reel, daring any comment or ridicule of their "music." Such bachelor flings were "big drunken spree[s]" according to early explorer Charles Larpenteur, in which the unruly men were finally subdued into a drugged sleep by laudanum-laced whiskey served up by the besieged officers of the fort. "This life makes a young man sixty in a few years," wrote trapper Peter Skene Ogden in 1825, describing an existence borne out in violence and survived by only the wary, the quick and the fearless. From 1820 to 1831 violent death had claimed 152 mountain men, their passing shrugged aside with the laconic phrase "Gone under, maybe."

By 1832 the first steamboat had reached the head of the Yellowstone River, bringing civilization to the far reaches of the fur trade society, but few women. Finding a wife became a full-time pursuit, since women—at least Anglo women—were scarce to nonexistent, so rare that at dances, any man with a female got in free, and those who brought more than one were paid for their presence by a reward of twenty-five cents a head. Describing a typical Canadian fling, Irishman Michael MacGowan wrote: "The music and the dancing started, the men all dancing together for there were very few women . . . "

Called "demi-savages" by the popular press and snidely commented upon by European critics, the hundreds of unwashed traders busily scouring Mandan villages for buffalo robes and horses, or luxury furs of beaver, otter, mink, weasel or fox, were, to most minds, "rude, fierce and repulsive," recognized by society only for their near-animal cunning and ability to keep the fashion world stocked with furs. They were hardly deemed marriage material for anyone, much less for genteel women. Yet the moral outcry raised by missionaries, in which the "poor" trappers were constantly thrown up as examples of moral turpitude for their habit of mating with Indian women, implied otherwise.

A pervasive fear of miscegenation fired the country in the mid-1800s. Even Indian women fluent in English drew the ire of anti-miscegenasts; subsequently, they would try to disguise their intelligence to avoid notice. Increased numbers of Anglo-European settlers stirred up greater hostility toward Native American women and the inevitable mixed-blood marriages. The Factors, or senior officers at the trading forts, urged their men away from Native brides—although often for selfish reasons. Their own sprawling half-breed families teemed with daughters of a marriageable age who should, by rights, marry European men, no matter how rowdy. In North Dakota alone there were more than forty forts and posts, all occupied by such likely bachelors.

Racial antagonism had not always been the case. The Channel Islands off the Washington-Oregon coast had largely been settled by former employees of the Hudson Bay Company, whose original policy of 1670 suggested that all employees should take Native American women as mates, to ensure peaceful trading prospects.

Mountain cabin in Virginia with ladder leading upstairs (Archives of the Episcopal Church, Austin, Texas)

Thus a large and thriving mixed-blood group sprang up on Orcas Island, led by Colonel May, the "King of the Squaw Men," who declared that he would fight to prevent the settlement of the island by white families. After statehood, a judge of the Washington State Superior Court declared that all "squaw men" had to marry legally, or relinquish to their wives a third of their property, then return them to their tribes. Citizens of the island forced to comply with his mandate were so outraged they burned the judge in effigy.

The Atkin Report of 1775 also encouraged soldiers at remote frontier settings to marry Indian wives to "strengthen the place" and to produce offspring, certainly a "valuable sort of Inhabitants." Oregon governor George Simpson endorsed "connubial alliances" with Indian women and encouraged the rowdy trappers to settle down and to pledge themselves to their Native American brides.

For trappers and traders, consort and companionship with an Indian woman offered explicit advantages. During the early 1800s there were less than a thousand trappers in the entire northwest who actually tended their own traps. Instead, they relied upon a network of friendly Native Americans to provide the furs in exchange for guns, steel axes or knives. A cooperative Native American bride assured the stability of this network, allowing her husband to control the tribal fur economy by forestalling tribal uprisings. A native helpmeet could also translate from the indigenous tongue, warn of upcoming raids and patiently explain to restless Indians the true intent of the fickle Anglos—no small feat for Native Americans inclined to match words to actions. Marriage to a Native woman ensured a husband's safety—who would fail to inform a spouse of an impending Indian attack?

A good wife also ensured the orderly progress of his scattered life; she would tidy his wardrobe, fold his furs, sort his moccasins and scrape hides into supple blankets for his comfort; she would point out favorite fishing spots and the tallest strands of trees for lumber; caulk canoe seams with spruce gum, sew rips and tears with deer tendons, fashion warm suits from furs, make moccasins in winter and mittens from moosehide, prepare animal scents for trapping and ably augment a dwindling food supply during the long and hungry winter months. One young trapper, George Nelson, was saved from starvation in 1815 by his Ojibwa wife, who in one month trapped fifty-eight rabbits and thirty-four partridges for their meals. Trapper Andrew Garcia's hunting plan also devolved upon his Indian bride, Inwholise: "I . . . ride along the edge of the trees," he wrote. "[S]he would do the hunting."

Yet "squaw man!" was a pejorative term hurled at the men who slept with, lived with and often loved their Indian mates; who were at home in the tall, conical, buffalo-hide tents; who slept beneath medicine poles crowned with healing bundles; who woke in the morning to the wafting scent of cooking meat, often dog.

One man, seen with his Indian wives and children, seemed comfortable and busy; when asked how he liked Indian life, he paused only briefly to note that it was "rather lonesome." Then he shrugged and silently padded away in his carpet slippers. According to the observer, "No one else appeared, but we had glimpses of the Indian women in the [tent] preparing the meal. After supper we all sat down on buffalo robes spread on the dewless grass."

Mixed-blood couples united freely, without covenant, or occasionally were wed officially in the style of the first mixed-blood marriage on the continent—that of John Rolfe and Pocahontas, wed by the Anglican Book of Common Prayer. In other unions, a Native woman would ask for a priest, or "black robe," to preside, knowing that a Catholic ceremony and a gold ring made the matrimony official, binding her legally to her footloose spouse.

Such formality was avoided by most mountain men, although one, Andrew Garcia, broke tradition when he suggested giving a ring to his bride, Inwholise, hoping to fashion the band from a ten-dollar gold piece. His friends were startled. Why waste good money? they wondered. Wasn't she only an Indian?

Most marriages were sealed *à la façon du pays*—"according to the custom of the country," in "country unions" that called for both a bride price and two-party consent, and were common wherever French and English mountain men mingled with local tribes. One match, between Chief Factor William Connolly and his Cree wife, was held lawful in a Canadian court. Occasionally, a couple would incorporate both Indian and Christian ceremony, as did the Colorado trader John Prowers and his Cheyenne wife, Amache. The two married in a ceremony that symbolized the cultural mingling that would meld their differences throughout their married lives, invoking the blessings of both his God and hers, along with those of the members of her tribe.

"Country unions" of long standing were often formalized whenever a priest came around—Jesuits were particularly assiduous in turning convenience into sacrament whenever possible, assuming that even these roughshod members of the Catholic flock desired an ordained wedding. Imagine the surprise of Father Christian Hoeken, who arrived outside Council Bluffs in 1831 to find, instead of a population in desperate need of instruction, a desultory collection of Canadians, half-breeds and Indians so "united among themselves" they were lukewarm concerning the sacrament. Although Hoeken baptized sixteen, only three couples from the dozens in the area actually sought his nuptial benediction. How could they reject the ministrations of the church?

Mixed marriages were not without dual benefits. Many tribes, particularly the Northwest Tsimshian, had a fixed awareness of class and rank, and viewed cross-cultural marriage as a sure ele-vation of women from their low tribal status—at least as identified by white observers.

Women were seen as inferior beings, valued more as property than as humanity; even the cry "Turn out your squaws," heard at the onset of every battle, was less chivalry than economics, as both horses and women were set free to seek safety and avoid injury. Horses were essential to trade, and women to peaceful relationships. Who would pay for their loss?

Mixed marriages sowed mixed benefits—Indian women found their low tribal status slightly improved, but the benefits were hard-won, as they traded the cuffs and blows of male tribesmen for the drunken attacks of their European husbands. On this harsh frontier, far from the socializing effects of church, society or law, men felt free to abuse their native wives. Trappers were, according to early explorer Charles Larpenteur, "more or less under the influence of Liquor" day and night and had rum to blame—or thank—for the routine desertion of their wives.

In one case, a trapper named Turcot had beaten his wife so unmercifully that "all inside the fort cried shame and . . . had to interfere." Often, the husband's payment of a bride price—fifty or so fine ponies among the Flathead tribes—caused sympathetic family members to hang back, but in this case, the outraged father broke tradition and struck the unruly husband before dragging away his daughter.

Women without family defenders had no choice but to wait out the storm of spousal abuse, some with obdurate, solemn truculence, growing more silent, more repressed and more stolid with each attack, quietly weathering each outburst until they could retaliate, while others, more forthcoming, or themselves inclined to drink, would break valuable glass windows or even thrash their husbands in return. In 1859, a trapper named McNeil watched "the women of the fort [do] nothing" while a smut fire spread rapidly through the kitchen. Amazed at their hostility, he realized that "they would have been pleased to see the Fort consumed."

The fort also represented safety, and to sleep at night within its walls at night was both status and security, for both Indian women and trappers. Larpenteur described the terrible fate of three trappers who bedded at night outside the fort, sleeping with their Indian wives. That night a rival tribe staged a war party. "We found one squaw dead, shot plumb through the heart; one shot through both thighs; one through the calf; and one of the white men with two balls through the left thigh. He died the same morning at ten o'clock."

Interestingly, men who completely embraced Indian culture and left the forts and encampments to live with their wives' tribes often faced a different kind of cultural discrimination. One man who deserted a fort to live with his Native wife and her family found himself a slave, according to author Helen Meilleur. No matter how loud his protestations of fealty and brotherhood-through-marriage, the tribe insisted that he was simply a slave, fit only to cut wood and haul water. He lasted a month before returning to the fort, begging for reinstatement.

Violence and cultural confusion aside, romance often blossomed, chivalry and devotion did occur, and love's languishing knew no race or barrier, surprising couples at every turn. Early diaries and journals record the successful stories of mixed-blood families who lived in the west, whose lives of civility, faithfulness and affection were in stark contrast to the popular, Euro-American view of mixed-blood matches as sordid, unnatural and brutal. One officer, surprised at his growing affection and interest in a Native American woman, began to find her "decidedly human"—an attraction in his isolated setting, far removed from the civilized women of his past.

In crossing the barriers of time, place and race, many stories of love and fealty are found: Trapper Andrew Garcia chastely

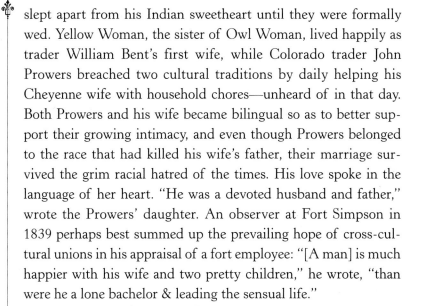

slept apart from his Indian sweetheart until they were formally wed. Yellow Woman, the sister of Owl Woman, lived happily as trader William Bent's first wife, while Colorado trader John Prowers breached two cultural traditions by daily helping his Cheyenne wife with household chores—unheard of in that day. Both Prowers and his wife became bilingual so as to better support their growing intimacy, and even though Prowers belonged to the race that had killed his wife's father, their marriage survived the grim racial hatred of the times. His love spoke in the language of her heart. "He was a devoted husband and father," wrote the Prowers' daughter. An observer at Fort Simpson in 1839 perhaps best summed up the prevailing hope of cross-cultural unions in his appraisal of a fort employee: "[A man] is much happier with his wife and two pretty children," he wrote, "than were he a lone bachelor & leading the sensual life."

DAVID CROCKETT

Both folk legend and family man, David Crockett managed to turn the ordinary ingredients of life into fame, humor and adventure, as seen in his narrative, *Written by Himself.* **Born August 17, 1786, in Greene County, Tennessee, he spent many years as an illiterate and impoverished youth, working for hire to pay off his father's debts. When finally able to marry, he faced the prevailing social condition of the day: a myriad of men, not enough women. After several attempts, he wed Polly Finley on August 16, 1806. Unhappily, she died after the birth of a daughter in 1815, and the distraught Crockett ultimately married again, reportedly more for convenience than romance.**

I have heard people talk about hard loving, yet I reckon no poor devil in the world was ever cursed with such hard love as mine has always been, when it came on me. I soon found myself head over heels in love with this girl, whose name the public could make no use of; and I thought that if all the hills about there were pure chink, and all belonged to me, I could give them all if I could just talk to her as I wanted to; but I was afraid to begin, for when I would think of saying any thing to her, my heart would begin to flutter like a duck in a puddle; and if I tried to outdo it and speak, it would get right smack up in my throat, and choak me like a cold potatoe. It bore on my mind in this way, till at last I concluded I must die if I didn't broach the subject. . . . And one day at it I went, and after several trials I could say a little. I told her how well I loved her; that she was the darling object of my soul and body; and I must have her, or else I should pine down to nothing, and just die away with the consumption.

I found my talk was not disagreeable to her; but she was an honest girl, and didn't want to deceive nobody. She told me she was engaged to her cousin, a son of the old Quaker. This news was worse to me than war, pestilence, or famine; but still I knowed I could not help myself. I saw quick enough my cake was dough, and I tried to cool off as fast as possible; but I had hardly safety pipes enough, as my love was so hot as mighty nigh to burst my boilers. But I didn't press my claims any more, seeing there was no chance to do any thing.

I began now to think, that all my misfortunes growed out of my want of learning. I had never been to school but four days . . . and did not yet know a letter.

I thought I would try to go to school some . . . so at it I went, learning and working back and forwards, until I had been . . . nigh on to six months. In this time I learned to read a little in my primer, to write my own name, and to cipher some in the three first rules in figures. And this was all the schooling I ever had in my life, up to this day. I should have continued longer, if it hadn't been that I concluded I couldn't do any longer without a wife; and so I cut out to hunt me one.

I found a family of very pretty little girls that I had known when very young. They had lived in the same neighborhood with me, and I had thought very well of them. I made an offer to one of them, whose name is nobody's business, no more than the Quaker girl's was, and I found she took it very well. I still continued paying my respects to her, until I got to love her as bad as I had the Quaker's niece; and I would have agreed to fight a whole regiment of wild cats if she would only have said she would have me. Several months passed in this way, during all of which time she continued very kind and friendly. At last, the son of the old Quaker and my first girl had concluded to bring their matter to a close, and my little queen and myself were called on to wait on them. We went on the day, and performed our duty as attendants.

This made me worse than ever; and after it was over, I pressed my claim very hard on her, but she would still give me a sort of an evasive answer. However, I gave her mighty little peace, till she told me at last she would have me. I thought this was glorification enough, even without spectacles. I was then about eighteen years old. We fixed the time to be married; and I thought if that day come, I should be the happiest man in the created world, or in the moon, or any where else. . . .

Just now I heard of a shooting-match in the neighborhood, right between where I lived and my girl's house; and I determined to kill two birds with one stone, to go to the shooting-match first, and then to see her. I therefore made the Quaker believe I was going to hunt for deer, as they were pretty plenty about in those parts; but, instead of hunting them, I went straight on to the shooting-match, where I joined in with a partner, and we put in several shots for the beef. I was mighty lucky, and when the match was over I had won the whole beef. This was on a Saturday, and my success had put me in the finest humour in the world. So I sold my part of the beef for five dollars in the real grit, for I believe that was before bank-notes was invented; at least, I had never heard of any. I now started on to ask for my wife; for, though the next Thursday was our wedding day, I had never said a word to her parents about it. I had always dreaded the undertaking so bad, that I had put the evil hour off as long as possible; and, indeed, I calculated they knowed me so well, they wouldn't raise any objection to having me for their son-in-law. I had a great deal better opinion of myself, I found, than other people had of me; but I moved on with a light heart, and my five dollars jingling in my pocket, thinking all the time there was but few greater men in the world than myself.

In this flow of good humour I went ahead, till I got within about two miles of the place, when I concluded I would stop awhile at the house of the girl's uncle . . . I was indeed just about ready to consider her uncle, my uncle; and her affairs, my affairs. When I went in, I found her sister there . . . She looked mortified, and . . . then burst into tears, and told me her sister was going to deceive me; and that she was to be married to another man the next day. This was as sudden to me as a clap of thunder on a bright sunshiny day. It was the cap-stone of all the afflictions I had ever met with; and it seemed to me that it was more than any human creature could endure. It struck me perfectly speechless for some time, and made me feel so weak that I thought I should sink down.

I, however, recovered from my shock after a little, and rose and started without any ceremony, or even bidding any body good-bye . . . My heart was bruised, and my spirits were broken down; so I bid her farewell, and turned my lonesome and miserable steps back again homeward, concluding that I was only born for hardships, misery, and disappointment. I now began to think, that in making me, it was entirely forgotten to make my mate; that I was born odd, and should always remain so, and that nobody would have me.

But all these reflections did not satisfy my mind, for I had no peace day nor night for several weeks. My appetite failed me, and I grew daily worse and worse. They all thought I was sick; and so I was. And it was the worst kind of sickness—a sickness of the heart, and all the tender parts, produced by disappointed love.

I continued in this down-spirited situation for a good long time, until one day I took my rifle and started a hunting. While out, I made a call at the house of a Dutch widow, who had a daughter that was well enough as to smartness, but she was as ugly as a stone fence. She was, however, quite talkative, and soon begun to laugh at me about my disappointment . . .

But I couldn't help thinking, that she had intended what she had said as a banter for me to court her!!!—the last thing in creation I could have thought of doing. I felt little inclined to talk on the subject, it is true; but, to pass off the time, I told her I thought I was born odd, and that no fellow to me could be found. She protested against this, and said if I would come to their reaping, which was not far off, she would show me one of the prettiest little girls there I had ever seen. She added that the one who had deceived me was nothing to be compared with her . . . so I shouldered my rifle, and started [to the reaping.] In the evening I was introduced to [the girl], and I must confess, I was plaguy well pleased with her from the word go. She had a good countenance, and was very pretty, and I was full bent on making up an acquaintance with her.

It was not long before the dancing commenced, and I asked her to join me in a reel. She very readily consented to do so; and after we had finished our dance, I took a seat alongside of her, and entered into a talk. I found her very interesting; while I was setting by her . . . her mother came to us, and very jocularly called me her son-in-law . . . I took care to pay as much attention to her through the evening as I could. I went on the old saying, of salting the cow to catch the calf . . .

We continued our frolic till near day, when we joined in some plays, calculated to amuse youngsters . . . In the morning, however, we all had to part; and I found my mind had become much better reconciled than it had been for a long time. I went home to the Quaker's and made a bargain to work with his son for a low-priced horse. He was the first one I had ever owned, and I was to work six months for him. I had been engaged very closely five or six weeks, when this little girl run in my mind so, that I concluded I must go and see her, and find out what sort of people they were at home. I mounted my horse and went away to where she lived. I found her father a very clever old man, and the old woman as talkative as ever. She wanted badly to find out all about me, and as I thought to see how I would do for her girl . . .

In a short time, my impatience was relieved, as she arrived at home from a meeting . . . There was a young man with her, who I soon found was disposed to set up claim to her . . . I began to think I was barking up the wrong tree again; but I was determined to stand up to my rack, fodder or no fodder. . . .I saw that she preferred me to all holler. But it wasn't long before I found trouble enough in another quarter. Her mother was deeply enlisted for my rival, and I had to fight against her influence as well as his. But the girl herself was the prize I was fighting for . . . I staid with her until Monday morning, and then I put out for home.

It was about two weeks after this that I was sent for to engage in a wolf hunt . . . I went as large as life, but I had to hunt in strange woods, and in a part of the country which was very thinly inhabited. While I was out it clouded up, and I began to get scared; and in a little while I was so much so, that I didn't know which way home was, nor any thing about it . . . I went ahead, about six or seven miles, when I found night was coming on fast; but at this distressing time I saw a little woman streaking it along through the woods like all wrath, and so I cut on too, for I was determined I wouldn't lose sight of her that night any more. I run on till she saw me, and she stopped; for she was as glad to see me as I was to see her, as she was lost as well as me. When I came up to her, who should she be but my little girl, that I had been paying my respects to. She had been out hunting her father's horses, and had missed her way, and had no knowledge where she was, or how far it was to any house, or what way would take us there. She had been travelling all day, and was mighty tired; and I would have taken her up, and toated her, if it hadn't been that I wanted her just where I could see her all the time, for I thought she looked sweeter than sugar; and by this time I loved her almost well enough to eat her.

At last I came to a path, that I know'd must go somewhere,

and so we followed it, till we came to a house, at about dark. Here we staid all night. I set up all night courting; and in the morning we parted. She went to her home, from which we were distant about seven miles, and I to mine, which was ten miles off.

I now turned in to work again; and it was about four weeks before I went back to see her. I continued to go occasionally, until I had worked long enough to pay for my horse, by putting in my gun with my work, to the man I had purchased from; and then I began to count whether I was to be deceived again or not. At our next meeting we set the day for our wedding; and I . . . returned to ask her parents for her. When I got there, the old lady appeared to be mighty wrathy; and when I broached the subject, she looked at me as savage as a meat axe. The old man appeared quite willing, and treated me very clever. But I hadn't been there long, before the old woman as good as ordered me out of her house. . . .

And so I told her girl, that I would come the next Thursday, and bring a horse, bridle, and saddle for her, and she must be ready to go. Her mother declared I shouldn't have her; but I know'd I should, if somebody else didn't get her before Thursday. I then started, bidding them good day, and went by the house of a justice of the peace, who lived on the way to my father's, and made a bargain with him to marry me.

ANDREW GARCIA

Garcia's travels through the Montana, Idaho and Wyoming territories were legend; he witnessed the last years of the Plains Indians, and the dwindling of the buffalo. A thoughtful man despite the rigors of his trapping environment, he fell in love with a Pend d'Oreille woman, Inwholise, whom he married legally in a Catholic ceremony, despite the incredulity of his fellow trappers. Marriage by a priest and bestowing a ring meant permanency— usually avoided by white men. After his bride's death, Garcia continued living among the roving bands of Blackfoot, Piegans, Pend d'Oreilles, Crows and Crees, and married several Indian wives. Resplendent in long hair and fringed buckskin, he bore the eponym the Squaw Kid.

It was in the fall of 1878 before the Priest came to the Cree buffalo camp on the Musselshell River, nearly one day's ride from the Pend d'Oreille camp. The Priest was a very good man, and while a whole lot more tough and rough looking than the priests and preachers of today, he was probably closer to God than some. He was called the Black Robe of the North, and his name was Father Landre. He followed the Cree buffalo camps in Canada and lived in the tepees with them . . . wherever there was a camp in Montana, and said Mass and preached to them in the Cree language. His church was a large one, the vaults of heaven and generally on a creek bank under a tree. His altar stood there, the tail end of a Red River cart. It was some sight to see, on the banks of the Musselshell, in the Indian camp, on that day when Inwholise and I were married.

Erecting a log cabin in Idaho (Idaho State Historical Society)

There were many tepees of different tribes, most of them ready to cut each other's throats . . . But here today in hypocritical brotherly love, Assiniboines, Crees, Bloods, Blackfeet, Gros Ventres, Piegans and Pend d'Oreilles met together to hear the wise words of the white man's God. More truthfully, they are here to race horses and gamble for horses at the game of playing hands. And it was certainly a wild and savage scene to see those warriors and some of the bewhiskered longhaired white men with squaws and plenty half-breeds and their women. All of us knelt down on the ground in the hot sun during Mass, when Father Landre preached to the Crees in their language telling everyone who did not understand Cree, with his hands and fingers. He made the prairie ring with his eloquence. . . .

Many of the squaws had come along to see Inwholise married to a white man, the same as a white squaw, by the Black Robe with a ring on her finger. And all of them thought it would be good medicine for a squaw to have a ring like that, and to have the Black Robe put Colon Suten's (God's) words in it. I was greatly surprised when I asked Father Landre, if I would have to get an interpreter to make Inwholise understand what he was saying to her. He asked, "I have talked with her and she can speak English as well as either you or I can, and has been to the mission school at Lapwai." I could not get her to say a word in English as long as she lived. When we were married, Inwholise thought she was nineteen years old and I was twenty-three years old.

The Indians, after going to church to hear the Black Robe's holy words till noon, made the air hum all the rest of the afternoon as they chanted . . . Toward night, many campfires lit up this scene of happy Indians gorging themselves on large chunks of broiled buffalo meat. After two days of this, the camp had a rude awakening.

Indians have many strange ways that a white man living with them had better learn quickly and heed, or he will soon come out

on the small end of the horn. [They] have what they call their Esalat (friend), and when two Indians make friends . . . it means that what one has got, the other one has got.

It was but a short while after . . . when I went in the Pend d'Oreille lodge . . . and was surprised to see my new bride in tears. Not without good reason, for squatted there was this Gros Ventre woman . . .

At first I thought it might be some kind of a squaw's pagan festival or seance, where no men are wanted, for this Gros Ventre woman was stripped to her bare pelt, without even a G-string. Before her in a small pile was her buckskin skirt with her leggings and moccasins, all a squaw is supposed to wear. While a short distance across the tepee from her was Inwholise in tears, with everything that we had brought to camp. Before her were namely three good new blankets and a few other things, while around the tepee squatted four Pend d'Oreille women silently watching this act. The Gros Ventre woman was bitterly haranguing Inwholise in Assiniboine and did not pay any attention to me.

I said to Inwholise, "What is the matter with her . . . and what are you doing with them blankets and the other stuff before you?" Inwholise said, "She is my Esalat [friend], and is saying what she has got, I have got and what I have got, she has got, and now says that because she is my Esalat she now gives me all that she has got . . . My pretty squaw skirt, leggings and shawl of white man's cloth, with my ring. I have said to her to do anything else but this, for you had already given her blankets and other things here, but she must not strip me of the clothes I was married in, and that I will not give her my ring even if she is my friend. But she is now mad at me and says she is now sorry that she did not let me die in the camp, then she would not today have a false Sapah-tan slut for her Esalat."

I then told [the Assiniboine woman] with my hands that she was not going to get the ring or anything else from Inwholise now or after this and to get back to her lodge, till she forgot this Esalat business. I then told Inwholise to put the blankets and other stuff back where she got them, and if I ever caught her giving away her or my stuff in this Indian friendship business, I would whale the camas [edible lily root, sweet to the taste and popular with many Indians] out of her.

Early next morning after promising the good Father Landre to say my prayers regular three times a day, to be a model husband and a whole lot of other promises that I did not intend to keep, we . . . bid the good Father good-bye . . . and started back to camp . . .

Now that we are ready to pull out, it is with feelings of sorrow and regret, and I hated to leave here, where I had so much happiness and hell all rolled up together. And as the warriors and women in camp stand around us, their swarthy faces show their regret, and they all say they are sorry to see me leave them and hope we will soon meet again.

The only one happy here is Inwholise, for the hour for her triumph has come at last. She is now all smiles to be on her way back to her people, but more especially to get me out and far away from the influences that dwell in this Pend d'Oreille buffalo camp . . . .

Arriving at Bozeman about noon [after traveling for several days], we went into camp about half a mile from town . . . [One of the local traders, Mr. Cooper] said, "So then it is as they are saying around town, that you had the gall to bring back with you an Indian woman." Knowing that I had a white girl in town, at first he did not believe I would do a foolish thing like that, and said that I would soon be sorry. And, if I would take his advice, the first thing for me to do in the morning would be to give that squaw a horse and some grub and send her alone on her way to her people at Lapwai, or back to the Indian buffalo camps in the Musselshell where I had found her. That he would put in a good word and smooth things over for me with my girl's people, and

help me out of this mess I had got myself into. Maybe, as no one could tell what a fool woman would do, [my white girlfriend] would forgive me and marry me yet.

I told him "So this is you the good Christian, a church deacon, who rants and prays to God every Sunday, yet you tell me to do this to her, who is my wife, just because she is an Indian? She is as good a woman as your own, and the only true friend I have got left. I told the priest the day I married her that I would stay with her till hell froze over. I meant it then and still mean it today."

When Mr. Cooper heard that I was married . . . by a priest, he apologized. He said he had thought I was like most other white men, who had Indian women and who did not believe in going to the bother of marrying them . . .

As I went on my way to the hitching rack, where I had left my saddle horse, I had to pass by several persons who had always been friendly to me. I could not fail to notice the black looks they now gave me. Instead of a friendly greeting, they went by me in silence. I knew the cause of this when I heard one fellow say to another sneeringly, as they went by me, "Squaw man."

Not long after their marriage Garcia and his wife, "Susie," rejoined the Pend d'Oreille tribe. "Like a fool," Garcia joined several of the young men on a horse-stealing raid against the Blackfeet; in the fray, his wife was mortally wounded when a Blackfoot warrior struck her on the side of the head with his coup stick. Within a few hours, she was dead. Garcia later married a white woman, Barbara, fathered four sons and lived comfortably on a ranch west of Missoula, Montana.

Unidentified emigrant family ("West" Collection, National Archives)

Overland Adventurers

"Oh! The power of love to win a sweet young girl from her parents and home to follow her young husband into the wilderness . . ."

—ELIZABETH BURT

"Except for love . . .
this is a wretched existence."
—ISABELLA BIRD, COLORADO, 1873

AS MEN AND WOMEN STRUGGLED WEST, UNSURE OF DAN-gers or even destination, they proved remarkably resilient on an equally formidable frontier—the emotional reaches of the heart. With every jolt of the Conestoga wagon, startled grouse flared through the grass, wings flapping with the same sharp sound as the snapping canvas tops. With every bump, strange longings stirred, for freedom, for companionship and for loved ones, near and far. The huge prairie schooners, weighted with goods and expectations, formed a link between east and west, and bore, as described by historian Dale Morgan, a cargo of "human nature on the loose." Freed of societal and familial restrictions, travelers could hurdle sex-role boundaries with the same alacrity as they forded rivers, with men learning to cook, women to shoot, and both viewing each other with newfound respect. On the overland crossing, "romantic" became a pane-gyric both for exceptional terrain and for the adventures of the heart.

Large-scale overland migration began in 1846, reaching a peak in 1850 when fifty thousand traveled west. The crossing formed one of the major societal shifts in the nation's history, irrevocably jostling family structure, cultural values, courting habits and patterns of domesticity. Customs of long standing were deeply shaken, stability undermined and families fractured. "Democracy unites brothers to each other," wrote Tocqueville. Yet democracy, and its spiritual mentor, manifest destiny, also tore families apart, causing a rapid rise in the rates of separation and divorce. Abandoned mates had few legal means of tracking a vanished spouse, or of obtaining financial support, other than

publishing notices; in one, posted in 1845, a Joseph Klepser of Delphi, Indiana, announced the elopement of his wife [the mother of three children] with a blacksmith "who had also left a wife and children behind." There was little chance they would be found, as United States legislation did not extend into the territo-ries. "[When] they got on the plains," Keturah Penton wrote, "they were out of reach of the law of God or man."

As the columns of exhausted emigrants continued west, their nine-hundred-pound wagons, packed with food, bedding and utensils, lumbered past unkempt cairns of bleached buffalo bones, hastily knocked together to commemorate unnamed vic-tims of cholera, Indian attack, scurvy, typhoid, malaria, dysen-tery and smallpox, all of which claimed two thousand trail-side victims in 1850 alone.

The journey west was always difficult. "Too slow," com-plained traveler Carlisle Abbott about the speed of a wagon train, then, changing his mind: "Too fast!" "Confusion!" cried pioneer Israel Hafle, his goods in one place, tent in another and wagon in a third. "Whoa!" echoed others, tired of the tedium of driving twenty-odd miles per day with hands, faces and clothes stiff with grime and dust. "Wife, wife, rise and flutter!" cried out one emi-grant each morning, fearing that she might linger too long in bed.

At night, with the chores done and children retired, the "female portion" of the train often met in the moonlight to pon-der the events of the day and muse about human frailties, mostly male, and always much in evidence. Heroism, they found, was a condition of the heart, unbound by gender, belonging to any per-son with an enterprising spirit, and often revealed during crisis. Women accustomed to relying upon men often found, like Mag-gie Hall, that fear could strike any heart. When she heard the cry, "Indians!" one day, she was startled to see frightened men "crawl . . . into the wagons" to join the women already huddled there.

But women, too, lost heart, becoming melancholy and delusional, occasionally trying to flee the wagon train and return home. One woman, racked with longing for her old way of life and terrified of the dangers ahead, set fire to the family wagon as a violent, emphatic statement of her desperation. Keturah Penton, traveling to Oregon in 1848, heard a "muffled cry and a heavy thud as tho something was thrown against the wagon box." It was a baby, flung by a furious, swearing husband, who warned his wife to "keep her mouth shut or he would give her more of the same." The baby lived and the journey continued, simply one more domestic outburst in which private anguish became public domain.

Some could not take the violence, despair and illness of the crossing and became "gobacks," who, according to historian John D. Unruh, in 1841 were nearly 10 percent of all overlanders. Traveler Ezra Meeker in 1852 was startled to see seven wagons thundering east, driven by women. Whether they were widowed, divorced, single or simply fed up, he never knew, but had he waited longer along the same trail, he might have seen another party of "gobacks"—that of forty-niner John Edwin Banks, who left his claim for the single reason that his wife was homesick, he loved her "more than gold," and he intended to take her home, just as she wished.

On the westward crossing, "the comforts of life could not be had for love or money," according to emigrant Harriet Sherrill Ward. Yet, countered Laura Winthrop Johnson, observing the vast, unbroken tract of prairie and sky, "there [was] something on the Plains that cannot be found elsewhere . . . something you must go there to find."

For many, "something" turned out to be a frontier romance, sparking up tinder-hot between the single men and women on the wagon train, or rekindled between couples already long wed. At night, as the campfire sparked and faded, so, too, did the rigid patterns that had once governed the ways of the heart. The old

Daisey DeGraff
(Photo by Frank B. Fiske. State Historical Society of North Dakota)

mores—chaperon and church—fell away on the frontier, and love's surprises often knew no restriction. The air was charged with the kinetic energy of struggle, quest, friendship and flirtation, with young men eyeing girls who giggled and whispered about their beaus, scrutinized by watchful sets of parents, who had seen tensions flare around girls as lovely as Agnes Stewart, and were prepared to intervene. Agnes, cited by historian Lillian Schlissel, was a campfire attraction. "Sometimes I think our Agnes is made of lodestone for she draws [men] to her [so] powerful," wrote her sister. While Agnes beamed and sizzled, others blushed and ducked, caught in a timeless, ceaseless courtship promenade that took on a different character wherever it was conducted.

"There is a great many young men loves me about Hear," a young girl wrote in 1852, her romantic musings accompanied, perhaps, by the nightly odor of onions mingled with pine or sage, and, after supper, by the stories, songs, good-natured rivalries and the courting that inevitably took place. One emigrant recalled an evening when "young ladies came over . . . and we had a concert with both guitars. Indeed it seemed almost like a pleasant evening at home. We could none of us realize we were almost at the summit of the Rocky Mountains." Helen Clark, from Plano, Illinois, remembered the fiddler from another camp who went from wagon to wagon, trying to raise a dance on the turf, inviting "ladies and gents" to come down and caper to his sprightly melodeon. Zilhart, an overland traveler, arrived at a camp on August 24, 1850, to find two hundred people gathered—travelers with a zest for merrymaking—whom he joined, spending two days with "danc[ing] to mid-night."

Newlywed couples created a honeymoon event out of the westward crossing, finding in the dusty trail west a way to combine two symbolic acts in one. A riverboat would take them down the Allegheny to Pittsburgh, or down the Ohio River into Mis-

souri. By 1855, they could take the railroad as far west as Iowa. But those wishing to go farther inevitably ended up beneath billowing canvas sheets or trudging behind the oxen toward the Pacific, as did eighteen-year-old Susan Magoffin, who rode along the Santa Fe Trail in 1846, comfortably ensconced in her own carriage, accompanied by "fourteen big waggons," and always under the watchful eye of a spouse. He tenderly built her a shaded blanket-and-saddle sofa at every stop, afraid she would overheat in the New Mexico sun. Nuptial journeys had been popular since the 1820s—vaguely tied to a Southern folk tradition that predicted bad luck if a wedding night was spent in a couple's permanent home. Thus, to travel became a kind of insurance for a successful marriage.

Few left home and family without regrets. "I knew it would be the last visit I would make . . . whether I lived or not," Keturah Penton sighed, leaving her parents' for her odyssey to Oregon. Ella-Elizabeth Spaulding, just married to Joseph Reed in 1854, treasured the last memento of her loving, exuberant Vermont family: shirt cuttings and fabric scraps pieced together by sixty-four friends and family into quilt blocks, each bearing a beloved memory, whether a scrap from a best friend's dress or the names of loved ones. On the honeymoon west, she traveled light, but, according to historian Linda Lipsett, took along her cherished friendship quilt, a bonnet with trimmings and a cloth album of family and friends.

The honeymoon west presaged the loss of innocence, for no bride would be shielded for long from the realities of life, death, the elements or the results of her own ignorance along the trail. What once appealed "as a romantic wedding tour" to Catherine Haun, a privileged young Southerner, turned tragic when the naive newlywed, so unskilled she could scarcely brew coffee, witnessed many tragedies; sudden death; the frantic entrance into the encampment of a brutalized young woman and her child

Young couple (Idaho State Historical Society)

Emigrants stopping to lunch on a white tablecloth in Greenwood County, Kansas (Kansas State Historical Society)

hotly pursued by Indians; petty theft; and pilfering. Undaunted, Catherine and her husband called upon all reserves—youth, health, education and their love—to buoy up their spirits.

Sorrows and hardships also faded away in the thrall of the frontier chivaree, a rowdy, rambunctious gathering of well-wishers and pranksters who congregated to celebrate a couple's nuptial night. Derived partly from the French charivari, partly from the English custom of publicly shaming deviate behavior, the traditional, the European charivari was a boisterous reminder of the hold which parents, tradition and village had on couples—not even their sexual conduct was private.

The American version was equally disorderly, involving rowdy well-wishers who might stuff a chimney with rags, partially saw through a bedframe or kidnap a groom. Diarist Rebecca Woodson observed pandemonium enough to "awaken the Seven Sleepers" during one chivaree. After pushing and pulling at the newlyweds' wagon, the party finally rolled it half a mile onto the prairie. "Then," wrote Woodson, "the fun began." Banging cans, wagon rocking, shooting guns and making "every noise conceivable" with "cow bells, whistles, horse-fiddles, and drumm[ing] on tin pans," the hecklers raised a ruckus until midnight, never allowing the frazzled couple to rest. Cheers and congratulations met the lovers as they strolled proudly into camp the next morning.

Part celebration, part persecution, one frontier shivaree was so mean-spirited that a young Nevada City, California, groom was saved from death by a lynch mob only by the pleas of his wife. The tender age of the groom coupled with the advanced years of his wife—no less than thirty—gave local hecklers much to deride. Everyone joined in the fun, which ceased only when the enraged groom pulled out a gun and peppered them with bird shot.

By the time of the crossing, many were already wed and well into maturity, but their stories of intimacy, freshly renewed, add a dimension of warmth and humanity to the text of overland writ-

ings. "Husband brought me a large bucket of snow," wrote Amelia Stewart Knight, pleased that he at least had thought of something. The single men of the wagon train had been offering her bouquets of prairie roses and clematis all along the trail, so why not he? Harriet Sherrill Ward enjoyed the "beautiful roses and Mexican cactus . . . in full bloom" gathered into bouquets by her solicitous husband.

Husbandly concern was not misplaced. An 1865 study cited mortality rates for women in Ohio and Illinois between the ages of twenty and fifty as 50 percent higher than those for men. Women's untimely deaths, often of childbed fever and complications, evoked a national mythology of longing and sorrow, reflected in popular sentimental ballads. "I am so very lonesom since my poor Rachel died," wrote settler John Biles, mourning the death of his nineteen-year-old wife in 1855. "The fact is," he mused, "no man knows how to appreciate a wife until she is gone from him forever." With illness and death so prevalent, men and women often reached intimacy through agony, comforting each other in their suffering. "We concluded to stay in camp and each take a vomit," wrote Amelia Stewart Knight, easily revealing the most private functions of illness as if it were the weather. "I am almost dead tonight. I have been sick two or three days with the bowel complaint," wrote Lydia Allen Rudd, suffering from a bilious condition that no amount of pepper, gunpowder, sage leaf or yarrow tea could cure, and to which all members of the wagon train, male and female, were inevitably subjected. Her husband also grew increasingly ill, his decline noted carefully in her journal. "Henry not any better" became a litany of both sorrow and surprising equanimity, inscribed in her journal day after day.

Yet few stories rival the sorrow of a grieving wife at the violent death of her young husband, killed one dewy morning by a freakish bolt of lightning that "struck the top of his head and . . . [ran] down his neck and side." Buried without a coffin, he was wrapped in a patchwork quilt and laid deep enough to prevent coyotes from scraping and pawing away the dirt heaped above his grave. "The last thing we saw," wrote emigrant Lydia Milner Waters, "was his wife clasping the grave in her arms and screaming." Lydia saved a burned lock of the man's hair for the widow as "No one else . . . thought of cutting it for her." Bereavement was also the lot of Mary Ackley's father, whose wife died along the trail and was buried, in 1850, beneath a wild rose bush. Grim and sorrowing, he became a recluse their first winter in Sacramento, unable to care for his children or stir from their home. "Our father was handicapped," Mary sighed, knowing that she would be the one to take charge.

In this, she was not alone. Like other women, she would emerge from the frontier experience stronger and more resolute than before; she could marry by choice, farm by hand and even, after suffrage was passed in Wyoming in 1896, vote alongside men. As a pioneer woman, she could tell time without clocks, bake cakes without eggs and face danger without flinching. One young bride, with high-pitched screams and a waving apron, averted an oncoming herd of buffalo racing toward their wagons, simply solving a routine emergency of daily life.

Even more terrifying was the threat of Indians to nervous and vulnerable emigrants, who were filled with fear and speculation by dime novels and lascivious captivity narratives, in which the deepest-held fear of the westward crossing was exploited: the capture and ravishment of white women by Indian men. Such fear, with its underlying threat of rape, mayhem and miscegenation, had a deep impact upon the women of the wagon trains. To prepare, some wagon masters even staged sudden mock Indian attacks, which were often more terrifying than the real thing. Actual statistics cited by historian John Unruh reveal that between 1840 and 1850, only 362 of the 250,000 whites who traveled west had died by Indian attack, but imagination brought the numbers higher. Every instance of capture or massacre served as justification for continued Indian decimation. When atrocities did occur, most were surprised that they had not happened sooner. "We lunched at a pretty creek," wrote emigrant Laura Winthrop Johnson, "a pleasant timbered stream, and a great place for Indian massacres."

Hearts beat quickly at tales such as the kidnapping of Sarah White, Anna Morgan, and Esther and Margaret Bell by the Sioux in Kansas, or the ravishment and murder of Mrs. Abigail Van Orman along the Snake River in 1860, or that most opprobrious of events, the death and mutilation of the beautiful Oregon missionary Narcissa Whitman, murdered by Cayuse Indians along with three of her seven adopted children, her husband, and seven overlanders staying at the Waiilatpu mission in Oregon. Yet another tragedy involved a lovely young Swedish woman, captured by the Sioux in 1862, who tried to gouge a bullet from her own flesh with a knife and died from the ensuing infection. Her last wish, conveyed to a fellow prisoner, was to send her love to her fiancée, a young blacksmith from Shakopee, Minnesota.

Some women were attacked and men massacred by white men in the guise of Indians, while in 1849 an emigrant couple was robbed and the woman cruelly raped by four renegade military riflemen.

When white women were captured, they were either used as chattel for trade or taken as slaves or into marriage. Captivity tales, always gruesome, were embroidered by sagas of pregnant women riddled with arrows, or exhausted teenage girls raped and mutilated and left dead along the retreat path. Yet often, female captives were treated simply as Indian women—often terrifying prospect in itself—and set to work about the camp, their virtue intact.

The measure of a captive woman was her ability to conform to tribal rules, hopefully with humor and courage, as did Mrs. Mar-

Family hiking into the Yukon, 1898
(Photo by Winter & Pond. Alaska Historical Library)

ble. A "small, but good-looking white woman" of twenty-five years, who had survived an Indian massacre on the Iowa-Minnesota border and been carried off as a captive with three other women. When rescued, she was "busily engaged with Mrs. Sounding Heavens in making a calico dress for herself" and had to be persuaded to return. "I am among my friends," she argued. Had they not clothed her in "the best style" of the Dakota women, given her "the best they had to eat" and furnished her with materials to dress again like a white woman? Another group of released prisoners, numbering nearly a hundred, had a different story to tell. When freed by their Dakota captors, the white women were "dressed up" as best as possible, but at the moment of release, began to wail and cry with such terrible tales of personal abuse that, upon hearing them, the soldiers arrested four hundred Indians and hanged thirty-eight.

The ultimate horror to most white settlers was the idea of a white woman loath to leave her captors, or one married to an Indian husband. Since happiness with an Indian mate was unthinkable, she would be viewed as demented, a woman as irrevocably scarred by her sexual odyssey as Olive Oatman, a sad-eyed woman captured with her sister by a Yavapai war party in 1851, then sold to the Mojave tribe and held for three years. Scarcely recognizable when finally released at Fort Yuma, she bore across her chin and arms a lavish network of tattoos—a startling and primitive emblem she could neither remove nor disguise.

Pioneer women were not entirely without recourse when it came to self-defense. Some frontier brides set aside skirts and bonnets for pants, hats and pistols—so-called anarchist impedimenta that, in the mid-nineteenth century, was in the east seen as a sign of sexual freedom and personal rebellion, but out west was deemed an occasional expediency. "With a few more lessons I shall make an excellent shot," wrote Lizzie Fisk from Montana.

And why not? The Indians had commenced their depredations in her territory, and, as she stated philosophically, "I might want to shoot them or somebody else."

No matter which hardship prevailed on the emigrant journey, relationships between men and women were affected—even in such mundane areas as hygiene. Countless diaries and journals, kept by both sexes, discuss the struggle to maintain standards with only the crudest of ablution tools—cold water and no soap. Oddly, the effects of grime on friendship, flirtation and intimacy are seldom mentioned. To bathe in a full-sized tub on a regular basis was unheard of, even in settled society, and most could only dabble and sponge in tiny nickel-plated basins—an entire family sharing the same water of a plunge, foot or sitz bath.

Like the forbearing oxen that pulled the wagons west, people, too, were coated head to foot with dust and grime, their clothes so stiff and caked they nearly creaked. Amelia Stewart Knight washed the dust from her eyes nightly to see enough to simply get supper, while Lydia Allen Rudd, ever mindful of appreciative male glances, often found her toilette interrupted by a "perfect cloud of dust, covering us all." Men and women schooled in politeness must have found the exposure to one another's most private moments daunting. Sanitary ablutions created "an unendurable stench," according to emigrant Charlotte Pengra, as thousands of emigrants made use of the same terrain for the same purpose. In addition, there were menstrual rags to be changed, wrung out and secretly washed—the hygiene of everyday life.

Obscure tales of birth control, abortion and "female complaints" were discussed, with information passed in whispers from one woman to another, many referring to the "female" drugs cited by historian Glenda Riley—Morrell's Magnetic Fluid, Yellow Dock Sarsaparilla and Henry's Invigorating Cordial. Such abortifacient potions were discreetly worded—they would "remedy all obstructions" if taken, particularly an unwelcome child. There were other concerns, less pressing, that struck at the heart of women's vanity in every assault of the burning sun and drying winds on chapped skin, turning the quest for complexion care into one as daunting as the crossing itself. No wonder the hundreds of freckle recipes, traded back and forth among wagon-train women.

Cosmetics came from nature or the pantry—cornstarch for powder, toothpaste to cover blemishes; soap root for hair "luster" tonic, lard for pomade, butternut hulls for hair coloring, sage for shampoo, olive oil and rosemary to wave hair, and grapevine tea to prevent it from turning gray. Occasionally, clay scooped from a riverbank was rubbed on as a complexion aid, fighting the effects of dirt with dirt. Moist chunks of saltpeter removed freckles, gloves lined with chicken fat softened chapped hands overnight and milk boiled with buckshot was a popular, if sticky, potion to clear the skin.

Occasionally, women would dart into the waving grass alongside the wagon and tear up handfuls of stalks and petals, rubbing the plant juices all over, or roll at night in the dewy grass, hoping that the essences released from crushed wild mint, parsley and sage would cleanse, scent, deodorize, and freshen their skin and clothes and, in some cases, repel the darting attacks of blood-hungry mosquitoes.

At night, young emigrant girls stared out the wagon back watching for a falling star, which, when spotted, would prove "lucky" if its trail lasted as long as the wish. If the star died out before the wish was finished, then, for luck, old shoes must be burned. Here the folkloric cycle was broken, as shoes were so highly prized that many walked barefoot to save shoe leather. Even Mary Ellen Murdock Compton, who struck out from Independence, Missouri, on March 23, 1853, with ten pairs of calfskin shoes, had none to spare—all wore out on the journey save the last, which she preserved by walking barefoot. Rachel Bond started with seven pairs; the last gave out after three hundred miles and she, too, ended up barefoot.

For most marriageable young girls, trailside fashion was a troubled litany of makeshift invention, with worn-out dresses that doubled as petticoats; ragged, ripped clothing patched with a thin wool lining, then hemmed at the bottom to complete the job; jeans cut into jackets, smocks and pinafores; and dresses turned inside out for fresh fabric and brighter colors. When Rachel Malick found that her slippers were too small, she simply "cut a little piece off [the] toes and heels." Rebecca Ketchum had only a single dress—a palm-leaf muslin, which immediately turned musty and was ripped "nearly if not quite twenty times" and remained unchanged the entire trip. What mattered fashion? she thought. "As long as I look as well as the rest, I don't care." Others, however, equated style and fashion with civilization, and fought to maintain standards of style in dress, no matter what.

The jaunty and self-assured Elizabeth Wood, journeying to Oregon in 1851, maintained her style despite the dearth of ribbons, thread, material—or even the time to sew. For the Fourth of July, she hastily hand-stitched a red calico frock, along with "a pair of mackasins, made of black buffalo hide, ornamented with silk" and, atop her head, fixed a "braided bulrush hat" trimmed with red, white, and pink ribbon. A young bride, observed by Helen Carpenter in 1857, crossed the plains wearing a phalanx of jiggling hoops beneath her skirts, prompting much spectator interest as she settled herself daily into the tall wagonbed. Hoopskirts might have helped maintain social distance from uncouth men in the city, but atop a wagon, they afforded a woman, according to an account, "less personal privacy than the Pawnee in his blanket."

Women were equally innovative when it came to bloomers, tacking up hems, stitching skirts into pantaloons and generally flaunting modesty in the quest for comfort. Strict cultural and moral codes, along with a strong desire to please men, inhibited many women from the divided skirts. In wearing bloomers, a woman sought both freedom of movement and a symbolic release from traditional limitations. For women thus outfitted, the freedom granted by such dress, particularly on the wagon route west, far outweighed the shock of tradition-bound men and women. To many, "bloomer" women were scarcely higher on the social scale than uncouth Missourians, or "pikers," or worse—forty-niners. They were seen as crazed and "emancipated," women who might just as well take up cigars and riding crops since they had already usurped pants, the recognized symbol of male hegemony. No more would a "bloomer" girl echo the sad refrain of emigrant Mollie Dorsey, who donned her father's old suit to better scramble through the underbrush, musing "How much easier if I were a man." Most men were loath to relinquish the "power of the pants"—if anything could discourage a suitor, even on a wagon going west, it was trousers on a girl. Unsavory stories of women such as "crazy" Mary Walker, a medical doctor who wore pants to her wedding, refused to take her husband's name and balked at the word "obey" convinced most young women not to adopt the costume. Yet as time passed and dress reformers of the 1850s urged women to free themselves from inherited, cumbersome and even unsanitary apparel, to exercise for health and even bathe recreationally, bathing costumes and bloomers settled into vogue. "With spirit and determination I wore my befringed, buckskin breeches," wrote Ann Bassett Willis of Colorado, eschewing the "puritanical sphere where girls' legs were strictly hush-hush, and anything resembling trousers for women or girls taboo." Married women were often the first to wear pants, preferring comfort over convention. And why not? With courtship days long past, they were less vulnerable to idle gossip and preferred, like Iowa settler Miriam Colt, dress "well suited" for women to "bound over the prairies like an antelope."

Those men who were staunch advocates of the bloomer were of a practical, not lascivious, turn of mind, since there is scant evidence that women thus attired were judged attractive. When gold miner Edmund Booth urged his wife to "adopt the . . . costume" and "cease to carry [about] 40 pounds of petticoats," his first concern was the health and well-being of his wife—not style. Marching west, men and women found in one another much to admire and much to change, from petticoats to voting laws, but like the frontier ahead of them, the results of that change would remain unknown for years to come.

HARRIET FISH BACKUS

As a young bride, Harriet was thrust into the wild heart of the Colorado mining industry in the San Juan Mountains, eventually ending up at the violence-tossed Tomboy mine near Telluride. Here any economic threat to the mining industry would set off bouts of mob terror among miners, who would riot, bomb or threaten worse. Harriet was married to a respected mining engineer with whom she raised two children and enjoyed a lifetime of happiness. She and her husband were a completely devoted, absorbed couple.

I was late for my wedding—so late that the date on three hundred engraved announcements had to be forever wrong. When my sweetheart of high school days telegraphed from Telluride, Colorado, saying he had found a position as assayer at the Japan Flora Mine, he asked me to meet him in Denver to be married. This caused considerable consternation in my family.

"Hattie, I don't think you should go alone," said my father with a worried look. "Young girls like you don't travel by themselves."

"I'm not afraid of her traveling alone," said my mother, "but it wouldn't be proper for her to be unchaperoned in Denver."

Working for the Telegraph Company after the San Francisco earthquake, preceded by two years of teaching school, had not conditioned me for "wild adventuring." But since George could not leave a new position for the trip to California, I must go to him.

A graduate of the University of California School of Mines,

Wedding of Sedda Strickler and Charles Hemry
(Hemry Collection, Wyoming State Museum)

George had been on guard duty in San Francisco after the earthquake and fire of 1906, which closed the schools. Released from that, he went to Colorado looking for work. Now he was ready to take a wife, and, since his uncle had arrived in Denver, my parents finally consented to our marriage away from home.

"Will arrive November twentieth. Arrange for marriage that day," I telegraphed, for that was the twenty-ninth anniversary of my mother's and father's marriage. . . .

It was a day of blue and gold, typical of Oakland in November, when my farewells were said and my big adventure began. There were few passengers and I was the only woman in the coach . . .

We reached Green River, Wyoming, in the evening and I was early asleep. Waking in the morning, I was aware of an ominous quiet, no chug-chug of the locomotive, no clackety-clack of the coach wheels . . . Something seemed very wrong.

Dressing hurriedly I called out, "Porter, where are we?"

Unconcernedly he answered, "Green River, Ma'am. Just where we were last night, waiting for the mail from a branch line that was delayed."

Like marbles spilled on a polished floor my plans scattered in all directions. At that moment we should have been in Cheyenne leaving for Denver. We still had four hundred miles to cover in thirteen hours, and that would have been really speeding.

Tears stung my eyes . . . [then] the conductor handed me a telegram which I feverishly tore open. Already George was aware of the delay.

"Under the circumstances are you willing to go directly to the minister?" he had wired. I wrote my reply on a telegram blank, "Yes, it must be tonight." I begged the conductor to send my message as soon as he possibly could.

That day I received three telegrams from George. The Reverend Dr. Coyle would wait for us and perform the ceremony. At seven we reached Cheyenne and boarded a special two-coach train waiting to run us to Denver. Barring another delay we would be there in four hours.

That [train] delay determined the date of our wedding. At one in the morning I stepped off the train for George's eager greeting. Together at last, our hearts pounding with happiness, we hugged each other tightly . . . From the depot we drove to the Hotel Savoy where the bridal suite had been reserved. To this I retired a very exhausted and lonely bride-to-be, while George joined his friend and best-man-to-be for the night.

Next morning he hurried to the jeweler to have the date corrected in the wedding ring, arrange for the ceremony, and order dinner sent up to our suite. Meanwhile, I spent the time laying our my wedding clothes.

My new corsets were too tight and the lacings had to be loosened. The silk feather-stitching of my long flannel petticoat recalled to mind my mother's patient needlework on my simple trousseau, consisting of three of everything. The white petticoat had three ruffles and I made certain the button on the waistband was secure. A white corset-cover with eyelet embroidery and white drawers with ruffles were carefully smoothed free of suitcase wrinkles. Black lisle stockings were more expensive than the customary cotton ones, but recklessly I had purchased three pair to wear with my shiny patent leather shoes accented by pearl grey buttons.

Mother had packed my wedding suit with tissue paper, and while unfolding it my hands trembled. It had cost such a big share of money saved from my school teacher wages of sixty dollars a month. I smoothed the satin-like reseda broadcloth, and the lovely jacket trimmed with gold and green passementerie that, once glimpsed, had become irresistible.

By my watch, time was flying, so I began dressing. Three times I coiled my hair and pinned it on the top of my head before being satisfied. George had often said it was my two long braids of hair that first won his heart on a well-remembered day in high school. The blouse of ecru net fluffed out of the front of my jacket. Petticoats and skirt were ankle length and correct according to Armand Calleau of the exclusive San Francisco shop where I bought my suit.

From a hat box came my crowning glory! Oh, that hat! White felt with a turned-up brim faced with black velvet and topped with a curving white ostrich plume, the ultimate in style. No bride, ever before, was so proud of her bridal outfit.

Smoothing on the fingers of my gloves I gazed into the mirror hoping George would be pleased. And so he was when he arrived with the ring and a velvet box containing a gorgeous sunburst of diamonds and pearls. With shaking hands I pinned it at my breast.

"The carriage and my uncle are here," he said.

In the manse of one of Denver's splendid churches, George placed on my finger the wide gold band which never has been taken off, and Dr. Coyle said, "I now pronounce you man and wife."

Unidentified (Library of Congress)

A. C. Wells, Eva Marsh and Clara Wells
(Photo by Frank B. Fiske. State Historical Society of North Dakota)

ANN RANEY COLEMAN

**Ann Raney Coleman was in the midst of a social
whirl in Whitehaven, England, when her father's bankruptcy
interrupted her active life. New fortunes awaited them in Texas,
at least according to her father, so on February 1, 1832, the family
sailed for New Orleans in order to reestablish themselves in
America. Texas was still a part of Mexico, and Ann's roadside
adventures reveal the rugged quality of life for travelers.**

The country was full of bachelors, but very few ladies. When
bedtime came we were ushered into a room where there were several beds. We did not like this much, as we expected a room to
ourselves, but on being told that the gentlemen slept on one side
and the ladies on the other side of the room, I opened both my
eyes and ears and looked again at my hostess, who did not seem to
be jesting. Presently several more ladies came in to go to bed.
They went through the undressing operation quickly and were all
in bed long before we had got over our surprise at this new fashion of sleeping. We soon undressed but did not divest ourselves
of all our garments, keeping on outside garments which were calico wrappers. We had been in bed about an hour when the gentlemen came in one by one until we had all retired. I watched with
breathless suspense the coming of the last one. This was something we were not accustomed to, and it was several nights before
I could sleep—not until nature was completely exhausted and
overcome with watching.

The ladies all laughed at us and said, "By the time you have
been in Texas a few months, if you travel in the country, you will
have to sleep with the man and his wife at the house you visit," as
houses were only log cabins with two rooms, one for the house
servants, the other for the family. I found this statement correct,
visiting some friends in the country two weeks after this who had
a small log cabin with two rooms in it, the servants and cooking in
one, and one to sleep in. I had to sleep with the man and his wife.
I slept at the back of the bed, the wife in the middle and the man
in front. They were settlers, and had gone into the woods to make
a plantation, and this was considered shelter for the present. This
was the way most of the wealthy planters lived when we first
arrived in Texas. . . . To make money was their chief object, all
things else were subsidiary to it.

Mrs. L's house was crowded every day with strangers out of
the country . . . Many came through curiosity to see the "Belles
with the Breeches" as they called my sister and self. Night after
night, Mrs. L's house was open for a dancing party. We, being
good dancers and our dress every way suited our figures and to
show our feet, were the chief attraction, there being very few
young ladies in the country. Those parties were very social, and
my sister and self enjoyed ourselves much. My sister had several
admirers, as well as myself . . .

After being a month at the hotel, we got two rooms next to the
printing office, also a kitchen to cook in . . . After we came to Brazoria we found many new acquaintances and many warm friends
. . . One, Mr. McN, who had always been deeply interested for
our welfare, had never proposed for my hand, much less my
heart. He often said, "I wish you to consider me your best
friend." He was far from being good looking, but was very interesting, his eyes keen and penetrating. He never said he loved me.
If he had, then our friendship would have ended. I looked upon
him more as a brother than a friend. I confided to him all my
secrets and sorrows. He was seldom my escort, and none sus-
pected that he had ever enlisted my sympathies.

Miss Evelyn Hettinger, right (State Historical Society of North Dakota)

Captain B was my constant companion walking, riding out for an airing; everyone said we were engaged to be married, and although unremitting in his attentions he had not proposed marriage. He had been bold enough to ask my mother and father for my hand, but had kept the strictest silence upon this subject to myself. Captain B was a great favorite with my mother. She thought him par-excellence. I admit of one thing; he had been a warm friend of our family and had been much in service to us on our landing in Texas. He introduced us to many families of the first standing and brought us many things from Orleans which we could not get in Texas. He was a general favorite amongst ladies and a welcome visitor in every family. He was Bostonian by birth, six foot high, fair hair and complexion, light eyes, very good looking, fine address. He was a handsome gallant, fond of dress and neat in person. He lived a good deal at our house, eating two meals out of three every day. Would have liked him better had I not seen quite so much of him. He was always teasing me or my sister with being called the Belles with the Breeches. I was not indifferent to him, but I liked Mr. mcN better. . . .

One or two weeks [later,] I saw a gentleman coming down the street go into the billiard room on the opposite side of the street. I asked Mrs. C. if she knew him. She replied that she did not. "I think it is some stranger just come into town." I should not be in danger of falling in love with him. She asked why. I replied he was too consequential. In one hour, the Doctor came home and said, "Miss Ann, I wish you would put on your best attire this evening. I am going to bring home a beau for you. He is a rich bachelor and wishes to get married very much. You must set your cap for him; he will be a good husband for you." I laughed and told him I believed he was getting tired of me and wished to get rid of me by marrying me off to some old bachelor. "Not so, Miss R," he said, "unless you could do well for yourself; and I know you would if you should get Mr. T. He is a man well known in the country, out of debt, and has a good home to take a wife to."

That evening after supper he came, and to my surprise, I found him the same little consequential fop I saw going into the billiard room in the morning. Mr. T was a man about thirty, black hair and eyes, good complexion, good looking, and a good address, a pleasant smile upon his features, and very communicative. He had one of his arms broken which turned a little out of its natural position. This gave his arm a swagger that I took for conceit of his own personal dignity.

I retired to the other end of the room to get my sewing. Mr. T drew his chair up to the table and commenced the following conversation: "I understood from Mr. B that you were to be be married to captain B." I told him "No, sir." He then remarked, "How do you like this country, Miss R?" I replied, "I like it well enough . . ." "As far as home is concerned," he replied, "Miss R, I think I can offer as good a one as any man in the country, if you will accept it. I am not like a terrapin that carries all on my back. I have plenty at home to make you comfortable. I know you have a great many suitors who can make many flattering speeches to you, which I cannot. I am as plain as a book."

This speech brought the color to my face, and I would have given anything to have left the room. He, seeing me silent, proceeded by saying, "I live thirty miles from here and the water courses are difficult to pass. If I come often to Brazoria, I shall make no crop, as I have no overseer. I should like, Miss R, if you could let me know if it is worth my while to come and see you again and pay my respects to you. I expect to leave town tomorrow morning, but will come back and see you again before I leave."

Before we had finished breakfast the next morning, in walked Mr. T. I was again caught for another day's courtship. I tried to excuse myself . . . but he would not let me off and made himself as agreeable as possible. When evening came I could hardly

believe I had been sitting all day in his company. Next day I was in hopes he would go home, but I was disappointed. He stayed this day also. He had been three days in town . . . he had appointed to return in one week from the time he left. I thought I would be absent, but he came in before breakfast and left me no chance to escape. It was during those visits he had been seen by Mr. McN coming to the house. Now Mr. T proposed marriage to me and waited my answer.

After many a debate in my own mind I determined to accept Mr. T's proposal. He had visited me about half a dozen times; he was well known in the country; everyone spoke well of him. This was satisfactory to me. He had given me several references as to his standing as a man in society.

It was on returning from seeing [a friend] and his family one evening, I was called in the street by . . . Mrs. A. She got hold of my arm and said, "I hear you are going to be married to Mr. T. Is it so?" I was silent. "If you marry him you will get a close stingy husband; and he has got a woman at home, one of his servants that will turn you out of doors before you have been home one month. He has lived a bachelor so long, he knows every grain of coffee that goes into his pot."

I listened patiently to this unpleasant news and said little in return. I made my walk as short as possible without seeming rude, and bid her good evening. I was determined to tell Mr. T of what his friend . . . had said the next time we met, for he was a constant visitor at their house. I was looking for him to come in town daily. Had my death knell gong been sounded, I could not have dreaded it any more. I was trying to summon up all my fortitude for the occasion when in walked Mr. T. He came up to me first and shook my hand and then passed on to the rest of the family. As soon as breakfast was finished Mr. T and myself were left alone.

He first broke the silence by saying, "I hope, Miss Ann, you have made up your mind to make me happy. It is to receive your answer I came to town today. I came near getting drowned crossing Linnville's Bayou, but I shall be repaid for the dangers I have passed if you consent to be my wife." My silence seemed to give consent, and he took my hand in his and pressed it warmly, while I burst into an agony of tears . . . I now told him what his friend had said. He seemed surprised and said, "Everyone is jealous of my expected happiness. You may pay no attention to anything you may hear against me . . ."

He then went into town to make arrangements for our wedding. He was determined that no expense should be spared to make a handsome supper, which was to be provided at the hotel . . . Mr. T gave me an order on Mr. M's store to get anything I wanted for the occasion. I was now busy as a bee making up my wedding suit, which was of rich white satin with blond lace, white silver artificial flowers, silver tinsel belt, black kid shoes with white satin rosettes and a gold bracelet, gold chain and no veil. This was all of my wedding dress. I had been in a fever of excitement all week, and with no appetite.

The day arrived. It rained in the morning so hard the streets were one sheet of water. Mr. T arrived early in the morning . . . The streets were very muddy from the recent rain. The sun shone out with all its brightness. There was a possibility that before night the water would dry up sufficiently to admit of our visitors to attend our marriage. The amphibious race, the frogs, were silenced by the subduing melody of the winged tribes; all nature was bespangled with smiles.

I alone seemed sad. Everyone else seemed cheerful.

My intended tried to cheer me, as he saw me look thoughtful, and never left my side only when obliged to. We had a private room to ourselves, and when it was time to dress he left me and went to dress also. Crowds of persons began to flock in from the country, and by seven o'clock in the evening the hotel was filled to overflowing by two hundred persons.

Ours was the first public wedding given at the town of Brazoria. At eight o'clock my bridesmaids arrived, one a Miss Anderson, the other a Miss Bailey . . . Mr. T had two groomsmen . . . at eight o'clock we entered the ball room to be married, it being the largest room in the house. The bridesmaids and groomsmen went first into the room, myself and Mr. T last. I felt much abashed in the presence of so many people . . . A breathless silence pervaded the room whilst the ceremony was being performed. The alcalde himself was so much excited that he paused once or twice whilst performing the ritual. I looked at the bridesmaids who were tastefully dressed. They looked like marble statues. As for myself, I trembled from head to foot, and when the ceremony was finished and the alcalde told Mr. T to salute his bride, I saw no motion made by him to do it. At last, feeling for his embarrassment, I turned my cheek to his so that he might more easily salute me, which he did. The same was done by the bridesmaids and groomsmen, the groomsmen kissing me first, then the bridesmaids . . .

I saw a multitude of people, half of whom I was unacquainted with. The ladies were dressed very gay and in good taste and might have vied with city belles . . . About ten o'clock that night I got liberty to dance for a short time . . . About twelve o'clock at night supper was announced by our hostess, Mrs. S, and we retired to the supper room . . . All eyes were on my husband and myself, so I ate but little; a cup of coffee was grateful to me, as it had always been my favorite beverage.

I hurried to retire where I would not be so closely observed. Everyone praised my dress, which I made myself, and said I looked charming but sad.

This was a truth.

I masked the feelings of my heart on this night that I might make him who I had chosen for my husband feel happy. At one o'clock I went up to my room with my servant Minerva, who, I had forgotten to state, was all obedience. I dismissed her shortly afterwards and I was left alone. My bridesmaids insisted on waiting upon me to disrobe me and see me in bed, but I would not permit them to and told them to go . . . I had been sitting in one position half an hour before a looking glass that reflected my form to my view, when I thought, "I am dressed and adorned for a sacrifice." I had been sitting in one position without a motion to undress. My thoughts were on my native land with my dear brother and Henry [a former beau] who I never expected to forget; my love was still his, and parted only by force of circumstances . . .

In the midst of these reflections, someone opened the door and the alcalde put in his head. "My dear, are you not in bed? Your husband wishes to retire for the night, and it is my business, according to the Spanish law, to see you both in bed." I felt indignant to this method of the Spanish law and promised to go to bed directly. With this promise he closed the door. My face, if anyone could have seen it, was crimson with blushes. And my husband came in and I was still sitting there with all my clothes on. He was surprised at seeing me still sitting there with all my clothes on. He was surprised at seeing me still up, and taking my hand and kissing it, he said, "My child, I will be a father as well as a husband. Do not sit there, but go to bed and take some rest, for you have need of it. Tomorrow you have a long and tiresome journey to take. The roads are bad, and without rest, you will be unfit for it. I want to start as soon as we get breakfast."

I hid my face in my handkerchief and wept bitter tears. Would he fulfill all he had promised? I had need of a father's and a husband's care. I was fifteen years younger than Mr. T and a child in appearance to himself. Without saying any more he went to the other end of the room, my back being turned to him, and in a few minutes he was in bed. I slipped off my dress and all my ornaments, blew out the light, and in a few minutes I was also in bed. Shortly afterwards in came my evil genius [the alcalde] with a light in his hand, opened a part of the bar and looked at us both the space of a minute and was gone without speaking. My husband laughed and so did I, though no one saw me do so for I hid my face with the cover.

In the struggle for independence from Mexico, Ann and her husband, John Thomas, lost all they possessed, never recovering financially. John died in 1847, leaving her homeless and with a child to educate. A later marriage proved even more unfortunate—her husband was cruel and dishonest. The resulting hardship finally led her to sue for divorce in 1855. In her later years, she struggled to support herself through teaching and doing household work, eventually finding solace in "prayer and quiet walks through the woods."

MOLLIE DORSEY SANFORD

"I do not know whether I will ever love any man well
enough to marry him or not..."
—MOLLIE SANFORD, MAY 5, 1857

"I don't know *why* I should call Mr. Sanford mine unless
because... I like him. He is the cutest fellow I ever met..."
—MOLLIE SANFORD, JULY 2, 1857

*When pert, black-haired Mollie Sanford emigrated from
Indianapolis to Nebraska Territory with her family in 1857,
she blithely dismissed both civilization and suitors for the
pleasure of "pure air" and "bright sky!" As a young, marriageable girl in the territories, she had many proposals
and suffered through countless attempts at matchmaking—
some with men as old as forty—before she found herself
charmed and won by Byron Sanford, whom she married on
April 8, 1860.*

SABBATH P.M., FEBRUARY 19TH, 1860
Finds me a happy bride. Our wedding did not pass as quietly as I
anticipated. Tuesday morning we were busy with preparations for
dinner, receiving and entertaining our guests, and it is something
to do that in as small quarters as we occupy. We were looking for
By[ron] every moment, but after 10 o'clock I began to feel nervous, for he had plenty of time to come, it seemed. I dreaded to
have the appointed hour pass without the ceremony. Twelve!

One! Two! Three! o'clock came, and no bridegroom. Many jokes
were indulged at my expense. I was fluctuating between hope and
fear, but never doubting but that he was unavoidably delayed.
Gedney came to me and said "Some of these chaps are slippery"
(he never did like By) "and I tell *you* I'd have got here or I *died*
trying to" (the last with a tragic emphasis). At three o'clock the
folks were about starved. The dinner was overdone, and it was
decided we "eat, drink, and be merry." Mr. Harris proposed
being groom by proxy. We all *tried* to be gay. Father and Mother
looked grave and anxious. After the dinner was ended and
evening approached, I could hardly stand the suspense. I would
steal off and weep and pray, and come to the house and smile and
be gay. The young folks played games in the sitting room, while
the older ones sat around the kitchen fire, regaling each other, for
my especial benefit, with harrowing incidents where the bride-
grooms *never* came, and the brides ended their days in insane asy-
lums.

Then dear old Grandpa meekly suggested that . . . *Byron* was
an honest young man (or we had thought he was) and that
stranger things had happened than—that—but he did not finish
his remarks, for I retorted with spirit that By was no horse thief,
or, if he was, that he as would soon run off with a calf, as poky old
Fox. After this the poor old gentleman sighed and groaned the
hours away until 8 o'clock, when he thought he had better go
home and to bed. . . . Then . . . I heard the sounds of a horse's
hoofs, and rushing to the roadside, I saw in the bright starlight
my truant lover.

His first exclamation was: "My gracious, Mollie, what do they
think?"

I said, "What do you suppose people think, Lord Byron?"

He was nearly frozen, so we hurried into the house, while Bro.
Sam, who too was on the lookout, cared for old "Fox" and then
dear Grandpa's fears were at rest. I made some tea and, while he

was thawing out, he told of his meanderings, and we made a little plan to have some sport out of what had so far been a prosy affair. Our wedding garments were down at the house, By's in his valise hanging behind the door, and mine in a small trunk also in the room where the young folks were. We would have to get them out without exciting suspicion, get them to the other house, dress, and suddenly appear before them and have the ceremony over before they could recover from their surprise, for everyone had given him up for the night. Father, Mother, Uncle, Aunt, Grandma, and Bro. Sam were all that were in the secret. I came in and said I would join in a game, and look no more for my faithless lover, at which I had an approving glance from Mr. Gedney.

In flying around I accidentally knocked the valise down. Bro. Sam was on hand to take it away. After a little I stumbled over the trunk and someone said that's a nuisance, so it was shoved into the other room. As soon as I could I got out of the play and went up to the house, where we dressed quickly as possible, helping each other with the finishing touches of our toilets. In the meanwhile Mother and Aunt had arranged the room. We came and stood outside the door, ready for the signal from Uncle Milton. Aunt stepped into where the company were, and said, "We will not wait for Mr. Sanford any longer. Come out to prayers." All marched solemnly into the kitchen. At a signal, the door opened, and stepping in, the ceremony was immediately begun, and Byron N. Sanford and Mary E. Dorsey were made man and wife together. Such a storm as followed, kisses and exclamations of surprise. Some of the best of the dinner had been preserved, and willing hands soon had a wedding supper, with a genuine Bride and Groom at their posts of honor.

And we were married in the kitchen!

MARIAN SLOAN RUSSELL

"Love, they say, is like the measles:
we take it only once."
—JEROME K. JEROME, 1889, "ON BEING IN LOVE,"
QUOTED BY MARIAN SLOAN RUSSELL

As a young girl, Marian had traveled the Santa Fe Trail so frequently that she was greeted familiarly by many as "Maid Marian," the daughter of a well-bred, handsome young widow who was struck by wanderlust. Marian's childhood memories were of prairie schooners, Kit Carson and her mother's incessant need to return to the Santa Fe Trail, which created a deep conflict in the daughter: to stay in Kansas City and "marry well," or pursue her own love of the west. She decided on "an old covered wagon" rather than "diamond rings and hoopskirts." When Marian finally married in 1865, a nomadic stint in the army seemed settled by comparison.

I was born in Peoria, Illinois, on January 26, 1845. The first child of my parents' union died in infancy. The next, my brother William, lived to manhood and shared with me many of the incidents of which I write.

My father, an army surgeon in the Mexican War, was killed at the Battle of Monterey . . .

[My mother] was a small very dark but lovely woman. She was courageous, educated and cultured . . . At times I seem to see her standing by a flickering campfire in a flounced gingham dress and a great sunbonnet. Behind her looms the great bulk of a covered wagon. I think I can hear her singing,

Flow gently sweet Afton,
Among the green braes . . .

Mother had remarried when I was but three years old and the memory of my step-father's kindness colors many of my childhood memories . . . To me he was always Mr. Mahoney . . . .[He] was killed by the Indians while he was out on a scouting expedition . . . I remember mostly my mother and how, when the news came, she leaned against the wall for support, one hand clutching at her throat as if she were choking. I remember the horror in her eyes . . .

After my step-father's death, mother, Will and I waited two long years in Kansas City . . . Grandfather Sloan had written that he was coming and would take us back to California with him. We might wash out much gold if we cared to. Mother was anxious to go. She was lonely and the interest she had had in life seemed waning. So we waited . . . but we waited in vain. That was the year of the cholera epidemic, and grandfather and both of his sons died with it and were buried in far away California . . .

When school closed in the spring of 1852, mother decided that we would go to California anyway. So we left Kansas City and moved to Fort Leavenworth where immigrant trains were wont to assemble in preparation for the trip westward . . . The dreaded cholera was raging in Fort Leavenworth the day our white-hooded wagons set sail on the western prairies. Our little city of tents dissolved like snow in a summer rain . . .

Minute impressions flash before me; the sun-bonneted women, the woolen-trousered men, little mother in her flounced gingham . . . Because I was one of the youngest, I may today be the only one left of that band to tell of the old, old trail that, like a rainbow, led us westward . . .

I was seven on this trip in 1852 across the prairies . . . [I remember] one night when the wind was blowing Captain

Aubrey [the train leader] came to help us with our tent. He drove the tent stakes deeper into the ground. Sparks were flying from the cooking fire that mother was endeavoring to keep ever so small. She stamped at the sparks with her little brogans. She had laid her sunbonnet aside and tendrils of her soft dark hair were blowing across her face. Captain Aubry and mother were friends of long standing, although I do not know when their friendship first started. I remember that he called her "Eliza," speaking her name slowly as if he loved saying it. Sometimes he would call her "Lizzie" and then mother would turn on him fiercely for she did not like the name . . . When mother would turn upon him, the laughter would leap up in the Captain's eyes, and watching him I always wanted to laugh, too . . .

The Cimarron Trail over which we came skirted [Fort Union] on the west side. [Here] our great cavalcade rested . . . How our hearts waited for a sight of the Santa Fe of our dreams. We thought it would be a city, and waited breathlessly for the first sight of towers and tall turrets. We were in Santa Fe before we knew it.

Our caravan wiggled through donkeys, goats and Mexican chickens. We came to the plaza and found there a man, a tall man, leaning on a long rifle. He had a neck like a turkey, red and wrinkled, but he was the boss of the plaza. We went where he told us. Under his guidance, wagon after wagon fell into place. Dogs barked at us. Big-eyed children stared at us. Black-shawled women smiled shyly at us. We were in Santa Fe . . .

As evening progressed young senoritas in crimson skirts, their black, mane-like hair caught up with great combs, began drifting languorously by. Tall vaqueros in sashes and peaked hats strolled among the wagons. Mother resented the vaqueros. She tried to shoo them away like chickens, for she did not speak Spanish.

As darkness deepened Santa Fe threw off her lassitude. Lights glowed in saloons and pool-halls and in the Fonda, a great mud-walled inn. As soon as our freight was delivered at the customs house, our drivers began eagerly to sign up and draw their wages. They washed their faces and combed their hair . . . There was a great hunting for clean shirts and handkerchiefs. From a dance hall came the tinkle of guitar and mandolin, a *baile* was forming. The cold air smelled of dust and sweating mules. We slept in the wagon, or tried to, but the noise and confusion kept us awake . . .

Marian and her family left Santa Fe for her grandmother's funeral in Ohio, then returned to Santa Fe again in the autumn of 1860. A year later, her nomadic mother was on the move again.

Mother moved to Kansas City. Once more I entered school, and Will found employment on the *Kansas City Journal.* I began putting my hair up in curl papers at night so that three shining curls might hang down over my shoulder next day. Gone were the blue pinafores and long brown braids. I was a young lady. In my dresser drawer was a small vial labeled "The Bloom of Youth." Secretly I encarmined my lips and my cheeks with it, and dusted my face with rice powder. Sometimes I applied a black beauty patch near the corner of my mouth. They were supposed to be fetching. I laced heavy stays over fine white muslin underwear and carefully arranged my fly-away hoops and big padded bustle. My petticoats were wide and flounced, and I had a taffeta one for Sunday. My ball dress was wide and caught up at intervals with bunches of artificial tea roses. My hats were small and flower-laden. My parasol was smaller still. On my hands I wore silk half-handers.

Mother had great expectations. Although she was home sick for Santa Fe and the old trail she was determined to stay in Kansas City until I should marry well. There was no one with a future out west, so she said. She encouraged many people to come to our home and the evenings were almost literary events.

A tall young man with dark commanding eyes came there one evening. He carried Harriet Beecher Stowe's newest book, "Dred," under his arm. The young man's name was Gerald Roberts, and he read "Dred" aloud to us that evening. Gerald was in the mercantile business and was of superior financial and social standing. Perhaps mother could be forgiven for having encouraged his visits. I remember how flustered I was when his dark eyes rested long upon me. He was not long asking my hand in marriage. It was long ago, but I remember him standing holding my hand in his saying, "Miss Sloan, will you do me the honor to become my wife?" I stuttered and stammered and said, "Ask mother." The ring that he gave me was a diamond and I liked the feel of it on my finger.

I thought mother looked relieved, and I was a bit hurt when she said, "After your wedding, I think I shall go west again." Go west without me? Such nonsense! The days that followed were most unhappy with mother planning my wedding with the left ventricle of her heart, while she used the big right one to plan going out west. Sometimes I would take off the hoops and the bustle, and then I would remove the diamond and lay it upon them. No one would want to wear diamond rings and hoopskirts in an old covered wagon.

Spring came. It was 1862 and mother was going to return yet again to Santa Fe. I was supposed to stay in Kansas City with Gerald who would soon be my husband. I just couldn't stand it. One evening I followed Gerald out on the stoop to say a good night and good bye forever. I left the ring with him and turned away from the hurt in his eyes to go tell mother that I was surely going to Santa Fe with her. For the first time she seemed disgusted. "I have tried so hard to do well by you," she muttered. Dear mother! She did better by me than she dreamed when she let me go with her . . .

After school closed in June of the year 1864 we moved to Fort

Unidentified couple (State Historical Society of North Dakota)

Union. We lived in a long, low adobe house whose six rooms were all in a row . . .

It was at Fort Union that I first met Lieutenant Richard D. Russell. I was rounding a corner rather suddenly, my green veil streaming out behind me . . . the wind . . . blowing my hair in my eyes and I . . . trying to keep my long skirts where they belonged when suddenly he stood before me. That was the moment the whole wide world stood still. My tall, young lieutenant stood and smiled at me while I struggled with my skirts, veil and hair. Then on he marched with his company, taking my ignorant young heart right along with him. For days the memory of his smile came between me and my prayers. Almost immediately he made an opportunity to be formally presented. Mother, it seemed to me, found many occasions to compare my lieutenant unfavorably with Gerald Roberts. Love, they say, is like the measles: we take it only once. . . . I am sure that was true in my case, for from that August day when I met Richard on the streets of old Fort Union, to that other August day twenty-three years later when an assassin's bullet took him from me, my love never faltered. Indeed, that love is a living part of the soul of me today, although the grass has waved over my lieutenant these forty years and more.

Richard was born in Canada in 1839. He was six years older than I. One evening he sat in our house at Fort Union and told mother and me about his adventurous life. Mother said she knew that evening that Richard had fallen in love with me . . .

When September rolled around, mother moved again to Santa Fe. I was sick at heart because so far she had never permitted Richard and me a moment alone together; always mother or some elderly couple was with us. Only our eyes could speak of the dawning love in our young hearts.

We moved to Santa Fe and a whole week passed, and I had not heard from my lover. Then one morning a great caravan was sighted coming in from Fort Union. I thought surely there would be a letter for me from Richard so I dressed up a bit and walked to the post office. I stood waiting among the jostling throng until my turn came at the window. There was no letter for Miss Marian Sloan. No news from my tall lieutenant.

I had dressed with special care that morning. My dress was of factory-woven cloth, in what they then called cotton challis . . . a glorious dress of a soft golden color [with] a tight little bodice buttoned down the front with little jeweled buttons. . . .

That day at the post office lies in my memory as faint and sweet as the scent of old lavender.

I had turned sadly from the post office window and was starting homeward when some one came up behind me and drew my hand through his arm. I turned quickly. It was Richard. He had come with the emigrant train from Fort Union. My heart overflowing with joy, I went where he led me and soon we were standing beneath the great wooden arch on the outskirts of Santa Fe. We were alone for the first time since the day of our meeting . . .

Six months from the day of our meeting Richard and I were married in the little military chapel at Fort Union; that was in February of 1865. I was twenty. Mother had sent to Kansas City for my trousseau. . . . My wedding dress was of soft beige and fitted to my slender figure. My hat, adorned with a single white feather, was small and turned away from my face at one side. My cape of blue velvet covered me from tip to toe . . .

I am afraid that I did not hear a great deal of our wedding ceremony, for something sacred and triumphant was going on in my heart. Somewhere on the hills of God, angels were singing . . . I heard Richard's deep voice beside me saying over and over, "I do" and "I do." Then all at once we were outside in the patio, and fine white snow was blowing little drifts in the folds of my new velvet cape. There were tears in mother's eyes, but Richard held my hand tightly. I was Mrs. Richard Russell.

ELSA JANE GUERIN

*"I buried my sex in my heart and
roughened the surface
so the grave would not be discovered . . ."*
—ELSA JANE GUERIN

**Charlie Parkhurst, or Elsa Jane Guerin, known throughout the
west as a "woman who dressed as a man," made her living as a
stagecoach driver, and had the distinction of being the first woman
to vote, in 1868, when she cast her lot along with "all the other men."
Disguising herself as a man took courage, as the labor she
performed was the most menial, throwing her in with the rough
and unruly wanderers of the west. Also, wearing clothes of the other
sex was illegal in some states, punishable by fines or jail. Added to
this was the mystery of being, reputedly, one of several women in
male attire who claimed the name "Mountain Charley."**

My husband was a pilot on the Mississippi—a fact of which I had
never thought to inquire prior to our marriage. He was a noble
fellow, and well repaid the sacrifice I had made for him. We made
a pleasant trip to various cities in the South, and at the end of a
month or so, came to St. Louis and determined to settle there per-
manently. My husband rented a small, comfortable house, and I
was installed as its mistress.

Life flowed on in quiet, uninterrupted beauty. My happiness
was . . . if possible, made greater when at the end of about a
year after my marriage, I found a breathing likeness of my
husband laid by my side. Three years after my marriage, another
stranger came among us—this time a daughter.

I believe that now the circle of my enjoyment was complete.
My husband, though much absent, was unremitting in his love—
I had two bright, healthy children, and what more could woman
ask?

Some three months after the birth of my last child, a thunder-
bolt fell into my Eden and destroyed its beauty forever.

My husband left one day to pilot the *Lady Poole* up the Ohio.
The day after I was engaged in a frolic with my son, when I heard
a knock at the door. I opened it, and a stranger stood there with a
countenance so full of evil tidings, that a shadow fell instantly
upon my heart.

"You are Mrs. F——?" he enquired.

"I am," replied I.

"I have some bad news for you."

"For me! Good Heavens, what has happened? My husband, is
he—" I stopped, not daring to pronounce the fearful word that
forced itself upon my tongue.

"Badly hurt," said he, concluding my question. And then as if
desirous to relieve himself of an imperative but unpleasant task,
he proceeded.

"It was three miles above Cairo, early this morning, that it
happened. He had some difficulty with his mate, a man named
Jamieson, about some old grudge, and Jamieson shot him,
wounding him badly."

My brain whirled as he went on, but yet there was a fearful
impression that the worst was not told.

"Are you sure he is only hurt?" I found strength to ask. "Is he
not—dead?"

"He is!"

I remember no more.

Then followed a dream-like succession of days and nights. I
remember . . . a collection of somber events—a hearse—funeral

trappings—the rigid body of my husband—meaningless words of comfort—whispered directions—until finally I was left alone with my children. One more shock, and the storm passed. A day or two after, my attorney called upon me, and gave me a statement of my affairs. My husband . . . had spent his entire income as it was earned . . . there was not a dollar remaining after his affairs were settled. I was completely a beggar. Even the house I lived in must be sacrificed—there remained to me absolutely nothing.

As my financial condition became more desperate, my desire for revenge increased in inverse proportion. Each privation that I endured served to make Jamieson more prominent as its author . . . I was bound to visit a terrible reparation. But how . . . ? This puzzled me for a while—I could conceive of no means by which I could reach him. At the same time my condition as to pecuniary affairs daily grew worse. I pawned . . . articles of jewelry, furniture, dresses, etc., until finally this resource was exhausted, and I knew not what to do.

At length, after casting over in my mind everything that presented itself as a remedy, I determined . . . to dress myself in male attire, and seek . . . a living in this disguise among the avenues which are so religiously closed against my sex . . .

In this apparel I should be better prepared to carry out my design of some day returning upon Jamieson, with interest, the heavy misfortune he had cast upon me.

Speaking of my husband's murderer, I will say that he had been arrested, tried and convicted, but escaped under some technicality. The matter had been carried into several courts, and ended by his being set free under some informality, and at the time I was arranging my plans for assuming a masculine dress, it was rumored that he had gone to Texas. This proved, however, to be false, as an event which I shall shortly relate will evince.

After I had fully determined to seek a living in the guise of a man, I went to a friend of my late husband, who . . . procured for me a handsome and substantial suit of boy's clothes. This point gained, I put my children with the Sisters of Charity, and prepared to commence operations. I cut off my hair to a proper length and, donning my suit, endeavored by constant practice to accustom myself to its peculiarities and to feel perfectly at home. Although not tall, my general appearance did not differ materially from that of any boy of fifteen or sixteen years—while a slight asthmatic affection which had visited me while at school had left a slight hoarseness in my voice that assisted materially in completing my disguise. I at first ventured abroad in my new dress only in the evening, and by degrees; as I saw that I attracted no particular attention, I made short excursions by daylight, and so rapidly did I progress, that at the end of three weeks I went anywhere and everywhere without the slightest fear of suspicion or detection.

My first essay at getting employment was fruitless . . . the many rebuffs I had met with in searching for a situation, though bitter at the moment, were in the end a benefit, for they removed to a large extent that timidity which accompanied my advent as a member of the stronger sex. I found myself able after a little, to address people without that telltale blush that at first suffused my countenance, and also to receive a rude reply without that deep mortification which in the beginning assailed me with terrible force. In short, I found myself able to banish almost wholly the woman from my countenance. I buried my sex in my heart and roughened the surface so the grave would not be discovered—as men on the plains cache some treasure, and build a fire over the spot so that the charred embers may hide the secret.

Once a month I visited my children; which I accomplished by going to the house of my friend of whom I obtained the suit, and changing my dress for a natural garb, in propria persona, visiting the place at which they were being cared for . . . For the first few months these absences were keen tortures. My children would haunt my dreams and play about me in my waking hours—the separation seemed intolerable, and for the first month an eternity.

I left the boat and determined to try my fortune on the land. With this view, I engaged a situation as brakesman, on the Illinois Central Railroad. This was in the spring of 1854, and I had been on the river nearly four years. It is needless for me to deny that during this time I heard and saw much entirely unfit for the ears or eyes of woman, yet whenever tempted to resume my sex, I was invariably met with the thought—what then?

[A]s the sensitiveness which greeted my new position wore away, I began to rather like the freedom of my new character. I could go where I chose, do many things which, while innocent in themselves, were disbarred by propriety from association with the female sex. The change from the cumbersome, unhealthy attire of a woman to the more convenient, healthful habiliments of a man was in itself almost sufficient to compensate for its unwomanly character. . . .

I was sitting one afternoon in the rotunda of King's Hotel, watching idly the throng that poured in and out . . . [when] two or three individuals . . . close by me engaged in conversation . . .

I was suddenly startled into listening by hearing one of the persons behind me say:

"I say, boys, suppose we go to Schell's and have a little game of draw. Won't you go up, Jamieson—you've had a few turns with the tiger, I reckon!"

The blood rushed through my veins as if propelled by electricity . . . It was some seconds before I could command my tumultuous feelings sufficiently to look around; and at length as my heart ceased a little its fierce throbbings, I turned slowly in the direction of the group. I easily recognized Jamieson in the person of a medium sized, swarthy individual, for . . . each of his features was burned indelibly in my mind. Pulling my hat over my eyes, so as to hide somewhat the emotions which thronged my countenance, I took a long look at the man whom I so long had sought. He was not a bad looking man naturally, but his appearance was that of one who has all his life yielded to the indulgence of fierce passions. He was haggard and careworn in appearance, I thought, which must have been the result of reflecting upon the friend he had slaughtered, and the widow and orphans he had made.

My fingers immediately sought and closed about the butt of my revolver and my thumb spasmodically forced the hammer upwards. In another instant I would have drawn it and sent a bullet into his murderous heart . . .

As the thought occurred to me, I replaced the hammer and drew my hand from the pistol. I need not hurry—he was here, he would not, could not escape me. I wondered what would be his feelings did he know that the wife of his poor victim sat within two yards of him—if he knew that his deadliest foe sat close before him, and only hesitated as a matter of policy from sending him instantly into that awful Unknown, whither he had driven a few years before, a husband, father and citizen. . . .

It was a little after midnight when the party broke up, and Jamieson arose a considerable winner. He asked the party to take some liquor, they all drank and went out. I followed close behind them, although at a sufficient distance not to attract attention. A few squares distant the party separated. Jamieson, keeping on directly toward the river. I quickened my step until I walked by his side. It was a bright moonlight night, and as I came up he turned and looked at my countenance, but seeing no one whom he recognized he said nothing.

"I wish to speak a word with you," said I, as he concluded his scrutiny.

"With me? . . . Well, what can I do for you, youngster?" said he, as he carelessly glanced at me, evidently supposing that I wanted some ordinary matter.

"You have done a good deal for me already, and I have come to thank you for it . . . A few years ago there lived in a city on the Mississippi a happy family, consisting of a husband, wife and two children. They were in comfortable circumstances—he able to earn a competence, kind, affable, affectionate, a loving husband and an indulgent father—the young mother trusting and happy in her maternal duties and the love of her husband."

"What's all that got to do with me?" broke in Jamieson, gazing at me with a singularly curious look. My strange language induced in him the belief that I was insane, while perhaps his conscience hinted to him that my conversation had reference to the act which had made him a murderer.

"Wait a moment and you'll see what it has to do with you. Suddenly the atmosphere of happiness which surrounded the family was overclouded. In one wretched hour the wife was made a widow, the children orphans, the husband hurried to an early grave!"

We stopped—he stood facing me and there was in his look an enquiring horror indicating that he very nearly, if not quite, appreciated the subject upon which I spoke.

"What of all that?"

"I'll tell you. The wife . . . swore to be avenged upon him who had drawn her into this ruin. For this she forswore her sex, she mingled with rough men, and sank her nature in the depths to which associations with rude characters plunged her. Through all these she persistently pursued the object of her mission. Her search lasted for long weary years—she followed it unweariedly, till at length she was rewarded. This night she followed him to a gambling hall, and when he left she met him, harrowed up his guilty soul with a narration of her wrongs, and then she did as I do now"—and I drew my revolver and cocked it—"and sent his black soul to the devil who gave it!"

Jamieson sprang backwards as I pressed the trigger, and instantly drew his revolver and fired at me. His shot like mine was harmless, and quicker than thought he cocked his revolver and fired at me again—this time with better aim, for a sharp pain shot through my thigh and I felt myself wounded. I braced myself with all my resolution and almost instantly fired at him again, when with a yell of pain he dropped his left arm dangling at his side and then bounded away.

Guerin, badly wounded in the thigh, was bedridden for the next six months, after which she again set out in her male guise to look for work. She accepted an opportunity to make the overland journey to California in the spring of 1855 with a party of sixty men. In California, she founded a pack mule business, flourished and sold the enterprise for $30,000. Even though stability and wealth were hers, the prospect of life in St. Louis as a proper matron seemed boring—she had sworn to avenge her husband's death. After an interlude in the fur trade, she settled in Denver, opened a saloon and took up the name "Mountain Charley."

One day . . . I discovered a stranger approaching, riding a mule. As we neared each other I thought his countenance was familiar, and as he got closer to me I found that I was face to face with—Jamieson. He recognized me at the same moment, and his hand went after his revolver almost that instant mine did. I was a second too quick for him, for my shot tumbled him from his mule just as his ball whistled harmlessly by my head. Although dismounted, he was not prostrate and I fired at him again and brought him to the ground. I emptied my revolver upon him as he lay, and should have done the same with its mate had not two hunters at that moment come upon the ground and prevented any further consummation of my designs. Jamieson was not dead, and the hunters, constructing a sort of litter, carried him to Denver.

I followed them along, assuring them that they need not concern themselves as to my appearance, for I was fully able to justify the whole transaction. Jamieson was taken to his boarding house and his wounds examined. The examination showed that three balls had entered his body, producing severe but not fatal wounds. He was cared for and soon after recovered enough to bear a journey across the Plains. He went to New Orleans but died almost immediately after his arrival with Yellow Fever.

Before his departure he revealed my sex, and told the whole story of my past life so far as he knew it, and exculpated me wholly from any blame in the attempts on his life. The story soon got out, and I found myself famous—so much so that [Horace] Greeley, in his letters from Pikes Peak to the New York *Tribune*, makes some allusion to my story and personal appearance.

I continued in my male attire notwithstanding the knowledge of my sex, and kept my saloon during the winter of 1859–60. I had a bar-keeper, named H. L. Guerin, whom I married, and in the spring we sold out the saloon and went into the mountains where we opened a boarding house and commenced mining. We left in the fall with a view of returning to the States.

We did so, and reached St. Joseph where my husband now resides.

Unidentified woman in cart (Library of Congress)

Unidentified (Photo by Frank B. Fiske. State Historical Society of North Dakota)

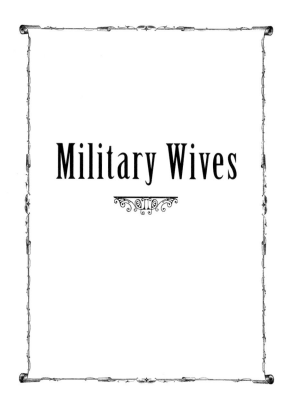

Military Wives

WHEN ARMY BRIDE MARTHA SUMMERHAYES DE-scribed terrain in Arizona "so horrible" that "even dogs committed suicide," she spoke for dozens of gently reared, cultivated New England women, whose wondering narrations of military life in the west create a travel literature of both terror and resignation.

Often their dismay stemmed from the stark contrast between the field and the fort. Many, like Summerhayes, had begun military life as brides in urban areas, wed to officers from elite academies, who found military society so "gay and brilliant" they "forgot the very existence of practical things" while dreaming over the strains of Italian and German music, lyrically played by fully uniformed military orchestras. So fond of good music was one regiment, the Eighth Infantry, that they imported musicians directly from Italy to Fort Russell, Wyoming Territory, creating an atmosphere in which brides felt themselves part of a vast, cosmopolitan social whirl.

What wives encountered next—following their husbands to remote outposts on the Indian frontier—was far removed from string quartets and white-glove affairs. Indians, outlaws, even unruly and imprisoned troops presented a constantly shifting and rowdy drama, often terrifying to the women, who also had to contend with a sharply divided class structure—the discomforting division within the military of rank and social status. Officers and enlisted men had their own duties—protecting traders and settlers, providing skilled labor and negotiating and maintaining Indian treaties, but women's roles were less defined, often limited to social graces, mending skills and the ability to organize a game of euchre. Their motivations were best summed up in the words of a young bride in 1827. What brought her to this rough country? she was asked. "I followed my husband," was her reply.

At the garrisons, she and other women found notorious squads of young bachelors, officers and recruits alike, who, when not in battle, whiled away their days polishing gear or courting ladies. "They were all there," wrote one bride, Katherine Gibson Fougera of Custer's Seventh Cavalry. "Few were married, and all carefree; they faced life with untroubled minds, without one presentiment of what fate had in store for them not so many months away." Fort Vancouver, Oregon Territory, had 234 single men in 1850, and only a few women. At a dance given near Hays, Kansas, which included local, nonmilitary men, there were ten men to each girl, with the men's behavior caught between wildly chivalrous and just plain wild. So notorious was the enlisted man's reputation for carousing that the father of an Oregon girl, Rachel Malick, pronounced her off-limits; no daughter of his would ever marry a soldier still in uniform.

Others viewed the "happy boys" more kindly, and numerous young, available girls would visit their married sisters at the garrisons, hoping to fall in love. A fetching girl would garner proposals within the hour; a homely one might marry within weeks. "It was remarkable how large the proportion of married men was," wrote Philip St. George Cooke of the Cantonment Leavenworth in 1829; of those who were married, a large number had brought their wives. Garrison men, shy or rowdy, often had skewed notions about the sexes. Because of the dearth of women at military bases—and those present usually married—officers, perhaps more than men in any other profession, harbored the notion of women as saintly and angelic. Lacking practical life experience, they created fantastic versions of "true" femininity—a vision which army post women gamely struggled to uphold. As if to justify such effort, Helen Chapman, a military wife in South Texas, praised "the true chivalrous feeling that I see no where else," which seemed to "counterbalance [the] slight annoyances that occur[red] in [military] life."

Some officers turned from chivalry to excess, finding other means of indulging their female fantasies. Major Marcus Reno

Mary Wintt Greenshield's wedding, 1902 (State Historical Society of North Dakota)

was so smitten by the beautiful young daughter of a commanding officer that he hovered outside her window by night, peering surreptitiously through the glass in admiration until stopped by a court-martial. Also misguided was one of the army's brightest luminaries—the blond and dashing George Armstrong Custer, whose interest in gambling and pursuing women, even though married, was legendary. Yet Elizabeth Custer, mature and tolerant, systematically tried to tame his extravagance and ameliorate the wildest rumors. This deeply reflective woman helped the younger military brides understand their role in history. "We army women . . . are . . . privileged. We are making history."

Indeed, the women who cantered sidesaddle over the prairies on frisky ponies, set up housekeeping in chicken coops and fashioned masks out of chamois skin to protect their complexions provided a stabilizing effect on military life, and helped further westering civilization by accompanying their husbands on duty.

To buoy their spirits and maintain standards, women spent hours trying to dress in fashion, kept up with the newest books and even donned tennis whites to play on makeshift courts. Ice skating in winter and riding in summer, they also would join their husbands on an occasional hunt, usually for grouse. Social life, when supply lines to the east were open, was occasionally lavish, the food opulent and, wrote military bride Katherine Fougera, the officers "resplendent in their full-dress uniforms," with "gaily gowned women" to lean upon their arms. Women, who lived on the fringes of army politics, made themselves central to every social aspect, passing the time with plans for musicals, charade parties, weddings and grand balls.

Women were often startled by the degree of military discipline they had to accept. Such obedience was second nature to their husbands but irked spouses who were scarcely more than teenagers, had never survived on a salary as meager as eighty dollars a month and were puzzled about the military meaning of "housewifely duties." Having no assigned work, women mended rips, organized gear, planned menus and sewed buttons. "The stitches . . . I put in the blue flannel shirts were set in tears," wrote Elizabeth Custer. Ellen Biddle, sick of army discipline, took great delight in discovering delicacies at the commissary— sometimes chocolate, raisins or prunes. But the utter loneliness of the bleak, remote outpost is best illustrated by Elizabeth Custer, describing three lone women who measured their journey, and their happiness, by their distance from the telegraph lines. Often, they lacked a permanent place to live, and once settled, could be "ranked" out of their abode by a higher-ranking married officer.

Women often spoke up about inequities; they protested unfair imprisonment of soldiers and were touched by the courtesies of the enlisted men. But only the special focus of hindsight acknowledges the similarities between the men without rank and the women without work, one imprisoned by military status, the other within the stratum of gender in civilian life.

In all, brides scarcely had time to ponder the practical side of life until the first glimpse of permanent housing, usually the bachelor quarters, where a couple would live for the next three years. Here the War Department turned a blind eye on nuptial bliss, often assigning lieutenants to a single room, symbolically denying the existence of wives and women, treating the men as lone recruits. Such economy cramped young women, whose silver, linen and huge leather trunks would scarcely fit into one room, even with a kitchen. Some shivered in sailcloth tents, sized and proofed to keep out rain, but not sturdy enough to block the raucous laughter of neighbors, the noisy *clip-clop* of passing mules or the racket of early-morning roosters. Late-night conversations echoed through the walls of surrounding tents, turning domestic discord into public domain.

Military life reflected the joys, tribulations and vicissitudes of the population in general. In Cantonment Leavenworth, designed

Wedding portrait (Museum of History and Industry, Seattle)

as one of a series of forts to protect trappers and traders as well as guard the Santa Fe Trail, women lived, bore children and even saw their daughters married, all within the confines of the fort's so-described "miserable huts." Anna Barbara Dougherty's marriage to Captain William N. Wickliffe, on November 14, 1831, was "solemnized in the presence of God and a large assembly of ladies and gentlemen" within the fort, who celebrated with a "jolification." All winter the fort had been on half rations—yet enough flour was scraped together to make a wedding cake. Army bride Alice Baldwin was greeted by a similar gala at the primitive dugout that served as Fort Harker, Kansas. A sign, THERE SHALL BE NO WEEPING HERE, set the tone of the revelry in her honor, where hardtack and coffee were drunk, and two violins and a squeaking accordion sprang to life.

Unspoken by most women was their deep dismay about prostitution, as soldiers consorted with the laundresses who followed the troops about, offering their services, both legal and illegal, for prices the soldiers could pay. The gathering of Indian women inside and outside the forts, and the continued dalliance between soldiers and Indian women, led to the edicts of the Banning Committee in 1876, which investigated the issue of immorality at frontier military posts—made public by the rumored liaison between Custer and the squaw Monasetah. The conclusion: that officers must maintain strict moral standards and give up Indian women. The army wives struggled for a charitable, Christian perspective toward the Indians, but were often repelled by Native habits, often calling them savage. Some army men, however, after years of observing Indian resiliency and stoicism took the view of Colonel Albert Brackett, who declared the lives of Indian women "unquestionably . . . happier than the do-nothing, thankless, dyspeptic life led by a majority of American women." Since military service on the Indian frontier was voluntary, men often used it as a means to escape their wives and families. Their ready liaisons

Unidentified
(Photo by Frank B. Fiske. State Historical Society of North Dakota)

with the "women at hand" continued, and never ceased to disturb and repel the white women of the army forts.

Yet many of these women were making their own cross-cultural discoveries. Exposed for the first time to actual Indians, rather than the warriors of popular fiction and newspaper stories, officers' wives discreetly noted in their diaries and letters home the beauty of the semi-clothed Indian form, usually male. Ada Vogdes, accompanying her husband to Fort Laramie between 1868 and 1871, carefully noted a Sioux warrior, Big Bear, whose casually draped buffalo robe "exposed to view the most splendid chest and shoulders [she] had ever set eyes upon." Whether the women's insights were shared with their husbands is not known. What has been recorded, however, is a racially based fear so great that the wives were routinely advised to gather in a specific spot, in case the garrison was overcome by Indians, where they would then be put to death—for their own protection—by the bullets fired by American officers. "When we ladies saw what might happen," wrote Sarah Canfield, "we preferred to be shot by our own officers rather than be taken captive." At Fort Phil Kearny, Wyoming, all the women and children were herded into the magazine and orders were given to light the explosives should Indians invade.

Officers' wives knew better than to complain; part of their role was to set an example for enlisted families and to encourage their own husbands. For Elizabeth Custer and other army wives, routine often replaced romance, yet occasionally the opposite was true and their versatility in accepting vicissitude became the mark of the mature military life. Grim or hopeful, the lessons learned on the Indian frontier were hard-won and, according to Elizabeth Custer, "lasted a long time."

Soldier and friend
(Photo by Frank B. Fiske. State Historical Society of North Dakota)

SARAH ELIZABETH CANFIELD

Sarah Canfield joined her husband at a garrison situated deep in Sioux territory—one of the most dangerous areas of Sioux and Crow warfare in the late 1860s. His assignment to police roving bands of Indians and to escort citizens safely through Indian territory was appreciably different from their honeymoon in New York, spent happily "doing" the city. Although well aware of the Indian massacres taking place in the Dakotas and Colorado, Sarah, in her journal entries, seems remarkably fearless. Perhaps she took courage from the fact that, despite the hysteria of the popular press, after 1861 not a single army wife had lost her life by Indian attack at a military post.

APRIL 13, 1867

This is a worse country than I ever dreamed of, nothing but hills of dry sand with little streaks of short shriveled grass in the hollows and on the river bottoms.

We saw several large groves of antelopes today—I suppose several hundred in all. And just before night a large grey wolf came down to the river bank to see us pass—We saw three Indians yesterday but nothing like a human today.

APRIL 25

The wild flowers are beginning to bloom, and today when the boat stopped to cut wood, we went ashore and gathered a few. The gentlemen armed themselves and acted as our escort, even though we did not go very far from the boat—for wild Indians are all around us. We do not often see them, but we know they are near, for this morning about daylight as our boat was just starting from where it had been tied to the bank all night (we run all night when the moon shines and the water good), the pilot was shot with arrows, no one knew it until he was found. The Captain says he will leave the body at Ft. Rice tomorrow for burial.

The Clerk of the boat has just brought me three letters from Mr. C[anfield] directed to my Iowa address. He said he found them in a gunnysack of mail which one of the men found on the bank of the river while we were getting wood. At first I was very much frightened but the Captain thinks the Officer at Ft. Berthold probably hired an Indian runner to bring mail down the river to the next Fort. That he either got tired of his bargain and threw it away or was attacked by his enemy the Sioux and was killed. The date of the latest letter was early in January, nearly four months ago, and what might not happen in four months, for I had not had a letter for a month or more when I left home. I had a hard cry over my letters but Capt. Ohlman told me not to worry, but if anything had happened to my husband, he would bring me back home all right which is very kind of him.

May 19

This is Sunday and a very beautiful day. I am out on deck pretending to read but my mind is not on my reading very much for the Captain has just told me that he hopes to reach Ft. Berthold to-night. Is my dear Husband alive? Am I indeed to see him soon? I am very anxious but am determined to appear calm as possible.

May 20

I was delighted to recognize [my husband] in the first man to step on the gangplank when we stopped. After introductions and the congratulations of my fellow travelers on the happy termination of my journey, I said good-by to all with many thanks to the kind old captain. I left the boat and went through the "Sallyport" into the two rooms "Uncle Sam" allows a 1st Lieut. to occupy.

I am at home with my dear husband. . . .

Our two rooms are very neat and cosy. One is a sitting room which contains a center table, an army cot for a sofa covered with a buffalo robe which is beautifully decorated on the flesh side with bright colors, a shelf of books, three chairs and a writing desk.

May 30

I was awakened last night by a great screeching, groaning, and a series of, to me, distressing sounds together with a great barking of dogs. Mr. C—— assured me I need not be alarmed. It is, he said, only a young warrior serenading or making love to his chosen one. The custom is for the young man to come late at night and tie some ponies in front of her tepee, then spend an hour or two on the roof reciting his own prowess as a warrior and praising the charms of his lady love. If the father of the girl thinks the number of ponies enough, he takes them and thus signifies his approval. If not, the lover will the next night bring one more and continue to do so until the father is satisfied. I do not know that they have any marriage ceremony. I think not.

June 3

The three chiefs came in today to hold a "Powwow" with the officer[s] . . . The costume of the Chiefs seemed to be buffalo robes, beads and moccasins, though one wore a large string of bear claws for a necklace.

The robes were only held by the hands and had a way of slipping down and displaying their splendid brown shoulders. They were magnificent specimens of manhood.

Saloon interior (Colorado Historical Society)

JUNE 10

Mr.C—— told me that one day last year the warriors started out, leaving the squaws and children at home. Encountering their enemy, the Sioux, [and] having killed one, they scalped [him], cut him up, and coming back to their camp held a regular Pow Wow over it, singing and dancing all day. They seemed to think [this] an act of bravery or at any rate a victory over their enemies.

[This] reminds me of the way they make warriors. They take a young man, cut two slits in the skin of his back just below the shoulder blades; raising the narrow strip of skin they insert a pole strong enough to bear his weight, then raise him off the ground and leave him to struggle until he breaks the strip and is free. Then there is a great feast made for him, but if, as is sometimes the case, he faints or cannot endure the pain—he is called a squaw man and works with the women.

JUNE 18

I heard today the story of my three letters found on the river bank. Capt. Osborne, having a large number of official communications and reports, together with many private letters to send to the states, hired a friendly Indian to take them to Ft. Rice. He had traveled about half the distance when he was captured by a bank of hostile Indians known as the Cheyenne Sioux. The mail bag was opened and examined by their big medicine man. And he, not being able to read any of it or to tell what it meant, who it was from, or who for, ordered it to be burnt.

DEC. 26

The winter is passing away. We have had little dinner dances and card parties to help pass the time. Some of the soldiers formed a theatrical troupe [and] have an entertainment once a month. The one at Christmas was especially fine—music, dancing, and a short play. Some of the men had seen a good deal of acting. . . .

Dance at Fort Stanton, New Mexico, ca. 1880
(New Mexico State University Library)

JAN. 1, 1868

Today the ladies of the Ft. received. The officers came calling, all in full uniform. We made as much of a ceremony of it as we could.

MAY 4

I shall remain at the Ft. until a steamboat comes up, goes on to Ft. Benton, and returns on the way to the States. Mrs. H—— is going home too. One of the ladies, realizing how lonely she would be, offered to board me if I would stay, but if I cannot be with my husband I think I shall go home.

MAY 5

We have had great excitement today. About 3 P.M. Indians in great numbers were seen coming over the hills South of the Fort . . . they were painted and mounted for war . . . They circled round three sides of the Ft. (the river being on the fourth) . . .

When we Ladies saw what might happen we held a "council of war" and decided if the Ft. could not be held that we preferred to be shot by our own officers rather than be taken captive. The officers promised to do so before surrendering . . . but while it would have been done, if necessary, we are still spared to tell about the attack of the Ft. by three thousand Indians. Now that the scare is over I remember that they came from the direction Mr. C—— went 24 hours ago. A new agony and nothing to do but wait for news.

JUNE 1, 1868

We left the camp at sundown. It was a sad parting. The life at . . . camp is so dangerous. I wanted to stay but could not, and it will be long before I get a letter.

Untitled ("West" Collection, National Archives)

Untitled ("West" Collection, National Archives)

KATHERINE GIBSON FOUGERA

When Katherine's father died, the ordeal of formal mourning plunged her into despondency and illness, which she tried to cure by visiting her married sister Mollie, who was roving gypsy-style with Custer's Seventh Cavalry up and down the Dakota frontier and camping in nine garrisons in eleven months. Also, Mollie had promised to find Katherine a husband. Katherine's last words before falling in love with the wavy-haired Lieutenant Gibson from Fort Lincoln, were: "Well, I wouldn't live in such a God-forsaken country, but as long as I am here, I want to see things."

[W]hen the Custers decided to give a *fête champêtre,* the news was received with enthusiasm . . .

And what preparations ensued! Soldiers who had distinguished themselves in rifle practice or military tactics were given the day off to scour the plains for plover or prairie chickens . . . The few women of the camp vied with each other in spying out patches of wild strawberries. . . .

Mollie [Katherine's married sister] and Mrs. Custer and I ranged these spaces, ducking bees that zoomed in and out of the bushes, and gathered armfuls of dew-dipped, spicy-smelling roses. These we placed decoratively in deep, rubber buckets, serving as vases, which we pilfered not only from the officers' tents but from the kitchen outfit as well . . .

Came the late afternoon, and with it, ambulances, buckboards, and rigs of all descriptions, teeming with the garrison crowd, who brought rations galore.

The influx of wives and overnight guests caused a temporary shortage of canvas shelter, so the bachelors were routed out of their so-called quarters and herded together in sketchy tent accommodations, from which would emerge loud protests of, "Where's my razor?" and "I'm shy a boot."

As for clothes? I was fairly well equipped, just coming from the East, but the other women dug down in their army chests and resurrected what finery they could, but no one would have taken a fashion prize.

However, with a full moon and the broad prairies for a ballroom, a regimental band, and feet itching to dance, what more could we want? . . .

Mrs. Custer received us in a faded muslin frock of ancient vintage, which she called her "valentine dress," "because," she explained, "I've had it since the year one."

I was the belle of the ball, not because of my irresistible charm, but because I was the only unmarried woman present . . .

Anyway, the hop was on, and did we dance? Ah, me—what space for the square dances and the Virginia reel and, best of all, the waltz with the man one loved!

Romance was abroad that night, and it seemed to me that I could have floated away forever on the strains of the "Beautiful, Blue Danube."

Under the clear, quiet sky, beyond the outskirts of civilization, for practically no ranches existed west of Bismarck before 1876, it was hard to realize how really isolated we were, yet Fort Lincoln and Bismarck comprised the white man's only oases in a desert wilderness stretching for miles in every direction . . .

However, seated on a bank of the little stream and fluttering a tiny, senseless fan, with Lieutenant Gibson beside me, I was oblivious to everything but my own happiness. A spell, woven in the starlight, seemed to reach down . . . and toss into my lap the things that my soul craved . . .

Untitled ("West" Collection, National Archives)

It might have been lunar madness that enmeshed my man and me, but, when we finally joined the others, I had signed up for a permanent enlistment with the Seventh Cavalry. I, who only a few weeks ago vowed never to tie my life to any impoverished lieutenant as Mollie had done, never to forsake the culture and green vegetables of the East for the crudities, hardtack, and perpetual canned beans of the army and the West . . .

Finally, alone in my tent, wakefulness sparring with sleep, I blew out my candle and sat huddled on my cot, my arms locking my knees. . . .

A light step crackled the dry grass in front of my tent, and a soft voice, lowered almost to a whisper, asked, "Are you awake, Katie?"

Mrs. Custer—and like a flash I was out of bed and across the tent to the fly. Like schoolgirls indulging in a forbidden midnight feat we sat huddled together on the cot in the lightless tent and whispered . . .

What a sane and satisfactory talk we had! She did not paint army life in the gay colors of an artist's brush . . . she spoke of dangers, real and imaginary . . . Her face was expressive of deep reflection.

[S]he continued: "We army women feel that we are especially privileged, because we are making history, with our men, by keeping the home fires burning while the soldiers are out . . . Yes, my dear, we are the pioneer army women, and we're proud of it."

In the moment of silence that fell between us, I sensed her unspoken challenge and advice. "If you have the courage, stay. If not, go. But be sure of your decision."

What a soul-satisfying message that woman brought to me! Next day, when I wrote home, I knew my heart thoroughly.

MARTHA SUMMERHAYES

As a bride in the early 1870s, Martha Summerhayes left her sheltered New England life to accompany her husband—a lieutenant in the army—to Arizona, seen by most as a fearfully primitive, uncharted wilderness. Frightened at night by bobcats that flew through open windows, frequent snake alarms and the constant dread of Indian ambush, Martha still took time to view her domestic situation humorously, tracing the path from bridal naïveté to the station of "old army wife." Between 1874 and 1878, she followed her husband through Wyoming and Arizona, where her story takes place. Later travels were to Colorado, Nebraska and New Mexico in 1889—after which she had "really good houses to live in . . . well-kept lawns and gardens." The following excerpt begins her married career.

Our quarters consisted of three rooms and a kitchen, which formed one-half of a double house.

I asked Jack why we could not have a whole house. I did not think I could possibly live in three rooms and a kitchen.

"Why, Martha," said he, "did you not know that women are not reckoned in at all at the War Department? A lieutenant's allowance of quarters . . . is one room and a kitchen . . . " After indulging in some rather harsh comments upon a government which could treat lieutenants' wives so shabbily, I began to investigate my surroundings. Jack had placed his furnishings . . . in the living-room, and there was a forlorn-looking bedstead in the bedroom . . . it was absolutely forlorn, and my heart sank within me.

But then I thought of Mrs. Wilhelm's quarters, and resolved to try my best to make ours look as cheerful and pretty as hers . . . We bought a carpet . . . a few more camp chairs . . . and a cheerful-looking table-cover. We were obliged to be very economical, as Jack was a second lieutenant, the pay was small and a little in arrears after the wedding trip and long journey out. [T]hen I turned my attention to the kitchen.

Jack said I should not have to buy anything at all; the Quartermaster Department furnished everything . . . and, as his word was law, I went over to the quartermaster store-house to select the needed articles.

After what I had been told, I was surprised to find nothing smaller than two-gallon tea-kettles, meat-forks a yard long, and mess-kettles deep enough to cook rations for fifty men! I rebelled, and said I would not use such gigantic things.

My husband said: "Now, Mattie, be reasonable; all the army women keep house with these utensils; the regiment will move soon, and then what should we do with a lot of tin pans and such stuff. You know a second lieutenant is allowed only a thousand pounds of baggage when he changes station."

Having been brought up in an old-time community, where women deferred to their husbands in everything, I yielded, and the huge things were sent over.

So Adams [a helper assigned to the couple] made a fire large enough to roast beef for a company of soldiers, and he and I attempted to boil a few eggs in the deep mess-kettle and to make the water boil in the huge tea-kettle.

But Adams, as it turned out, was not a cook, and I must confess that my own attention had been more engrossed by the study of German auxiliary verbs . . . than with the art of cooking. Of course, like all New England girls of that period, I knew how to make quince jelly and floating islands, but of the actual, practical side of cooking . . . I knew nothing.

Here was a dilemma, indeed!

The eggs appeared to boil, but they did not seem to be done when we took them off, by the minute-hand of the clock. I declared the kettle was too large; Adams said he did not understand it at all . . . I appealed to Jack. He said, "Why, of course, Martha, you ought to know that things do not cook as quickly at this altitude as they do down at the sea level. We are thousands of feet above the sea here in Wyoming."

So that was the trouble, and I had not thought of it!

My head was giddy with the glamour, the uniform, the guard-mount, the military music . . . the new interests of my life. Heine's songs, Goethe's plays, history and romance were floating through my mind. Is it to be wondered at that I and Adams together prepared the most atrocious meals that ever a new husband had to eat?

I related my difficulties to Jack, and told him . . . we should never be able to manage with such kitchen utensils . . . "Oh, pshaw! You are pampered and spoiled with your New England kitchens," said he, "you will have to learn to do as other army women do—cook in cans and such things, be inventive . . ."

After my unpractical teacher had gone out . . . I ran over to Mrs. Wilhelm's quarters . . . and saw the most beautiful array of tin-ware, shining and neat, placed in rows upon the shelves and hanging from hooks on the wall. "So," I said, "my military husband does not know anything about these things"; and I availed myself of the first trip of the ambulance over to Cheyenne, bought a stock of tin-ware and had it charged, and made no mention of it—because I feared that tin-ware was to be our bone of contention, and I put off the evil day.

Martha and her husband traveled from Wyoming to Camp Verde, Arizona, about forty miles east of Prescott, and then to Camp Apache.

Captain Brayton, of the Eighth Infantry, and his wife, who were already settled at Camp Verde, received us and took the best care of us. Mrs. Brayton gave me a few more lessons in army house-keeping, and I told her about Jack and the tin-ware; her bright eyes snapped, and she said, "Men think they know everything, but the truth is, they don't know anything; you go right ahead and have all the tin-ware and other things; all you can get, in fact; and when the time comes to move, send Jack out of the house, get a soldier to come in and pack you up, and say nothing about it."

"But the weight—"

"Fiddlesticks! They all say that; now you just not mind their talk, but take all you need, and it will get carried along, some-how."

Now [at Camp Apache] came the unpacking of the chests and trunks. There . . . was no closet, there were no hooks on the bare walls, no place to hang things or lay things, and what to do I did not know. I was in despair; Jack came in, to find me sitting on the edge of a chest, which was half unpacked, the contents on the floor. I was very mournful, and he did not see why. . . .

I could never get accustomed to the wretched small space of one room and a hall . . . The forlorn makeshifts for closets, and the absence of all conveniences, annoyed me and added much to the difficulties of my situation. Added to this, I soon discovered that my husband had a penchant for buying and collecting things which seemed utterly worthless to me, and only added to the number of articles to be handled and packed away. I begged him to refrain, and to remember that he was married, and that we had not the money to spend in such ways. He really did try to improve, and denied himself the taking of many an alluring share in raffles for old saddles, pistols, guns, and cow-boy's stuff . . .

But an auction of condemned hospital stores was too much for him, and he came in triumphantly one day, bringing a box of antiquated dentist's instruments in his hand.

"Good gracious!" I cried. "What can you ever do with those forceps?"

"Oh! They are splendid," he said, "and they will come in mighty handy some time."

I saw that he loved tools and instruments, and I reflected, why not? There are lots of things I have a passion for, and love, just as he loves those things, and I shall never say any more about it . . .

HARRIET NEWELL JONES DODD

Harriet's husband, Captain William Dodd, was killed in an Indian attack on the Norwegian settlement of New Ulm, Minnesota. Described by an observer as "indomitable" for his political involvement, and by a fellow pioneer as "a considerable mimic and an actor" whose clever acts and gesture drew "roars of laughter" from the audience, his energetic presence was sorely missed by all—particularly Harriet, whose sorrow was carefully recorded in her journal, kept between 1862 and 1863.

18TH

Terrible Indian massacre

1862 AUG. 19

W. B. Dodd left his home before daylight to prepare to march to the defence of New Ulm.

20TH

Armed men constantly passing through St. Peter.

21ST

Soldiers arrived from St. Paul, Sick soldier, James Hill, came to my house.

22

Burning at the Norwegian settlement. Great panic among the citizens of St. Peter. All rushing into the ware house.

1862 AUG. 23
William B. Dodd at New Ulm. Saturday.

25TH MONDAY
Heard the rumor that he was killed but did not believe it.

26 TUESDAY
The Kniff boy came and told me he helped to bury him!

27
On Wednesday Dr. David came and brought me his last words. *last*—oh shall I *never* never more hear his voice?

28 THURSDAY
The Bishop came and helped to nurse the wounded in the hospital.

SEPT. 1
Mrs. Seeger called and took my bonnet and got my black dress.

TUESDAY
Mrs. Parker came to help me sew and Mr. Livermore came.

WEDNESDAY
Mrs. Parker helped me sew on William's clothes and Augusta Sylvester took his shirts home to make.

SAT. SEPT. 6
Walked up to Henry's for the first time since— Read some lines entitled "the Wife" and felt reproached that I had not loved more faithfully and singly— Now let my heart be set on loving him thru his children. Oh the darling Lucy. Let my prayer be not that she may be rich, beautiful or great in the world's eyes, but that she

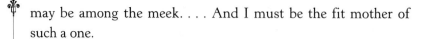

may be among the meek. . . . And I must be the fit mother of such a one.

SUNDAY, SEPT. 7TH 1862, 12TH AFTER TRINITY
Mr. Livermore had service this morning—this afternoon I walked around the barn and yard observing what I have to take care of and considering how much *diligence* and method is necessary to manage a household. How can I learn method? I begin this evening some mental cultivation. I will attend to German. Oh how much I have to learn for my darling. Thank God that my labor of study is so great. I must find some time every evening for study when my darlings are asleep but never to go beyond the hour of 10—then I must retire.

Dr. Daniels stopped in today and talked of the last hours of my husband. I must not live in the past. My whole thought must be of my present duty, to improve myself in mind in heart and manners, to cultivate in my children habits of neatness, order and diligence.

MONDAY, SEPT. 7
To day went to the commissioner's office to get the bill of the oats we had furnished the goverment certified . . . I thought when I came home of writing a sort of memorial . . . asking for aid for myself and children on the ground that our husband and father fell in the front of battle, I thought of asking aid for all such widows and orphans but I reflected at last that I was rather desirous of drawing attention to myself and then children, than of making any such profit for them. *This must be my rule*. Do nothing for the praise of men. Let your single motive be, the Glory of God and your own salvation. . . .

Unidentified wedding (Denver Public Library, Western History Department)

PART III THREE

The

Marryin'

Kind

Woman at dressing table
(California Museum of Photography, Keystone-Mast Collection)

Homestead Brides

*"And so I told her . . .
that I would come . . .
and bring a horse, bridle,
and saddle for her,
if somebody else didn't get
her before Thursday."*
—DAVID CROCKETT

THE HOMESTEAD AND RANCHING REGIONS OF THE WEST, touted by land brokers and rail companies as an "earthly paradise" and a "Garden of Eden," fulfilled biblical prophecy in at least one way: there were hardly any women. So severe was the gender imbalance that frontier men often resorted to courting teenagers. With prostitutes and Native American women ruled out as bridal material, men would eye the youngest women around. "Hurrah for the girls!" a group of bachelors shouted in Nebraska City as a settler marched his brood of young girls through a hotel parlor. The "whoops and cheers" that celebrated the adolescence of young Jane Malick of Oregon had less to do with her ability to gallop to fling aside parental restrictions on horseback through the countryside than the fact that she was extremely young, and also a hard worker. "It was customary in early days for girls to marry at fourteen, fifteen and sixteen years of age," wrote California emigrant Mary Ackley. Often, they were even younger.

Some children were spoken for at eleven and twelve. So desperate was one man for a bride that he rode from house to house with a long pole, tapping at each door and crying out from horseback: "Are there daughters within to marry?" Junior officers at Fort Simpson, Oregon, during the early years of the old Northwest fur and trading company, resorted to wooing the children of their senior officers—girls so young they needed "finishing" before matrimony, and fathering after. One fourteen-year-old bride, the betrothed of a Colonel Hearne, clung to her dolls at the altar, one of a long line of children who would be grandmothers before turning thirty.

Age disparity in marriage was not uncommon. Older, widowed women were desired by younger men—particularly if they had property—while older men, widowed or long-term bachelors, sought energetic young women, ideally between the ages of fourteen and sixteen.

For most, a young wife was highly desired; youth meant malleability—a girl to comply with authority, raise children and act as nurse in a man's elder years. For the bride, matrimony offered financial asylum. The freedom to oversee her own household, humble or not, was a welcome alternative to working "as a drudge" for hire.

Rebecca Woodson was married at the age of sixteen. "I have never for one moment regretted my marriage to George," she recalled, even though her teenage years were an endless regimen in which she had to "cook and do the housework for twenty men, sometimes more."

Eliza Spencer, married at seventeen, found age difference immaterial. One day she sat atop a gatepost, "gazing at the world," according to diarist Mary Hallock Foote. The next, she had met George Austus, a forty-year-old bachelor who spied her sitting there. They courted, loved and married. She bore him twelve children, presided over his table and cheerfully performed as hostess to legions of visitors. Each day that passed lessened the gap of age: love had worked its claim on their hearts.

Not all were so sanguine about the age difference. Bernhard Marks, writing in 1850, was troubled by the "lack of a *grown* lady, from twelve upwards" to dance with, much less to marry. Lala Ketchum, a sixteen-year-old from Maine, decided to "get her dresses long" before marrying. Hadn't we better? she wondered.

Washington Territory pronounced that marriage applicants must be eighteen. But, according to reporter Roger Conant, the "marryin' man of choice" was Elder Bagley, a clerical scofflaw who simply cut out two shoe-sized pieces of paper, marked them with the number 18 and placed them underfoot for the bride to stand upon, reasoning that she was then "over" eighteen.

Parents often tried to ward off older suitors, knowing that the departure of a daughter depleted the household's real, and potential, income—no small loss in a struggling rural economy. Thus,

Abigail Malick tried to avert the attentions paid to her young daughter by a Mr. Pearson, who "had no business to notice a little school girl." Persistently, he was "Alwais Stuck to Jane . . . until he had her," and besides, "they Loved each other very Mutch." In fact, Abigail finally admitted, "his hol hart hung on her and no one elce." Missouri Senator Thomas Hart Benton objected to the courtship of his fifteen-year-old daughter, Jessie, by the noted explorer John Charles Frémont. Both age and birthright were in question, since Frémont's family was not only poor, but also undistinguished. Although she was only fifteen, Jessie was considered an original thinker. She knew her own mind and was old enough to know that what her father would not approve, she would simply take. Lovestruck and headstrong, she accepted Frémont's offer and the couple eloped—her independence presaging a growing desire in women for freedom in politics, economics and matters of the heart.

Such autonomy made men nervous. Some would "fly into their state rooms to hide from the females," according to riverboat passenger Mollie Dorsey—perhaps fleeing by a woman's mature age rather than her politics. According to *Godey's Magazine and Lady's Book* of 1844, a gentleman trying to shake off the attentions of an "ancient lady" informed her that a man's prime was at fifty and a woman's at thirty: "I have barely climbed to the top of the hill," he explained, "while you have passed over it, and are . . . down the wrong side."

Yet widows were often prized as wives—they were solvent, competent and valued for their life experience, child-rearing skills and household acumen, not to mention inherited property, jewelry and money in savings. Marriage-minded widows might itemize their assets, present the list to a helpful—and possibly prominent—male relative, then hope for the best. "Excuse me for not riteing Sooner," penned one young widow to her cousin, John Binckley, in 1819. "I must inform you I have five children . . .

[my parents] are deceast . . . [I own] some home, [and have] seven hundred and thirty nine Dollars remaining." Would he help her find a responsible mate? Colonel John Thornton, a well-to-do landowner, noted that about "three-fourths of the rich widows" he had known had "lost all or most of their estates for want of business knowledge," with one widow allowing her life's savings to vanish between May and December of a single year by loaning it without security and against all advice to a "smooth, pleasant, plausible talker." Naive and trusting, such women were, according to Thornton, "overreached and cheated by numerous and plausible sharpers"—examples of what Samuel Johnson termed the "triumph of hope over experience."

Widowhood did not mean complete inexperience. Despite the prudery of the times, many females brought certain sexual expectations to their new unions—they would not go lacking. Historian Merrill D. Smith cites an 1805 case in which the heartbroken Jacob Collady confessed the shameful inability to consummate his marriage to his mature bride, Sophia. The bride's "considerable uneasyness and dissatisfaction" after the wedding night soon grew to epic proportions. Jacob was clearly "not fit to know" his wife—even after long consultations with a minister and a physician. Sophia won a divorce on the grounds that she was a healthy young woman, had enjoyed normal relations in her first marriage and deserved them in her second.

"Grass widows," on the other hand, were seen as women of suspect virtue, in search of younger mates or, failing that, secret consorts. Truth and fantasy intermingle in the telling, since most grass widows were simply women unable to remarry because their husbands lived far afield; couples could neither reunite nor divorce. Men routinely left their families to join the army, to mine the mother lode, to work as field hands or to simply disappear. They promised to write, send money or summon for the wife when the new home was established, but time worked its lethargy in even the strongest union. When Jerusha D. Merrill's husband, who had "taken up a tract of land and commensed a farm . . . about fifty or sixty miles" distant finally wrote to his wife, not even the lure of his eight employees, apparent prosperity and "two yoak of cattle two mules an[d] a lot of chickings" could entice Jerusha to pay him a visit. Other women, however, pined for their missing mates, as did Rachel Malick, who discovered at the end of her husband's four-month absence on a surveying job that life without him "haint as much fun as I thought it would be."

What to do? Widows wanted husbands and bachelors longed for mates. Although more than 800,000 women trudged west during the peak years of the overland migration, most of them were already married—there were simply too few single white women available, even counting all the Civil War widows and Eastern spinsters. A staggering imbalance—16,584 bachelors to 1,426 single women—made Idaho a spinster's paradise, according to a survey taken by the *Ladies' Home Journal* in March 1899; Arizona and Wyoming were considered the next best destinations for bachelors.

An advertisement in the *Des Moines Register* of March 19, 1868, cited by Glenda Riley, read "wanted—thirty-seven thousand, five hundred farmers!" to settle in Iowa. Left unmentioned was the fact that each man would want a wife. "Let the Yankee girls take the hint!" cried another newspaper at the time, sounding the universal challenge to single women: "Go West and marry!"

Toward the end of the 1900s, personal correspondences sprang to life, linking men and women across the country in numerous brides-by-mail schemes, some successful, some not. On March 9, 1911, the *Wahpeton Times* of North Dakota described the odyssey of two girls, one of whom was to become a bride-by-mail:

GIRLS TELL A STRANGE STORY

. . . the girls left their homes . . . several weeks ago to come to Buford, N.D. One of the girls had been corresponding with a farmer . . . and their correspondence had progressed to the point where he had popped the question. The girl immediately started for Buford from far away New York, but her friend insisted on [coming] . . . probably with the hope that she, too, would become entangled matrimonially. But when they arrived in Buford and the elder of the two had gazed upon the face of the man . . . the spell was immediately broken. He didn't suit. In fact, he wouldn't do at all. The other girl fully acquiesced in the decision so they started back again . . .

Another "want ad" romance ended better, according to the *Devil's Lake Daily Journal* of May 8, 1912—also in North Dakota.

. . . about a year and a half ago, John Bartley, a prosperous farmer . . . advertised in some rural paper for a wife with which to share his prosperity . . . The ad found its way to Mcintosh, Minn., where Mrs. C. E. Davis, who is devoted to her grand daughter, Margery . . . answered the ad without consulting the young lady. When the gentleman's answer came, it not only pleased her, but met with the approval of Miss Davis and immediately a lively correspondence sprung up. This continued a year and [soon] . . . the date was set. The young lady accompanied by Mrs. Davis reached Lakota last evening. It was agreed beforehand that . . . each should wear a bouquet of flowers so there would be no difficulty in recognizing one another. Mr. Bartley was at the depot at Lakota with a large number of friends. It was a case of complete satisfaction and they lost no time in coming to the county seat to secure the license.

He has showered the bride with gifts.

Into the gender breach stepped a sober, intelligent widow with a plan to bring "migrating women" to California from the East Coast. Eliza Farnham's motives were altruistic; she believed that well-bred women, clergy-recommended and sound of character, could check the rampant evils of all-male living, so sadly apparent in the west. The concept was not new—in 1619, ninety women were sent to the Virginia colony to settle amid the all-male population and guarantee the colony's future through progeny—yet Eliza's efforts were met with hilarity and gossip, she was called a procuress, and resultant snickering innuendo made her so ill she canceled the plan and sailed for California with three women, rather than a hundred.

In 1866, entrepreneur Asa Shinn Mercer sensed an economic windfall in transporting women west, and to recruit them he lectured throughout the east, filling the heads of eager female listeners with bright hyperbole and stories of gold, land, men by the thousands and boundless employment to be found in the state of Washington.

Occupationally, the western tilt favored men, while the majority of women remained home- or factory-bound, trapped in minimal domestic occupations, sewing for dimes or working as impecunious teachers, an occupation revealed by early statistics to have the lowest rate of marriage compared to the other female occupations of nursing, domestic or manufacturing work. Manufacturing paid three to twelve dollars weekly; sales about eight dollars a week and theater or ballet arts, ten dollars a week, less the cost of costumes. With five to six dollars as the typical weekly rent and seventy-five cents paid out for washing, little wonder that working women struggled to live. Targeting thirty thousand single women under the age of twenty-five, Mercer promised to deliver to the eager Pacific Coast bachelors a "passell of genuine ladies" and a "suitable wife of good moral character," already evident in the cluster of eleven females delivered to Puget Sound,

Unidentified young girl (American Images, National Archives)

where they immediately found jobs or marriage.

To the lonely men of the Pacific Northwest, Mercer seemed a savior; to the press, a probable charlatan. To the women he enlisted—dubbed a "Hegira of Spinsters" and a "Cargo of Females"—Mercer was banker, chaperon, tour guide and matchmaker, all for the price of the two-hundred-dollar passage. He also proved manipulative, if not criminal, by cleverly soliciting money from the eager bachelors for prospective brides, then double-billing the women the same amount for their passage, even adding landing costs. As his funds dwindled, Mercer would fix random fees on personal belongings—trunks and suitcases—and refuse to sail further until "proper financial arrangements" were made. Or he would stall the ship in port, refusing to sail unless the women would sign notes for money in the names of the future husbands. Naive women meekly signed—others flatly refused.

On matters of shipboard behavior, Mercer insisted upon a strict code of conduct: early curfews and no flirting or mingling with officers or crew. Two women were compelled to leave the ship in Brazil, labeled "unfortunate" in the ship's records, their offense and their departure shrouded in mystery. Eventually, boredom forced one high-spirited girl to "flirt with [the] officers as much as . . . she pleased," which panicked Mercer. She was "no better than a ruined girl," he exhorted. What would the bachelors think? Her upstart spirit sparked the women's slumbering dissatisfaction into full mutiny—flirting, singing and dancing broke out day and night, long after the ten o'clock curfew had passed.

Scarcely had the ship landed when the weddings began—one of the first being Mercer's. According to one passenger, the "very gay and flirtatious" Mercer had fallen in love with one of the passengers, been soundly rejected, then met another whom he wed when he reached Seattle.

In the spirit of western enterprise, another businessman, Fred Harvey, became one of the west's most active marriage brokers. In 1882, he opened his first restaurant in the sagebrush desert of Raton, New Mexico, by hiring "women waiters and mop squeezers" who had never been away from home. Young rural girls throughout the country penned eager applications to work in whistlestop restaurants along the Santa Fe line, serving fresh fruit and filtered spring water to "distinguished" passengers, at stopover points that numbered a hundred in 1917, and ranged from Chicago to Galveston, Texas, to the West Coast.

Food servers were traditionally men, while the word *waitress* was a popular euphemism for prostitute. Since to be served food for money by an unknown woman seemed a metaphor for much deeper intimacy, Harvey's experimental decision to use women, not men, excited much attention. Insisting upon finding "young women of good character, attractive and intelligent," Harvey made sure the girls were well chaperoned, had strict visiting hours, were not harassed by profanity in the workplace and dressed decorously. Each girl's contract required her to remain single for a year, to live in a chaperoned dormitory and entertain callers only in the "courting parlor." Unspoken was the fact that she would save a handsome nest egg on her salary of nearly twenty dollars a month.

Although profiting from male fantasy and female expectation, Harvey still offered women a chance to improve their working conditions, their social skills and, ultimately, their marital status. He attracted entrepreneurial women seeking a direct route to better jobs and, often, matrimony. "I honestly never believed anything that good would ever happen to me," wrote Bertha Spears, a farm girl from Oklahoma who happily complied with the Harvey House rules, knowing that when the year's contract was up, so, too, was her obligation to stay.

So popular were the demure, black-clad young women that toward the turn of the century, nearly five thousand of them had wed, many happily. They met distinguished male travelers—generally engineers and local merchants or ranchers who would order up a four-course meal, complete with capon, roast sirloin of beef and seven vegetables, and then fell in love with the spry young waitress who could be enticed into the courting parlor if the right man came along. For a period of time, Fred Harvey "kept the West in food and wives," with as many as 100,000 Harvey Girls employed between 1883 and 1950.

In reality, the U.S. government was the west's largest wedding broker, making marriage financially worthwhile for both men and women through its homestead land policies. With a simple "I do!" a man could get 640 acres of land and a working partner—if he could find a woman to say yes. The economics were simple: a single homesteader could claim 320 acres and a family, twice that amount, or one square mile of unbroken prairie. The only drawback for women was in the fine print, for property legislation designated a married woman's land to her husband, leaving her unable to trade or sell her 320 acres. By marrying, she bolstered the family's holdings; by staying single, she would become a landowner. Her dilemma fostered the solution of common-law couples staking out parallel claims, their adjacent wooden shacks back to back, connected by a roofed wooden catwalk for back-and-forth travel and conjugal visits. One house was used for sleeping, the other for dining and family life; thus a couple could live legally as lovers, common-law partners and separate landowners.

For the remaining unwed, newspaper matrimonial advertisements were wildly in vogue and used by both sexes, in which true motives, finances, status and physical appearance were construed from veiled—or oddly candid—descriptions. *The Matrimonial News,* a San Francisco matchmaking newspaper of 1873, desired to "promote honorable matrimonial engagements and true conjugal felicities" for "amiable" men and women "edifying in conversation, truly chaste and partial to children." In fact, only the amiable needed to advertise, since all others, particularly those with "questionable objects in view," were urged by the newspapers not to apply. In case of a scoundrel, the paper would break a code of privacy as "sacred as life itself" and reveal the culprit's name. And those who truly wished to marry? Advertising rates were $1.50 per word, names were secret, unless a nom de plume was used and, if a wedding occurred, both parties would pay a fee within one month.

PERSONALS—1873

I.S.—I TOLD YOU TO LOOK IN THE MATRIMONIAL NEWS FOR MY ANSWER. IT IS THIS: I AM FIRM. IF YOU AGREE TO MY VIEWS MEET ME AT WOODWARDS GARDENS ABOUT 3 O'CLOCK SUNDAY AFTERNOON.

MAGGIE—GEORGE IS DECEIVING YOU AND I CAN PROVE IT. HE WILL SEE THIS ADVERTISEMENT AND I AM READY TO MAKE GOOD MY ASSERTION EITHER BY PROOF OR THE OTHER WAY. H.M.S.

BESSIE—A WEEK'S ROMP OUT THERE WOULD DO US BOTH GOOD. SAY WHEN. AGNES.

TOM—SECURED TWO SEATS NEAR THE FRONT. BE WAITING EARLY. KATE.

J.V.G.—DECLINE TO MEET YOU AGAIN UNTIL YOU WRITE AND EXPLAIN YOUR INTENTIONS. YOU HAVE HAD TIME ENOUGH AND OUR LAST [ENCOUNTER] WAS DISAGREEABLE TO ME, AND CANNOT BE REPEATED UNTIL WE ARE ENGAGED. A.S.C.

D.J.C., MARKET ST.—I KNOW IT WAS YOU WHO FOLLOWED MY SISTER IN AN OFFENSIVE WAY ON SATURDAY EVENING

Woman looking at photographs
(Photo by Wilcox. Museum of History and Industry, Seattle)

Unidentified man reading a letter
(Arizona State University Libraries)

LAST. TAKE THIS NOTICE THAT YOUR CONDUCT IS OBJECTIONABLE TO HER, AND BEING SO I SHALL NOT SHRINK MY DUTY, AND THIS FAIR WARNING TO YOU WILL BE GIVEN IN EVIDENCE ON MY BEHALF. I AM *YOU KNOW WHO.*

A BACHELOR OF 30, TALL, WELL CONNECTED, WOULD LIKE TO HEAR FROM 58 OF JAN. 17TH, OR ANY OTHER LADY OR WIDOW, WITH SMALL MEANS. PROPRIETOR HAS ADDRESS.

THE ADVERTISER WISHES TO FORM THE ACQUAINTANCE OF A MIDDLE-AGED LADY, WHO HAS SOME MEANS, FOR THE PURPOSE OF GOING INTO A RURAL PURSUIT THAT WOULD PAY WELL.

A BACHELOR OF 40, GOOD APPEARANCE AND SUBSTANTIAL MEANS, WANTS A WIFE. SHE MUST BE UNDER 30, AMIABLE, AND MUSICAL.

A LADY, 23, TALL, FAIR, AND GOOD LOOKING, WITHOUT MEANS, WOULD LIKE TO HEAR FROM A GENTLEMAN OF POSITION WANTING A WIFE. SHE IS WELL EDUCATED, ACCOMPLISHED, AMIABLE, AND AFFECTIONATE.

"CANDID" SEEKS TO IMPROVE HIS CONDITION BY MARRIAGE. AGED 27, HEIGHT 5 FEET 9 INCHES, DARK HAIR AND EYES, CONSIDERED BY ALL HANDSOME, HIS FRIENDS UNITE IN SAYING HE IS AMIABLE AND WILL MAKE A MODEL HUSBAND. HE HAS NOT RESIDED IN CALIFORNIA LONG. THE LADY MUST BE ONE IN THE MOST EXTENDED ACCEPTATION OF THE WORD SINCE THE ADVERTISER MOVES IN THE MOST POLISHED AND REFINED SOCIETY. IT IS ALSO DESIRABLE THAT SHE SHOULD HAVE CONSIDERABLE MONEY.

I AM 33 YEARS OF AGE, AND AS REGARDS LOOKS CAN AVERAGE WITH MOST MEN. I HAVE BEEN AN OFFICER IN THE UNITED STATES NAVY; HAVE TRAVELED ALL MY LIFE, AND HAVE SEEN THE WORLD. FOR THE PRESENT I AM FOLLOWING A PLEASANT OCCUPATION AT A FAIR SALARY. I AM LOOKING FOR A LADY TO MAKE HER MY WIFE, AS I AM HEARTILY TIRED OF BACHELOR LIFE. I DESIRE A LADY NOT OVER 28 OR 30 YEARS OF AGE, NOT UGLY, WELL EDUCATED AND MUSICAL. NATIONALITY MAKES NO DIFFERENCE, ONLY I PREFER NOT TO HAVE A LADY OF IRISH BIRTH. SHE MUST HAVE AT LEAST $20,000. I HAVE A QUIET DISPOSITION, LOVE COMFORT ABOVE EVERYTHING, AND, IF MARRIED, WILL MAKE A MODEL HUSBAND.

A YOUNG LADY OF GOOD FAMILY AND EDUCATION, CONSIDERED HANDSOME, WOULD LIKE TO CORRESPOND WITH SOME GENTLEMAN OF MEANS, ONE WHO WOULD BE WILLING TO TAKE HER WITHOUT A DOLLAR, AS SHE HAS NOTHING TO OFFER BUT HERSELF; WOULD LIKE TO HEAR FROM AND EXCHANGE CARTES WITH A GENTLEMAN NOT OVER 40.

I SEEK A CONGENIAL SPIRIT, IF SHE IS OF THE **EARNEST, BRAVE** AND **TRUE,** WITH WELL DEVELOPED BRAIN AND BODY, A WARM AND WILLING HAND: . . . AM 22, MEDIUM HEIGHT, SIZE OF BRAIN 23 INCHES: TEMPERAMENT, NERVOUS-SANGUINE: . . . ANTI-RUM, SLAVERY, DRUG, TEA, AND COFFE AND AM A VEGETARIAN . . . SHALL BE HAPPY TO COMMUNICATE WITH ANYONE INTERESTED. [FROM THE *WATER-CURE JOURNAL,* 1856]

The first frontier correspondence may have begun with a brush and a bucket of tar, with which thousands of overland travelers passing Independence Rock daubed across the tortoise-shaped rock their initials, names or the names of their loved ones. Such insignia was the mark of the lonely traveler, calling up beloved faces, memories and names. Equally poignant was the lonely frontier woman, who according to writer Louis L'Amour, sadly penned dinner invitations, over and over, then attached them to tumbleweeds which she tossed into the wind, hoping that someone—some man—might be lured across the plains that evening to enliven her solitary supper. Later, the Pony Express thundered cross-country, bringing letters a month or two old. Some were discarded along the way because sealing wax, the mark of elegant, cosmopolitan correspondence, melted in the desert heat and turned to waxen sludge, and the letters were thrown away in disgust by the post office. "It took a letter about four weeks to come from New Jersey to Ohio, and twenty-five cents to get it out of the office," wrote Keturah Penton. "So we did not get Many letters in them days."

In the Dakotas in 1866, Sarah Elizabeth Canfield's letters came "at long intervals, usually three or four at a time as the mail is sent . . . [first] by Indian runners . . . then to Omaha by stage" —a random correspondence little appreciated by suitors.

Chautauqua views
(Photograph by E. A. Bishop. State Historical Society of Wisconsin)

ELINORE PRUITT STEWART

Elinore Pruitt Stewart was one of hundreds of widowed women who came west seeking independence and a means of support. Uneducated and trying to raise her child by cooking and washing, she found the prospect of moving to Burnt Fork, Wyoming, as a housekeeper to a Scottish farmer ideal. Once there, she homesteaded her own land and eventually married her employer, facing each day with good humor and an endless reserve of charity for those hapless wanderers in need who came her way.

DECEMBER 2, 1912

Dear Mrs. Coney,

. . . I have often wished I might tell you all about my Clyde, but have not because of two things. One is I could not even begin without telling you what a good man he is, and I didn't want you to think I could do nothing but brag. The other reason is the haste I think I married in. I am ashamed of that. I am afraid you will think me a Becky Sharp of a person. But although I married in haste, I have no cause to repent. That is very fortunate because I have never had one bit of leisure to repent in. . . .

The engagement was powerfully short because both agreed that the trend of events and ranch work seemed to require that we be married first and do our "sparking" afterward. You see, we had to chink in the wedding between times, that is, between planting the oats and other work that must be done early or not at all. In Wyoming ranchers can scarcely take time even to be married in the springtime.

That having been settled, the license was sent for by mail, and as soon as it came Mr. Stewart saddled Club and went down to the house of Mr. Pearson, the justice of the peace and a friend of long standing. I had never met any of the family and naturally rather dreaded to have them come, but Mr. Stewart was firm in wanting to be married at home, so he told Mr. Pearson he wanted him and his family to come up the following Wednesday and serve papers on the "wooman i' the hoose." They were astonished, of course, but being such good friends they promised him all the assistance they could render. They were quite the dearest, most interesting family! I have since learned to love them as my own.

Well, there was not time to make wedding clothes, so I had to "do up" what I did have. Isn't it queer how sometimes, do what you can, work will keep getting in the way until you can't get anything done? That is how it was with me those few days before the wedding; so much so that when Wednesday dawned everything was topsy-turvy and I had a very strong desire to run away. But I always did hate a "piker" so I stood pat. Well, I had most of the dinner cooked, but it kept me hustling to get the house into anything like decent order before the old dog barked, and I knew my moments of Liberty were limited. It was blowing a perfect hurricane and snowing like midwinter. I had bought a beautiful pair of shoes to wear on that day, but my vanity had squeezed my feet a little, so while I was so busy at work, I had kept on a worn old pair, intending to put on the new ones later; but when the Pearsons drove up all I thought about was getting them into the house where there was fire, so I forgot all about the old shoes and the apron I wore.

I had only been here six weeks then, and was a stranger. That is why I had no one to help me and was so confused and hurried. As soon as the newcomers were warm, Mr. Stewart told me I had better come over by him and stand up. It was a large room I had to cross, and how I did it before all those strange eyes I never knew. All I can remember very distinctly is hearing Mr. Stewart saying "I will," and myself chiming in that I would, too. Happening to glance down, I saw that I had forgotten to take off my apron or my old shoes, but just then Mr. Pearson pronounced us man and wife, and as I had dinner to serve right away I had no time to worry over my odd toilet. Anyway the shoes were comfortable and the apron white, so I suppose it could have been worse; and I don't think it has ever made any difference with the Pearsons, for I number them all among my most esteemed friends.

It is customary here for newlyweds to give a dance and supper at the hall, but as I was a stranger I preferred not to, and so it was a long time before I became acquainted with all my neighbors. I had not thought I should ever marry again. Jerrine was always such a dear little pal, and I wanted to just knock about foot-loose and free to see life as a gypsy sees it. I had planned to see the Cliff-Dwellers' home; to live right there until I caught the spirit of the surroundings enough to live over their lives in imagination anyway. I had planned to see the old missions and go to Alaska; to hunt in Canada. I even dreamed of Honolulu. Life stretched out before me one long, happy jaunt. I aimed to see all the world I could, but to travel unknown bypaths to do it . . . I want a great many things I haven't got, but I don't want them enough to be discontented and not enjoy the many blessings that are mine. I have my home among the blue mountains, my healthy, well-formed children, my clean, honest husband, my kind, gentle milk cows, my garden which I make myself. I have loads and loads of flowers which I tend myself. There are lots of chickens, turkeys, and pigs which are my own special care. I have some slow old gentle horses and an old wagon . . . Do you wonder I am so happy? When I think of it all, I wonder how I can crowd all my joy into one short life. . . .

Elinore often wrote her humorous letters from a "creaky old rocker" overlooking a bower of pansies and sweet alyssum— the "memory-bed." Her joy in life was extreme and before her death in 1933 she wrote: "I [realize] anew how happy I am . . . and how many of life's blessings are mine."

Chautauqua, Winfield, Kansas, 1888, with professor Charles Fazel, standing at left (Kansas State Historical Society)

Unidentified women
(State Historical Society of North Dakota)

Mercer
Girls

ROGER CONANT

"I, A. S. Mercer, of Seattle, W.T., hereby agree to bring a suitable wife of good moral character and reputation, from the East to Seattle, on or before September, 1865, for each of the parties whose signatures are hereunto attached, they first paying me or my agent, the sum of three hundred dollars, with which to pay the passage of said ladies from the East and to compensate me for my trouble."

—A. S. MERCER, SEATTLE, W.T., MARCH 1, 1865

The steamship Continental *embarked from New York bound for Seattle in 1866 carrying one hundred single women recruited by entrepreneur Asa Mercer. He appealed to "high-minded" women to go west, hopefully to marry the eager bachelors who awaited them. The seventeen-week voyage was designed to end the Great Male Shortage in the East and the lack of women in the west. Drawn by the publicity aspect,* The New York Times *reporter Roger Conant came along— a thirtyish bachelor who delighted in the abundance of feminine company on board.*

TUESDAY, MARCH 27TH [1866]

The day after we left Talcuhuano Mr. Mercer commenced writing out some very suspicious looking papers. On Sunday he was so busy that he could not find time to preach one of Mr. Beecher's sermons. Yesterday he brought matters to a climax. The first lady he called into his state room was Mrs. Chase, and after stating that he had been to great expense in bringing out this party, told her that she must give him her note for two hundred & fifty Dol-

lars [a legal acknowledgment of debt] . . . [and that] she would probably get a husband as soon as she reached Seattle, and he would pay the note. "Yes, Mr. Mercer," said she, "if I can find a man with white hairs, his pockets well lined with gold, one foot in the grave and the other just ready to go in I might get married, but mind, none of his money shall ever find its way into your pocket . . . "

With his next subject he was more successful. Poor old Aunt Berry was the victim. After stating what he wanted, he told her with a beaming smile that she would find a husband in Seattle, who would pay the note.

"Oh! Mr. Mercer," she exclaimed. "Do you think that there is any body up there who would be willing to marry me?" "Certainly," said he. "Certainly. There is a . . . farmer who lives near me, who wants a wife, and he promised to take whoever I brought."

"If that is the case," said she, "I will give you my note for any amount, if you will promise to recommend me to him." "I picked you out on purpose for him," said Mercer, at the same time handing her a note to sign, which she did without reading it . . .

Some [women] gave him their notes and some did not . . . the whole affair has created great excitement on shipboard. Some of the ladies came to us and asked if Mercer would not be obliged to carry them through on the tickets which he gave them in New York. We were very sorry to . . . tell them that Mercer was not a responsible person, and as he had received no consideration, the tickets were not worth the paper they were printed on.

THURSDAY, MARCH 29TH

In order to draw their attention away from the officers, Mr. Mercer has been trying to invent some new games and induc[e] the young ladies to play them. Among them were "Spiritual rappings," and guessing Proverbs . . .

THURSDAY, APRIL 12TH

The flirtation between the officers and some of the ladies has gone so far that the Captain felt compelled to interfere. The younger officers have begun to neglect their duties for the girls and the Captain has determined to put a stop to the whole thing. He has ordered the younger officers not to speak to or have anything to do with any of the ladies . . .

FRIDAY, APRIL 13TH

The Captain finds the enforcing of his order rather up hill business. The girls have denied his right to issue such an order, and have combined together to break it, and they seemed determined to flirt as much as they please. Last night the Captain told them that they must all be in their state rooms by ten o'clock. They did not go, and were determined not to go. It was a splendid little case of mutiny. The captain saw that his orders must be obeyed or all discipline would be at an end. Placing the 1st Officer at the head of the stairway leading from the upper into the lower saloon, to prevent them from coming up, he went up to one of them and taking her by the arm, marched her down into the lower saloon with out any ceremony. The balance at once saw the joke and scattered in all directions. It was a long and hard chase for the old man, but he finally captured the last bird, and peace once more reigned . . . The girls . . . went quietly to their state rooms.

MONDAY, APRIL 16TH

Yesterday during dinner time one of the girls and the 2d Mate drew a chalk line from the railing to the door on both sides of the main saloon and wrote underneath, "No subordinate officer allowed aft of this line." When the Captain came and saw it he was in a perfect rage. He threatened to put all the girls under arrest and keep them in close confinement during the remainder of the voyage. He then put on a sweet smile and promised to for-give the one who did it and give her all the molasses she wanted for the rest of the voyage . . .

TUESDAY, APRIL 24TH

We are now passing through the Golden Gate, and before night the cruise of the *Continental* will come to an end. Most of the party however will proceed to Washington Territory, by some means or other . . .

WEDNESDAY, APRIL 25TH

This morning the ladies were taken from the ship and are now fairly settled at the International and Tremont [hotels]. Fifteen have already broken away from the party, and more will probably follow. Those who wish to taste the beauties of a territorial life will probably be sent north in lumber vessels.

TUESDAY, MAY 29TH

We . . . took the plunger *Maria* . . . for Seattle. The day was beautiful and we had a delightful sail of 15 miles . . . [W]e have seen nothing, with the exception of here and there a little one horse settlement, but water & pine forests. We reached Seattle at 5 in the afternoon, and went at once to the Occidental Hotel . . .

I don't see what Mercer meant by bringing all these women up here for, where there is nothing for them to do . . . The people were all opposed to it, and not knowing what to do with the women . . . hearing that . . . 500 of them [were coming] to that state. The people have warm and hospital [sic] hearts, and have thrown open their doors . . . and promised them a home till they can find something to do.

TUESDAY, JUNE 5TH

We have been here one week and two or three strange incidents have occurred. There were some men in the Territory foolish

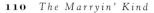

enough to take stocks in Mercer's Company. He was not at all particular as to the character of the men who held stock, and it mattered little to him into whose hands he placed the happiness and keeping of the deluded females, who were crazy enough to place themselves under his charge, with the promise of a future home, so long as he obtained their money. Among those who took stock in the company, and who, hearing of the arrival of the party, hastened to Seattle with the full expectation of receiving a wife . . . and upon being indignantly refused by the girls who wouldn't even speak to them, went away vowing vengeance against Mercer for bringing women that wasn't "on the marry" . . . [were] Humbolt Jack, Lame Duck Bill, Whiskey Jim, White pine Joe, and Bob tailed and Yeke.

There was a young man who owned a little farm up the White River twenty miles back from Seattle. . . . All he wanted to make his life perfectly happy was a wife . . . Hearing that Mercer was going to the States he placed $300 in his hands to bring out this lady . . . But Mercer put the money in his own pocket, and never communicated with the young lady at all. It so happened that another lady of the same name . . . a tailoress . . . came out as one of the party. The young man saw her name among the list of passengers published in the Seattle *Daily;* and with [red] cheeks . . . he arrived in town . . . and learning where the lady was stopping, made his way to the house . . .

There was an awkward pause of a minute or two . . . At last he [said], "I'm the [one] what sent $300 by Mercer to bring you out for my wife . . ."

"Sir," said the young lady, "I do not wish to marry . . ."

"Well," said the youth, "if you didn't come out to get married [why] did you come out . . . ?"

"To make pants, coats and vest," she laughingly replied, "for such fellows as you . . ."

FRIDAY, JUNE 8TH

This morning an old back woodsman who could neither read or write, visited Seattle to inspect the party, and see if he could secure a wife. He was introduced about 3 this afternoon to widow W. who brought out with her a Mother and three interesting sons, the neck of the youngest of whom we were on the point of wringing at least a dozen times during the voyage. At six he offered her his heart and hand; was accepted and at 9 o'clock, just one hour ago, they were married.

We do not know which of the two has been most badly sold.

The following marriages have already taken place:

Miss Mary Grenold to Mr. McClellan of the White River country

Miss Sarah M. Davidson to Mr. Baxter of Seattle

Miss Maria Kinney [or Kenney] to Mr. Tingley

Miss Almira Huntoon to Mr. Reichner of Stockton, Cal.

Miss Mary Martin to Mr. Tallman of San Francisco. This lady is over 40 years of age, and the frisky youth . . . is about 25. He came out on the Continental *as oiler.*

Mrs. Horton to Mr. Buckley of Seattle

Mrs. Amanda Chase to Mr. Harry Wiggins . . . She is eight years the oldest . . .

Miss Robinson to Mr. David Webster of the White River country . . .

Miss Griffith to Mr.——— of Olympia, W.T. This lady married a gentleman worth $100,000

Mail Order Brides and Child Brides

Mr. and Mrs. John Kaliscal. Note that the bride wears a dark dress with a white veil. (Photo by G. G. Machann, "traveling artist." The Institute of Texan Cultures, San Antonio)

ELINORE PRUITT STEWART

**As an observer of the western scene, domestic-turned-homesteader
Elinore Pruitt Stewart is unrivaled. Self-educated, she learned to
read from scavenged newspapers. Self-sufficient, she opted to leave
low-paying domestic service in the city to try her hand at western
life, becoming both a bride and a homesteader in southwestern
Wyoming. Her letters, here quoted, sketch with humor and keen
observation life on the frontier.**

IN CAMP ON THE DESERT
AUGUST 24, 1914
Dear Mrs. Coney,

At last we are off. I am powerfully glad. I shall have to enjoy this
trip for us both. You see how greedy I am for new experiences! I
have never been on a prolonged hunt before, so I am looking forward to a heap of fun . . .

So early the next morning we were astir. We had outfitted in
Green River, so the wagons were already loaded . . .

So we set out. There was a great jangling and banging, for our
tin camp-stoves kept the noise going. Neither the children nor I
can ride under cover on a wagon, we get so sick; so there we were,
perched high up on great rolls of bedding and a tent. I reckon we
looked funny to the "onlookers looking on" as we clattered down
the street; but we were off and that meant a heap.

Soon after noon we could see white clouds of alkali dust
ahead. By and by we came up with the dust-raisers. The children
and I had got into the buckboard with Mrs. O'Shaughnessy and
Miss Hull, so as to ride easier and be able to gossip, and we had
driven ahead of the wagons, so as to avoid the stinging dust.

The sun was just scorching when we overtook the funniest
layout I have [ever] seen . . . In a wobbly old buckboard sat a
young couple completely engrossed by each other. That he was a
Westerner we knew by his cowboy hat and boots; that she was an
Easterner, by her not knowing how to dress for the ride across the
desert. She wore a foolish little chiffon hat which the alkali dust
had ruined, and all the rest of her clothes matched. But over them
the enterprising young man had raised one of those big old sun-
shades that had lettering on them. It kept wobbling about in the
socket he had improvised; one minute we could see "Tea"; then a
rut in the road would swing "Coffee" around. Their sunshade
kept revolving about that way, and sometimes their heads
revolved a little bit, too. We could hear a word occasionally and
knew they were having a great deal of fun at our expense; but we
were amused ourselves, so we didn't care. They would drive along
slowly until we almost reached them; then they would whip up
and raise such a dust that we were almost choked.

Mrs. O'Shaughnessy determined to drive ahead; so she trotted
up alongside, but she could not get ahead. The young people
were giggling. Mrs. O'Shaughnessy doesn't like to be the joke all
the time. Suddenly she leaned over toward them and said: "Will
ye tell me something?" Oh, yes, they would. "Then," she said,
"which of you are Tea and which Coffee?"

Their answer was to drive up faster and stir up a powerful lot
of dust. They kept pretty well ahead after that, but at sundown
we came up with them at the well where we were to camp. This
well had been sunk by the county for the convenience of travelers,
and we were mighty thankful to find it. It came out that our
young couple were bride and groom. They had never seen each
other until the night before, having met through a matrimonial
paper. They had met in Green River and were married that

morning, and the young husband was taking her away up to Pinedale to his ranch.

They must have been ideally happy, for they had forgotten their mess-box, and had only a light lunch. They had only their lap robe for bedding. They were in a predicament; but the girl's chief concern was lest "Honey-bug" should let the wolves get her. Though it is scorching hot on the desert by day, the nights are keenly cool, and I was wondering how they would manage with only their lap-robe, when Mrs. O'Shaughnessy, who cannot hold malice, made a round of the camp, getting a blanket here and a coat there, until she had enough to make them comfortable. Then she invited them to take their meals with us until they could get to where they could help themselves.

I think we all enjoyed camp that night. . . . We sat around the fire talking as the blue shadows faded into gray dusk and the big stars came out. The newly-weds were, as the bride put it, "so full of happiness they had nothing to put it in." Certainly their spirits overflowed. They were eager to talk of themselves and we didn't mind listening.

They are Mr. and Mrs. Tom Burney. She is the oldest of a large family of children and has had to "work out ever since she was big enough to get a job." The people she had worked for rather frowned upon any matrimonial ventures, and as no provision was made for "help" entertaining company, she had never had a "beau." One day she got hold of a matrimonial paper and saw Mr. Burney's ad. She answered and they corresponded for several months. We were just in time to "catch it," as Mr. Haynes—who is a confirmed bachelor—disgustedly remarked. Personally, I am glad; I liked them much better than I thought I should when they were raising so much dust so unnecessarily.

I must close this letter . . .

With a heart full of love for you,

E.R.S.

KETURAH PENTON BELKNAP

Keturah Penton began her journals as a young girl living in a log cabin near Cincinnati in the early 1800s. In typical migrant fashion, the Pentons moved twice across the country, followed by Keturah's own migration to four locations after her marriage. As a marriageable girl on the frontier, she had no lack of suitors, but refused them all until inspiration struck and she knew she had fallen in love.

[M]y mother had looked quite sober all day   I was getting ready to go to take care of a sick neighbor woman toward evening we was getting supper . . . and we had got through the fried chicken and short cake   Father had left the table and had gone to his work (him and Mother always worked in the garden after supper till time to milk)   I noticed Mother lingered over her tea and I thought she looked a little sad. Like she wanted to say something that was hard to say, so I said Mother, if you have anything you want me to do I wont go   She Said She did not need me. but said She, Kitt if I was you I [would] get married and be fixin up a home for myself and not be a drudge for the whole country their is plenty of these fellows that wants you and could give you a good home, and with the tact you have you could soon have a nice place of your own. but says I Mother, I dont like this country and I dont want to leave you and pap alone well, she Said, if I could better myself she had no objection. they could get along very well now they had land enough cleared to make them a good liveing on, and if I staid their till they died I would be an old bro-

Louise Tasher and Charles E. Neil
(Cyanotype Collection. Colorado Historical Society)

ken down old maid and maybe so cross nobody would want me and then would be kicked about from one place to another without any home.

So I told her then when the right one came along Ide think the matter over and let her know in time to get ready but now I must go if she had said her Say. So now I began casting about to see if their was anyone I thought I wanted (for their was about five single men to evry girl)   so their was a young Preacher on the circuit that year and he had all ready filed his intentions to go to conference a Married man so I thought that was my chance to do lots of good.

I was quite a good nurse and I thought we could visit the Sick

and I could help them in two ways   by administering to their bodily wants I could lead them on to love the Lord, so I had almost decided to say yes at the next appointment, but before that time came his Presiding Elder informed me to go a little slow as Brother D did not belong to the conference and was only a supply and it was not recorded that he could get in for he would not study. So for my good he would advise me not to waste my talents on So unpromising a youth.

So that ended my romance of Marrying a Preacher and that I was so providencialy led out of the scrape   but when his next appointment came he wanted to rush matters right through   as it was nearing the time for Conference the whole thing must be got through in a month. I told him that he must go acording to the laws of the church, had he counceled with his Presiding Elder? he said, no, nor would not. he was capable of doing his business and would not ask advice of anyone so I told him if he was that Smart that ended the matter, and we would quit friends   he said their was plenty of other girls, and I told him there was plenty of other men.

the next one that appeared on the sene was a rich young doctor but he was to lazy to practice and he did not know how to do anything else. he had been raised in the South and had Slaves to wait on him So he was no good.

the next was an old Batchelor with a head as red as fire. he had two Sections of Land and lots of money. he Said it was waiting to be at my disposal but he was too stingy to get himself a decent suit of cloaths   So he was Shiped perty quick. but not long after one pleasant Sabbath morning we saw a man comeing walking up the road dressed up with a Stovepipe Hat on and I said to Mother, their he comes now   but we did not know who it was, but when he got a little nearer we Saw it was George Belknap.

Mother wondered how he came to come that five miles a foot for She knew their was meeting at his fathers that day. oh I said he wanted to hear Perkins preach. So after meeting father asked him to stay to diner and my brother had his girl their so after diner we all took a walk   we two girls Started out together but we did not get far till we paired off   we went out in the medow and sit on a log awhile then went to the house and pretty soon my brothers girl went home and he went with her and pretty soon Mr B went also. . . .

but that was not the last of it   in two weeks their was preaching at one of our neighbors a mile and a half from us and as the roads was not very good we Generally went on Horseback or on foot   that day we all walked and about the same time we got their up rode my B and (verily) we thought he must like our meetings better than his own   but when meeting was out and I started home he met me in the yard and wanted to know if he could see me home and in my Surprise and excitement I said I had no objections   so I thought as he was on horseback he was going to ride a long to see that I did not stick in the mud or fall off of a log . . . . Some of the time we would walk side by side and sometimes we had to go Indian file and sometimes Coon it on the logs . . .

from that [day] on the visits became more frequent and more interesting   About the middle of September he came one day and Said they was about to Sell their place and wanted to go west to a Prairie country and if we went along we must bring matters to a close pretty soon   So him and mother had a long talk out by the well that evening in the moonlight and before morning it was Settled that we would be Maried on the third of october 1839 so then we had to get ready for the wedding and also for the Journey.

Keturah and George emigrated to Oregon, raised five children and buried six in Iowa and Oregon. George died in 1897 and Keturah passed away August 19, 1913—the honored elder of an extensive western family to whom she was lovingly known as Aunt Kit.

ANNA CORA MOWATT

Although Anna was selected as a future bride in her early years, child brides were found less in polite society than on the frontier— there were more women available for marriage in the cities. A high-spirited, dramatic young girl from an affluent home, Anna had to convert her boarding-school skills into income when her husband fell bankrupt. She became an actress, forged a successful career and, ultimately, supported and cared for her husband in his elder years, as he had for her during childhood.

I must go back to my thirteenth year, to relate one of the most important incidents of my life, the one which [would] govern my whole future existence. My eldest sister Charlotte, with her two little children, passed a summer at Rockaway, for the enjoyment of sea bathing. Among the guests at Rock Hall was James Mowatt . . . a young barrister of education and fortune. He was much charmed with my sister, imagining her to be a youthful widow. This mistake she never discovered until his admiration was expressed in open terms. When informed that he was addressing a married woman, his chagrin was so great that she laughingly consoled him by saying,

"O, I have plenty of young sisters at home, and one of them very much resembles me. Call upon me . . . and I will make you acquainted with her."

In a few weeks she returned to the city. Mr. Mowatt made no delay in paying his respects. The school, which four of us children attended, was directly opposite our residence. While we

Unidentified young couples (University of Wisconsin–Lacrosse Murphy Library)

were in the midst of our studies one day a messenger came to say that the eldest of the schoolgirl sisters must come home. She was the one that most strikingly resembled our sister Charlotte. I asked the servant if anything had happened. She replied, "No, there . . . was only a gentleman in the drawing room, who entreated that my sister might be sent for."

I had heard Mr. Mowatt much talked of in the family, and felt a childish curiosity to see him. Without permission, I accompanied my sister home, and watched her while her beautiful hair was recurled, and her school dress laid aside for a more becoming attire. She was ushered into the drawing room; and I, of course, dared not enter.

After waiting half an hour, I remembered that I had received no permission to leave school, and, certain visions of black marks rising up before me, I thought it judicious to return. But to go back without having seen this much-talked-of beau—I could not do it.

I would enter the drawing room on some pretext.

After hesitating a while, I opened the door, ran across the room, threw down my satchel of school books upon the centre table, as though that must be their proper place, gave one look toward the sofa, and ran out again.

"Who is that?" I heard the gentleman exclaim.

"Only one of the children from the nursery," answered my oldest sister.

"Do call her back," he urged.

My sister came to the door and called out, as I was flying up the stairs, tolerably frightened at what I had done. "Anna, Anna, come back and speak to Mr. Mowatt."

"I don't care for Mr. Mowatt!" was the saucy reply that reached his ears, and away I went.

A servant was sent to summon me, but I refused to comply. I waited until I heard the gentleman take his leave, then hurried down stairs to return to school. Mr. Mowatt was standing at the foot of the street door steps and placed himself in front of me with extended arms. There was no retreat, and he kept me prisoner for some time . . . I answered his many questions with saucy, merry frankness, and every now and then imploring to be freed. Finding he would not consent, I watched my opportunity, suddenly slipped beneath his arm, and ran across the street to school. I well remember the expression of his face as I looked back, laughing heartily at the astonishment of my discomfited jailer.

I have very many times heard Mr. Mowatt describe this first interview to his friends . . . and I only regret that I cannot convey his impressions in the same language. Soon after he left the house, he encountered an intimate acquaintance. The subject turned upon courtship and matrimony. His friend asked him how long he intended to remain a bachelor.

"Not long," he replied, "if a little girl whom I saw to-day would only grow up." He then related what had taken place, and added, emphatically, "I feel as though I should never marry unless I marry that child."

From that moment he conceived the project of educating me to suit his own views—of gaining my affections, and, the instant I was old enough to be considered marriageable, of taking me to his own home—his child wife.

His visits to the family became very frequent . . .

I thought it very grand to have so devoted a lover, and played the tyrant at thirteen and fourteen to my heart's content. Yet I owed almost entirely to Mr. Mowatt the rapid progress which I made in my studies at these ages. He directed my reading, furnished me with books, examined all my compositions, and (what I thought most delightful of all) supplied me with an endless quantity of flowers, as a species of reward for my industry.

He was present at my performance of Alzire and was naturally the most enthusiastic . . . The next morning he . . . offer[ed] himself, although I was not yet fifteen. It was Saturday, and there was no school. He called very early and asked for me. While my sisters were making their toilets, I hastened to the parlor in my morning dress. I was eager to listen to praise of the last night's efforts. But I was not more disappointed than astonished when the gentleman awaiting me commenced a serious conversation, without making the slightest allusion to the play. I only comprehended enough to be alarmed. I did not reply, but, jumping up, called to my sister Charlotte to come downstairs quickly. She did so, inquiring what was the matter. Of course, this was an *unanswerable* question, and the situation . . . must have [seemed] particularly ludicrous. . . . A schoolgirl of fourteen pondering over . . . an offer of marriage from a man many years her senior. It was in itself an amusing situation; yet I found it a painful one. I carried the important document to my sister Louisa, and, making her promise secrecy, placed the letter in her hands . . .

She told me I must write a letter [back] and she would correct it. . . . [The effect of the letter] was very different from the one anticipated. Mr. Mowatt merely laughed at what he considered girlish shyness. He increased, rather than diminished, the number of his visits and assumed the bearing of an accepted, instead of a rejected, lover. This went on for some time . . .

My father's consent was asked. He could find no objection to Mr. Mowatt, and made my extreme youth the only barrier. He replied that if we were both . . . of the same mind when I was seventeen, he would give his sanction . . .

More earnestly than ever he entreated me to become his wife without further delay . . . I was much grieved by . . . the sight of his deepening melancholy. Of my own free will, I gave him a promise that we should be united within a week.

Young as I was, and totally incapable of appreciating the importance of the step I was taking, I did not come to this determination without much suffering. But once having resolved, once having *promised,* nothing earthly could have shaken my resolution. . . .

What was I to do? And who was to aid me? I could not leave my father's house alone. I could not be married without a *bridal wardrobe.* These were huge barriers to be surmounted; but I went resolutely to work, determined to overcome them . . .

All necessities for a wardrobe were next to be purchased. It was raining in torrents; we were very much fatigued, and . . . hired the first carriage that could be found. For several hours we drove about shopping as long as our money lasted, and filling the carriage with our purchases. Amongst other things, I insisted on buying a large wax doll to comfort little Julia in my absence, and a huge basket full of sugar plums for the other children, which I hoped would have a similar consolatory effect. Rather juvenile "bridal purchases."

We could not drive home in the carriage without being questioned. We left our parcels at a confectioner's very near our house, dismissed the carriage, gave orders that the bundles should be sent to our number, addressed to the nursery maid who was to accompany me on my bridal expedition, and walked home.

The next question was: how could the newly-purchased wardrobe be made up? There was no resource but to make it ourselves, with the assistance of the nursery maid. But at what time could this be accomplished without our being seen? It must be at night; we must work instead of sleeping.

At length the 6th of October came—the day on which I had promised to be married. My slender wardrobe was completed—all our arrangements made. The day dawned magnificently—every thing looked propitious.

There had been some difficulty in procuring a clergyman to perform the ceremony. Mr. Mowatt first applied to Bishop Onderdonk. But [the bishop] knew my father well; he had children of his own—it was not a good example to set them. He preferred that some other clergyman be selected. I desired that Dr. E——, whose church I attended . . . should be asked.

He also refused.

A third refusal came from Dr. J—— N. Mr. Mowatt, nothing daunted, then applied to the Rev. Mr. V——, the French pastor. This gentleman's own had been a runaway marriage, therefore he *could not* object. He consented. The bridal party were requested to assemble at his house at ten o'clock.

My sister dressed me in a plain white fabric dress. My little straw bonnet chanced to be trimmed with white ribbons, and the veil and white gloves which we had purchased she carried rolled in her handkerchief. They were not to be put on till we were out of sight of the house. I kissed my father before he went out, but felt myself becoming so agitated that it was well he was in haste and did not notice me. Just as I was opening the street door, my mother came into the entry, and I kissed her also. She remarked on my white dress, and asked if I were not too lightly clad for such cold weather. I answered that I felt quite warm, and she allowed me to depart.

My poor sister, I think, suffered even more that I did; the blame was all to fall on her. She had done her utmost to dissuade me, and now had to assist in depriving herself of a beloved companion . . . her unselfishness touched me deeply.

We left the house, and, turning the first corner, she threw the bridal veil over my bonnet, gave me the white gloves, and begged me to try and look composed before I met Mr. Mowatt and his friends.

Wonderfully composed I was. Of the future, I did not even think. My only grief was leaving my parents, my sisters, my home . . . What could a girl of fifteen know of the sacred duties of a wife? . . . I had always been lighthearted to a degree that savored of frivolity. I usually made a jest of everything—yet I did not look upon this matter as a frolic. I only remembered that I was keeping a promise. I had perfect faith in the tenderness of him to whom I confided myself. I did not in the least realize the novelty of my own situation.

At St. John's Park we met Mr. Mowatt and his two groomsmen. I took his arm . . . we were ushered into the drawing room. Mr. V—— entered in his robes. He, of course, did not know which of the sisters was the bride. He took a seat, opened a large register, and asked the names and ages of the parties to be married. When I replied, giving my name, he looked at me steadily and with some surprise.

"Your age?" he inquired.

"Fifteen."

He put down his pen and repeated the question. For a few seconds he seemed doubtful whether he ought to proceed. I was thought to look younger even than my years; and I was dressed in a childlike manner, which probably made me appear younger still.

The law sanctions the marriage of a girl of fifteen and he could not make any reasonable objection . . . We rose, and the ceremony was performed in French. At its close he delivered a beautiful address . . . wished us both much happiness, and we took our leave.

Our groomsmen had just left us. We had hardly walked a square when we encountered my father! My sister and I were greatly confused. My father joined us, and entered into conversation with Mr. Mowatt. All at once he exclaimed, looking at me, "Why, how like a bride you look! One of these days, Mowatt, she will grow up to be quite a fine girl!"

I could not repress a terrified exclamation at the word "bride" and trembled from head to foot. Fortunately, my father was just leaving us and did not notice my agitation.

We returned home, and I passed the rest of the day in gathering together my little possessions and in writing to my parents. I was to leave the next morning and pass a few weeks in the country . . .

Mr. Mowatt passed the evening with us as usual, but my sister's grief greatly depressed me. When he left, and I retired to the nursery, I could not help sighing to think that I should no longer be looked upon as one of the children. I began to have strange forebodings of the future, and again and again I repeated to myself, "O, if this were only a dream, and I could wake up!"

The next morning, immediately after breakfast, I was to join Mr. Mowatt, and, accompanied by the nursery maid, we were to take the steamboat for [our honeymoon]. His sister-in-law was there, and to her he proposed to take me.

When breakfast was over, I made some laughing excuse to kiss every one present . . . As I stooped to kiss my father for the second time . . . my courage nearly gave way. In another instant I should have told him all.

He looked at me anxiously and said, "What ails you, child?" I did not reply. I could not have answered. I hastened from the room and . . . hurriedly left the house . . .

"Let us run! Let us run!" I said to my sister, for all my courage was melting away and I could trust myself no longer. And we did run, rapidly and without speaking, until we reached the spot where Mr. Mowatt was waiting for us. There I had to bid adieu to my faithful sister. She must go home and bear all the blame . . .

My mother soon after visited the nursery and found upon my dressing table a sprig of geranium. It grew, and she tended it carefully for the short remainder of her life. She called it "the bride's flower."

It was different with my father; he was indignant with the whole party, with me, with my sister, and, most of all, with Mr. Mowatt. My letter failed to pacify him. He at first declared that he would *never* forgive me, and it was three days before a letter was received, bringing his pardon. Those days seemed like a "never," indeed, to me . . .

But the pardon came and an invitation to return home . . . My father, mother and all welcomed us with open arms and without one chiding word . . . Mr. Mowatt they received less cordially, but still with kindness . . .

Caroline Lockhart
(American Heritage Center, University of Wyoming)

BETHENIA OWENS-ADAIR

As the youngest of nine children, Bethenia learned to be
provident and resourceful—traits that served her well as the
fourteen-year-old bride of a slothful and incompetent husband.
After four years she petitioned for a divorce, deciding
that she could educate herself, raise a child and, ultimately,
attend medical school without the help of a spouse.
She obtained her medical degree in 1880, at the age of forty.

On May 4th, 1854, [Mr. Hill and I] were married. I was still
small for my age. My husband was five-feet eleven inches in
height, and I could stand under his outstretched arm. I grew very
slowly, and did not reach my full stature until I was 25 years old,
which is not 5-feet 4 inches.

Just prior to our marriage, Mr. Hill had bought a farm of 320
acres on credit, four miles from my father's home, for $600, to be
paid for in two years . . .

I had high hopes and great expectations for the future. My
husband was a strong, healthy man; I had been trained to work,
and bred to thrift and economy, and everything looked bright and
beautiful to me. My soul overflowed with love and hope, and I
could sing the dear old home-songs from morning to night. My
happy buoyant nature enabled me to enjoy anything, even cooking out of doors, over a smoky fire, without even a covering over
my head; for at first we had neither fireplace nor stove . . . And
yet, from a child I was practical and methodical. I had everything
packed, and ready to move to my new home as soon as we were
married, and I insisted on going there the next morning, knowing

Unidentified couple
(Utah State University, Special Collections)

that the garden ought to be in. Within a few days it was planted. We depended upon wild game for meat, and as my husband was a good marksman, he kept us well supplied. I always went with him, and we never came home empty handed. He often killed two grouse from the tree by shooting the under bird first. The upper one seldom flew, and the hunter could bag it at the next shot. This seemed to be characteristic of the grouse . . .

Mr. Hill was always ready to go hunting, no matter what work was pressing to be done . . .

In the beginning of our married life, my father had advised my husband to begin at once to fell trees, and hew them, and put up a good house before winter set in. There was an abundance of suitable timber on our land, near by, but he was never in any hurry to get down to work. In one way and another he managed to idle away the summer, going to camp meetings, reading novels, and hunting.

Legrand Hill's "want of industry and perseverence" contin-ued until the couple was unable to pay the first year's mort-gage on the farm. They went to stay with his aunt in Jackson County, Oregon.

We moved into our new house in March, with the $150 mort-gage hanging over us. On April 17th, 1856, our baby was born, and then Aunt Kelly begged me to give him to her, addressing me thus:

"Now Bethenia, you just give him to me. I will take him, and educate him, and make him my heir. I will give him all I have, and that is more than his father will ever do for him. I know very well that Legrand will just fool around all his life, and never accom-plish anything."

She seemed to think my consent to her having the child was all that was necessary. But my baby was too precious to give to anyone . . .

Mr. Hill neither drank or used tobacco, but, as his aunt said, he simply idled away his time, doing a day's work here and there, but never continuing at anything. Then, too, he had a passion for trading and speculating, always himself coming out a loser; and thus the time dragged on, until September, 1857, when who should drive up, one glad day, but my father and mother. Father had heard how things were going with us, and had come, pre-pared to take us back with them in case we were willing to go, but he was too discreet to let this be known until later. He and mother wanted to see the country . . . they especially desired to see my baby.

It did not take them long to understand that we were barely living "from hand to mouth" as it were, with most of the work coming on me, so father said:

"How would you like to go back to Roseburg? It is a growing town. I have several acres in it, and if you think you would like to make a change, I will give you an acre of land, and the material for a good house, which you can put up this fall . . ."

To say that we were delighted with this proposal expresses it but faintly. We sold our house and lot in Yreka, realizing less than $100 out of the transaction . . .

On reaching home, father told me I could go over and select my acre of land, and out-building spot, which I gladly did. He told Mr. Hill he could have the team, and he and the boys could haul the lumber for our house, so that he could get to work on it at once.

They hauled the lumber, but, in the meantime, Mr. Hill had been talking with a man about burning brick. This man had some land a mile from father's, and a team, and he offered to go into equal partnership with Mr. Hill . . .

Father endeavored, in every way, to dissuade him from going into this undertaking . . . [but] Mr. Hill put all the little money we had into the venture, and so he moved me and my young child into a tent in a low, damp valley, near the river, and their work and mine was begun. But it was never half completed, for when they had only a few hundred brick molded, it began to rain continuously, and put a stop to their work, and in addition to this ill-fortune, I was stricken down with typhoid fever. Father and mother came with the wagon, and moved us back to their home. It was now late November; winter was upon us, and still our house was not touched.

When I became convalescent, father urged Mr. Hill to begin the house. He replied that he wanted a deed to the acre of land before beginning the house.

Father then told him that he and mother had talked it over, and had decided to deed the property to me and the boy; that he had given us one good start, and now after three and a half years, we had nothing left but one horse, and that he thought it best to secure a home for me and the child in my own name.

This enraged Mr. Hill, who said he would not build on the lot unless the deed was made to him, as he was the head of his family. Father advised him to think it over and not act rashly.

He sulked for a time, and then bargained for a lot in town, after which he hired a team, and hauled the lumber off from the acre to the lot, and began to build the house. All this time we were living off father, who said nothing; but furnished the shingles, and told Mr. Hill to get nails, and anything he needed at the store, on his account, which [Mr. Hill] did. In time, the roof was on, and the kitchen partly finished, and we moved in. The kitchen was so open that the skunks, which were very numerous in that region at that time, came under the floor nights, and up into the kitchen, where they rattled around among the pots and pans, even jumping on the table, and devouring the food, if I did not keep everything securely covered . . .

My health was poor. I had not been strong since the baby came, and I could not seem to recover from the effects of the fever. The baby was ill and fretful much of the time, and things were going anything but smoothly. A short time before the climax, I went home and told my parents that I did not think I could stand it much longer. My mother was indignant, and told me to come home, and let him go; that "any man that could not make a living with the good starts and help he has had, never will make one; and with his temper, he is liable to kill you at any time."

Father broke down, and shed tears, saying:

"Oh, Bethenia, there has never been a divorce in my family, and I hope there never will be. I want you to go back, and try again, and do your best. After that, if you cannot possibly get along, come home." I went back, greatly relieved, for I knew that if I had to leave, I would be protected.

Our trouble usually started over the baby, who was unusually cross. He was such a sickly, tiny mite, with an abnormal, voracious appetite, but his father thought him old enough to be trained and disciplined, and would spank him unmercifully because he cried. This I could not endure, and war would be precipitated at once. A few days before our separation, his father fed him six hard boiled eggs at supper, in spite of all I could do or say. I slept little that night, expecting that the child would be in convulsions before morning. And thus one thing led to another until the climax was reached.

Early one morning in March, after a tempestuous scene of this sort, Mr. Hill threw the baby on the bed, and rushed down into town. As soon as he was out of sight, I put on my hat and shawl, and gathering a few necessaries together for the baby, I flew over to father's. I found my brother ferrying a man across the river, and I went back with him. By this time, I was almost in a state of collapse, as I had run all the way, about three fourths of a mile. . . . The next day father saw Mr. Hill, and found he had been trying to sell the house and lot. Father told him that he would come with me to get my clothes, and a few things I needed, and that he (Mr. Hill) could have the rest. That he (father) would take care of me from that time on, and that when he (Mr. Hill) sold the house and lot, I would sign the deed, as the lot was not paid for, and the unfinished house would, according to law, go with it.

However, before Mr. Hill found a purchaser, he had repented, and come several times to get me to go back to him. I said: "Legrand, I have told you many times that if we ever did separate, I would never go back, and I never will."

And now, at eighteen years of age, I found myself, broken in spirit and health, again in my father's house, from which, only four years before, I had gone with such a happy heart, and such bright hopes for the future . . .

Mrs. William Lauder (State Historical Society of North Dakota)

PART **IV** FOUR

Calico

Courtin'

Haying in Livermore (Fort Collins Public Library)

Farm Life

*"They are a strange lot,
the men . . ."*
—EMILY FRENCH, 1890

*"I feel lonely tonight . . .
I do so crave love."*
—EMILY FRENCH, 1890

MARRIED LIFE ON A FARM TOOK ON THE SAME REGU-larity as the weather, an incessant, measured pace, with generations of friends and family barreling apples, plowing furrows, courting and marrying on the same farm site, some staying on after marriage, others moving to plots near by. "I was never away from [mother] till I was 50 years old," wrote farm woman Margaret Archer, a spinster whose continued, domestic presence satisfied the expectation that one child, always female, would stay at home as parental caretaker—a middle-aged woman prized as a widow for her nursing and "caring" skills. No matter how many generations sprang forth on a rural farm, each hearkened back to the first family members, often "earnest, industrious, upright men & women" whose work seemed endless on the dry, tractless plains, but whose origins in rural Puritan America had prepared them well for a lifetime of punishing struggle.

They came from a society that was squeamish about sex in general, to create one that was less so. In fact, a kind of lazy forbearance of sexual vicissitudes evolved, in which even cousins were free to court at will, providing they were second- or third-generation removed and differed considerably in looks and size—mating with look-alike relations was considered taboo. The arrival of "woodpile" children born out of wedlock to rural couples seemed as predictable as each month's new moon. "A number of our married women [were] in the straw," mused the Reverend Timothy Dickinson, noting the spate of pregnancies begun during a recent eclipse of the sun.

On the farm, windmills were turned, relentlessly, by hand, on hot, breezeless days, while hay was turned to dry in the meadow, then stacked in long ricks for winter use. The tough, jagged furrows were sown with corn. So fatiguing was the daily work that no amount of friendship, celebration, food or romance could erase its effects. Though at times the settlers feasted on buckets of ripened wood cherries, and sucked, with laughter, great hunks of wild honeycomb brought from the prairie on a day's roaming, thoughts always returned to the daunting work at hand. "We farmed our crops," said one woman. "It took so much work . . ."

Those who married found solace in the home, comforting one another within the rough shelter of a frame cabin, roofed with sod for insulation, from which rye grass would spring high when the rains came, lending a comical air. Such domesticity touched both men and women, causing deep yearnings for home and spouse, when one or another was absent. "Home, with me, was always delightful," wrote Ethan Allen Crawford. "To be able to sit down and have half a dozen little ones come and rest themselves upon me, all of them having good reason and proper shapes, was a blessing." James Tulloch ached for his cabin in Washington Territory, which Annie, his wife, had gaily surrounded with seventy-five vigorous breeds of ever-blooming roses. "We took pride in our home," he wrote. "We dreamed of what we would make of it in years to come."

Yet men often left, striking out for the gold fields or herding cattle. Women, bleakly supportive, were left to tend the homestead, nurture children, harvest crops by hand and count the days to a husband's return. Surrounded by desolate prairie, cut off from supplies, neighbors and mail, married women often found an empty panorama, not the vibrant partnership once envisioned. "How can I ever call this place my home?" wondered Mrs. A. M. Green, from Union Colony, a homestead experiment in Colorado. What joy, women wondered, without an ally? Harriet Dodd grew sorrowful at the loss of her husband, William, in an Indian raid in 1862. "Oh, shall I never more hear his voice?" she cried. "I feel homeless," sighed cleric Isaac Owen, writing to his wife Elizabeth in 1851 from California. "What would home be without your smiles?" he added. When this tack failed to lighten her spirits, he tried another. "Cheer up," he wrote, "and try to get fat by my return."

Loneliness was often pushed away when travelers, neighbors, drifters or field hands claimed overnight hegemony, moving in, "tinker and tinsmith alike," sometimes with livestock included. Such enforced intimacy made life hellish for a frazzled frontier hostess, her tiny quarters packed by footloose strangers, her sleep rent by the odors, harsh sighs and muttered dreams of snoring passers-by. So beset were they that few married couples could claim what they needed for marital bliss, which was privacy.

The problem was not solved by inns, bunkhouses or teeming ranch "hotels"—the typical way stations of the west. In the Texas borderlands, in the years before statehood, outlaws, vagrants, wayward clerics, gentry and cowhands mustered at local hotels, distressing the occasional woman traveler who needed shelter for the night. Also distressed was English explorer Richard Burton, who recoiled from the "promiscuous heap" of "men, women, children, lambs and puppies" bedded together on the stage stop floors. Women routinely bunked with men, particularly if the women were domestic servants, or "day workers." Emily French, a housekeeper from Colorado in 1890, recalled a "poor bed" she was forced to share with two males: "Mr. Jackson the first, the Sweed boy the second, I the third."

Inconvenience bred its own, rural etiquette, calling for staggered dressing times, less modesty and revised standards of cross-gender behavior. Usually, the men rose first, skipped quickly into boots and breeches, then drifted outside to "check the weather" while the women hastened to dress. One thoughtful relative, quoted by historian Glenda Riley, sauntered outside to dress so regularly that the children decided "outdoors" was "Uncle Ed's bedroom." Equally perplexing was the act of seeking personal relief without a refined, indoor privy, or "secret." Easterner Anne Raney Coleman, lodging in way stations in Texas in the mid-1800s, was awed indeed by the sight of different sexes sleeping together in "uncurtained beds," but was stirred to the depths of Yankee propriety when, to "change her linen"—a euphemism for relieving herself—she had to "haste away to the grove," seeking privacy in the breezy acres of prairie grass. The protocol of mixed-gender sanitation, according to an Iowa woman, demanded "thick brush or a couple of fallen tree-trunks; one for men, one for women." Or another option: a tin-walled chamber pot, equally unwieldy, which served to remind a young bride that marriage was both less, and more, than what she had bargained for.

Women travelers felt threatened and embarrassed by the migrating masses of unwashed and scowling men who jostled along the back roads, drank outrageously and shared their coaches, trains and wagons. In Pierre, South Dakota, according to Walker Wyman, "the decent women didn't venture out much at night alone, and when they did they carried long hat pins or twenty-two revolvers for protection from the drunks." Yet generally, in the United States, an actual attack upon a woman was a capital offense, judged legally with "inexorable severity."

But men, too, were skittish. Some bachelors were so edgy, claimed traveler Mollie Dorsey, they would "fly to their state rooms to hide" from any females they chanced upon to meet, en route west on a riverboat.

Chivalry prevailed, thanks to southern arrivals after the Civil War, whose gentlemanly codes of behavior eventually were adopted as western traits. "There was nothing more precious than a woman's honor," noted French critic Alexis de Tocqueville, surprised at the relatively esteemed position of American women compared with that of Europeans. British traveler Isabella Bird was impressed by the entrance of a woman in a train, her presence heralded by the call, "A seat for the lady! Get up for this lady." While the American men leapt to their feet, an English traveler refused, protesting, "I've paid for my seat and I mean to keep it." He was booted out the door amid a "chorus of groans and hisses," so shaming Bird that she hid her British identity, adopting "every Americanism" she could think of.

Such deference to women was not lost upon such canny male travelers as the soon-to-be silver baron of Colorado, Horace Tabor, who wisely relegated his gold dust to his wife's underskirts while traveling, certain that even the most audacious bandit would refrain from frisking a woman. Women, meanwhile, were less concerned about bandits than a subject of even greater dread—conjugal intimacy. When intimacy proved unsettling, it was often to middle-class women of "elevated" tastes, whose protected girlhoods offered little preparation for the vicissitudes of conjugal life. Such virginal timidity was addressed in a number of popular publications, beginning with bridal bed descriptions—some were stuffed with prairie grass or buffalo hair, but most popular was the cornhusk bed, advertised by one newspaper in 1858 as "cheap, durable, healthful to sleep on and liable to last twenty-five or thirty years." An 1890 manual even allowed that "parties in good health" might use one bed chamber without suffering any disadvantage, "if sufficiently roomy."

For Helen Davis Benton, virginal modesty was short-lived; the Victorian penchant for creating complications through rigid rules was quickly flung aside after her marriage in 1878. Instead of problems with intimacy, she found that her main difficulty was getting *out* of the bed in which she and her new spouse frolicked. "After dinner I went to bed," she wrote. "Leroy also. We laid till chore time."

On the frontier, women wed at a younger age than their European counterparts, often as young as fifteen, sometimes as old as twenty-three. Their weddings, mused rural dweller Daniel Drake, were "scenes of carousal, and merriment of no very chastened kind," bringing relatives from afar to join in the merrymaking, as well as neighbors, who gathered to trade information, cooperate in food preparation and celebrate. Weddings were planned to match the rural rhythms of an agricultural world, marking the seasonal shifts between crops, plantings and harvest. Spring offered an ideal time, hearkening new life and occurring in the seasonal pause before the rigorous months of harvest time, when the work was heaviest.

Of lesser concern was the denomination of the marryin' pastor, since the presence of a preacher at all was often highly unusual. Californian Rebecca Woodson, in 1852, left the choice up to her father, who "went and got [a Presbyterian] preacher" from Nevada City; a year earlier her sister wed Robert Bailey at the family home near Bear River, the wedding officiated by a reverend from Nevada City. "I think he was a Baptist preacher," Rebecca wrote, but perhaps not. Those clerics actually summoned often had to work for the privilege; they traveled great distances, braving inconvenience, as did the Reverend Cyrus Townsend, who thought nothing to swim "two rivers and one creek" to reach a wedding twenty-seven miles away in Indian territory—such distances were standard. His church was a converted saloon decked out with tumbleweeds, through which the bride kicked her way to the groom's wagon. But what matter? Townsend reasoned. "The bride was pretty and the groom was manly and those are the things which count."

A more elaborate wedding reception was hosted by the parents of Sophie Parker Stapley, in which the entire community turned out, a crowd of two hundred people "over the age of fourteen" who feasted on "three or four varieties of meat, hot potatoes and gravy, several kinds of vegetables, three or four varieties of pies and cakes, with other desserts such as puddings." The bride's cake was white and the groom's a dark spiced fruit. Sweet wines were sipped by the ladies after dinner, while brandy and sweet Dixie wine were drunk by the men.

In the rural west, home weddings were standard, ready-made dresses unthinkable, gift-giving sporadic, and the color white

Hemry family and Ohio visitors, ca. 1917 (Wyoming State Museum)

impractical—how could it be reused? Instead, a touch of white lace might edge a gown "here and there," for a romantic variation. Rachel Malick studied English pattern books to figure out the proper ratio of flowered material to plain for a stylish wedding dress, sending material snippets to a friend. "I haint Maryed yet," she confided, but "I will enclose some of My White Matrimonial Robe."

At the low end of the hospitality scale was the wedding of Martha Farnsworth, who, for personal reasons, refused to "ask any one at all." Likewise, the wedding of New Yorker Annie E. Osborn, in 1864, fell short of social expectations. Whisked immediately away by stagecoach to the preacher's remote cabin, she was shocked to find the officiating witnesses were his wife and children, still in bed, sleep-rumpled and drowsy. She was further disturbed to see, dangling from the rafters of their nuptial suite, a raft of butchered hogs stored overhead for safekeeping.

Frontier singles, ever hopeful of being wed, would meet and mingle at rural shindigs which often began early in the morning with a women's quilting bee. During the quilting, wrote pioneer Daniel Drake, young men would assemble to "plague the gals," their efforts gaining momentum until the event became a "frolic," partway between a "bee" and a dance, and which was, according to one settler, a "neighborly meeting that generally conclude[s] with feasting and dancing but sometime[s] lasts two or three days." Here, passions came into play, casting a spell upon married couples and singles alike, drawing men and women by horse, buggy or spring wagon [buckboard] from a fifty-mile radius with burdens of food and quilt-snuggled babies, encouraged to doze while the parents danced. Couples, young and old, would hop and sway over a skidproof floor scattered with slivers of sealing wax for traction, or trot through the steps of a "bran dance," gaily working the flakes of the tough cereal scattered upon the floor into a a skidproof pulp.

Dancing leveled community contradictions, convening neighbors and kin for a festive night of swing-your-partner set to the jaunty wail of "a sassy fiddle bow," according to Kansas homesteader Mary Lyon. It was music to "melt a rock and split a cabbage head," at least for one young boy, entranced by a lively folk quadrille in Idaho:

I grabbed her femail hand, she squeezed mine, we both slung each other but she slung the most because I think she loved me for a little while; then . . . I dosed a doe and hopped home again . . . then we two forward four, the ladies changed . . . I backed to place, she diddoes; side couples to the right, to the left . . . all hands round . . . light gentlemen balance to heavy ladies, duplicate, promenade all.

Not all revelers embraced all music, as schoolteacher Tommie Clack discovered in her staunch Baptist community in Tarrant County, Texas. One of the "few things strange" about country parties, she noted, was the freedom of a French harp or a Jew's harp to trill, but the minute anyone "let a fiddle string crack" the elders would immediately rise and depart, saying: "This is no place for decent, respectable men and women. . . . We've got to get out of here!" A fiddle meant dancing; dancing was a sin and, for this very reason, offered young, courting couples a means of rural rebellion—a way to cast off the inhibitions and prohibitions of the elders and follow where the fiddler led.

When viewed by sophisticated, "city" eyes, such rural dances often became the material for mockery. "Oh Gust I must tell you one thing," wrote a young soldier to his sweetheart. "I saw . . . a Country Dance. Oh Snow Banks and Plank Roads! What a time! I would have given a great deal to have had you there a few moments. You would have killed yourself laughing. I did very near."

In the farming heartland, early fall nights lured young couples

Mr. and Mrs. Alex Krueger fixing up a Christmas tree in Watertown, Wisconsin, on December 24, 1901 (State Historical Society of Wisconsin)

out for a moonlight stroll, blending hearts together and sometime melodies too. One heart that remained aloof belonged to the flirtatious Nebraska homesteader Mollie Dorsey, for whom a boy named Dick had employed a string band, hoping to win her interest. As ballads trembled and rose outside her window, Dick's voice blended in with a pleading version of "Meet Me by Moonlight Alone." When he later asked her opinion of the music, Mollie shrugged; she informed him that she "loved nobody" and seemed surprised to hear of his serenade. "Dick," she smiled, "was that you?"

"Kissin' wears out, cookin don't," claimed the Pennsylvania Dutch, invoking an adage even older than the better-known folk homily: "Food is the way to a man's heart." Victorian women were restrained by modesty from direct avowals of love; thus savory pies, box lunches, coconut cakes and stoned-cherry roly-poly could safely bear a direct message from the heart. After all, wasn't wifely devotion the ability to feed a husband until he grew stout? To view such lavish food preparation as communication lent new meaning to dishes called "flummery," "slump," "buckle," "grunt" or the ubiquitous dish known as "Gosh!"

The path to love was also strewn with steaming tins of cherry buckle, perfectly browned and served with a feminine flourish, at the pie social, where men might vie for layer cake "light as a feather and laid up with a cream filling," baked by their favorite girl. Half of the fun in outbidding a rival suitor was to drive up the price. With bidding prices reaching an outlandish forty dollars per basket, matching hearts with pocketbooks became an important issue, and any man who failed to recognize his wife's basket was worse than inattentive—particularly if he ended up sharing the layer cake of another woman. Not all food events were a harmony of inspiration. Oregon physician Bethenia Owens-Adair was surprised at a frontier festivity at the cranberry barrel by a "small, stuttering Englishman" who seized his romantic opportunity while she was stirring the cranberries—tiptoed up behind her and grabbed her around the waist to plant a kiss. "Like a tiger, I leaped between him and the door, gave him a whack with the broom handle," Adair recalled. "[I] plunged his head into the cranberry barrel!" She then proceeded to spank him with the broom until he nearly drowned.

Food, and its sharing, occasionally bred jealousy and ill-will, giving rise to notions of infidelity between couples already burdened with complaints and grudges. Cookies were considered a covenant—the first batch was always given to the best beloved, the second noted for its lesser status. Even such innocent food distribution might be carefully watched by a jealous spouse. Emily Hawley's husband, James, "twitted" her about "getting good meals of victuals when Insurance agents or a young man came from town." Stung by his accusations of flirting through food, she never "[saw] a happy day" after the first two weeks of her marriage. Likewise, Elkanah Walker begrudged the meals prepared by his wife, Mary, at their remote Oregon mission, and cheerfully offered to the spry young naturalist whose visits, to Elkanah, "never seemed to end." Shouldn't his wife hasten to resume more important domestic pursuits, and cease her frivolous entertaining?

The basket dinner and pie social disguised a deeply symbolic and often combative aspect of rural feminine community relationship. In a public arena, a man bidding for a woman's pie acknowledged his romantic interest, without the ordinary subterfuge that often accompanies small-town wooing. On another level, the pie social sparked a fierce competitiveness among pioneer women, who, according to historian Lillian Schlissel, went to the most grueling extremes to maintain domestic standards—crisp white aprons, for one, while all about was mud—in a spirit of genuine competition. Women had their own sphere, and public affirmation of skill translated, also, as avowal of worth. In the sexually repressed milieu of a rural setting, the intensity poured into housecleaning, starching and pie making could be seen as an emotional proxy for thwarted love or failed ambitions, or other travails of the heart. Electric with the stress of competition, at times pie socials were like frontier shootouts, with women eyeing one another's pastries and pinafores as if contemplating gunplay.

This same intensity spilled over into the courting life of sons and daughters—often the designated bearers of parental dreams. Wyoming settler Connie Willis dressed her daughter, Lennie, in finery she had lacked in her own youth, even though she was still poverty-stricken. "I am going to put all the beauty on her that ma would have liked to see on me," Willis sighed, as with great difficulty she assembled the clothes. While some wished the gift of emotional happiness and health for their wedded children, suitability weighed heavily upon parents. Others insisted on financial well-being. Abigail Malick's own joyless marriage convinced her that her daughter, Rachel, should have only the best suitor:

I must tell you that the young Man that is courting Rachel Henrietta is here At present . . . And he is A very good work Man. I supose you know what sort of A traid he has. His traid is A wagon And Coach maker. And he can make all kind of furneture. And he is Avery in dustru[ous] young Man and is well be loved by All hoo knos him. And he is very handsom. He has blue eyes And light hair And is very pretty spoken. He dose not Sware nore Spake eney bad wordes And is A butiful form. Nore he dose not drink nor play cards nor is not guiltey of eney bad habits what ever And is very saving. I think that he will Make Avery good husband for hooever gets him. He is a pennsylvanian. He is from near philadelphia. he is Ahelping father to Make the paorch now.

With reasons ranging from petty to profane, men and women squabbled between themselves; men seemed disinterested, inert

or beaten down from work, while women still struggled to understand life, aided by the outpouring of advice from novels, romances and advice columns in newspapers, and the confidentiality they enjoyed at sewing bees or quilting circles. Tantalizing glimpses of city life came in magazines such as *Godey's Lady's Book* or the Sears, Roebuck catalog. Women longed for their mates when gone, and fretted about their flaws when present.

Oregon farm wife Abigail Malick admitted that she had "not Mutch Com Fort" with her husband, whose only credit was that he remained the father of her children, while Colorado day worker Emily French "craved" love, and dreamed of a mysterious paramour who would meet her on the stairs at night to talk and dream and make plans together. "I cannot, must not forget this dream," she reminded herself upon waking. Mollie Dorsey, working as a cook, found her employer disagreeable—but his wife was the one who bore the brunt. "O! Sam," she would cry, her lip quivering, each morning when he "fired off" a biscuit out the window because it was too hard. Likewise, coffee was routinely spilled from the end of the table—his way of saying the taste was off. Why did she stay? Apparently, as long as the wife stayed "meek" and obliging she was given "plenty of money." And, Mollie added, "she does like to dress." When Sarah Anderson wondered, in her diary, if "Dr. O will be all that I want in a husband," her heart was crying out for an elusive dream of both men and women: romantic love.

For many, happiness was fleeting, sorrow ever-present and strains of melancholia, an illness now partially credited to vitamin loss or even mercury poisoning, were common. While Abigail Malick believed her daughter Jane's "wastrel husband . . . was the Caus of Her Incainety," others pined away from bereavement, dementia, despair, malnutrition or, in some cases, the angst of the female cycle, referred to discreetly as a woman's "time" and traced by a series of *x*'s in diaries and journals. Nature, harsh

Unidentified couples (Dresher Collection, Kansas State Historical Society)

enough under the best circumstances, dictated to rural women a regimen of secret washings and wringing-out of menstrual rags, embarrassing in the extreme to young girls thrust uncomfortably into male company. Such unpleasant details were seldom mentioned in diaries and journals, yet each monthly occurrence must have lent a grueling perspective to lives already stretched to the limit. "My time commences today," Emily French remarked at the beginning of a forty-two-mile ride by horseback across plains and valleys, riding until her clothes were soaked and she was physically sick. "I am bad in my periods these days," she concluded. "I feel bad unwell."

"Unwell," in fact, became a metaphor in the lives of rural women who could no longer face multiple pregnancies yet felt a moral obligation, as staunch Christians, to bear adversity with equanimity. Unlike their middle-class, urban counterparts, whom often turned into "delicate" women with "nervous" disorders due to the stresses of childbirth and bad marriages, frontier women were economic partners whose illnesses could cause a family financial despair. Their maladies, accordingly, tended to be more serious—even fatal—rather than "constitutional."

Women were not alone in their anguish. Men, too, would gaze at the horizon, drinking in the loneliness of unlimited vistas, which moved Kansas homesteader Edward Fitch to exclaim, "One week from today I shall be 27! Such an old man I am, with a wife and family to take care of." Fitch was sure his years were already too many, his "sheet . . . about full." Other men turned sour and cantankerous, like the husband of Abigail Malick, whom "the older [he got] the More he like[d] to scold," by his wife's account. "It is imposibel to pleas him . . . So we do the best we Can and let him scold." Benjamin Alfred Wetherill, living on the Alamo Ranch on the Mancos in New Mexico, admitted that the "winters [brought on a] serious case of the blues for the reason that often we were snowed in . . . "

One of the sadder aspects of women's complaints and men's despair was the frequent occurrence of suicide and murder in the rural setting, often the final result of lives gone awry. Old newspapers and court records recall a surprising number of murder trials held throughout the country. At one, Mrs. Hannah Kinney was held for the "alleged murder of her husband, George T. Kinney by poison, 1840." Mary Meadows, a Granville, North Carolina, housewife, hired a slave to kill her abusive husband in 1846. The court found both guilty of premeditated murder, but only the slave was convicted and hanged. Emigrant Lorena Hays, writing in the 1850s, recalled attending the funeral of a Mrs. Lyons, who, it was supposed, "was murdered on the fourth of July by her husband, who was drinking, probably choked her to death, then, to hide his crime, hung her in the well and called it suicide. He is in jail awaiting his trial." Jack Sheridan of Nevada stabbed his wife in the back with a bread knife, while Ann Sims, a friend of Emily Hawley Gillespie in Iowa, in 1866 "killed herself & her four children . . . *O what awful news.*" Later, Emily reported the death of family friend James Canalstine by hanging. "No reason is yet known," she wrote, "only that he told his wife he was too much trouble to her & began to cry." Emily's own husband grew paranoid, believing that his wife wished to kill him, and warned her to "tell . . . if you do. I want to meet my God prepared." So caught up with death and mayhem was he that he often poisoned Emily's prized chickens with salt, perhaps to watch them die, and took a rope to the barn "to hang himself" until interrupted by his children and fetched back to the house. When not obsessed with his own suicide, he accused Emily of plotting his murder. "Emily, I believe you mean to kill me sometime" was a horrible and familiar litany to the besieged woman. Despair came from geographical isolation, financial burdens, years of prolonged incompatibility and a chaotic and far-flung justice system that was little deterrent.

What fortitude did author Ann Grench display when forced to put up with a husband "as black as her fancy" could paint him? "It would be better for her to stay with him awhile," her friend Ellen Slayde advised, "during Lent, for instance." Did not a husband, after all, have "a steadying effect on a woman, abbreviating her flights and keeping her feet on the earth?" Others were less intrepid than Grench, fighting to leave their mates, no matter how costly or long the process. "Susan and her husband are parted," wrote Abigail Malick in 1860, calling her son-in-law a "Worthless Retch" who "Got Mad At Susan [and] Swore He Would Cut her Throat." Abigail delighted when Susan decided "She would Not Live With No sutch A Man, So they parted." Another woman's husband grabbed their five-month-old baby and ran into the rain, shouting, "I'll never return!" It took four years to earn the money to file for divorce.

Desertion was the common resort before divorce, for those too poor or too disorganized to separate legally, and was the common lot of women whose husbands had simply drifted west. "He has eloped from me, but not I from him," a woman mused, aware that her status as a "grass widow" made her suspect in the community, completely diminished her finances and imperiled any chances she had to remarry, unless officially divorced.

While some grew resigned, others grew restless, finding in the liberal and mobile society of the west an ideal milieu in which to start anew. With wagons, pack trains and stagecoaches leaving daily from routes along the major emigrant trails, transportation west was readily available—all options to leave a spouse were within means, often without the deserter having to give a second thought to children, debts, work or spousal support. Under the old English common law, desertion of the common-law partner was no crime; nor could a legally wed spouse be imprisoned for debt, under the terms of the U.S. Constitution—making it easier for men to dodge the debt of support owed an abandoned wife.

"Holding Down A Lot In Guthrie"
("West" Collection, National Archives)

Without legal constraints, husbands and wives often fled, pursued only in the newspaper Missing columns. "For Humanity's Sake, Help Me Locate Walter L. Davis," began one impassioned message. "When thou readest this, suppress thy sobs, sue out a divorce, and set thy cap for another . . . more happy swain," announced another, written by a fleeing husband in the *Missouri Intelligencer*, in 1824.

Others sought a clean and legal break, as did one of Seattle's founding citizens, Doc Maynard, who, while riding overland on a mule, met a wagon train and found himself helping out a widow whose husband had just died of cholera. One thing led to another, and before long, Maynard told friends, "I just shifted my duds to the widow's wagon" and continued on to the Pacific Coast. Because he was already married, honesty dictated that he obtain a difficult legal divorce in order to remarry, but not before his original mate in Ohio decided to visit. After a shave and trim, Maynard proudly showed Seattle a new sight: the well-trimmed man strolling the city streets with a wife on each arm.

ANNE ELLIS

**Anne Ellis grew up poor, the daughter of a barefoot Missouri
mother and a "charming, good-looking, artistic" father with no bad
habits other than that he "hated work"; rather, he enjoyed most of
all "getting ready to do a thing." Raised in Custer County,
Colorado, Anne sampled the bravura, excitement and
"strike it rich" mentality of the silver boom era. Her long yellow
hair and friskiness attracted many suitors;
she faced a problem common to young women on the frontier—
whether to marry Jim for love or Jamie for the long run,
or perhaps neither one.**

I am really having the best time in my life and look forward to being married, and do have my wedding dress made . . . It was a sage green cashmere, made with a gored skirt and lined and interlined with goods called fiber chamois; on the bottom was a circular flounce headed with a narrow silk braid. The tight-fitting waist was made with a puffed silk yoke running down in points . . . As hard up as I am today, I would give a hundred dollars to have it. I take care of the dressmaker's children for making part of it . . .

Now Jim sees how popular I am, and starts to pay attention to me. He can make me tremble by looking at me, and so weak by touching me. Jamie [the fiancé] was frantic with jealousy, but through it all he never said one cross word to me or blamed me in any way. (I think he was the only man who ever really loved me.) These are troubled times at our house. Mama cries over the one who happens to be talking to her at the time. (She really knows

Jamie ought to have all her sympathy, but Jim has a way with women.) Jim explains the cause of his coldness. He said that the boy who was out berrying with us told him a story about me which he believed for a time. I have always had my doubts of this, as I think Jim soon grew tired of any one woman . . .

Jamie has my father get our engagement ring in Salida . . . but Jim says our engagement still stands. I recall leaning on the window and thinking, "Did ever such trouble come to a girl before?" [I ran] over in my mind anything I had read of a girl being engaged to two men at once and how she handled it.

Mama, trying not to play favorites, asked both to a Sunday dinner, killing one of her precious chickens and making ice-cream. This was no small job, as first the ice had to be got from an old mine or prospect hole where the water had dripped and frozen. After she sent one or more children after the ice . . . she has in the mean time made her custard and it is now in a ten-pound lard pail, in the creek cooling. Once we had the dreadful misfortune to have it upset. When the ice comes, it is pounded fine and put in a tub, a good deal of salt sprinkled in, the custard is brought from the creek, the cream added . . . the lid then put on the bucket and placed in a nest in the ice . . .

To this Sunday dinner Jim comes early in the morning. Jamie knows of it and, not to be outdone, soon follows. The chicken is not on yet, and Mama, so confused, puts the chicken on without cleaning the gizzard, and she cries into the bread. Jamie gets so wrought up that he goes out and paces the yard. Mama goes to console him. He says, "to think of him in there talking to my wife," and at this, through her tears, Mama has one of her big laughs. Then dinner, gizzard, rocks, and all are served, but I remember no more of this day.

I can come to no decision. (I would like to have them both, one to love and one to love me—wonder if this is not the cause of a good many triangles?) I want Jim so—but know all the time he doesn't mean it. And Jamie wants me. They get together and have some sort of an understanding, and Jamie gives Jim one evening to tell me good-bye . . . I heard afterwards Jamie walked the hills raging [that night].

Jim comes, and what a wonderful night! . . . We say good-bye, dozens of times. And he leaves, after having me promise that if ever I am in trouble [to send] for him from . . . the ends of the earth. This old, foolish, and dear promise, always given and never used! Had I sent for him each time I have been in trouble, he would have had a steady job. I hear he is making preparations to leave town, but am too heartsick to care much . . .

A day later, just as it is getting light, some one is in my room. I am wide awake at once, but never speak. It is Jim come to tell me good-bye for the last time. He leans over the bed, takes me in his arms, kisses me, and walks out. And to this day, this brings a lump in my throat . . . I never see Jim again, but, there is never a day in all these years I do not think of him. Never a day, up to nine years ago, that I have not dressed for him, thinking and hoping he might come.

And, I thank the Lord for this love. I have been able to understand life so much better. Many people have said to me, "Do you think there is anything in this love you read about?" I say, "I don't know . . . " But, I know there is. This is the first time I have ever written or spoken of this.

Just the other night I dreamed that it was my wedding day. I am very happy and run eagerly forward to meet my lover—Jim—thinking, as I run, of our life and the wonderful children we will have. When I reach him, he is holding out both hands to me. I awaken to find myself a very sick, almost old woman with grown children. The man I ran to meet was not their father. Still, mine are wonderful children. Romance is not nor ever will be dead, not in the heart of a woman, anyway.

Anne married Jamie, but he left her after fathering several children. Alone but optimistic, Anne continued to work in mining camps, feeding miners and eking out a living. "I . . . will marry the first man who asks me," she once joked, and within minutes had netted a proposal from a third man, her future second husband, George.

Unidentified (W. L. Sutton, Hornellsville, N.Y.)

Harvey family (Pikes Peak Library, Colorado Springs)

MALINDA JENKINS

Born in an Illinois log cabin in 1848, Malinda Jenkins was married three times, once for forty-three years to a professional gambler. She moved constantly, from Arkansas to the Klondike, in the frantic, uprooted manner of the frontier. Her decision to leave her children and first husband in order to better her life—and ultimately get them back—reveals deep love, unusual courage and the determination of a woman who felt free to leave as well as to stay.

At Thorp Spring I met Johnnie Ellis that had the grocery store. He wanted to call on me but I wouldn't let him. He didn't know that I was married—everybody called me Miss Jenny, or Miss Page. It wasn't none of his business and I didn't tell him. I said I hadn't no place to entertain in . . .

I was feeling that I was a wife and didn't want no company. But Johnnie kept on. "You're dang right!" He said, "Why can't I come down Sunday afternoons?" Well, I let him come. I thought it wasn't no harm, so I said all right.

Johnnie was a fine fellow and good looking. He was sure attentive and nice, it looked like every thought of his was to do something for me. He come Sunday afternoons; he got coming nights, too. One day, setting out in the shade under a big oak by the schoolhouse, I thought that I ought to tell him how it was with me, a married woman with three children—and I did.

And one thing more, too. "Even if I was a widow tomorrow," I said, "I never would marry again. One husband is plenty." I felt it, and thought it was the truth. "Still, even at that," he said, "let's go right on and be friends . . ."

One day a man turned up from Ladoga, Indiana. Jonah Small; he'd worked for Willie and lived with us for many months. Back in Indiana I helped him take care of his two little girls when his wife was sick and dying. We got to be very good friends, and in that way he knew that I had a sister down in Texas. So when he come down to Stephenville the first thing he done was to hunt up Mary. Wesley Cunningham told him that we was at Thorp Spring and here he was to see me.

With news, too! Jonah Small asked me, "When did you hear last from Willie?" [Then] he gave me a look. "Don't you know," he said, "that Willie's divorced you?"

"Why, my God no!" Not that I was so in love with Willie but I never counted on nothing like that . . .

I didn't tell Johnnie Ellis for nearly a month. I let him keep calling on me and I begun liking him. I wasn't in love, I just liked him. One night I up and told him. I didn't intend to be mealy-mouthed about it, I put it to him plain; "I ain't married no more," I said, "I'm divorced."

"All right, what about you and me pairin' off?" It come so fast the breath went out of me. Johnnie sure had a mind of his own and a quick one . . . So the next time Johnnie come, that nailed the thing. "Let's be married . . ." he said.

"No," I told him, "I want to go with my sister, but after I get there we can talk about it some more."

Johnnie aimed to sell out and move to Fort Worth; he liked the idea of a bigger place. But he seen he couldn't rush me. Besides he knew he didn't come first, as much as I liked him. He told me, "Jes' as soon as we're married, or before if you want it, I'll give you money to go after your kids." We pulled out in about three days, us two women and Mary's boy Johnnie. We had eggs, bacon and ham, and we camped just like men . . .

As hard as I was working, every other day I went to the post office for Johnnie Ellis' letters. Me and Johnnie had arranged our plans; he could sell out his business any time for cash but until I wrote him to come he wouldn't do nothing. The last time I was with him he told me, "I want to be honest with you, and you be honest with me the same way. If you find anybody you like better, you jes' write and say so; I'll take it standin' up!"

After a little while Johnnie's letters stopped coming. Well, he proposed the arrangements and it was him left off. I wasn't going to let it break my heart . . . Besides, I was seeing Jonah Small. He drifted in to town and got him a job. I went out with Jonah Saturday nights; I hadn't no time for gallivanting week days . . .

Jonah Small was around asking how I was getting along and trying to help out every way he could. And after a few months we was engaged to be married and I had his ring on. I was mighty happy. He knowed Willie and the babies; he was the only one around there that did. He was good and kind, promising how we was going back for the children. He meant all he promised. It was that more than love; I was grateful to him for his understanding ways . . .

How is it that so many things comes up in one person's life? It was probably six months after me and Jonah was engaged—I just don't know how long it was—when I went over to the post-office, and my land, if there wasn't a letter from Johnnie Ellis! He wanted to know what had happened, why I hadn't answered his letters. Asked me to tell him didn't I care no more.

Well, the way things had turned out, that's so. I didn't care no more. Not hearing from Johnnie I'd kind of forgot him and I'd stopped going to the post-office regular . . . But here was something else. I was sure now, somehow it come to me, that Jonah Small had been stealing my letters. He knew about Johnnie for I'd told him everything . . .

When Jonah come to see me in the evening I asked him, "Where's my letters?"

"What letters . . . I don't know what you mean?"

"I mean this; I want them letters from Johnnie Ellis that you stole out of the post-office. I got one here saying as how he was writin' right along!"

Jonah was dumbfounded. He thought there wouldn't be no more letters, after Johnnie got disgusted and quit writing for a while.

I told him, "Do you know I could send you to the penitentiary? The only thing you have to do is tell me why you done it."

Yes, he owned up; what else could he do? "I done it because I wanted you to marry me. I knew the kind of woman you was ever since I lived at your house. I made up my mind to court you, and marry you, and help you take care of the children . . . I seen that Ellis stood betwixt us and that's why I done it."

There was a little ravine close by where we was setting. I throwed Jonah's ring down there in the bushes. "Now you jus' follow it!" I said. "I never want to see your face again."

Malinda later met a wealthy middle-aged widower, Mr. Chase, whom she married on the condition that he pay for her children to join them. Reunited with her family, she lived happily together with them for many years. Malinda finally had the financial security to develop her talents— she eventually became a millionaire by breeding and selling horses, passing away at the age of eighty-three. Her slogan, "to make good like I always done," was the touchstone of her troubled life.

Unidentified bride (Library of Congress)

TOMMIE CLACK

A pioneer resident of Taylor County, Texas, "Miss Tommie" was known as the First Lady of Abilene—an educated woman so starved for culture she taught her children to play the piano by painting keys on a board and humming the chords and notes. She was born April 29, 1882, alongside Lytle Creek in the dry plains of West Texas. The marriage she observes is unusual in one sense: many of the men who remarried and reestablished in the west did so in secret, and were never exposed.

The first wedding I ever saw was at the Colony Hill schoolhouse. It was the most impressive—and the most exciting wedding I ever attended. I was not invited, but as usual I was at Sunday School that morning and witnessed the whole affair from start to finish.

In the intermission between Sunday School and church services, a quiet fell over the little building as a stranger with a long black mustache appeared in the doorway. His bold air was in strong contrast to that of the rather pretty girl who leaned on him for support.

Down the narrow aisle the couple edged their way, through the staring country people, to the platform where the preacher stood to receive them. The wheezy organ began droning out something which sounded like "Can Jesus Bear the Cross Alone?"

Things went well while the minister was lecturing the couple on the hazardous step they were taking and the solemnity of the occasion. Then he came to the clause in the ritual "if anyone here knows the reason why this couple should not wed, let him speak now—or don't make trouble afterwards."

A profound stillness settled down over everything until a sort of mumbling came from the rear of the building where a tall woman, dressed in black, was trying to make her voice heard. "I object," was her message.

The minister, rising to the occasion, called out, "Speak up. We can't hear you. State your objections."

Sadly, through copious tears, the poor woman answered. "He's been married before."

In the awful calm that followed, the minister leaned over to the prospective bridegroom and whispered a question. The man with the black mustache whispered something in return. The ceremony then proceeded to its fatal end. The organ burst forth with "Joy to the World."

As a child I questioned, "What did the preacher say? What did the man answer?" And for years I never went to a wedding that I did not wonder: who is going to object to this one?

JESSIE HILL ROWLAND

As the daughter of the local justice of the peace in a small, unnamed town in Kansas, Jessie witnessed many humble weddings, some held in dugouts and puncheon-and-sod cabins, each reflecting the rustic character of the times, including the following ceremony.

My father, being one of the early pioneers and a justice of the peace, was called upon many times to report "Wilt thou, Mary?" and "Wilt thou, John?" Then came the test of trying to live happily ever after.

On one of those occasions my father was asked to preside at a wedding ten miles away from our home and my mother received an invitation to accompany him. Upon arriving at their destination they were ushered down six steps into a dugout, where the mother of the bride was preparing a wedding feast. There was but one room and the furniture consisted of two chairs, one with only two rounds to the back and bottoms. A bed made of scantlings, a board table, a short bench, a stove and a motto hung over the door, "God Bless Our Home."

There was no floor, and a sheet had been stretched across one corner of the room. The bride and groom were stationed behind this, evidently under the impression it would not be proper to appear until time for the ceremony, but they were in such close quarters and the sheet was so short it put one in mind of an ostrich when it tries to hide by sticking its head in the sand.

Mrs. Brown, we will call her, was grinding something in a coffee mill but arose to receive her guests with all the dignity of the first lady of the land. She placed one chair for my mother and one

Lebanese wedding in Utah (Utah State Historical Society)

for my father; seating herself upon the bench, she continued turning the coffee grinder. Soon after some of the neighbors came in and at the appointed time the bride and groom emerged arm in arm from behind the temporary curtain and, stepping forward to where my father was sitting, all became quiet and he pronounced the words that made them one.

Soon after all sat down to the wedding supper. The sheet that hung across the corner of the room was taken down and spread over the table for a cloth. Mrs. Brown's efforts at the coffee mill had turned out some delicious coffee, made of dried carrots. There were seven different kinds of sauce, all made out of wild plums put up in seven different ways. The rest of the menu was quite simple and consisted of plain bread and butter, and fried pork. The table was shoved close to the bed and three sat on that side while three sat on the bench. The chairs were occupied and two or three kegs finished out the number of seats.

After supper the bridegroom took my father to one side and asked him to accept some potatoes in payment for performing the ceremony. He readily accepted and returned home.

ANNA BREWSTER MORGAN

The capture of Anna Morgan stirred the peaceable settlers in Kansas to a frenzy; nothing would do but to regain the blond, blue-eyed bride stolen by Sioux warriors in 1868, along with a fellow captive, Sarah White. Anna's plight epitomized the deepest-held fear of the European—the kidnapping and ravishing of a light-skinned woman by her captors. Yet by her own account, she was treated kindly by her Indian husband, and the death of her half-breed son, two years after her release, plunged her into despair. According to stories, she languished and finally died in an asylum.

I was a bride. My maiden name was Brewster. My brother and I were orphans. Mr. Morgan and I were married September 24, 1868, and I always went with him to the field. On the morning of October 23, it being very foggy, Mr. Morgan thought there was no danger, so he told me that I could stay at the house and do what work I most needed. While I was busy at work, I heard the clatter of horses' feet and rushed to the door to see what was the matter. There were our horses near the door, snorting and looking back. I could not see anything, and thought that Mr. Morgan might have been hurt and managed to free the horses. So I slipped the harness off at the corner of the house and strapped on my revolver. I mounted one horse and led the other and started in search of him.

I came to the river and started up the opposite bank. The Indians saw me, then they jumped and grabbed my horse by the bridle. They had all risen to their feet and there seemed a regiment of them. Everything turned dark to me and when I came to

consciousness, I was in a strange country among the hills, bound tight to my horse. They travelled until night, and then camped on a creek. Another band of Indians came in soon after, having a Miss White as their captive, having captured her somewhere near Concordia.

Then they took us to their village and put a guard over us. They made us do menial service such as carrying wood from the creek for the more favored squaws. We obeyed all orders and gained the confidence of the Indians. During this time, we were laying by a supply of dried buffalo meat so we could escape for civilization the first opportunity presented.

The warriors came in one day from the warpath and had a big pow-wow. When all was quiet we crawled out past the guards unnoticed. Then we struck the Indian trail and travelled for dear life. We travelled until morning and then hid in some secluded spot where we could see the Indians passing to and fro on the trail seeking for their lost captives. When night closed in we again took the trail and repeated the same until one morning we saw a light on the hill and knew it must be Fort Dodge. We thought it best to keep hidden until the soldiers came out, but we were so hungry to see a white face that we agreed to pass on.

[We] had not travelled over a half hour when the Indians recaptured us. I fought hard and said I would not go back. But they took me by main force and whipped me and bound me onto the pony. They took us back to the Indian village and they were more strict with us, giving us no privileges whatever. We felt that we would never gain our liberty as we settled down to hard work.

An Indian chief proposed to me and I married him, thereby choosing the least of two evils and never expecting to see a white person again. My Indian husband would come in from the warpath bringing many things he thought would please me. The squaws were now waiting on me, bringing me wood and laying it down at my door. All my Indian husband expected of me was to tend his horse when he came in off the warpath. He would throw the lariat to me, and I would picket out his horse. I began to think much of him for his kindness to me, and when they brought the news that there were two white men in the camp, I did not care to see them. I was surprised to see my own *brother* walk into the tent. I had on Indian garb.

The government had captured five Indian chiefs and was going to hang them. Only on one condition would the government free them, and that was to free myself and Miss White. The Indians took young Brewster [her brother] and White down to their village, where they found their sisters.

There were many things that I have not spoken of. We were piloted back to the Fort, where the officers' wives took us in charge and furnished us with clothing from their own wardrobes. We were then sent back to our former homes. After I came back, the road seemed rough, and I often wished they had never found me . . .

HARRIET ANN AMES

Harriet was thrice married, her life a litany of "tragic and eventful" occurrences during the frontier years in Texas. By her own account, she was called "the bravest woman in Texas." She was abandoned by her first husband, courted by and wed to her second in a "Texas wedding" (those who remarried as Catholics had the weddings legalized after statehood); was widowed, then married for the third time in 1841. Throughout, she maintained the decorum of gentility, impressing all with her beauty, diminutive size and pure spunk.

In the first sad years of my married life one of the hardest things to bear was my husband's indifference to his children. He did not seem to care anything at all about us; he never once bought a dress for one of his children.

Night after night the lonely hours sped by; usually he did not come home until three o'clock in the morning.

My heart fell one day when I saw him come in at an unusual hour; I knew that something must be the matter—something perhaps to add to my troubles.

I waited until he told me. He had just seen a man from Texas, the Captain of the *Amos Wright,* and he had given a glowing description of the town of Brazoria and all the country about there.

My husband had set his heart on going to Texas; he said that I could get a piece of land if I went; that the Government would give it to me, and, best of all, promised he would go to work.

"But what can I do?" What if, after we got there, he should fail me, what if he did not keep his promise?

Wedding photograph of John Ducho and Barbara Hauser
(Photo by Gey's Photographic Studio, Cuero, Texas, ca. 1890.
The Institute of Texan Cultures, San Antonio)

My father, Francis Moore, lived just five miles from Brazoria on one of his ranches. I thought perhaps things might go on well if we were near him, so I made ready to carry all my belongings that it was possible to take on the vessel to Texas. I had accumulated nice furniture and clothes during my years of work; besides these I bought two barrels of flour, supplies of coffee, sugar and other necessaries, and with a hopeful heart, set out for Texas . . .

When we got to Bailey's Prairie I thought it was a very paradise on earth. The breeze bore on its invisible wings most delicious odors and in among the brilliant wealth of flowers clusters of luscious grapes hung purpling in the sunshine.

In front of my brother sat my little girl and behind him clung my little boy, both radiant with delight at the strange things they saw, and the novelty on horse back.

It was also strange and beautiful to me. To the westward a deep belt of timber curved like a great protecting arm, and just on . . . my father awaited us . . .

He asked me if I had brought any flour. I told him that I had two barrels and that one of them was for him. He was so eager to get the flour saying that now he could get well, and that he would pay me any price for it, so he made them hitch up the wagon and go after it, telling them to bring all they could that evening and next morning they must go after the remainder of my things.

Anxiously I looked after the wagon as it grew smaller in the distance . . . and anxiously I watched for its return.

At last it came in sight. I strained my eyes to see what it had brought me. I could not believe my sight when it showed me one barrel of flour only; no one can imagine what I felt . . . when I realized that my husband . . . had gambled away everything that we possessed. He got down off the wagon, and I went and asked what he had done with my things, why he had not brought more with him.

"I got into a game of cards and lost your things," he answered.

I tried to quiet my brother's anger for fear my father might hear and the bad news might make him worse . . . [but] he overheard us talking about it, and he told me to leave Page [her husband]; my brother, too, insisted that I should leave him.

I have often regretted that I did not do it then, but there were my two little children to think of, and my stepmother was so stingy that she did not take proper care of her own . . . so I said to my Father, "What can I do? I am here in a wilderness. What can I do if I leave him . . ."

I think that I shed more tears than any woman could ever have shed before. My brother and Dr. Jones, who was afterwards President of Texas, went to Brazoria and finally managed to get back all of my things except the groceries . . .

Then my husband went off and when he returned . . . he informed me that he had gotten a house on Austin Bayou, twenty miles away from the nearest settler and that I must get ready to go there. A few days saw us domiciled in a little log house containing one room and a shed. The room was neatly sealed and finished and I tried to make the little home . . . as attractive as possible. I was tired and heart sick and when my husband said that he must leave us and go to see the man who wanted someone to keep his stock, I was willing that he should go and get employment, and I felt that this time he was in earnest . . . I had a little money and as we had nothing to eat except one quart of blackeyed peas I gave him $10 to get us some provisions, urging him to get back in three days time . . . I remembered that in this house, the Merrick it was called, a family had died of starvation and as the quart of blackeyed peas grew less and less, I anxiously thought of my husband's promise to be back in three days . . .

At last the peas were all gone. I searched the Prairie with anxious eyes, but I strained them in vain. There was not a sign of a human being on all that wide expanse of glowing flowers, and only the wind ruffled the heads of the tall grasses . . .

I gathered the sweet scarlet bunches of parsley haws that grew tall and luxuriant about the door, and fed the children with these.

I was afraid to let them play about the haw bushes, because the wild beasts would have killed them . . . at night panthers and wolves howled hungrily about our home . . .

Hope was not dead yet . . . when I saw my husband coming towards me. He had not brought one thing to eat.

I asked him what he had done with the money I had given him? He said he had bought some clothes to go to war in [the Civil War]; he said that everybody was volunteering to go and that he did not want to be called a coward. Then, I said, "What am I and the children going to do?" "You will have to do the best you can," he replied.

"If you go off and leave us to starve," I cried, "I hope that the first bullet that is fired will pierce your heart, and leave you time enough to think of the wife and children that you left to die of starvation in this wilderness."

Day after day came and went, and never a sign of a human being came over the lonely prairies, and I gathered the parsley haws for my little ones to eat with starvation daily staring us closer in the face . . .

Twenty miles [distant] . . . lived Mr. Merrick on his farm. For three nights Mr. Merrick had had a bad dream about his tenants in the lonely little house out on Austin Bayou . . .

Mr. Merrick's dream disturbed him and . . . he made up his mind that something had happened and saddled his horse and went to see what it was. He did not know that Mr. Page had gone to war, and was horrified to find that his wife and children were alone and starving. It was nine days after Page left that Mr. Merrick arrived.

I was never so glad in my life as I was when [he] rode up that day, and I felt that my little ones and I had a protector. He lost no time in getting us something to eat, but staked out his pony and went off with his gun. He soon came back with a turkey which he skinned and cutting the breast off he sharpened a stick and ran through it and stood it up before the fire to cook. We had never seen anything cooked that way before, but the odor was most appetizing and I thought I had never tasted anything better than that turkey . . .

I asked Mr. Merrick if there was not some way of getting away from my unhappy little home, to a settlement of some kind. He shook his head seriously, "No, I cannot see any way," he said, "everyone has gone to war."

"Your husband certainly did not go away without making some arrangements for you; I think some one will come for you." So we waited . . .

On our way home from the Brazos we had stopped overnight at the house of Mrs. Abit, and in the morning, when I asked her the amount of our bill she refused to take any payment whatever, saying that we were very welcome to anything that she had, that she did not charge anything to persons who lodged with her overnight . . . Mrs. Abit and I parted with very friendly feelings for each other; and journeying all day we got to our destination that night.

Somehow, when my husband left me, Mrs. Abit heard that he had gone to the war and left me unprovided for on the prairie. She was very sick, and she sent for a minister to come and pray with her, and . . . she made him promise to go and hunt me up.

She said that she could not rest easy until he found me and saw that I was cared for, or that I was alive . . . I shall never forget my feelings when he walked up and spoke to me. I had thought at first that he was a lost traveler, but he had a smile on his face. I asked him in and gave him a chair for I had brought my furniture with me . . . He spoke of Mrs. Abit's long illness and death . . . he knew that my father and brother were in the war, and said he had heard that we had nothing to eat . . .

Presently he came back from over the bridge, bringing with him a quantity of things; and then he unpacked cold biscuits, brandy, candles, and a host of things too numerous to mention. I said thankfully, "God has been taking care of us, for you see we are all alive and now he has sent you to take us away." He said that he knew the way to Bayou Austin and that he would go back and send wagons for me in three days time.

At the appointed time the[y] came, and Oh, with what joy we began our journey towards civilization, leaving behind us in the lonely little house sorrow and loneliness, hunger and despair.

I looked back at it in the distance till it became a mere speck and was swallowed up in the great wide prairie. So, I hoped, would its terrible memory fade from my life . . .

When I lived once more with other families in a settlement, I could make some money selling my little store of notions . . .

When I went to Texas, country life was a sealed book to me. I knew how to make a stylish dress; all about the fashions, and how to dress my hair in the latest mode of coiffure, and how to make a living in New Orleans . . . My sister-in-law taught me how to raise chickens and set a hen, to milk a cow and make butter, and to do all the pleasant tasks that fall to the lot of a housekeeper on a large farm.

I was quick to learn, and began to enjoy the busy life until one day the famous Norton Panic occurred. There was a man named Norton . . . who was known as a "very hard drinker." His supply of whiskey gave out and he . . . wandered about on the verge of delirium.

Some one had set fire to a cane brake . . . and the cane was popping like volleys of guns firing. Norton was seized with fright and ran down the prairie shouting that the Mexicans were coming to make an attack, burning and murdering as they came. The terrified people soon gathered . . . and hastily prepared to flee for their lives . . .

I gathered my baby in my arms, and got a man, who was driving a wagon loaded with meat, to let my little boy ride on the wagon, and for nine miles I trudged the heavy trail that alone served us for a road, carrying my little one who seemed to grow very heavy as the way grew longer . . .

It was not long before we learned that the negroes had risen and were burning and destroying everything in a savage, senseless way, too ignorant to appreciate the value of what they destroyed, or to carry off the spoils . . . When this was learned, we all prepared to go home . . . [then] Col. Robert Potter rode up with Col. Hall and two or three others and said that his party had just come from Austin with orders to take all of the people to Galveston for safety . . .

In a moment everyone began to get ready to go except me. I was alone among strangers; how could I carry my little ones all the way to Velasco? Besides that, I was distressed and embarrassed at the way people stared at me. One would have imagined that I was some very strange animal . . . I shall never forget the dress that caused me such uncomfortable regard. It was a black silk, somewhat the worse for wear after my forced march over Texas prairies, and with it I wore a white crepe shawl and a black velvet hat with trimmings of white satin ribbon and feathers. I was young, and even I could not help but acknowledge, very pretty, so that the gaze of so many strangers was more embarrassing than I can well describe.

Col. Potter stepped up to Col. Hall and they spoke together a moment; then he came over to me and in a gentle and courtly manner offered me a seat behind him on his horse, saying that his servant would carry my two children. My little boy was large enough to ride behind the servant, and I accepted his offer with a very thankful heart. So we began our eventful ride that changed the whole course of my life.

Col. Potter told me that he had asked Col. Hall about me, wishing to know who I was, and that Col. Hall had said that he knew my Father well and that I was a lady.

Never was a woman treated in a more kind and thoughtful manner than was I by Col. Potter. Himself a perfect gentleman, he treated me with all the deference due to a queen, and I began to look up to him as a protector; somehow he heard that I had said I would never again live with my husband, Mr. Page, and from the time he learned . . . he was most kind and attentive to my little boy, until I thought that there was nobody like the Colonel. . . .

One day he came up to the house and said that he had some important questions to ask me if I would answer them, and when I assented he inquired whether my marriage with Page had been solemnized by a priest. I explained how the ceremony had been performed. We were not married by a priest. "Very well," he answered, "your marriage with Page was not legal, because in Texas a marriage not solemnized by a priest is not valid. Therefore you are just as free, according to the laws of Texas, as if you had never married."

"Yes," I told him, "I have heard my father say that people had to be married over again by the priest before they could get land." "Don't you see," he said, "that you are just as free to marry again as any one else?"

I listened to all he said and promised to think the matter over. He loved me very devotedly, and the more I thought about it the better way it seemed out of my difficulties.

So one evening, according to the custom of the country, the little assembly gathered to see us wedded; the ceremony was a very simple one in those days in that country, but it was just as binding as judge and clergy were present. The only guests at our piney woods wedding were Joe Miller, George Torenta, Paddy Roling and Martha Moore.

Col. Potter was always a very devoted husband to me, and never did anything to distress me until the time when he made his will in Austin; and I have always believed that he thought I would never hear of his action then, because the first thing he told me on his return was that he had introduced a bill into the Senate making all marriages like ours legal.

Ironically, just as their marriage was legalized, Potter became irrationally infatuated with a beautiful young married woman in Austin. It was a brief whirl, but he foolishly deeded their homestead land at Potter's Point to her upon parting. He was murdered in 1840, and before he died tried to tell Harriet about the will, but failed. She found out some years later when it was sold to a third party, who demanded Harriet's eviction.

GEORGE W. RILEY

George Riley kept a personal diary in which the passage of time "was marked with introspection." When four months away from his twenty-fifth wedding anniversary, he noted his devotion to his wife, Lucy Ann, with the following recollection, showing how closely his identity had become linked to hers.

31 DECEMBER 1880
today ends anotyher year of our lives and this is my Sixteenth Diara

am able to give an account of my Selfe every day for the past 16 years or 5640 days. Perhaps I cannot give as good a record as I ought to be able to give but am glad that things have gon no worse for us than they have, but on the Contrary have great reason to Praise the giver of all good gifts that our lives have been spared and So many blessings have followed us during the whole time of my Diara Keeping together with our whole lives. but Many has ben the Changes, with all its disapointments and trials that this world of cares are hier to, during that tiem our little seven year old girl has grown to womanhood got married got to be Mother over four years ago. Juddie has ben Born and grown to be a Man in size and is a great help to us. and we have ben able to pay all our debts, bought the Frost place, built a new Barn on it, got Ida and Bert on it and Started. Built our wagon house, an addition on our house, wood mill and shops, Cleared and improved a good deal of our place. helped to Build a church at Maine and have tried to do what little I could towards helping the Cause of Religion along.

during the sixteen years manye afflictions have befalnus in the loss of my Father, Lucys Father, one of my half Brothers and one half Sister, together with Scores of Friends that have gon to there last resting place. but death has not ben permitted to enter into our little family for which we cannot be to thankful and with all the rest we have had maney good times which is pleasant to reflect on . . .

it is a fact that ever aparent to me that during all of the quarter of a century that has past in my Married life   The greatest good that this world has afoarded me has ben my Ever True and faithfull Wife to Stande by and helpe and encourage doing all in her power to make every thing pleasant to all around. May God Bless hur guide and direct and keep and save us all is my earnist & sincere prayer.

Unidentified couples
(State Historical Society of North Dakota)

On the Ranch

"*The cow custodians did not have me fooled. I knew how harmless and afraid of women they really were.*"
—ANN BASSETT WILLIS

Katherine Folstrom Forse, Dunn County homesteader, ca. 1907–1908 (State Historical Society of North Dakota)

THE DREAM OF SOME COWBOYS WAS TO SAVE ENOUGH money to "nest," or own a small ranch somewhere along the great cattle trails, marry a local belle and achieve respectability. Occasionally, such happiness occurred, but more often, low wages of three dollars a day, coupled with spendthrift habits and a streak of sentimentality, isolated many "prairie troubadours" into a morose state of perpetual bachelorhood.

Or, when it came to women, they simply lacked nerve. Accustomed to wielding searing-hot branding irons, castrating bulls and facing down runaway herds that thundered toward them, hell-bent, it seemed odd that so many lost courage and turned morbid when confronted with the female sex. Campfire ballads upheld the myth of the "poor lonesome cowboy" who never found love, either due to his own ineptitude or to the high mortality rate of women on the frontier, which in 1859 and 1860 was 22 percent higher than for men in the more settled regions of Dakota, Nebraska, Utah and Wyoming.

While other men, particularly homesteaders, hurried to marry, the cowboys hurried out of town. They drifted up and down the cattle frontier like dust devils, stirring up the ladies and the locals, angering the town sheriff, then moving on.

Supposedly, good cowboys made bad husbands, although the prostitutes with whom they consorted had few complaints. To them, the cowhands, with their aloof, tongue-tied courtesy, were like dusty, trail-sore medieval knights who thundered into town, shined their boots, shook the dust from their creased hats and found a dance-hall girl to hole up with for a spell. They treated their harlots like ladies, giving them gifts while buying their time, even, on occasion, bestowing a symbolic cheap tin "wedding" ring. "We married a girl for a week," said cowboy Teddy Blue, at the end of which, the honeymoon over, the footloose cowhandleft and the so-called bride remained behind to ready herself for the next mock marriage to come her way.

In the wide reaches of the far west—Wyoming Territory, Texas, Colorado and beyond—ranch hands were gruff, weathered and hard-drinking, their hands callused from hauling yearling calves or flinging a lasso, their eyes in a perpetual squint from scanning the far horizon. Untalkative, more at ease with animals and inevitably stiff and standoffish with women, they were hardly husband material. Often, they had trouble with banter, and ended almost every phrase with the word *ma'am*. To them, decent women were an idealized myth, elevated to inaccessibility, to be admired from afar but seldom touched. In fact, the men were often thwarted in love by their overblown, Victorian notions of "true womanhood."

No matter how often they met and mingled with town women, the men never seemed at ease. And no wonder: without exposure to ladies, few had developed the manners to succeed; their ineptness around women was legendary. Thus when Miss Ethel Edmunds of Virginia commanded her fiance, Mose Drachman, at the count of three to help her back onto her horse, she expected the gallantry and savoir faire of southern gentility—not to land, arms and feet dangling, across the saddle as he stood there stupidly. "Why didn't you hold my foot?" she cried to the perplexed cowpoke. Mose's only reply: "I never helped a lady before."

Respectable women had other, deeper concerns when it came to range hands. To their credit, the men were soft-spoken and often reserved, but they earned minimum and sporadic wages, drank heavily and, like cattle, were prone to seek farther pastures. Some were so marginal they possessed only boots, quirts and saddles and had to borrow a horse from the boss's outfit in order to work. What kind of a provider, women wondered, would not even own a horse? Furthermore, there was the history of long-standing habit. Many of these men had spent decades huddled out in the solitude of a line camp, living, as historian Ramon

Adams wrote, "the life of a buck nun," with little or no socializing. "My comrade was my horse," wrote cowhand Jim Christian, a type of camaraderie that often failed to translate into social graces.

Marriage-minded or not, single women sometimes let down their guard at a moment of emotional low ebb; perhaps desperate at the everyday repetition of their lives in the same whistle-stop, with a single grocery store, dry goods emporium, barbershop, boot shop, livery stable, bank, two saloons and a scattered house or two, they would view cowboys as a welcome diversion. A woman might take a cowboy in hand, instruct him in dress, diction, and even education—all in the spirit of social reform.

An enterprising cowhand might pursue his own social mobility, as did Walker Wyman, riding herd in the Texas Panhandle, who spotted an opportunity for social advancement when he read of dancing lessons offered in a local paper at the bargain rate of twelve for three dollars. "I was so awkward . . . I couldn't join hands and circle to the left," he admitted, but quickly gained the sympathy of a young townswoman adept in dancing, who suggested they practice at the public dance halls. Later, at a local shindig, Walker found a Mrs. Winn, the "most friendly and best looking woman" at the dance, to show him how to follow the caller and guide him through the quadrille. "My earlier shyness was gone," Walker marveled. "I danced with others."

More adept and mannerly than his peers, Walker stood in contrast to another cowboy, described by ranch hand William Timmons, whose favorite stunt to attract women at a dance was to "catch with his mouth anything thrown across the room," never missing a peanut, candy or apple projectile, flaunting his ability to catch food and dance at the same time.

Dancing provided a way for the inarticulate to shine socially, and became increasingly popular with cowboys on the range. At the Charles Goodnight ranch, a huge preserve sprawling over vast sections of Texas that sporadically employed hundreds of trail hands to ride the line, dances were not left up to fate or town dandies; instead, the cowboys would plan their own ball, pooling their money for supplies, making exhaustive lists of young ladies within a day's ride, scrubbing the bunkhouse to a shine and setting out abundant food for a midnight spread of lemonade, oranges, apples, peanuts, popcorn and candy, followed by a daylight breakfast of bacon, eggs, flapjacks and brown-sugar lick, "all the little extras" they could think of to please "the girls," who would depart in the morning by wagon, buckboard, buggy or on horseback, sleepy and pleased at the grand social event. Goodnight's affairs were a rousing local success to which no pretty girl ever failed to be invited. Such bunkhouse flings were, to Ann Bassett Willis, brimming with attractions. There "saddle-galled cow punchers congregated to sing range ballads and squawk out doleful tunes on the fiddle."

Cowboy William Timmons was philosophical about such merriment; he viewed a dance like a storm wind, strong and gusty at its peak, then growing feeble as life drifted back into the unvarying routine of spring bog riding, fence mending, dogie throwing and windmill greasing. He'd seen enough festive affairs to know that occasionally, hearts came together with a clash, bridging the gap between town and saddle, bringing cowboys into the married state and town women into ranch life.

Dusty illiterates on the range soon found their ranks sprinkled with the well-bred sons of the genteel, seeking a middle-class rite of passage by running away west. Cowhands who could read poetry—who could even read at all!—were increasingly seen. The changing status of the cowhand, as seen by the enormous popular interest stirred up in Europe and on the East Coast for wild west shows, was also reflected in dress. Those who flaunted the insignia of cowboy rank—the duster coat, the leather chaps and the silver-etched belts and buckles—found themselves eyed appraisingly by women, both respectable and not.

In 1898, more than twenty Wyoming and Colorado newspapers decided to capitalize on the cowboy attraction, stirring up a frenzy in western wedding mania by promoting, in Cheyenne, a public frontier wedding and a Bridesmaids Ball for bridal candidates chosen from nearby cities. The pioneer wedding took fourth place on the day's agenda, along with a half-mile cow pony race, a running free-for-all and a bucking and pitching contest. According to reports, the wedding was the highlight of the show, featuring a young applicant who read the ad in *The Denver Post,* was twenty-four years old, and eager to wed a young lady—eighteen years old and "handsome too." He was disappointed in his marriage bid by a more substantial citizen, a Dr. M. C. Matthews of Denver, who dressed "in full frontier garb" to marry his intended, Miss Cora Baer. Amid the blare of a band, the bridal party repaired to its position "under the grandstand" in "full view of thousands of spectators." The Bridesmaids Ball, held afterward, was one of the most enjoyable events in Cheyenne's history, according to an article in the *Sun-Leader,* "aside from the unfortunate accident of the bleachers falling down." From the Bridesmaids Ball to the turkey trot, men and women of the ranching frontier would rise up when the fiddler played and do-si-do with abandon, finding in the country dances a risk-free opportunity for men to actually touch a woman, and for women, the chance to inspect the men up close, while pondering the meaning of those words "for better or for worse."

NANNIE ALDERSON

Nannie Tiffany Alderson was "bred to leisure" in the plantation world of the South, but on a trip to Kansas, fell in love both with the west and with her future husband, a cowboy. Neither event was anticipated; she began life as a rancher's wife completely unequipped. Yet love, enterprise and enthusiasm created in Nannie an indomitable pioneer spirit. "I led a hard life," she wrote, "but I don't think an easy one is ever half so full."

The year I was sixteen a new world opened up for me. My father's sister, Elizabeth Tiffany, had married a Mr. Symms and had pioneered in Kansas in the Fifties. On one of her periodic visits to Virginia she stopped to see me . . . The result was an invitation to visit her in Atchison, Kansas, from September to June.

What an experience that was! Kansas then was the West. I felt that the very air there was easier to breathe. In Union [West Virginia] you had to have your pedigree . . . to be accepted anywhere, but in Atchison it didn't matter a bit who your ancestors were or what you did for a living; if you were nice you were nice. What impressed me most was the fact that a girl could work in an office or a store, yet that wouldn't keep her from being invited to the nicest homes or marrying one of the nicest boys. This freedom to work seemed to me a wonderful thing. I wanted to do something useful myself . . . but Auntie wouldn't let me; she knew my mother would never consent.

So many little foolish conventions that we were brought up on at home didn't apply in Atchison. There was much less formality there; when people went visiting they took their darning or their

Hilda Satterlund, ca. 1905 (State Historical Society of North Dakota)

knitting with them in the friendly old-fashioned way—but when I tried it after returning to West Virginia, mother was shocked. In Union on Sunday we were never allowed to open the piano nor to visit anybody except relatives; in Kansas we all did as we pleased bout these matters . . .

On this visit I first met my husband. One evening in June, 1877, I was invited to take supper and spend the night with a Baptist preacher's family named Alderson, who were West Virginians like ourselves. There were several brothers in the home, and three or four girls had been invited. After a jolly supper one of the boys excused himself from the parlor and went out on the porch to smoke a cigar.

In a minute he was back, saying excitedly: "Mother, Walt's home!"

This announcement produced a great effect. "Walt," I learned, was a brother who had run away to Texas when he was twelve or thirteen years old, and they hadn't seen him for nine years.

They made him come inside—a cowboy in sombrero and chaps. We girls were not impressed; we thought he was funny-looking. I remember that he was rather silent and ill at ease, and soon excused himself, saying he was going to bed. In the morning the brother brought the startling news that "Walt" had not slept in bed, but had gotten up in the night, taken a quilt, and lain down on the floor of the bedroom. This strange visitor, they said, had come up with a herd of cattle to Dodge City, the wild, tough cowtown which was then a northern terminus of the great cattle trail from Texas. He left the house very early . . . and I didn't see him again, except once at a crystal wedding party, before going back to West Virginia.

Much later I found out what lay behind his sudden appearance that night in his strange cowboy dress. . . .

His parents were conscientious, high-minded people who

thought their first duty was to the church, not to their children and home. There was a good deal of strictness about certain matters, such as the observance of Sunday, but Walter was always wild and irrepressible. The people in Atchison used to tell a story of his riding home on a horse afternoons, behind his father . . .

[A]t thirteen he ran away to Texas. Two other boys ran away with him; their fathers went after them and brought them home, but Mr. Alderson, Senior, was very wise. He said: "No, since that is what he wants, let him go and learn for himself."

He was tall—just half an inch under six feet—blue-eyed, and of a fine appearance . . .

He told me much about his early life, and one thing he said I have always remembered; that he had never known any pleasure in his home until I was in it. I believe that was one thing that gave him such a strong feeling for home afterwards. He told me, too, that he had made up his mind never to marry, but that I had changed it. He was already planning to go out and start a cattle ranch in Montana, and he asked me if I would be afraid to share that kind of life with him. I told him I wasn't afraid, and we became engaged soon after his father died.

My aunt and the relatives in Atchison did not approve the match at first. This was not because he was taking me to the unsettled West; they all thought the ranching business had a wealthy future, so that was looked upon as a good thing. No, they disapproved because of his wild reputation. But I had perfect confidence in him, believing then, as I do now, that it's not what a man has done before marriage that counts, it is what he does after.

I wanted to see my grandmother again before going so far away, so I went home to West Virginia and spent the next year there, getting ready to be married . . . I made all my trousseau myself. Thanks to Auntie I did have sense enough to make my underthings plain according to the standards of the day . . .

I made my own wedding dress of white embroidered mull,

and I earned the money to buy my wedding veil . . .

While I was at home making these preparations, Mr. Alderson was in Montana hunting a site for a ranch . . .

He stopped at a road ranch up Tongue River run by some people named Lays . . . That year the buffalo were still so thick that Mrs. Lays had only to say: "Mr. Alderson, we're out of meat"; and he would go out and find a herd and kill a calf, all just as easily as a man would butcher a yearling steer in his own pasture. Yet when I came out, one year later, there was nothing left of those great bison herds, which had covered the continent, but carcasses . . .

With the ranch selected and the cattle bought, Mr. Alderson [came] East. We were married at my mother's house in Union, on April 4, 1883.

For weeks and weeks it had rained, as it can rain only in the West Virginia mountains, but that morning the sun came out, and I was awakened by my niece's voice exclaiming: "Why, the sun is shining on Aunt Nannie's wedding day!"

The servants' faces were all wreathed in smiles.

The ceremony was at ten, and in the afternoon Mr. Alderson and I went across the mountains by stage to Atchison, where we were to be entertained by his relatives before we took the train. As we went down into the valley toward Atchison we saw the sun setting in a great mass of gold and purple clouds; before we were through dinner it was raining again, and we heard it on the train that night. Mother wrote me afterwards that it rained for weeks . . .

I went with romantic ideas of being a helpmeet to a man in a new country, but I was sadly ill-equipped when it came to carrying them out. Before I left Union a dear old lady had taught me how to make hot rolls, but except for that one accomplishment I knew no more of cooking than I did of Greek. Hot rolls, plus a vague understanding that petticoats ought to be plain, were my whole equipment for conquering the West.

CLARICE E. RICHARDS

**Clarice Eastbrook accompanied her new husband,
Jarvis Richards, to his recently purchased western home,
a Colorado ranch in Elbert County. Jarvis (called "Owen" in her
account) was an intellectual who had studied languages in Berlin
and Leipzig, but took a fancy to western jargon and raising cattle.
Clarice, ladylike yet vigorous about her new life, learned daily the
lessons of the wilderness yet also managed to establish herself in
Denver as a prominent member of local womens' clubs.**

We were living in the land of the unexpected. Six weeks on the ranch demonstrated that. The possibilities for surprise were inexhaustible, and the probabilities innumerable and certain, if Owen happened to be away.

On one of these occasions the cook eloped with the best rider on the place . . . Twenty-two husky and hungry men wanted three square meals a day, and one inexperienced bride stood between them and starvation. The situation was mutually serious.

In my need, help came. Tex, our coachman . . . saved the day. Shortly after the elopement he came in for supplies for the cow-camp. I was almost hidden by pans of potatoes, and was paring away endlessly . . . [Tex] hated "messin' 'round where there was women," as he expressed it. Here was sacrifice indeed! Tex scrubbed his hands until they fairly bled [and] enveloped himself in a large checked gingham apron . . .

Something deepened in me. I was seeing a new thing.

After the meal was over, there was such a general shaving and donning of red neckties that I could not restrain my curiosity. I called Tex aside and asked him where they were going. He looked a little sheepish, as he replied:

"Why, we ain't goin' nowhere." Then in a burst of confidence, "I don't know as I'd order tell you, but the fact is, you folks is goin' to be surprised; all the folks 'round is goin' to have a party here, and we're expectin' 'em . . ."

Tex saw I was really troubled. "Why, Mrs. Brook," he said, "you don't have to do nothin'. Just turn the house over to 'em, and along about midnight I'll make some coffee—they'll bring baskets . . ."

"Me and the boys"—Tex spoke somewhat apologetically— "we kind of thought maybe you and Mr. Brook would like to get acquainted, seein's how you're goin' to live here; but I guess we oughten to have did what we done . . ."

At eight o'clock, Tex, self-appointed master of ceremonies, ushered in the first arrivals . . . From eight until ten they came, ranchmen, cow-punchers, ex-cow-punchers running their own outfits, infant cow-punchers, girls and women, until kitchen and sitting room were filled to overflowing, and every chair and bench on the place in use. Among the last to arrive was a tall, languid Texan, accompanied by two languid, drab-colored women. They were presented to us as "Robert, Missus Reed and Maggie." "Maggie," I immediately concluded, was a sister, but not being quite certain, I sought enlightenment from Mrs. Bohm.

"She ain't Reed's sister," she informed me in a low tone, "she's his girl."

"Oh, works for them, you mean?" I said, somewhat puzzled by the Reed connections.

"Works nothin'," Mrs. Bohm replied, scornfully. "She's got the next place to 'em and goes with 'em everywhere. Ella don't seem to mind. I'd just call her 'Maggie' if I was you," and Mrs. Bohm departed to join a group of women near the door.

I looked over at the two with a new interest. They were chat-

Unidentified ranching scene (Garrison Collection, Colorado Historical Society)

ting and laughing together, the "girl" and the wife seemingly on the best of terms, with no sign of rivalry for the tall Texan's affections. Here was a situation fraught with latent possibilities that made me tremble, yet—"Ella don't seem to mind."

The kitchen had been converted into a ballroom by moving the table up against the wall and placing three chairs upon it. Unfortunately the sink and stove were fixtures, but everything else, including the bread jar, found a temporary resting place in the yard . . .

The music, if such could be dignified by that name, was such as to defy description . . . The two men sawed their violins, and the third was purple in the face from his efforts on the mouth-harp; all were stamping time with their feet, and he of the harp was slapping his knee with his unoccupied hand . . .

However, music mattered little, for all had come to have a good time, and the "caller-out," with both eyes shut tight and arms folded across his breast, was making himself heard above all other sounds.

"Birdie in the center and all hand around!" he commanded. Then fiddles and mouth-harp began a wild jig, couples raced 'round and 'round, while "Birdie," a blond and blushing maiden, stood patiently in the midst of the whirling circle, until the next order came:

"Birdie hop out and Crow hip in!
Take holt of paddies and run around agin"

"Crow" was a broad, heavy-set cowpuncher, wearing chaps, and in the endeavor to "run around agin," I found my progress somewhat impeded by his spurs, which caught in my skirt and very nearly upset me. All the riders wore their heavy boots and spurs, and it required real agility to avoid having one's skirt torn to ribbons. I was devoutly thankful that tulle ball gowns were not worn on ranches.

Easter-egg boil
(Pikes Peak Library, Colorado Springs)

There was more to avoid than spurs. We had to dance about the kitchen and avoid the stove, the sink and the tabled musicians, to say nothing of the nails in the floor. But after a few hours' practice, I began to feel qualified to waltz on top of the House of the Seven Gables, and avoid at least six of them . . .

I danced—my head fairly spins when I think *how* I danced—for, since the party was given in our honor, dance I must with every man who asked me.

Owen, not being a dancing man, made himself agreeable to the wall-flowers and the children, stealing upstairs about once an hour for a few moments' nap on the bedroom floor. The beds themselves were occupied by sleeping infants, whose mothers were going through the intricate mazes of those dances below.

At one o'clock Tex began to make the coffee, whereupon the

musicians descended from the table, and the expectant party sat down. But where were their baskets? My heart sank, as Tex approached holding a very small one. He informed me in a stage whisper it was all there was!

The basket contained a cake and a one week chick, evidently fried soon after leaving the shell. It was the smallest chicken I ever saw. I hastily produced our cake and roast, and then took one despairing look around at the forty individuals to be fed. I shall never be able to explain it, unless Tex had an Aladdin's lamp concealed in his pocket, for cake, roast and chicken appeared to be inexhaustible, and the supply more than equaled the demand . . .

It was six o'clock Sunday morning when one most thoughtful person suggested that "they'd orter be goin'"; and by seven the last guest had departed. Then Owen and I, weary and heavy-eyed, donned our wraps, climbed into the wagon, and started on a sixteen-mile drive to the railroad to meet his brother, who was coming from California to see "how we were making it."

I was almost too tired to speak, but one thought was struggling for expression, and as we started up the first long hill, I had to say:

"Anyone who ever spoke of the 'peace and quiet of ranch life' lived in New York and dreamed about it. In twenty-four hours I have discovered that we have an ex-convict for a trusted cook, and have received as guests a man with his wife and resident affinity. We have had a surprise party and I have danced with all the blemished characters the country boasts of, until six o'clock in the morning of the Sabbath day, with never a qualm of conscience . . ."

WILLIAM TIMMONS

Born in 1878, Bill Timmons began his life on the range in Texas and continued it in the empty expanse of North Dakota during the peak years of the cattleman's west—a time when range hands who hungered for sociability far outnumbered the women who could provide it. The cowboy dance near Hebron, North Dakota, was one of many attempts at a social event that began hopefully, with "one girl and a fiddler."

Bill drove up in his spring wagon, accompanied by a well-dressed young lady and two city men from Satoughton, Wisconsin. The men were bankers—George and Read Dow. The young lady was their niece, Miss Georgia D. Townsend, whose mother and uncles were interested in three townships of railroad land they'd bought. They were there to look over their holdings.

Bill came down and said, "There's a young lady up here I want you to meet. She'd like to eat with you cowboys." I told him he knew which way the pleasure lay. Then I met Miss Townsend . . . We invited her to have supper at the chuck wagon! She thought it quite a treat.

Then Bill said, "I'll bet Miss Townsend would like to dance with some cowboys. My hayloft's empty, and it's a good place to dance."

Georgia said she'd like that. And we told her, "Miss Townsend, if we can locate a fiddle and somebody to play it, you'll certainly have a chance to dance with some long-haired and whiskered cowboys."

Charley Partridge and I hitched up our lead chuck-wagon

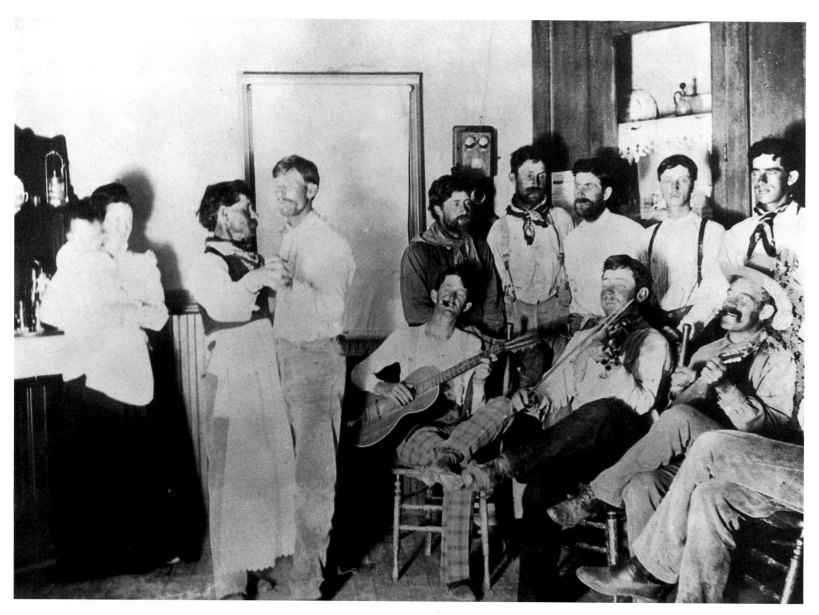

Stag dance at Lubbock
(Archives Division, Texas State Library, Austin)

team to Bill's spring wagon and drove out to see if we could get one girl and a fiddler. As the big percentage of cowboys then were like me and not very graceful at such things, the dances were mostly square ones. To have four women—one more besides Georgia, Mrs. Connolly, and the Connolly hired girl—we had to get another.

We knew where to find her—six miles east. She was Sophia Beaner. But when we got to Mr. Beaner's house, Sophia said she wouldn't go to the dance unless Sam Pelton was going to be there. She was engaged to Sam and wasn't going to a dance unless he was there.

This was a desperate situation. We didn't know where Sam was. Luckily we didn't let on to Sophia that we didn't know, for to get things going something had to be done. It wasn't that making up some sort of ruse would have bothered Charley or me. We were used to that. It was that we knew any scheme we thought up would be found out in a few hours. We didn't wait long to decide, though. We took the chance.

We told Sophia that Sam would be there, that he'd just gone to his brother's ranch, several miles away, to dress up so he could meet her at the dance. He was expecting us to bring her, we said.

Sophia came with us. Ten miles farther on we got Paul Palson and his fiddle. By eleven o'clock we were back at Bill's barn.

The dance started with Sophia, Charley, and me expecting Sam at any moment, but he didn't come. Mrs. Connolly wasn't feeling well, so she couldn't take part. But with a boy taking the place of a girl and one or two sets of boys dancing together, the dance was on.

Panch Arnett showed the most signs of trying to spruce up for the occasion. His hair had grown so long that unless he kept his hat on, stray locks would flop down in his eyes. At the barn he'd found some old sheep shears, which Billy Connolly kept to trim fetlocks, and he'd trimmed the front of his hair almost even with

Dance held by Texas A&M college students, 1912
(The Institute of Texan Cultures, San Antonio)

his head. It was a sort of a bangs appearance. He looked cute, and seemed to have a wonderful time.

At two o'clock Dick stopped the dance to serve beefsteak, fried potatoes, corn, hot biscuits, and coffee. It was evident that the first gray-pink streaks of dawn would soon be appearing, and we'd have to tangle with Sophia, no matter what.

Her manner left no doubt that by now she knew we'd lied to her and that she looked upon us as contemptible frauds. Earlier in the evening she'd been cherry-voiced, charming, and delightful. Now she wouldn't dance anymore.

A heavy fog hugged the country for miles around, and nobody could leave until daylight. Time dragged. Still I couldn't muster enough courage to face Sophia.

Just as the first rays of the sun were filtering into the barn I went to Charley, dumped the job of handling Sophia on him, and walked out into the crisp morning air. She was very mad at first, but she got over it . . .

Wedding party at Union Church, Barry, Colorado
(Pikes Peak Library, Colorado Springs)

Old World Traditions

"I like best those who come up, take me by the hand and say, 'Well, we wish you welcome to America!'"
—Elisabeth Koren, Iowa, 1853

To the inflow of emigrants from disease-ridden Europe, the deep hungering for America was part wishful thinking, part an overdrawn imagery that glorified even the most mundane aspects of the new land. Travel rhetoric touched off wild speculation among all classes, drawing the cramped and dispirited Europeans to America's shores to find a verdant tabula rasa, inviting private dreams of enterprise, autonomy, and for some, prospects of marital choice.

Between 1717 and 1775, fully 200,000 hungry English from Ulster sailed the Atlantic, with more than 11 million Europeans emigrating from the British Isles to America by 1890. From Germany came 2.5 million by 1776, while a million or so Irish sailed to America between 1846 and 1854. More than 153,000 Poles arrived between 1875 and 1900, and 182,500 Italians by 1890—among all shuddered an uneasy cultural pluralism, described by Irishman Michael MacGowan, recalling a backwoods gathering: "There were people . . . from every corner of the globe. . . . I heard languages spoken that night that I never knew existed."

For women, emigration was often linked to marriage, just as male migration turned on the tide of economic demands. In Europe, "hordes of girls" who were tied financially to the paternal household and faced declining marriage opportunities as they aged, sought exit to America. Dowries were dear, and few parents could afford to marry off more than two daughters. One German parent of ten sadly bid his five youngest daughters farewell as they sailed away to America to work as servants, and, with luck, find husbands. Spinsterhood loomed unless emigration was possible, and the fare for five young maidens across the Atlantic cost considerably less than a dowry.

Upon arrival, immigrant girls from eighteen to twenty-five were already older than marriageable American women. Disparaged as "Brigits" if Irish, their nationality threw up a quick social barrier between the immigrant girls and the local girls, who sel-dom worked as servants, married younger and had an increased life expectancy. "I pity the Irish. I pity cooks and blacksmiths and red-haired people," mused Lorena Hays, echoing a popular, nationalistic sentiment of the day that refused to recognize at least one similarity between cultures and classes: both American girls and immigrants were occasionally pregnant when wed.

Opposition to emigration mounted from second-generation European Americans. To them, the land was already spoken for, and increasing xenophobia translated into stock rejection of the immigrants, popularly cast as a "brutalized peasantry" and a "wild and motley throng" to be summarily rejected by those more established. Egalitarian notions were cast aside, prejudice reigned and myriad groups settled in nervous proximity—victims of their own ethnicity whether attempting assimilation or segregation.

Many ethnic groups clung to their old ways, as did a group of two hundred Polish families from Upper Silesia who settled in rural Texas. So repelled were they by the "strange and barbarous customs of the Americans," they retreated ever further into the intimacy of their traditional circle. Without the usual guidance of a priest, members could pray at will, sing whenever, and arrange love matches with no interference, relying upon the fact that bold and decisive Polish women often took the upper hand in courtship. Among the Silesians, only one barrier existed to wedded bliss: men and women who shared godfathers and godmothers could not marry.

Few could claim absolute serenity within marriage. The effects of nationalism, faith and denomination were far-reaching, leaving Catholic and Protestants in such pitched discord that not even love could smooth their contradictions. Those brave enough to cross-wed were true pioneers, bound to find their own solutions of the heart. Thus when two Irish immigrants, William Hatton and Kate Harney, fell in love and wed, their theological opposition—Catholic versus Protestant—led to a unique solution. Lovingly, they elected to mate, cohabit, bear children and raise a family of fourteen, but, to avoid conflict, seldom speak.

In America, such cross-culturalism chipped away at prejudice. What better way to thread together European communities, polarized and insular as in the Old World, than by the brave intermingling of lovers? Clan commixed with culture, resulting, over time, in greater understanding, muted ethnic hostility and a strengthened population. "Well I suppose we are just a mixture of different nationalities," said Margaret Archer, with unusual tolerance. "A little Welsh and little Irish & a big lot of Dutch well any way I am glad I am what I am."

Ethnic colonies were so close-knit as to blur the lines between aristocracy and peasant. All became immigrants together, subject to new courtship ideas, kinship rites and bonding. Often, formality was flung aside; the mandated "time of acquaintance," or engagement, was shortened. Young men had to get back to the crops, women to their household chores.

In Europe, kith and kin presented one another with suitable youngsters for marriage, or, failing that, advertised in a newspaper or engaged a marriage broker. Since traditional dowry marriages were sporadic in the New World, children of the lower classes were allowed to meet randomly at festivals and church or social activities. After all, what impoverished dirt farmer could scrape together a hundred dollars for a bridal price? Why exchange money when both the girl and the boy were desperate to marry? America turned customs inside out—new rules were laid, futures forged and paths traveled without precedent.

Russians, however, clung to the practice of arranged marriage. Their inflow into the midwest brought companion practices— particularly *Koopla,* or arranged marriage, which drew in recent émigrés such as the hulking young arrival, Ludwig, whose intended, Christina, met his every expectation. Ludwig was entranced by her at work in a sunlit kitchen, her strong arms removing freshly baked loaves from the oven, each, significantly, the size of a baby. Industry and energy seemed to be hers; and, she was attractive. With or without a marriage broker, Christina would have been his choice.

In a traditional European nuptial ceremony, parents first agreed upon the match, whether the families were acquaintances or not. Elder women of the community would scrutinize the bride, pinching her strong forearms and noting the shine of her freshly scoured kitchen, part of a tradition that extended across the Atlantic. Nowhere were Old World customs more in evidence, however, than in the traditional wedding rituals— marriage, celebratory meals and gift-giving. Foods remained unchanged with "a typical German repast"—served in a German Mennonite community in Pennsylvania, in 1780, an array of foods "biled and roasted to rags," embellished with spiced red cabbage and followed by a savory, deep-dish apple pie.

Habits of dress also persevered, as evidenced in the 1876 wedding of a plump German-Russian bride in Hays, Kansas. The daughter of a prosperous immigrant family, she could afford to marry in the required number of gowns, beginning with a "changeable green silk dress," in a ceremony that lasted five days. The festive event was replete with butchered cattle and fancy cakes and a traditional wedding bowl of soup and meat communally shared. According to an observer, as cited by historian Joanna Stratton, the *hoch-zeit* was danced, men smoked long-stem pipes, and the bride's gown was aflutter with greenbacks, lavishly pinned on by the guests.

In a German household, women were seldom pampered and even less frequently given authority. Pedigree, power and respect were invested by German men in their sons. Any true German male scorned the "weak" Yankee custom of making a wife a partner—as unthinkable as allowing her preeminence at the table.

Young women, immigrants or national, still took time to collect a trousseau within their cedar-scented hope chests, daydreaming, all the while, of the future. From time to time, the bride-to-be would delve into the chest, pulling out a welter of finely woven sheets, embroidered pillow slips, and ornate hand-knotted or woven bed coverings for all to admire. High lace caps were a particular favorite, embellished with flowers, securely anchored with pins and worn at weddings. The largest flounce of lingerie and "whitewear" separated women of means from those without.

Traditional Russian customs drew strongly from nature's imagery: the bride's wormwood crown mourned the bitterness of the married state, a handful of hops sprinkled on her head by the priest wished her the grain's fruitfulness and the festive exchange of a rough goatskin called forth fertility—a prayer for as many children as the skin had hairs. Bread and salt were ceremonially shared, while a chorus of giggling children would blurt out stanzas from the *epithalamium,* a grossly obscene wedding song. Czech settlers flounced out their plaudits to the pair with polkas, mazurkas and a lively quadrille, dancing until the bride's early-morning announcement of the nuptial consummation—the binding up of her hair with long, slow emphasis. If the couple was modern, they would put aside one of the mainstay canon laws of the Russian Orthodox church—a law that changed most radically in America and was considered a primitive observance: the forbidding of conjugal intercourse on Mondays, Wednesdays and Fridays.

Italian immigrants came west after the turn of the century, steeped in Catholic customs, echoed in distinct configurations from France to Mexico. A wedding day, for the Catholic, should be spent in humble dress, to discourage vanity's sensuality, reflecting upon the upcoming holy state. Most important: a Catholic would marry on a workday, sure in mind and spirit that none of the fourteen impediments to marriage, as listed by Latinate Catholicism, were in evidence, including lack of chastity, an unbaptized spouse, a history of homicide or apostasy.

Italians recognized constraints on conjugal intimacy: no coupling on fast days, feast days and during pregnancy. In America, the practice of arranged marriages had fallen away; couples married for love, which undercut the historic Italian system of concubinage, or routinely having a "love" match, or mistress, after marriage. American Italians, always practical, had brief and spirited courtships and married without ceremony. Who was to know?

In Italy, grown daughters often bedded down at night with their parents, perhaps to ward off surprise attentions from an overenthused suitor. There is no record of the custom's continuance in America. Nor was the traditional fear of age difference carried over to western life. In some Italian states, a man under thirty could not wed a woman over forty, and if she were older than forty, her husband must be at least thirty-five. Conversely, a man older than sixty could not marry a woman less than thirty.

The Dutch, often seen as "dull and stolid" by their native-born neighbors, clung to the home as the center of all activities—including the social ritual of courting. During Christmas, homes bustled with activity and blazed with lights and good cheer, thrown open to an endless round of young men who wished to "see" the family's daughters while enjoying punch, oysters and treats of the season. Dutch-Americans considered a young man maladroit if by the age of eighteen he lacked a *luffee,* from the Dutch word *liefje,* or sweetheart. At weddings, the *luffee* was toasted with ceremonial waffles sizzled to crispness on heavy, indented waffle irons. Dutch domesticity often resembled the paintings of the Dutch masters—the women of each generation identical to their foremothers, prim in a starched nightcap with a crisp, pleated border.

Yugoslav wedding in Utah (Utah State Historical Society)

Swedish settlers, coming from a country where marriages were historically governed by the will of the parents and where such indiscretion as a "stolen match" was ordinarily frowned on, found their American offspring scandalously independent in their marital choices. But then, they finally concluded, wasn't that what the country was all about?

German immigrant Jews, suffering the memory of European prejudice and racial isolation, found on the west coast respite from their troubled history. From a recorded 6,000 Jews in 1825, their numbers increased to 280,000 by 1880—often single men who moved quickly from village to rancho, setting up businesses, fluently trading in Spanish, being skilled in weaponry.

When possible, they married Jewish wives, but eligible women were so scarce that many men sent for wives from their hometowns, often women they knew only by reputation, if at all. The groom paid for the bride's wedding apparel and her passage to America, without complaint, heeding the dictum, "[Jewish] girls were scarce and every home needed a mother."

In reverse of the typical European system, it was anxious American-Jewish men who were willing to pay a dowry, although historically, a "money marriage" turned upon the woman's *mitgift*—both social contract and economic transaction, arranged by a professional marriage broker for a percentage of the dowry, and accompanied by much dickering among parents. The *mitgift* was also a means of redistributing capital within a society. A typical marriage contract of the 1870s stipulated the exact amount of the bride's dowry and her portion of the wedding gifts if she died childless.

Prospering in their new freedom as merchants and professionals, close-knit Jewish-American families clustered in the major urban centers, cementing comfortable futures by intermarriage, often through family connections, rather than a broker. As respected citizens, Jewish urbanites sought culture, progress and reform—delighting in a social whirl alive with neighborly and civic gatherings. Jewish families prospered and proliferated, the times changed, matrimonially. Where once Jewish brides in the west were rarely found, by the late 1870s, the market was so overstocked, according to an article in *The American Israelite*, that eligible Jewish women would "go a begging." Furthermore, an eligible Jewish girl must be "good-looking, well educated, and have a father [with] a large bank account."

The aristocracy would meet at garden parties and social gaieties, where, according to a society column written in Oakland in 1912, "many innovations in the way of entertaining" were being "thought out" by members of the social set. Young socialite Clara Hofer Hewes recalls the discreet elegance of her girlhood in Carson City, Nevada, where French menus graced the dinner table, candelabra glittered and the men were resplendent with gold-handled canes, stovepipe hats and swallow-tailed coats. "They were all aristocratic," she wrote. "Everything was done according to etiquette." Even as a girl, however, she noted the clannishness of Nevada Jewish society. "The plumbers went together and the tradesmen went together and the saloon keepers kept to themselves."

In the west, the children of the founding families had a life of ease, often living in households that included a nurse, a governess, trained cabinetmakers, German tutors, mending women, a laundress—even a "woman who came and washed" hair once a week. "I wouldn't say our Jewish families were high society," Jewish writer John Newmark Levi determined. "But we were nice society." Men dallied nightly at whist, families lived within earshot of one another and social life, including that of courting couples, was, according to Levi, "mostly yacking and card playing." Some critics claimed that women, particularly Jewish women, were all too comfortable with the evils of gambling, particularly poker. As cited by historian Rudolph Glanz, one article railed that "nearly every house in the city is the rendezvous of gamblers of both sexes" where even young girls would "poker away" the night in the company of their mothers. Such freedom proved shocking to the Orthodox, and as time went on, a sharp demarcation occurred in Jewish society between "good" and "fast."

John Levi recalled the intimacy of the social life of Los Angeles's Jewry during the early 1900s, which carried out the *mishpahah,* or the warmth and solidarity of a complex family: "We were all cousins or close friends with cousins in common, or we were closer than that." Levi's parents stayed silent when he escorted Gentile girls about, but hoped that he, like other Jewish youngsters, would meet the right girl, perhaps at such gathering spots as Kramer's Dancing Academy, where boys learned to bow formally and girls to follow their lead.

A Jewish marriage was a civil contract, with both parties in clear agreement of their marital obligations. The husband must provide "food, raiment and conjugal duties" while the wife undertook all household chores. A Jewish bride must understand the concept of *trayf,* or "forbidden," knowing whether a fowl was improperly slaughtered, or if the dietary laws had been violated—meat and milk mixed, or the regrettable use of lard. In a moneyed home, she would juggle nursemaid, cook, servants and social life and excel at needlework, knitting and embroidery while "sending east" for the latest fashions. "They were not snobs," wrote Clara Hofer Hewes. "But they were exclusive."

Traditionally, procreation was the civil duty of married partners; if one failed in this duty, the other was free to move on, to find a man or woman capable of being a parent. Anything else would be a "sectarian" marriage, one that placed pleasure before the duty of bearing children.

In early years, Jews moved freely throughout society, their presence noted in society columns by the eponyms "Jewess" or "Jewish." When prejudice existed, it was often among the Jewish elite, found in the rift between established German Jews and indigent latecomers, usually Russian or Polish emigrants—landlords of pushcart and pawnshop, who filled the air with the chatter of Yiddish and threatened the hard-won dignity of the established elite. Middle-class Protestant animosity against Jews burst forth occasionally in unguarded moments, a reminder that no matter how acculturated, how affluent or how accepted, a Jew always retained a vestige of "difference." Typically, young Harriet Levy commented upon a girl she saw on the street as "slender and beautiful . . . refined looking, quite Gentile."

Even in Salt Lake City, where Mormons, like Jews, referred to nonbelievers as "gentiles," there was deep suspicion of Jewish men. Mary Prag, an educator who stayed for ten years in the city, was shocked by the local reaction toward her husband. The couple was often "shadowed" by a hulking, six-foot-tall figure dressed clumsily as a woman in a sunbonnet—a "guard" in disguise sent to "protect" Mary Prag, mistakenly believed to be Mormon, from the overtures of a Jew.

On the other hand, many Christian women saw Jewish men as successful partners and excellent providers. Were the Gentiles, according to one report, not "improvident" spouses who refused to "go out and peddle, and . . . climb the steep mountains in Indian territories in order to keep . . . wife and children comfortably?" Many must have agreed, for in 1883, as reported by Rudolph Glanz, in San Francisco only 39 Jewesses married Gentiles, while 163 Gentile women married Jewish men.

A surprising number of Jewish emigrants were homesteaders and farmers, the descendants of early, communitarian settlements founded in the early 1800s by Eastern European Jews who had briefly settled in the grassy plains of the midwest, hoping to escape the dark memories of anti-Semitism, poverty and depression. Many were intelligentsia, former scholars and merchants, who glimpsed in the huge prairies a chance to return to nature in the spirit of the Russian peasant commune, so idealized by socialism. Amateur farmers only slightly informed by their textbooks, they settled in tiny, communitarian enclaves, "spent lavishly for fine horses . . . choice cattle and lumber," quickly wasting their meager savings.

The "one married couple [and many] young and strong unmarried men" who comprised one of several Jewish colonies in the midwest, Bethlehem Yehudah, were "determined to rouse the slumbering spirit of Israel" through agricultural output. Instead, the spirit seemed to be one of dickering and discord. They were viewed with surprise and suspicion by nearby settlers, since their ethic of equality for women was in marked contrast to the local practice of complete patriarchy. Ultimately, crop failure, isolation and the allure of urban enterprise drove the gentlemen farmers on to other enterprises. Better suited to merchandising than agriculture, they quickly established themselves as shopkeepers and merchants, selling and bartering with the stream of rough passersby, their communal efforts collapsed.

The more remote the setting, the less likely Europeans were to encounter prejudice. Flora Spiegelberg, the adventuresome "Tenderfoot Bride" cited in many historical documents, spent her honeymoon jolting over the plains in a stagecoach with her young husband, Willi, en route to the Spielgelberg Brothers' store in Santa Fe, New Mexico. The year was 1874; as the thirteenth American-born white woman in Santa Fe, she found that her Jewish heritage on the Catholic frontier was ignored by most; generally, there were more pressing issues to resolve. Besides, her own penchant for Jewish mysticism gave her much to admire in the "choir boys, monks, hymns . . . [and] opulence" of a candlelight Catholic procession. Rather than a religious threat, she found the church and its pomp "a grand sight."

Surviving marriage customs, such as the portable canopy, the wedding ring and the glass cup, were general, well beloved and commonly practiced—although medieval. For generations, a bride would gaze skyward to the *tallith*—a cloth suspended overhead—then ritually break a wineglass underfoot. The ornate *ketubah,* an illustrated parchment once used to announce dowry provisions was read aloud, then given to the bride. Jewish law dictates that this contract would bind a couple to a lifetime of mutual support. So cherished was this object that traditional couples even took it along when traveling. In the gathering of ancient symbols, German Jews hearkening back to a fifteenth-century custom might shout "mazel tov" upon shattering the glass, startling evil spirits or commemorating the destruction of the Temple in Jerusalem. According to the Old Testament's Jeremiah 7:34, a marriage brought "the sound of mirth and gladness, the voice of bridegroom and bride." Guests danced the *sherr,* similar to a square dance, or the Russian *kazatsky,* while dining from a groaning table filled to overflowing with rural bounty: challah, relish, roasted goose, delicate strudel, honey cakes and wine. Amid the festivities, it was never overlooked that a man's highest obligation was to honor his wife, whether the tallith overhead was fashioned from elegant silk or from a tattered quilt.

HARRIET LEVY

One of three vivacious Jewish sisters who grew up in San Francisco, Harriet recorded with utter frankness her family's social insecurity and their agonizing envy when other Jewish families forged brilliant matches. To Eastern European immigrant families—even second generation—the cultural zenith seemed to be marrying a Bavarian, while least prestigious was a Pole.

Many [of my sister's] friends were of the superior caste; Evelyn Taussig was Polish, but Proudy Dinkenspiel, her aunt . . . had married a Bavarian in a mining camp in those early fifties when girls were few and a dance was divided among five partners. We knew that the Taussigs had aspirations to break through the walls of their set and we feared their success. The number of the boys in the rich family offered opportunity for excellent connections. When Elias, Jonah, Nathan, Benjamin, and Morris had acquired Bavarian wives, the family would be entrenched in social security forever. Though Evelyn was not comely, but large and bouncing with blue eyes leaping from a florid face, her social potentialities commanded respect. Leopold Stone, tall, handsome, erect (a tree, mother said), man of the world, was known to have visited the Taussig home twice in two weeks. Anything might happen. The possibility of a marriage was often discussed in our family.

"If he needs the money badly enough, he might," Mother said, and then followed the blighting dictum that condemned us within the pale forever: "No [Bavarian] marries a Pole unless he is *krumm* or *lahm* or *stumm* [crooked or lame or dumb]."

"But if one fell in love with a girl?" Polly protested.

"If he fell in love, he'd fall out again," came the answer . . .

We, alas, had no relative on whose social standing we might hope to erect a claim, and our position remained a precarious one. We lived on the verge, without the aggressiveness to force our way across and establish ourselves within the zone of privilege . . .

In the midst of the Bavarians, I was sensitive and uncomfortable. In the home of the Kahns, I shrank before the double grandeur of their ancestry, which was not only Bavarian but Parisian . . . My social uneasiness, being constant, stimulated the development of a strong conversational offensive . . . I never completely belonged, never felt that I might stretch myself comfortably and doze in the circle in which I lived, but must keep alert, protecting weak places . . .

Not only were we disquieted by the possibility of new Bavarian affiliations among the members of our group, but any advantageous betrothal was greeted by Mother with resentment and with reproach of Father for his social shortcomings. No sooner had an engagement been announced, a younger brother or sister bringing the glad tidings, than a shadow fell upon the house for the day. Often the prospective groom would be a stranger, perhaps an old bachelor brother of a friend of the family who, after years of seclusion, had been persuaded that the last bell had rung for marriage; or he might be a rising merchant from Nevada . . . On the other hand, he might be a young city merchant already enjoying good credit; or worse, the son and heir of a member of an old firm; or, worst of all, an attorney with high degrees at the Odd Fellows, equipped at any moment with an elaborate speech for a wedding dinner, or a B'nai B'rith banquet. Beneath the blow of such a betrothal Mother sat still, her hands folded . . .

One afternoon Addie's friends had gathered in the music room, their fingers crocheting, embroidering, and pointing shuttles as they talked . . . The front doorbell rang and I answered it. . . . at the door stood Benjie, the little Taussig boy.

"Evelyn is wanted at home," he said. A strange message. Nobody had ever been wanted at home. I went into the music room. "Evelyn is wanted at home," I said. "Benjie came to let her know."

Everyone stopped working to regard Evelyn, who awkwardly gathered up the cloth which she was embroidering and dropped it into her basket unfolded. She looked at no one. Self-conscious, happy, helpless, she left the room.

An hour later, while we sat at dinner, the front doorbell rang.

Mother answered it. She came back alone. "Evelyn Taussig is engaged to Leopold Stone."

So must an ancestor have announced the destruction of the Temple of Jerusalem.

"No!" cried Father, bringing a fist down upon the table. A running fire of self-condemnation encircled the table. We felt ourselves weaklings in the struggle. Father tapped three times upon the table with one finger, his signal of concern. Mother's face veered away from him slowly and rested at her angle of accusation.

Two couples on a crescent moon
(From the private collection of Eric Wogsberg)

PART **V** FIVE

Courtin'

with

Faith

Man and woman at table (Sharlot Hall Museum)

Clerics and Saints

"I pity omnibus horses and ministers."

—Lorena Hays

America's Christian worship veered away from the traditional, staid Protestant service to the "red-hot" oratory of the camp meeting, in which praise, revelry and spiritual ardor offered a kind of social quarterdeck for emotional freedom; hundreds would gather by the flickering light of bonfires, in thickets and groves throughout frontier America, to sing, cry, groan in ecstasy, share food and generally be "sunk in praises to God." They were "hair-hung and breeze shaken over hell" by revivalists who turned faith into frenzy for rapt crowds of the faithful and the frolickers, in numbers from eight hundred to twenty thousand at a time. Some came to worship, others to sip lemonade or whiskey, smoke and, often, view devout ecstasies with cynicism or scorn. The first camp meeting began in Cane Ridge, Kentucky, in 1801—its carnival spirit drawing so many assembled faithful that politicans also turned out; camp meetings turned into precursors of the political rally, drawing candidates from all walks to meet the public. Camping and deep conviction marked the early Methodist revivals—huge, shambling affairs where, wrote historian Charles Johnson, "horse thieves and women of easy virtue plied their respective trades." One revival even offered teeth pulling.

"Is this a proper way to worship God?" wondered a Universalist minister, perhaps responding to the growing evidence of overactive fraternity between men and women who strolled at night among the shadowed groves and were often "overpower'd" by an inappropriate spirit. One young girl experienced both religion and social success at a Georgia camp meeting in 1846, thanks to "beaux in abundance," while another was delighted with the many boyfriends she had met "at meeting."

Emotionalism ruled the revival, sparked by oratorical "sons of thunder" who lectured by day and exhorted, weeping, by night, barraging the crowds with the promise of "free grub . . . and free salvation." One woman at a Colusa County, California, revival

was so stirred that, according to early diarist H. C. Bailey, she jumbled her bed, bedding, children and clothes into a huge pile, jumped on top, bareheaded, and "defied husband or friend to remove her." By morning, the mood had passed; she climbed down and rode away on a wagon with her husband, never to be heard from again.

Critics found such behavior intolerable. Minister Benjamin Lakin was convinced that Methodists who attended such revivals "were sinking into . . . Epicurianism"—perhaps for want of a better word—and called for stricter fleshly mortification than ever before. But where to start?

Men and women had grown used to acting out their innermost spirituality, often passing long hours together, supine on the floor, in the "Mourner's tent," or bowed in penance, their heads supported by mounds of straw. Emotionalism reigned and spiritual conversion was often accompanied by tears, protestations and a series of physical convulsions called "the jerks." Added to the melee were close-knit prayer groups, where all hands clasped together in a "circle of brotherly love," sparking both reverence and revelry. "The town was getting religiously hot," wrote Methodist preacher Reverend Sullins, observing a small "revived" southern village, speaking for the multitudes who claimed a new, emotional kind of faith.

Such activity had mixed effects. Critics noted the penchant of young men to "run, jump, wrestle, play, yell, swear, talk vulgar" and be generally rowdy, while newspapers questioned the religious application of "beer, whiskey, profanity, and quarrels." Critics were legion, led by rival denominations—usually Lutheran or Episcopalian—who saw their flocks being whittled away by competitive evangelists who claimed to be "in the lead." Everyone, however, expressed dismay at the number of unmarried women suddenly pregnant after revival week.

Pastor William Hickman, normally "like thunder in the dis-

Brother W. Van Orsdel
(Montana Historical Society, Helena)

Unidentified Californian (Holt-Atherton Center for Western Studies,
University of the Pacific, Stockton, California)

tance" when animated, became, according to observer John Taylor, "like thunder at home" during a revival, exerting "prodigious force on the consciences of his hearers," particularly on the themes of fornication and adultery. Many also complained about "frolicking and dancing," while members of the Baptist church were "excluded" for gambling. Others were victims of the growing evil of drunkenness, having "C[ome] too Much in Licker." But then, were not "Satans bulwarks were Very Strong," and according to many male clerics, often manned by women?

In fact, women posed a threat to male ministers, were greatly feared by church officials and were often chastened far in advance of any possible wrongdoing. Methodists were the most judgmental. When Methodist bishop Richard Whatcoat railed against "Thos Wyches in the evening," he meant not only strangers, harlots or spiritualists, but also God-fearing women of his own congregation. They, in turn, were resigned to yet another "long Nervous Discourse" against frivolous display—the flaunting of ornaments, curls, even showy gold glasses.

So tempting seemed womankind that in 1774 Methodist bishop Francis Asbury cautioned a circuit rider to "stand all possible distance from the female sex" to avoid temptation, as any sexual shadow on his record would "blast" his future ministerial prospects. Those straying too close to such temptation ended up married and bound to support a wife and family.

Most circuit riders adhered to the dictum: "it is better to itinerate than marry," and put off finding a wife and raising a family on a paltry thirty-three dollars per month, which only increased to seventy dollars by the late 1800s. Benjamin Lakin, writing in 1814, agonized over whether it would be proper to make choice of a station in life for himself, "I can not chuse." He sighed," I am not my own, But belong to God, the Church, and My Country and where they call I must go . . ."

But as red-hot exhortations gave way to a stabilized Christian population, ministers and preachers began to embrace more than their spiritual calling, finding wives and sweethearts to help them preside over a pastorate of settled emigrants. "Settled" ministers were more likely to wed, with entire rural communities taking a strong interest in the pastor and his wife. Gossip, conspiracy and intervention were the village matchmakers, just as the romantic interests of friends and neighbors never failed to arouse interest. "Don't you think Brother Bateman ought to have a wife?" cleric Isaac Owen pressed his wife, Elizabeth, in private conversation. When the Reverend Storm, a "big, powerful man with very bushy eyebrows and a heavy mustache," came to Wells County, North Dakota, he antagonized nearly everyone he met, according to settler Barbara Levorson, yet intrepid local matrons began a bridal search for him, "no easy task as marriageable girls were few thereabouts." Ultimately, Storm's growing eccentricity left him unmarried, and without a congregation as well.

A cleric's wife must be a light, a guide, a clarion call to all, in addition to being able to think quickly, anticipate the worst and, like Christ himself, multiply her scanty stores to feed the populace. So discovered Elizabeth Koren, the wife of a Norwegian Lutheran minister in Iowa, who was pining away in the kitchen for her husband, warming his soup and brooding, when she happened to see two wagonloads of people drive up. "They will certainly not come here," she thought, only to see her husband dismount and shepherd the group in. Suddenly, a party was brewing, and she was the presiding hostess. "I knew what the situation was and hurried to clear the table . . ."

No one realized the importance of a wife more than missionaries, the success of whose petitions to the American Board of Foreign Missions to preach the Word to the Sioux in the Dakotas, Nez Percés in the Northwest and all other tribes farther west, including Iowas, Sacs, Omahas, Winnebagos and Kickapoos, often depended upon having a wife. More than 270 Presbyterian missionaries were sent to the Indians during the years 1838–1869, and only one among them, Robert Loughridge, was without. He complained that he had "not yet succeeded in finding a partner for life—I have for several years been looking for a *Missionary wife,* but I have not yet found her." Shouldn't it be simple to get "some pious woman" to unite with him in his work? The success of his mission would rest upon "her character & qualifications," so none but the best would suit his needs—and the bravest, too, since there was still considerable animosity toward Christian missionaries in his region.

Ministeral politics dictated that a settled cleric with a church should also have a wife, thus relegating Oregon itinerant A. J. McNemee to the forlorn and solitary circuit of the byways and back trails. He also failed to win a desired appointment in Alaska because of his persistent bachelorhood. "That made the third time I have missed a good appointment because I did not have a wife," he sadly wrote. Awkward and partially troubled, McNemee was destined to roam about on the Whatcom County circuit in Oregon footloose and underfed, alive with self-doubt and alienation, as each year took him farther from the joys of marriage and a position.

On the other hand, missionary-minded women were also rejected. "A Miss Narcissa Prentiss of Amity is very anxious to go to the heathen," announced a broadside of the Board in 1834, avoiding the greater question: "Are females wanted?" Though "her piety was good" and even "conspicuous," unmarried females were urged not to apply without a fiancé in mind. Ideally, the missionary couple would meet in training, fall in love and pursue their calling in the field together.

Many Americans were "blown hither and thither by the different winds of doctrine," becoming members of cultish, utopian communes or bickering among themselves over dogma and belief. Yet nothing excited the national interest more than the notion of harems, concubines and the lascivious goings-on in the remote, private realm of Utah, where the Church of Jesus Christ of Latter-day Saints began its campaign to practice polygamy, outraging Christian sensibilities throughout the country. Visitors to the remote state came back with tales of abuse and anguished quotes from anonymous wives, who agreed great public sympathy with the dictum that "polygamy [was] tolerable enough for the men, but . . . hell for the women."

Although less than one fifth of the church population lived polygamous lives during the fifty years in which polygamy was legally practiced, and because Mormon women were admonished not to criticize the process, many reports relied upon gossip alone, and often centered around the chief purveyor of the system—patriarch Brigham Young. One observer, editor Samuel Bowles, took a different critical approach, musing about the "sorry selection" of wives made by Young, although, to his mind, "handsome women and girls [were] scarce among the Mormons" in general. He, like the rest of the nation, tried to grasp the motivation of Mormon polygamists; what could possibly tempt women to live such a life? Non-Mormons, or "Gentiles," could not fathom the idea of Latter-day rewards, such as becoming a "queen in heaven" through a polygamous earthly union, or that of "eternal marriage." Nor did Gentile men accept the concept of heavenly blessing through progeny—the more children sired by a Mormon man the greater his status, and the closer he came to godhood. Gentiles, in fact, could hardly think of any words for polygamy at all, save "slavery," "concubinage" and "barbaric."

Founder Joseph Smith cited, as Scriptural justification for polygamy, the Bible's parable of the hidden talent. If the "talent," or wife, were "hidden away" and not shared, shouldn't she be given to one who had more? Sexuality, it seemed, had become the earthly means to celestial glory.

Given the lurid portrayal of polygamy in the national press, little wonder that church patriarchs hurried to describe the practice in the most conservative terms. Joseph Smith and a few energetic associates first began the practice of polygamy in the mid-1840s, although they publicly denied the practice until 1852, when, one by one, leaders of the church were bullied, forced and persuaded to perform their "religious obligation" with a seemingly endless procession of threadbare young immigrant women from the Scandinavian countries. Many husbands and wives were distraught by polygamy and nearly abandoned the faith, caught between their belief in Smith as a prophet of God, their dependence upon the goodwill of the Mormon community, and a traditional practice of monogamy.

To its credit, polygamy had provided many older, unmarriageable women with provident spouses, and had been a means to absorb single female converts, often penniless European immigrants, into the community, so they could gain established husbands rather than marry poor, or remain single. From 1869 to 1887, a total of 33,000 Latter-day Saints emigrated from Europe, an average of about 740 per year—many were older women unable to compete with spry, younger girls. In a study of two thousand male polygamists, historian Stanley Ivins found that 66 percent had taken two wives, 21 percent had taken a third, 6 percent a fourth, and 6 percent, five or more. Polygamy fostered a useful division of household labor and promoted independence in the women, who often had to fend for themselves when their husbands were overseas on missions, or, during the underground years when Mormons were persecuted, in hiding from the law. Plural marriage was also a safeguard of female virtue and innocence, a sure protection against "the fearful sin of prostitution and its attendant evils." There had never been a bordello in the early Mormon communities. Wasn't that proof enough?

"Take thee wives, this law obey," proclaimed an angel to Joseph Smith, who, along with the 66 percent of Mormon men to marry more than one wife, followed the angel's dictates in all things, including discreet and practical plural courtships.

"Married men didn't do any courting of their plural wives," said the fourth wife of Hyrum Stratton. "Why, we would have thought it dishonorable for a mature married man to go sparking around like a young man." Weddings were quiet and practical, often occurring when the husband quietly slipped into town on an errand, to return with a prim young bride. Often a maid, seamstress or governess imported from Europe would quietly step into the role of wife, her marriage ordained as a religious, not a romantic, "mission."

An efficient courtship was carried out by John W. Taylor, who wooed two women at once and then married in the same ceremony. In some cases, young girls sought older, polygamous husbands for their proven stability and financial security and would boldly demand, as did the twelfth wife of John D. Lee, that he "take charge of her and her effects." Joseph Smith, by the time of his death, had wed forty-eight wives, including one group of five sisters, and one as young as fifteen. His first wife, Emma, resisted his wishes for more wives as long as possible, but in 1843, reluctantly agreed to plurality if she could choose the brides. To her horror, the two selected candidates had already married Smith two years earlier and been living conjugally in their home.

Not all courtships went smoothly, since the first wives often succumbed to periods of weeping, horror and deep repugnance. Annie Gardner had an "awful feeling" when she heard President Woodruff read the manifesto announcing polygamy—yet she voted in favor of it because protest would have meant ostracism, robbing her of husband and home. How could her daughter bear it? Annie's mother simply couldn't understand. Crying, Annie "raised [her] hand" and "voted for a thing that would make [her] an unlawful wife."

Others flatly refused the arrangement—one wife told her husband: "you get another wife and I'll get another husband." Mary Prag, an educator who stayed for ten years in Salt Lake City, tells of the grief and near-hysteria of Mormon women when their husbands first entered the polygamous state. Promises were made and broken—anything to calm the women's fears. One husband promised his wife to keep the bride in another town and see her only once a year. When the rival became pregnant, the first wife took to her bed, ill for a year. Particularly poignant is Prag's story of a Mormon official's wife who scrimped for a year to buy her husband a gift for his return with the emigrant train, only to watch, horrified, as he swung down his pretty new wife from the buckboard.

Because polygamy was a fledgling concept, couples were free to fashion their own techniques. Obedient wives would help select the younger brides, organizing the marriage ceremony in sporting fashion and serving up a cheerful wedding feast. Plural weddings were common events, so much so that on a typical day, Brigham Young noted in his diary: "This afternoon Spent in the endowment House, Sealed [married for eternity] a great many couples in the altar."

More women meant more discord—even Brigham Young tired of the women's incessant complaining and often reminded them that since they had voted to comply, they should do so without complaint.

Not all reports were negative. Margaret Smoot had "thirty-six years of experience in Plural marriage," and with her husband and his wives, had twenty-one children. "I have lived under the same roof with his other wives . . . and I hold them as a part and portion of our family."

The greatest irony was that so many wives submitted to polygamy only after intense pressure, resistance and prayer, tried to reconcile themselves to it, and then were persecuted for their acquired beliefs after it was outlawed. Even though supposedly "freed" by the Edmunds-Tucker Act, which banned polygamy in 1890, these long-married wives and respectable citizens were turned into outlaws, subject to harassment, surprise searches, fines and imprisonment. Moreover, their children were branded illegitimate.

Regardless of religion, denomination or location, men of the cloth, cult followers and religious women struggled to keep priorities simple and faith first, even in matters of love and romance. Perhaps the view of Reverend Calvin B. West epitomized the ideal Christian perspective: "Keep a good heart," he wrote in 1909. "Don't get it too full of the world, groceries & etc. Such things are of but little use in heaven."

Comer's 60th wedding anniversary
(Photo by Frank B. Fiske. State Historical Society of North Dakota)

HANNAH CROSBY

Hannah Crosby was born April 25, 1853, in Ogden, Utah, while her father was on a church mission to Europe. Her girlhood was filled with normal activities—none could have predicted her decision, as a Mormon from a nonpolygamous household, to enter a plural marriage. She had a steady suitor—a well-to-do contractor who loved to dance and drink—but she recognized him as a "tippler" and refused his hand, explaining that she would "lose her salvation" if she did. Inexplicably, she then chose to marry a "poor man who already had two wives and a family of seven children." Often polygamous wives were young immigrant girls trying to earn a living. Her choice was locally unpopular, it being not financial, as for so many, but spiritual.

My decision to marry into a plural family tried my family, all of them, and in giving them trial I was sorely tried. I had studied out the matter. I knew the principal of plural marriage to be correct, to be the highest, holiest order of marriage—I knew too, that I might fail to live the holy life required and lose the blessings offered . . .

Having decided to enter this order . . . I could not go back . . . It made me miserable beyond endurance when I tried to recede from the decision I had made . . . My only relief was in prayer . . .

When the final decision was made known to my family . . . the storm broke upon my head. It was not marriage of love, they claimed, and in saying so, they struck me a blow. I could not say that I had really loved the man as lovers love, though I loved his wives and the spirit of their home. I could not assure my family

that my marriage was gotten solely on the foundation of love for man. The fact was I had asked the Lord to lead me in the right way for a place in his kingdom. He had told me how to go and I must follow in the path he dictated.

On November 20, 1869, we started for Salt Lake City to be married. On Monday, December 6th we were sealed [religiously married in the Church of Latter-day Saints] in the old end House. I received my endowments the same day . . .

On our way to Salt Lake City we called at McCarty's [a family friend] and I felt grateful to them for not mentioning my marriage in the few minutes we stayed. But McCarty's brow was dark and lowering. I dreaded that but a little less than his scathing tongue . . . On our way home we gave McCarty's another call. We were well treated and McCarty gave me much good advice that I did not forget. He having a second wife knew wherewith he spoke . . .

I rejoiced that I had been able to take the step I had taken, but I soon saw that every day was to be a day of sacrifice. I had thought that when I entered that home of peace and prayer and Gospel alive, that all evil, unrest, and sorrow would be ended and I would have "Arrived in Zion . . ."

It had always seemed to me that plural marriage was the leading principle among the L.D.S. [But] when I came to know how generally my action . . . was denounced, especially the fact I had married into poverty, I was saddened as well as surprised. When in my mind I took a survey of our little town, I could locate but a very few men, not one in fifty of the whole city, who had entered it at all. One who had been my admiring friend said: "it is all very well for those girls who cannot . . . get good young men for husbands to take married men, but she (me) had no need to lower herself for there were young men she could have gotten." And she and other friends "cold shouldered" me and made uncomplimentary remarks. The good kind women whom I had chosen to share the burdens of life with gave me strength and comfort with their sympathy and love, and I retired within the home, but like the porcupine, rolled myself into a ball when my enemies approached and showed them my quills only. But in thinking it over, I [came] to the conclusion that the public dealt with me as charitable as I could expect it to do, and I blamed no one—not even my own family—for their coolness toward me.

I began to realize my own imperfections. I was grateful to my Father in Heaven that I had wisdom from him to seek and know them.

Adopting the rules and regulations of my husband's family . . . I had to submit to an almost entire reversal of my nature and habits. The greatest . . . I had to meet was the hot Irish temper that had always swayed me when occasion aroused it. Many times the words of McCarty would be brought to my mind "Remember in your plural home to speak no words when angry." When I disobeyed that injunction it brought me sorrow . . .

To eat a dinner without meat, and salt rising bread without salt in it was two pretty trials I had to put under my feet. And I hankered for a sip from my mother's tea-pot. I thank my Father above that he gave me a strength to comply with all the rules of our house. The main rule being perfect obedience. The first year of my married life gave me more experience in the duties of life than I had ever learned before . . .

We [wives] had our work so systematized and so well ordered that we could, with ease, do a great deal. One would for a period superintend the cooking and kitchen work with the help of the girls, another make beds and sweep, another comb and wash all the children. At seven thirty all would be ready to sit down to breakfast. Lizzie was always ready to go to her sewing at eight or nine o'clock. She was also the best sales woman of the house. She generally did most of the buying, especially the shoes. She was a good judge of leather. Auntie did darning and repairing. I seldom patched anything, she did it all for me. She never ironed the clothes, I did most of that. When wash day came all hands were employed except the cook. On that day we liked the boiling pudding. Noon saw our family wash on the line.

We usually bought cloth by the bolt and whoever needed most was served first. In fact we had in our home an almost perfect United order. No one can tell the advantages of that system until he has lived it. We enjoyed many privileges that single wiferey never knew. We did not often all go out together. One always stayed home and took care of the children and the house. In that way we generally came home with a correct idea of what was given in the sermon.

Whenever one was indisposed she was not obliged to tie up her head and keep serving around the house but she could go to her room and lie down knowing that her children and all her share of the work would be attended to. No one was obliged to bend over the wash tub when she was in delicate health or condition. All stepped into the breach and helped each other.

We acted as nurses for each other during confinement. We were too poor to hire nurses. One suit or outfit for new babies . . . did for us all, and when one piece wore out it was supplied by another. For many years we lived thus, working together cooking over the same large stove with the same great kettles, eating at the same long table without a word of unpleasantness or a jar in our feelings . . . The children we bore while we lived together in that poor home loved each other more than those that came to us after the raid on polygamists came on, and we were obliged to separate and flee in different directions.

To me it is a joy to know that we laid the foundation of a life to come while we lived in that plural marriage, that we three who loved each other more than sisters, will go hand in hand together down all eternity. That knowledge is worth more to me than gold and more than compensates for the sorrow I have known . . .

ANN HAFEN

Ann's parents embraced the Mormon faith as converts in Switzerland, then emigrated to the hot mesas and rocky hills of southern Utah to live out their beliefs with Brigham Young's southernmost settlers. There the twenty original families ate pigweed [spinach] boiled in water, usually without bread, butter or milk. Ann's matter-of-fact acceptance of polygamy reflects a religious obedience found in many smaller Mormon communities.

I was now almost a young woman and began to take an interest in parties, husking bees, dancing, and different kinds of fun. Naturally I had young men callers. But none of them appealed to me so much as did John Reber, my Uncle . . . He was much older than I, was married to my father's sister, and had four children. But he was kind and joyous and everyone liked him. Before this time Brother Hafen had called and taken me to several dances with him. John Reber did not dance so I had not been out much with him, but when he asked me to marry him I was ready to say yes. His wife, Aunt Barbara, helped me make my wedding outfit, a simple dress of blue material with little pink flowers and a white petticoat which would be very common now. I was then nineteen years old.

My sister Rosena was to be married too. So we decided to make it a double wedding. We had to go all the way to Salt Lake City to be married in the endowment house. With our two outfits loaded with dried peaches for the northern brewery, we set out that morning, August 4, 1873. Rosena's husband-to-be was a widower and his mother traveled along with them. Our ten days

of travel were happy ones. On August fourth both couples were married. In ten days we were back again in Santa Clara, happy and satisfied with our lot.

The day after we returned home, my husband took me and Aunt Barbara and her four children for a ride down to the field to see how the crops looked. We started back feeling very happy for the corn was so thrifty, but our joy soon turned to sadness. On the way one of the horses caught its bridle under the wagon tongue and started running with the bridle off. I jumped off, so did Aunt Barbara. The frightened horses turned down a lane, ran over a woodpile, throwing my husband under the wagon where two wheels ran over him and he died the next day. That was a sad finish for my honey-moon, and I went back home to live with mother and father. Inasmuch as they were getting old and times were hard, they thought it best that I should marry again. Soon John Hafen came courting me. I told him I would be his wife, though my heart was not in the answer.

Just four months after my first trip to be married, I was journeying again to Salt Lake. Again the wagon was loaded with dried peaches for the brewery. But this trip seemed different. I cried when I left home, and cried often all the way up and back. John was kind to me and did everything he could to comfort and please me. But somehow I could not get over caring for my first husband.

For three years I lived this way and had no babies. We were not happy. Besides, his first wife seemed unable to reconcile herself to my coming into the family. I decided it would be best to leave John, but first I would fast and pray to find out if that would be the right course. After three days of fasting I woke in the night. The indifference, and the bitterness had all gone from my heart, and I loved him. I could hardly wait until morning to tell John my change of feelings. We were happier then than at [any other] time. . . .

Brigham Young (Photo by Charles W. Carter. Church Archives, the Church of Jesus Christ of Latter-day Saints)

FLORENCE A. MERRIAM

Florence, an urbanite from New York, was viewed with "polite amazement" by her friends for spending a summer bird-watching in "rustic" Utah. She viewed everything with the eye of a traveler, from irrigation systems to polygamy—interested and generally attempting sympathy. Her voice joins countless others in providing an outsider's view of the practice of "celestial marriage," or polygamy.

My first inquiries on getting settled in Utah were for a horse and saddle, [and thus I] got a hint of the dark undercurrent of the outwardly peaceful village life. Going to the house of one of the white-haired patriarchs, I asked if he would rent me his saddle. He smiled in an embarrassed way, and mumbled, "The girl has got it," looking at the house across the street, where I had been told his second wife lived. I covered his confusion by a few remarks on the weather, and then said casually:

"Could I see the saddle?"

"Yes," he answered hesitatingly, "you can go over."

He crossed the street with me, saying in a masterful way, "The girl is away, but I can show it to you." However, he rang the bell, and stood uneasily fumbling with the door waiting for an answer. As none came, he finally led me into the house. It was he who explained my errand to his wife, but she looked past him at me. I thought she would not meet his eye at all, but saw her at last look up at him; and that look gave me my first real understanding of polygamy. It was as if they were separated by an impassable black

Portrait of unidentified Mormon family (Church Archives, the Church of Jesus Christ of Latter-day Saints)

"Outgoing missionaries" at the Episcopal Church Mission House
(Archives of the Episcopal Church)

gulf of hatred. He lived across the street with his other wife; and she and her children lived alone here.

In this case, however, I consoled myself by reflecting that it was the younger wife, not the old woman, who had the worst suffering. But at the next house where I looked for a saddle—"the girl" having lent this one—the old white-haired wife was living alone, her husband having gone to Canada with his young wife . . .

We had become so engrossed in the peaceful side of village life—what with chickens and cows, and our views of mountain and lake—that we had almost forgotten where we were. One day, however, something was said about polygamy, when some one quietly remarked that our cook was one of the former bishop's *sixty-three* children, and that her mother was one of his *seven*

wives. We awoke with a start, remembering with a sense of shock that we were in Utah.

Not long after, the mother wanted some peaches from the bishop's orchard, and I volunteered to go for them on horseback, secretly glad of an excuse to get sight of this marvelous family.

When near the place I inquired discreetly not for the bishop's house, but for the house where Mary's mother lived. But it is hard for the youthful mind to classify sixty-three children—even if they be his own half brothers. And although children fairly swarmed about the doorsteps and in the yards, at each inquiry they told me that "Mary's mother" lived in "the next house."

When I finally found her, I did my errand, and then sat in the saddle pondering the situation. Here were three houses—an adobe, a rock house, and a brick one—that made three. Across the street were two more—five; up the road, another—six. The [first] wife was dead; she had gone insane and died when the second wife was taken. I drew a long breath before I could realize the situation. I caught sight of a gray beard in the shrubbery, but did not really see the patriarch that day . . .

The domestic tragedies I stumbled on in looking for a saddle were saddening enough, but one day we got a sharper flash of light upon polygamy. My friend and I were wandering about the village looking for nests to watch, and were led by the song of a grosbeak down a byway to a farm-yard gate. As it looked peaceful and quiet, we let ourselves in. The cows were lying in the shade chewing their cud, "red-wings" were feeding their young in a flowering bit of marsh at the head of the broad sunny meadows, where the bobolinks' voices rang merrily . . .

Through an open door I looked into [a] neat little kitchen, its window bright with house plants, and saw a slender young girl swaying back and forth over the ironing board—I could almost smell the warm iron on the fresh linen. When I went to ask for a drink she was no disappointment—with her big blue eyes, fair hair, rosy cheeks, and a fresh happy face it did you good to look at. She took a glass and went out to fill it at an ice-cold bubbling spring.

When we spoke of the big locusts, she said her mother had lived there thirty years and would not have one of the trees cut down. She had had large offers for the place last winter, but would not sell, and would not let a tree be cut down.

We went home full of our discovery. What a place to spend a summer in—birds nesting all about you, and an atmosphere of peace and quietness that would rest the most wearied soul. It seemed a Garden of Eden. We afterwards learned that the woman had been *branded* by her husband—with a red-hot iron cattle brand—because she refused to keep his saddle in her parlor! The husband was a fine-looking man of more than ordinary intelligence, shrewdness, and cruelty. Years ago he was convicted as one of the ringleaders in the Mountain Meadow Massacre [when Mormons dressed as Indians and killed emigrants passing through], and a bounty was offered for his head. Forced to flee from Utah, he sought refuge in Northern Arizona, where, on the outskirts of the dreaded "Painted Desert" he built houses for two of his wives at distant points in a secluded canyon and lived in comparative comfort, beyond the reach . . . of the law.

Last year in a quarrel over pasturage for his horses, he was killed by a Navajo Indian.

Joseph W. Summerhays
(Utah State Historical Society)

Wedding, stereo view, taken in Wyoming, ca. 1850
(Wyoming State Archives)

REVEREND CYRUS
TOWNSEND BRADY

"Western dioceses are bishop-killers at best," pastor Cyrus Brady wrote of the difficult task of Episcopal ministry in the west. Within his own diocese he estimated that he rode "over ninety thousand miles by railroad, wagon or horseback ... marrying and baptizing," trying to alleviate the hardship through writing. Calling upon memory, he relived the humorous and poignant moments of his ministry in a series of books, including the following.

I had a wedding one day at [a] frontier town. There was no church there, and as we sat waiting for the bride and groom to come into the parlor, one man spoke thus:

The bride, who was a head taller than the groom, was a bold, vigorous, red-faced, masculine-looking woman, while the groom was a rather timid, sallow little man. She said she was twenty-two and he was twenty-one. It was midsummer, and as they stood under the hanging lamp the perspiration poured off the bride's face in streams. When we came to that part of the service in which the woman promises to obey her husband to be, there was a pause. The big bride looked down on the little groom, and evidently felt the incongruity of the situation.

"Can't you let that pass, parson?" she whispered pleadingly.

I was inexorable, however, so she finally complied with the requirements, but with an exceedingly bad grace, and we finished the service.

I think the company were all surprised that I did not kiss the bride. But I remembered a story told by another missionary,

Wilbur Raymond marrying Jetti Walker, Pikeville, Kentucky (Seaver Center)

[about a time when] he did kiss the bride, whereupon the husband became abusive and threatened him, at which the lady promptly interfered. Laying aside her bridal veil and catching her husband by the shoulder, she shook him vigorously, remarking at the same time that she "didn't allow no man to interfere with her religious privileges, even if he was married to her!"

I used to have other weddings from time to time, and on one occasion I had two in the same town on the same day, one in the morning, one in the afternoon. The first wedding fee I received was ten dollars, a very large remuneration for the place and people. After the second wedding, the best man called me into a private room and thus addressed me:

"What's the tax, parson?"

"Anything you like, or nothing at all," I answered (I have frequently received nothing).

"Now," said he, "we want to do this thing up in style, but I have had no experience in this business and do not know what is proper. You name your figure."

I suggested that the legal charge was two dollars.

"Pshaw!" he said, "this ain't legal. We want to do something handsome."

"Go ahead and do it," I said; whereupon he reflected a moment, and then asked me how much I had received for the wedding of the morning.

"Ten dollars," I replied.

His face brightened at once. Here was a solution to the difficulty.

"I'll see his ante," he remarked. "Raise him five dollars and call." Whereupon he handed me fifteen dollars.

Student evangelists (Corrie Lee [Acuff] Brashear album, Abilene Christian University, Texas)

LORENZO DOW

"...If I find no one that I like better than I do you, perhaps something further may be said on the subject."
—LORENZO DOW

Lorenzo Dow, known as "Crazy Dow" in the backwoods of the Mississippi Valley, was a thin, earnest saddlebag evangelist so idiosyncratic he often forgot his coat or shoes as he preached the Methodist "heart" religion to agitated camp meeting crowds. He was not above emphasizing biblical injunctions by staging his most dire prophecies to coincide with a natural event, such as an eclipse, or those unnatural, such as a trumpeter hidden in a tree to sound a warning blast at surprised sinners. Born in 1777, he lived during the most climactic years of the Great Revival, in which Dow, with his door-to-door admonitions and accusatory style, was a fervent, and often unwelcome, participant.

[A Methodist friend] came to a big meeting in the woods, and heard that CRAZY DOW was there, and after some time sought and found me. He accompanied me to my appointments, consisting of about one hundred miles' travel. He kept what some call a Methodist tavern, i.e., a house for the preachers. One of my appointments being near his house, he invited me to tarry all night, observing his daughter would be glad to see me. I asked if he had any children! He replied, a young woman I brought up I call my daughter. I staid all night, but so it happened that not a word passed between her and me, though there were but the three in family. I went to my appointment where we had a precious

time, but whilst preaching, I felt an uncommon exercise (known only to myself and my God) run through my mind, which caused me to pause for some time.

In going to my evening appointment, I had to return by the house . . . I asked [my friend] if he would object if I should talk to his daughter concerning matrimony.

He replied, "I have nothing to say, only I have requested her, if she has any regard for me, not to marry so as to leave my house."

When I got to the door, I abruptly asked his wife, who had been there, . . . what they had been about in my absence. She told me . . . that Peggy was resolved never to marry unless it were to a preacher, and one who would continue travelling. This resolution being similar to my own, as she then stepped into the room, caused me to ask her if it was so. She answered in the affirmative; on the back of which I replied, "Do you think you could accept . . . such an object as me?"

She made no answer but retired from the room. This was the first time of my speaking to her. I took dinner, asked her one question more—and went to my neighboring meetings, which occupied some days. Upon [returning] I staid all night, and in the morning, when going away, I observed to her and her sister . . . that I was going to the warm countries, where I had never spent a season, and it was probable I should die, as the warm climate destroys most of those who go from a cold country. But, said I, if I am preserved about a year and a half from now, I am in hopes of seeing this northern country again, and if during this time you live and remain single, and find no one that you like better than you do me, and would be willing to give me up twelve months out of thirteen, or three years out of four to travel . . . (and never say, do not go to your appointment, &c., for if you should stand in my way, I should pray God to remove you, which I believe he would answer) and if I find no one that I like better than I do you, perhaps something further may be said on the subject.

Woman with husband's photograph (Denver Public Library, Western History Department)

And finding her character to stand fair, I took my departure . . .

In my travels, I went to Nachez county, where I found religion low . . . but [she] lay on my mind . . . But now I find she was still single, and willing to comply with my request . . . so our bargain was drawn to a close.

I thought not to have the ceremony performed until I should return from Europe, but upon reflection, [I considered that] the circumstances would require a correspondence, [and] my letters might be intercepted, and the subject known, prejudice arise, jealousy ensue, and much needless conversation and evil . . . result. Wherefore, to prevent [this], a preacher [came] in, [and] we were married that night, though only we five were present, this being the 3d of September, 1804.

PEGGY DOW

Peggy Holcomb, of Fish River, Missouri, was a Methodist equally as ardent as Dow, and whose idea of marriage—that her husband be home "no more than one month out of thirteen"—coincided exactly with his need to travel. They were, for one another, providentially matched.

I set out to seek my soul's salvation, through many trials and difficulties. The Methodists' preaching and zeal were new in that part of the country where I lived at that time, and my sister's husband was very much opposed to them, so that it made my way very trying. But I was determined, come what might, that I would take up my cross and follow Jesus . . .

I was willing, and gave up all my young companions, and all the diversions of which I had been very fond, such as dancing, and company that feared not God. The Lord, who giveth liberally, and upbraideth not, gave me peace and consolation in him. My sister and myself joined the first society that was raised in that part of the country, at a neighborhood called Fish Creek, about four miles from where we lived. We attended preaching and class meeting once every week.

And the Lord was very precious to my soul in those days . . .

About this time, "Camp Meetings" began to be introduced into that part of the country, and were attended with the power of God in the conversion of many precious souls!

At this time, there was one about thirty miles from where I then lived, and my brother-in-law attended it. [Here] he met with Lorenzo Dow, on his way to Canada, and invited him home . . . to

Woman reading
(University of California at Berkeley)

He was invited to my brother-in-law's, but did not come for several days. He had appointments to preach twice and thrice in the day. However, at last he came, and tarried all night. The next morning he was to preach five or six miles from our house: and little did I think that he had any thought of marrying, in particular that he should make any proposition of the kind to me. But so it was. He returned that day to dinner, and in conversation with my sister . . . he inquired . . . how long had I professed religion? She told him the length of time. He requested to know whether I kept wicked company? She told him I did not, and observed that I had often said, "I had rather marry a Preacher than any other man, provided I was worthy, and that I would wish them to travel and be useful to souls." By this time I happened to come into the room, and he asked me if I had made such a remark? I told him I had. He then asked me if I would accept of such an object as him?

I made him no reply, but went directly out of the room—as it was the first time he had spoken to me, I was very much surprised. He gave me to understand that he should return to our house again in a few days, and would have more conversation with me on the subject, which he did, after attending a meeting ten or twelve miles from where I lived. He returned the next evening, and spoke to me on the subject again . . .

He told me I must weigh the matter seriously before God, whether I could make such an engagement and conform to it, and not stand in his way, so as to prevent his usefulness to souls! I thought I would rather marry a man that loved and feared God and [who] would strive to promote virtue and religion among his fellow mortals, than any other. I felt myself inadequate to the task without the grace of God to support me!

Yet I felt willing to cast my lot with his, and be a help, not a hindrance to him, if the Lord would give me grace, as I had no doubt but he would, if I stood as I ought—and I accepted of his proposal.

preach at our preaching house, and [announced him] a day or two before hand, so that the people might get notice. And as he was a SINGULAR character, we were very ANXIOUS to see and hear him. The day arrived, he came, the house was crowded, and we had a good time! I was very much afraid of him, as I had heard such STRANGE THINGS about him!

Unidentified Mormon family (Utah State Historical Society)

Miners, Maidens and Camp Lives

"I'm all alone without a friend/No one for my trousers to mend/I wish I had a wife."
—WESTERN FOLK RHYME

Unidentified saloon (Colorado Historical Society)

"The society of men makes one wish for the sight of . . . a woman."

—ALF JACKSON, MINER

GOLD ORE WAS WEALTH AWAITING DISCOVERY, AND THE argonauts who flooded west after 1848 flung everything aside in their frantic quest for its riches. Bearded and hungry, hundreds of men fought and scrambled to stake their claims, stumbling through the foothills and mountain passes of California, Nevada, Colorado and Alaska, buying and bartering, sluicing, picking and panning in their quest for the precious metals—silver and gold. Suffering was rampant; mud, dirt, danger and chilly tents routine. "Let me tell you," wrote one woman who witnessed the nonstop, backbreaking labor of men in the mining camps, "it is a good deal like work to dig gold."

Drawn by such appeal, men left mothers, sisters, wives and mistresses behind to "find the elephant" or "make a pile" in rowdy mining camps, lured by the promise of "Free gold for the picking up—it fairly glistens!" yet discouraged by the reality of a typical day's take: usually no more than one half ounce of ore. Yet delusional miners continued to spy glistening nuggets lodged beneath the rocks, then would drink away their disappointment at finding clay instead.

Immediately, men noticed the dearth of women; in the silver-rich Comstock Lode in 1875, "fewer than one miner . . . in three was living with a woman," wrote historian Mimi Goldman, while frontier journalist E. Hazard Wells offered an unstructured guess of thirty women to six thousand men in the Klondike in 1897. Men in California in 1850 outnumbered women twelve to one, while in Montana, the shortage of women caused a general grooming decline, with young miners going "nearly four days without blacking their boots or oil[ing] their hair." Worse, they

also wore "paper collars a week without turning them," according to a newspaper account. At Selby Flat, California, only one woman was found along with three hundred men, but most allowed that even one female was enough "to keep the camp a-boiling."

"There wasn't a wife in Leadville," confirmed Mary Hallock Foote, the bride of a mining engineer in Colorado. "Ladies are very scarce in the mountains," prospector Edmund Booth agreed. There bachelorhood prevailed, men boarded in brotherly domesticity in makeshift rooms, spartan tents or tar-papered shanties and "paired up" with a partner in rough approximation of married domesticity. In each duo, one partner was assigned as the "wife," a sexless eponym completely free of ridicule or scorn, since it only indicated that the two had achieved an efficient division of labor. "There is nobody to boss us," wrote Alf Jackson of his life with his partner. "I suppose we are contented." Those truly scorned were loners so reticent or awkward they could boast no "wife," no pal, no special fireside of their own.

"We don't want to live this way forever," admitted a miner who had to fend for himself. His lot was to bake bread in a Dutch oven, brew his own pain remedies, thread needles, mend rips, hem overalls, resole boots and grill game in a cast-iron spider, bearing adversity with equanimity, managing adequately without a wife. No task was too difficult for a man alone, save housecleaning, which was generally seen as an affront to the prevailing ethic of squalor. So accepted was the slovenly that when E. Hazard Wells procured a dustpan for tidying up, his neighbors in Dawson were indignant: "It looked bad to see such an article hung up in a pioneer's cabin!" they complained. Besides, bachelor shanties were identified more easily by the pyramids of rusting tin cans out front.

As the boom years unfolded, some of the same honest miners who had struggled so much for so little often began to rake in "from a hundred to a thousand dollars daily" from their claims, according to Mark Twain, gambling it away in bouts of Monte, Red and Black, Chuck-a-Luck, Rondo and big stakes "brag" until they "hadn't a cent the next morning." Letters from home flew back and forth; wives and sweethearts feared the worst and sent anxious queries about domicile, health, job and, more subtly, a husband's free time and faithfulness. Throughout ran allusions to the married woman's deepest fear: "Without me, what will he do?"

The answer, for many, was found in the ubiquitous pocket-sized French postcards, whose pin-up images of scantily clad models, photographed in dreamily seductive poses, were in compelling contrast to the buttoned-up Victorian women. Many men were honestly ignorant of female anatomy and the "girlie cards" offered them the pleasures of imagined intimacy, all for a price. One westerner staunch enough to resist temptation—or too poor to pay—recalled the candy butchers offering to sell him a "pretty interesting-looking book filled with pictures of naked women." He refused to pay a steep $1.50 and "the butcher," wrote cowboy Walker Wyman, "was sore as a boil."

Carnal longings were not long ignored. Answering the plea for "more women and [more] good restaurants," ladies of easy virtue flooded into the mining centers of the west—"pioneer prostitutes" who dazzled and delighted with flounced skirts and flirtatious ways, filling the saloons, brothels, boardinghouses and bagnios from Deadwood to Portland, and fulfilling, however briefly, some of the basic requirements of "wife." As the women shook nightly profits from their hair in a shower of gold dust, or fetched up small nuggets from bags and bodices, they discovered, for a brief, heady time, what many had only dreamed of: on the mining frontier, all that glittered really *was* gold.

The women sparked endless civic debate with their misbehavior. Author Bret Harte wrote of "ladies in dreadfully disorganized drapery" who dove into doorways in the San Francisco streets, while Kansas resident Catherine Cavender was "wall-eyed" at the sight of a woman in a "low-necked, short-skirted dress" rushing screaming through the swinging door of a saloon, pursued by a man firing a pistol at her feet. The drunken cowboy was simply "having a joke" and shooting at the sidewalk to "see her run."

"Great rascality is carried on," wrote early settler Jerusha Merrill in 1851, describing a West Coast setting where harlots from the East Coast, Mexico, South America and Europe arrived by mule, by cart, by wagon and by sea, lured by the prospect of steady work and high pay in a profession that was, in fact, the single largest occupation available to women on the mining frontier.

As art, indenture and industry, prostitution added substantially to local revenues and helped to stabilize and pacify a chaotic population spinning free of the usual societal restraints. At the peak of the boom in 1849, nearly 20 percent of all women in California were involved in the flesh trade, having joined for myriad reasons. The lure of wealth and the hurly-burly atmosphere of the mines were an entrepreneurial opportunity to turn female companionship into a high-priced endeavor in the dusty streets and the muddy mountain passes of western mining towns. Unskilled women, from east or west, trapped in low-paying domestic or clerical jobs, earned less than five dollars weekly, and even those with specialties, such as dressmaking or shorthand, spent so much on food, transportation and lodging that, to amass a simple down payment of twenty-five dollars for rent might demand loans from credit brokers, friends or family. One woman, a skilled secretary with a "fine Spenserian hand," had to address a thousand envelopes, then put the cards inside, to earn a mere seventy-five cents.

Conversely, girls in the boom camps selling cigars might charge sixteen dollars—the price of an ounce of gold—simply to sit with a gambling hall patron. Anything more cost "a fabulous

Women on Main Street in front of a Chinese laundry (State Historical Society of Wisconsin)

amount," often earning women between fifty and four hundred dollars a week, according to a 1916 Wisconsin legislative report. For many, a night's take ranged from a twenty-dollar gold nugget to several hundred dollars, plus the price of champagne. Prostitution, for some, was a female version of the gold boom: speculative, adventuresome and with a sharp ring of profit.

Many of the "working women" who flooded west were blessed with youth and beauty, groomed to perfection, draped in silks and lace, and coached patiently by the madam of a class house to serve as pampered favorites of select patrons—men who San Francisco observer B. E. Lloyd described, in 1876, as those who "could afford to be perverse." So refined were these women, he added, that they resembled "graduates of the best female seminaries" rather than the constituency of brothels. "There have been a lot of drunken women in Deadwood," wrote a bar girl in the *Denver Pioneer.* "I for one am an exception."

As youth and beauty faded, the women sank to a different level of trade in seamy second-class brothels, servicing uncouth men for pocket change and a slight percentage of the house profits. Whereas an establishment such as as Bertha Cahn's in San Francisco set the tone in its legend, "No Vulgarity in This Establishment," others were unremittingly grim. In one case, even the owner of a Virginia City brothel was repulsed. "That damp, dreary house makes . . . me sick to think that I have to go back to it," wrote Cad Thompson, who, like so many women in the trade, could not afford to leave. Nights were measured by the intake of brass tokens, each worth several dollars, given to men to redeem "in trade" with a woman of the house. Fatigued, diseased and in decline, such women could tempt only the poorest clients along the boardwalks and gutters, where they earned fifty cents per visit, or less. Bargain rates bred high turnover, with men so hurried they kept their boots on, and women so besieged they seldom had time to dress. The squalor glimpsed in these tiny rented cubicles shattered forever the skewed dream of a courtesan's glamour. As B. E. Lloyd noted, such women were in "the last stages of human degradation." Added observer Thomas J. Dimsdale: "The girls in the cribs . . . got wore out fast." Given the general squalor and poverty of many women's lives and the medical ignorance of the day, little wonder that many women, and particularly whores, died young, and those who lived regretted an unhappy past. "A large proportion [are] fifth-rate humanity, morally [speaking]," wrote the Reverend William Taylor, summing up the prevailing view.

For some women, the flight into whoredom was a getaway from marital abuse, or simply from marriage. According to 1880 census reports, nearly half the population of prostitutes on the Comstock Lode had been married, with few bothering to divorce before the next liaison. One wife fled her home, moving the family furniture into the bagnio while her husband was away—her defection blamed upon the terrible angst of wedlock.

For others, marriage held deep allure, calling up images of a life they could only envy, and that seemed, in imagination, far better than the life they lived. After seeing her first wedding, Laura Davenport wrote to a fellow prostitute in Virginia City: "I was just wishing I was a good virtuous girl and it was Joe and me but no such good luck. If I had my life to live over, I would never do wrong." She might have tempered her yearning had she witnessed the typical miner's wedding that took place in 1849, at Rose's Bar along the Yuba River. The buckskin-clad bride and groom were united by the district mining recorder according to the local mining laws in a ceremony that began with "Swear 'em in, Joe," and was finalized when they signed their names to claims.

Marriage meant "striking it rich," presenting the certainty of partnership and even a financial future. "When I married him," wrote prostitute Maimie Pinzer of her husband, Albert Jones, "I reasoned it all out as one would a business proposition."

Marriage was the hidden dream behind each client encounter, an almost-magical way out of a dead-end life suffered by "working women." Prostitutes were painfully aware that "rags to riches" was admired in men but suspect with fallen women who seldom achieved legitimacy. "A parlor house is where the girls go to look for a husband and where the husbands go to look for a girl," expounded Cock Eyed Liz, mistress of the Palace of Joy sporting house in Buena Vista, Colorado, folk analyst of both "her" women and "her" trade. For "working women," even the briefest stint of promiscuity shunted them far from the ranks of respectability.

By the turn of the century, prostitution was an acknowledged, if exorable, aspect of American life, carried on in red-light districts in nearly every major American city from coast to coast, reviled by society at large but perversely condoned by an odd, Victorian notion—the "Volcano Theory" of male nature so "explosive," so dangerous and powerful in sexual outlet, that no self-respecting wife could, or should, be expected to provide relief. In fact, the dictum "spare the wife and spoil the mistress" seemed apt and chivalrous, turning prostitution into therapy rather than social prohibition. Fancifully interpreted, whoredom was socially justified because it kept men from consorting with Indian women—a dire consideration at the time. B. E. Lloyd was horrified at the number of brothels in San Francisco, frequented by a preponderance of married men; he proposed keeping a register of all visitors, a notion that would drive "many husbands and fathers . . . from the city" and create a "breeze of indignation" that would ruffle the feminine ranks of society.

Excuses aside, the men continued to visit "red-light districts"—the term supposedly coined in Dodge City, Kansas, to refer to the red light of the brakeman's lantern that was left by railroad workers outside the whorehouse door as a kind of "busy signal" to warn away upcoming customers.

The bedrock of prostitution was a steady influx of naive young girls recruited for the so-called white slave trade. Tales of procurers, or "agents," who scouted the ranks of female seminaries, churches and hotels searching for innocent young girls, preferably from out of town and visiting alone, were nearly apocryphal, steeped in prurient appeal and touted in countless reformist pamphlets and tracts. Some girls were lured by newspaper ads promising high wages for experienced servants, while others worked as waitresses, or worse, in wine rooms or as chorus girls. According to alarmed religious broadsides, even ice cream parlors harbored "scores of girls [who] have taken their first step downward," falling prey to female agents, usually older women who performed small courtesies with the intent of drugging and abducting them. Often the procurer was a refined, fatherly gentleman who proffered advice or suggested accommodations. Too often, according to reports, such contacts led to a girl's drugging and violation; only rarely were the victims able to escape. "I am a respectable woman and I supposed I was being taken to a ladies' café," cried a terrified woman, fortunate enough to be rescued by a bystander from two "escorts" who were forcing her through a doorway.

Once she was drugged and captured, a girl's clothes were replaced with gowns too flimsy to wear in public—modesty thus preventing her escape. These gowns, in fact, were charged back against her "account," sometimes at amounts as high as $1,500, binding her to the trade through a system of indebtedness impossible to repay. Once a virgin was violated, she often grew resigned, or was beaten or starved into submission, or faced with the ultimate threat—exposure to her family. In the rigid Victorian patriarchy of America, there was no ambivalence over the loss of virtue. Marriage to a respectable man was ruled out of her future, forgiveness all but impossible and a virtuous life forever denied.

Unidentified women (Photo by P. E. Larss. Alaska Historical Library)

In a society that assumed females were the property of males, there was surprising intolerance for unmarried "property."

Reformer Ernest A. Bell wrote a detailed account of this shameless traffic in 1910—in a book designed "to awaken the sleepy and protect the innocent" and titled with the strong invective "For God's sake, do something!" Most girls died within ten years of capture, he noted, and many took their own lives. Little wonder that the popular drinks of the day were dubbed "Moral Persuasion" and "Sweet Ruination"—and that young girls trembled at the notion of an enforced life of sin.

Punishment of this heinous crime was called for, invoking both the ire of and participation from numerous religous groups. Rampant vice brought its own ruin, however, in the growing incidence of syphilis and gonorrhea in at least "half the adult male population," according to Bell. The antiseptic washes, lotions and injections available through newspapers were largely useless, and in countless cases, the wives of philandering men were also infected. Blind children were born to contaminated mothers, and in the cases of diseased prostitutes, countless experimental, "charitable" operations often left them bereft of reproductive organs, or crippled or sightless. Medical advice ranged from abstinence to premarital physical checkups; one writer arguing that "syphilis could be virtually eradicated . . . through the universal practice of circumcision," while others advocated the female equivalent, the clitoridectomy. So persuaded were a number of middle-class women that ideal, virtuous femininity meant sexual purity, they willingly requested this bizarre and experimental operation. In seeking the aescetic norm of passive womanhood, surgical excision of sexuality seemed normal.

Feminine idealism also tempered the moral dynamics of the frontier, as settled women arrived to organize and reform, sweeping the cool winds of prudence over the frenzy of gamblers, faro dealers, hustlers and whores. Gone were the notions of wealth for the taking and pleasures by the pound, as church spires shadowed the doorways of boarded-up bordellos and as Sunday meetings replaced weekend revelry. The settled women, the civilizers and the civic servants, moved steadily to right the rocking boat of male morality on the mining frontier. Women were eager to start new homes, "school" children and eliminate vice. Men who had once lamented the "crying need for women" were startled by the changes these same women undertook, and often wondered, if the women came, would ministers be far behind?

To police prostitution, an immigration act of 1875 prohibited importing immoral women; later, the Mann Act of 1910 forbade interstate trafficking in vice. Women joined in, founding such reform clubs as The Steadfast Club to promote "The Three P's—Purity, Perseverance and Pleasantness" and the fanatical Purity Movement of 1885–1900. Gamblers, hustlers and whores moved out of the mainstream: the civilizing of the west had begun.

Hundreds of young brides emigrated into the far reaches of the mining and trading frontiers, inheriting the hand-me-down chairs and tables and stoves of earlier occupants, gazing out over deep canyons at the lonely horizon. Many a bride seated her guests in a parlor consisting of a potbellied stove and a single mattress on legs, cooked on a coal range and bathed from a tin basin. Privies were outdoors and, in shoulder-deep snow, often inaccessible.

Those who came west were usually wives of the better-paid mining superintendents, educated, genteel women highly critical of their new homes, interested in sanitation and civility, sometimes to the extreme. Often, the ladies "were not much pleased" with the west, and planned, according to Jerusha Merrill, to head east "at the first opportunity." They took a dim view of using as a postmark such town names as "Damn," Delirium Tremens," "Freeze Out" and "Hell Out," lobbying for more conservative names, such as "Ione" and "Noon."

Not all women were middle-class wives. Many young immigrants took up legitimate work on the mining frontier, seeking early marriage or independence and transforming domestic skills into paid positions of cooking, laundering or running a boardinghouse. Such women readily married, creating a servant problem for employers. "I am very fortunate," wrote Louise M. Palmer of Virginia City, "only five cooks within the last year."

The tenor and texture of the bawdy mining west was changing. Desperadoes, shootouts, gamblers, evil passions, the demon rum, ill repute and faro gave way to churches, schoolhouses, and the Women's Christian Temperance Union. Dance halls, saloons and pool rooms were largely replaced with residences. "The excited state of things cannot long exist," explained mining wife Jerusha Merrill. As virtuous women came west, a moralizing tone crept into the writing of the day, imposing upon the greed and profit-based social order a new, feminine idealism. Prostitutes "were not allowed to recognize their guests on the streets," wrote westerner Walker Wyman since no virtuous women wished to risk meeting a harlot, or possibly a dance hall girl, while browsing the boardwalk. Even when the prostitutes were restricted to separate areas, the classes of women were not inclined to coexist.

Who was decent and who was not was clearly defined by dress, vocabulary, activities and, especially, by address. Diarist Tillie Mayer recalled the "big dance hall" near her home in Gordon, Colorado, where young girls, ostensibly "boarders," would entertain so many bachelors that many "got to callin' her boardinghouse the Sporting House"—and with reason. Boardinghouse confusion seemed to reign, with young girls often discovering, to their utter horror, that their boardinghouse of choice was also a house of ill repute.

One of the most fascinating accounts of a woman in and out of the sporting life is told by Maimie Pinzer, a Jewess who married, fell in and out of prostitution, even losing an eye to venereal disease—and whose letters chart a lifelong attempt to reform. In her search for respectability, Maimie was struck by the change in male attitudes when she moved from a boardinghouse to live with a family and share their "decent life." "[If] the men whom I know . . . met me 'boarding' or 'visiting,' they'd start to hunt me down," she wrote, "whereas [now] they are just as polite as though [I was] . . . being thoroughly respectable."

Usually, brothels were discreetly enclosed behind doors marked only by the smallest of numbers—with one exception. Mattie Silks, the queen of Denver's red-light district, emblazoned in tile on her front door her twenty-two years of success with the bold insignia "M. Silks," defying propriety to claim her position as a local entrepreneur. "Sin was a business, like shoes and real estate," wrote historian C. L. Sonnichsen, and as such, it flourished in the gaudy parlor houses, dance halls, brothels and cribs of Dawson, Leadville, the Frazier River, Sonora and San Francisco. But just as the gold boom ended, so, too, did the sexual frontier. The spirit of reform raged through the California foothills and other mining boom sites, casting sporting women into social exclusion, even causing an entire parlor house in Marysville, California, to be dragged away by a team of horses, Ladies of the Night ensconced on board.

Occasionally, women from within the community's own middle-class ranks went awry, raising questions about the meaning of *circumspect,* which altered daily. Should married women go out on the town with escorts? Should decent women dance? Puritan reticence and Victorian obfuscation mingled with brash western effrontery—cultural confusion reigned. Married women in boomtowns such as Virginia City seemed, like socialite Louise Palmer, to have an "unnatural craving" for balls and parties that their husbands refused to attend. Like other men of his class, her husband, John, preferred to talk stocks at night rather than escort his wife to a ball, whether a fancy dress, masquerade, policemen's or even, in San Francisco, the Prostitute's Ball. However, the social scene was rife with young bachelors eager to escort mature, financially endowed women about town.

The essence of the frontier was change, industry and opportunity; many women who found themselves abandoned for long spells by prospecting, cattle-driving or military husbands ventured into the realm of outside male company. Lizzie Fisk, whose newlywed husband had returned east to raise money for his newspaper, was both shocked and pleased by a request from a male friend to keep him company on a buggy ride. "This is the first and only time I have ridden with him," far too early to "set the gossips talking."

Victorian women of the nineteenth century, even reformers, inadvertently courted scandal in their dress, having only to look in their own closets to see the influence of French prostitutes on everyday attire. From décolletage to lip rouge, scandalous frocks and shady mannerisms attracted middle-class women.

The dilemma had a certain irony. Women engrossed in moral reform by day would frizzle their hair, don a silk mask and glide through the streets by carriage, escorted by a handsome bachelor to a midnight masquerade ball or the shadowed recesses of an upstairs room in a French restaurant. Picnics, junkets, beer gardens and Sunday theatricals beckoned Sabbath-breakers rebelling against formal devotion, supporting Harte's contention that the new "boom" society was "hard, satirical, incisive, iconoclastic and illusive." And further, he pointed out, "Californians did not take kindly to moral legislation."

While America's social conscience wobbled between altruism and avarice, unhappy couples struggled free of social and religous constraints; where once only murder or desertion were options to end marital discord, scandalous "divorce resorts" of Illinois, Indiana, Oklahoma and Nevada now beckoned. So common had divorce become that in Dayton, Nevada, a town of crazy "wooden buildings" and deep winter mud, the redbrick courthouse was busy as an anthill. Only the stupid would be "so . . . blind as to cling to his or her first love," noted Louise Palmer. Although accounts were often exaggerated, statistics show that even in Connecticut, far distant from the divorce-happy west, by 1880 one marriage in eight was shattered by divorce.

Wild moral fluctuations created statistical chaos not because of increased numbers of people to marry, but because the few married so often. In Montana, newspapers had two ongoing columns—Divorce and Marriage—often with the same name appearing in both columns. "Californians are fast," it was agreed. "The divorced wife revels in her new freedom [and] is the constant envy" of the married woman, wrote Bret Harte. As pioneer Daniel Dustin wrote from French Corral, California, in 1853: "It would almost astonish you to notice the frequency of family difficulties resulting from the infidelity of husband or wife or both. It is proverbial that a woman's virtue cannot stand the test of California and that *flattery* and *fine presents* are poured upon them in such profusion that they soon forget themselves . . . they have passed the rubicon and once gone are gone forever." Sarah Royce, the quintessence of feminine virtue, observed with dismay the custom of boom-rich men, in an "offhanded, jocular way," bestowing female acquaintants with expensive gifts. Did this not presage future evil? Royce was shocked to see expensive jewelry and "even pieces of coin," thrown at young girls on stage at school exhibitions, or at literary entertainments, and blushed to discover that, instead of coldly rejecting such attentions, both the daughters *and* their mothers wore "looks of exaltation." Not only were such gifts countenanced, but mothers would boast of the amount their daughters had received.

Increasingly liberal divorce laws and the rise of outside jobs for women promised unhappy wives greater autonomy. "Aunt Mary talks of getting a divorce after being married over fifty years," wrote Iowa settler Emily Gillespie. "How strange, it is too bad." Like Mary, many long-suffering wives discovered that they could divorce, receive alimony and in many cases, even keep the children—all had hitherto been awarded to the fathers without undue recrimination. "Divorces are fashionable here," wrote Lizzie Fisk of Helena, Montana, in 1868. "It is . . . common . . . that a man in the mountains cannot keep his wife." In freewheeling Nevada, so many migratory divorces occurred that statistics exploded into a rate of one dissolution for every two enduring unions. B. E. Lloyd, writing from San Francisco in 1875, noted that during a twelve-month period, there were "more than six hundred applications for divorce," of which 350 were realized. Europeans, whose divorce rates lagged far behind, were stunned by American statistics: between 1850 and 1900 divorce rates had increased so rapidly that by 1890 at least three in every hundred marriages, according to historian Roderick Phillips, had crashed upon the "rocky shoals."

Such was not always the case. Divorce policy in the Colonial states had been generally restrictive—with the exception of Massachusetts and Connecticut—with warring couples often turning to violence or "divorce from bed and board," a form of legal separation. Old court records show a high incidence of spousal murder, with equally disturbing numbers of institutionalizations, assault and suicide. Even when divorce was recognized, the grounds varied wildly: in some states, only adultery, cruelty and desertion were grounds, while New York recognized only adultery and South Carolina had no provision at all. "It was wives who had to prove that they were blameless, pure and virtuous," wrote historian Merrill D. Smith.

The once-notorious act of dissolution had grown into a social disaster, and the idea of being able to begin anew held sway in the popular imagination. One politician, Fayette McMullen, accepted the position of second territorial governor of Washing-

Keystone Hall, Laramie, Wyoming, 1896
(American Heritage Center, University of Wyoming)

ton only after learning that the territorial legislature could grant divorces. According to historian Murray Morgan, McMullen spent eight months in his new post—from December 1857 to July 1858—long enough to divorce legally and remarry the virginal Mary Wood of Olympia before heading back to Virginia.

Nor was bigamy uncommon. When Asa Mercer brought would-be Yankee brides to Washington Territory to marry local bachelors, he was shocked to find that one prospective groom, Mr. Webster, was already married. Why, he railed, didn't Webster obtain a divorce, since it cost only fifteen dollars? The criminal offense of bigamy was more expensive to defend and was also a crime against society. However, for the sum of five hundred dollars, Mercer was willing to overlook the indiscretion. After all, the "young" lady was over thirty-five, and "looked as if she could paddle her own canoe." Typically, the best protection went to the young, the beautiful and the fetchingly vulnerable.

Money wove allure and sparkle throughout the gold-boom population, casting aside old, formal courtship structures in favor of brief, almost nonchalant encounters and giving rise to a body of myth and history that often framed the truly sad and ruined lives of women for hire in a froth of folklore, including the saga of the much-touted "whore with the heart of gold." Her generosity and quick-witted outreach led her to feeding hungry miners, raising funds during emergencies, backing politicians, doctoring the ill and boarding itinerants—an angel of good works. "I am what I am," stated Maimie Pinzer, underscoring the fact that, like many other women faced with thankless choices, she had chosen her career, and like the men who visited her, was not about to stop. Like other men and women of the mining frontier, she was drawn west by the prospect of gold, then drawn to others in hopes of an even greater and more dazzling discovery—love.

MARY JANE HAYDEN

Gold fever, like wildfire, could be stamped out one year, then flare to life again in one form or another. When faced with her husband's decision to go west, Mary tried to dissuade him, and he promptly postponed his plans, showing a tenderness and regard for her feelings seldom found in frontier accounts. But when the fever struck again, it led the couple to Oregon to farm, not seek gold.

In 1849 there was great excitement about the discovery of gold in California and nearly everybody had what was called the *gold fever,* my husband with the rest, and I soon discovered by their evening chat as we sat about the fire, that he was making plans to go to California.

At that time I was in very feeble health, having an ailing infant six weeks old. I knew it was impossible for me to go with them. (My uncle, Mr. Sumner Barker of Maine, and Mr. Edward Copeland of Massachusetts, were to be partners with my husband.) I listened to their plans which they had gotten pretty well formulated, when I thought it was time for me to take some interest in affairs, and so put the question, "what do you propose to do with me?" "Send you to your mother until I return," was his answer, which did not meet with my approval, but I made no answer at the time.

I was very fond of my husband and was nearly broken-hearted at the thought of the separation. It was getting late in February and if they went to California they would have to start by the tenth of March, and it had to be finally settled. This was the way it was done.

I said, "We were married to live together," (he saying "Yes"), "and I am willing to go with you to any part of *God's Foot Stool* where you think you can do the best, and under these circumstances you have to right to go where I cannot, and if you do, you never need return for I shall look upon you as dead." He answered, "Well, if that is the way you feel about it I will not go." Mind you—no word of this was said in anger, for we had never differed in our two years of married life, and so it was settled that we should go the next year to the California gold mines.

Man and woman on porch
(Sharlot Hall Museum)

MARY McNAIR MATHEWS

A brusque and outspoken resident of Virginia City, Mary Mathews's ten-year sojourn began in 1869, when she traveled to the tunnel-riddled Comstock Lode in Nevada, to investigate the mining properties of her dead brother. As a widow, she lived frugally with her young son, sewing and taking in laundry, as well as using her college experience at Oberlin to organize a soup kitchen and write letters for others. Her salty intolerance of "lawyers and railroad conductors" seemed to extend, in most cases, to the suitors who came her way.

I never lived in a place where the people dressed more richly or more extravagantly than in Virginia City. It is not only a few millionaires who indulge in it, but every woman on the Comstock who has a husband earning $4 or $6 a day . . . And many families live up to every cent of their wages or salary.

Some of my friends were very extravagant, and I used often to tell them so, and in return they would call me a miser, because I would not follow all of the silly fashions.

Mrs. Calvin often laughed at me, and said: "If you would go down in that old stocking, and get out some of the gold you have hoarded up, and put it on your back in fine clothes, you would stand some show to get a rich husband, for they would know then that you did have something; and now they don't know you are worth anything."

I would tell her I was not in the market, for I had determined never to bring a stepfather over my child, no matter how good he might be. I told her that if I ever married, it would be after my boy had grown to be a man, and then it would not be a fortune-hunter, but a *man* I could respect.

I do believe that if I could have married every man that she and Mrs. Beck picked out and tried to make a match with for me, I would have had as many husbands as old Brigham Young ever had wives.

They finally gave up all hopes of ever dancing at my wedding, although both offered to be bridesmaids, and furnish the wedding supper. But I told them all that I had too much business on hand to get married . . .

[I did not go] shabbily dressed . . . I never bought needless finery, as I had other uses for my money; besides, I never believed in dressing to catch a husband. I think this is one reason of so many divorces in California and Nevada . . .

[It was not that] I never had an offer, for I have had several, one . . . from a merchant. Now see how business-like he popped the question. He came to bring me some goods. As he stood in the door, looking around, he said: "Do you own this place?"

I replied that I did.

He said: "It is a fine little property." He stood a moment as if in deep thought, and then turning to me, said: "I wish the Lord you would marry me. I have got four or five children, and I have not time to take care of them. I want a good, smart woman to bring them up—some one that will be kind to them."

I told him if that was the case, he had better get some one else, for I would not do for a stepmother. I was afraid I should abuse them.

"I guess not," he said. "I have heard you were just splendid—humor Charlie [her son] to death. Now, I want just such a woman for my children."

Oh! yes; I am pretty good to Charlie; he is my own, you know; but I dislike other children, and would be apt to be a cross step-mother.

"Well, you won't do for me, then, for I won't have my children abused by any woman. But I don't believe a word you say. I guess you are only gasing."

I had done a great deal of trading with this gentleman, and always got goods cheaper than at any other place. But the first time I called there after the above conversation, I found he had raised on his prices. I suppose he did not intend to sell cheaper than his neighbor, with no prospects of a wife.

Well, who blames him? Not I.

Another offer, or almost one, was from a young Englishman. It was the first winter I lived in Virginia City. I had but a short acquaintance, having done some sewing for him. He was rather good-looking, and was bigoted enough to think he could get any woman to marry him by asking her.

He called one evening, and said: "Why didn't you tell me when you moved? I have been looking for you for the last six weeks."

I told him that I did not think it necessary to give an account of myself to anyone.

"Well, I have some very important business I wish to see you about."

I was quite surprised, and waited to hear what he had to say.

After a little hesitation, he said: "Well, I am on the marry." (That was the old country way of speaking.) "I think I know a lady that suits me."

Well, why do you not go and ask her? I do not see that I can assist you, for I never break nor make matches.

He laughed at me, and said: "Let me tell you what kind of a woman I want. She must be an American, and good-looking; one that knows how to do all kinds of work; one that can keep her own house, for I can't afford to pay $40 a month for help."

Get a Chinaman for $15, said I.

"I don't want any . . . Chinaman in mine. I don't care for a young girl; I would sooner have a widow about twenty-five or thirty."

I now began to see which way he was drifting.

I said: Would you, indeed? What a pity I am not *fifteen* years younger. I might stand some chance!

"How old are you?" said he, as though I were in duty bound to tell him.

Oh! too old for you, altogether—forty-five.

"I don't believe a word of it. I took you to be about twenty-five."

Well, you see appearances are often deceitful, said I.

"F-o-r-t-y-f-i-v-e!" said he.

Yes, said I.

"'Pon honor?" said he.

Yes, honor bright, I replied.

"Well, that settles it," said he, reaching for his hat; "I don't mind marrying a woman about my own age, but I don't want one quite so old. Good evening!"

And this did settle it, for he never called again.

Remember, reader, I only said forty-five. I did not say years.

Another man came and took a room at my house for a month. After he had been there a week, he came one day and rapped at the sitting-room door. I opened it, thinking perhaps he had called for something I had left out of his room, and stood waiting to see what it was; and to my astonishment he came in and sat down, and asked me if I owned the place. I said I did.

"I heard so," said he.

I expected the next question would be, Do you want to sell? But no such question came. His next words were: "Well, you want to get some nice man to take care of it for you. I heard you were a widow, and came and took a room on purpose to get acquainted with you."

Well, sir, said I, I am afraid you will have your labor for your

Mining-town scene (Library of Congress)

pains. I made this property, and I think I can take care of it without the assistance of any man. Good-day, sir! said I, holding the door open for him.

The next day he called and paid my week's rent.

He had his trunk by the handle dragging it along.

Are you moving? said I.

"Yes; I am off."

I thought you wanted the room for a month.

"Well, I did; but you know I have been terribly disappointed."

Indeed! said I. Perhaps you will have better success the next time you go fortune-hunting.

This is about the way one-third of the people of the coast propose and are accepted. This is the reason why their honeymoons end in divorce. It is no trouble for a woman in any class of society to get married, especially if she is from the East.

SARAH OLDS

**Sarah Elizabeth Thompson was born in Iowa in 1875,
the youngest daughter of a family of nine. She cared for her ailing
parents until their deaths, and in 1897, at twenty-two, followed her
brothers to the southern Mother Lode of Stent, Nevada, to "batch"
alone and work as a dressmaker. Pretty and popular, she had many
offers of marriage but settled, to her own surprise, on A. J. Olds, a
footloose, gold-fevered scion of a distinguished California family
who was sixteen years her senior and did what he could to discourage the match. But her instincts prevailed; they wed, and, to determine who would be in charge, they stepped on the scale. She tipped
them at 168 (he at 165) and she was the "boss" from then on.**

Although I had never met Mr. Olds, I had often heard Mrs. McNeal tell what a wonderful man he was. At the time of our first encounter, he was trying to work nights at the mine and sleep in the daytime, and we in our hilarious fun [she was in a boisterous snowball fight] had disturbed his rest.

"Oh, Mr. Olds," I said, "I'm very sorry we disturbed you."

"It's too late to be sorry now," he snapped. "There's no apologies accepted." He turned abruptly and went back into the house, leaving me thinking he was the darndest old crank I'd ever met.

I told everyone what I thought of him, wanting them to share in my opinion. Perhaps I was a little egotistical and stuck on myself, for I was used to hearing compliments rather than a tirade like this. The world in general had gone wrong with Mr. Olds that morning, and after his rude awakening he went down to the mine office, drew his time, and left town.

We didn't see him again for some time. I felt so bitter about him I really hoped he would never return . . .

In the meantime I was . . . interested in a dashing young Irishman named Murphy, who was foreman of one of the mines. He had a wonderful baritone voice, and I realize now that it was the voice and not the man that I thought I was in love with . . .

Mr. Murphy was very methodical in his courting. He called me every Sunday and Wednesday . . . promptly at seven P.M. . . .

One afternoon while I was sitting on my porch sewing, I looked up and saw the most handsomely dressed gentleman walking my way. He wore a tailor-made suit and derby hat, which was the fashion in those days. He stopped, tipped his hat, and said, "Good evening, Miss Thompson. I came over to apologize rather belatedly for my rudeness in speaking to you the way I did the morning of your snow battle."

It was then that I recognized the well-dressed gentleman as Mr. Olds, the "old crank" . . . he was now a handsome young knight with a pleasant smile, and a very pleasing personality. . . . [H]e came upon the porch and sat down for a friendly visit which lasted for hours. It was the beginning of a strange courtship that held never a word of love or affection, but a very real companionship. He called me either "Sister" or "old lady" from the beginning, which pleased me, for I thought it more interesting than the endearing terms the other young men used. I called him A.J. from the first, and so it was—A.J. and old lady (till we were married and the babies came, when he became Daddy to all of us).

A.J. liked to hunt and fish. He would come by my shop after coming off shift at the mine and say, "Come on, old lady, let's take to the hills." I would neglect my work, and we would go for a glorious tramp, either hunting or fishing along the Tuolumne River.

One day while fishing, we found an old raft tied up to a stump. Some children had made it and anchored it there. It was rather a crude affair—just two big logs with boards nailed on top. We thought it would be fun to row the raft out in the middle of the river where the water was deep so A.J. could fly-cast from it.

It was great fun. A.J. finally caught his fish, but in the excitement of reeling it in he stepped too close to the edge of the raft, dumping both of us into the water. I had learned to swim barenaked as a child, but we never knew what a bathing suit was. This was a different proposition. Swimming now in the swift-moving current with all my clothes on was quite a struggle. I was fully dressed in the costume of the gay nineties—high-topped button shoes, black lisle stockings, two full, ruffled petticoats, and an ankle-length dress. It was topped off with a wide-brimmed sailor hat fastened on with two ten-inch hatpins stuck in from opposite sides of the crown. It would have been an acrobatic feat to remove my hat. I laboriously swam in all my cumbersome attire through the fast-flowing stream. Fortunately I had only a few strokes to swim till I reached shallow water and waded ashore.

I think A.J. must have glanced my way and seen that I was making it all right, for he kept right on with his fish. Soon he followed me to shore with both fish and raft. After depositing his hard-won fish on the bank, he came over and gave me a rousing smack on my wet back and said, "By George, old lady, you're all right!"

We went on our hiking and fishing trips almost every evening except Wednesday and Sunday. These nights were still reserved from Mr. Murphy. A.J. insisted that I keep those dates. I was becoming very fond of A.J. and wished he would say some little word of love or ask me to discontinue seeing Murphy, but there was never a word, and when Murphy's name was mentioned A.J. had only the greatest praise for him.

One evening while A.J. was hurrying me home to keep my Wednesday night date I said boldly, "A.J. , I have lots more fun with you than I do with him. I'll quit him if you'd like me to."

Much to the deflation of my ego A.J. replied, "No, old lady. Don't you do it! Never give up a good man for a poor one. Murphy has everything a young girl would want. He's a handsome fellow with a wonderful voice and a social position. He's foreman of one of the biggest mines around here, and he must have money. Then look at me. Just a hobo miner . . . I want to rove, to ramble, to venture . . . Someday I'll strike it rich—then everything will be different . . .

"No, old lady," A.J. repeated, "you grab Murphy if you can."

On the other hand, Mr. Murphy's attitude toward A.J. was so different. Some little bird had told him of A.J.'s calls, and our delightful companionship irked him. . . .

Of course we quarreled, and I told him not to come to see me anymore. I was honestly glad of a chance to break our friendship, but when I told A.J. about it he seemed very sad. He said he was sorry that he had ever come into my life, but we still continued our rambles.

I had a sister living on a ranch five miles from Stent by wagon road . . . At that spot the canyon opened into a little valley with a view of a fruit ranch below . . . We would stand together . . . and I would exclaim in awe at the beauty of the scene below, "Beautiful, beautiful, beautiful!"

A.J. would look down on the same scene and say, "Who in hell would live there? It's isolated. The only place you can see is up."

"What difference does it make if it's in the heart of Egypt," I would retort, "if it's a home and a beautiful one." I think I was subconsciously longing for a home and wishing that little ranch was mine. We realized then for the first time what a difference of opinion we held on almost everything. A difference which we carried all through life. But I believed then, and still believe, that if there is enough love it can surmount any difficulty.

In a mining camp where there are so many men and so few women, a girl gets lots of attention and many proposals of mar-riage. But A.J. was so different from the rest. I will admit now that from his very first visit I was madly in love with him . . .

Then the roving spirit struck him and the hills were greener on the other side. He left for Bodie, a mining camp across the Sierra mountains, where miners' wages had reached the fabulous sum of four dollars a day. . . .

The morning he left he came by my shop and bid a friendly good-bye, asking me to write to him. "Just Bodie, California," he said in reply to my request for his address. Then he added, "All girls seem to have a weakness for writing, so practice on me."

This made me think, "Well, you old crank, I bet I never do write to you."

How I missed him! I listened each evening for his decided and individual footsteps on the newly macadamized road that ran by my door. In my mind I was sure I could hear him coming. Then I would remind myself that if he didn't think enough of me to say one little word of love, it was a good thing for me that he was gone . . . Then I'd add for my own satisfaction, "He was an awful old crank anyway."

A week or more had passed when I received a friendly little note from A.J. at his Bodie address. I didn't answer it . . . I was being entertained by a thriving, handsome young doctor, who had a beautiful horse and buggy in which he took me riding every evening. . . .

Then I had another note from him saying that he had written to me but received no reply . . . I didn't answer that one either. Thought I, "Old boy, you'll have to declare some interest in me before I ever so much as write a line to you." I was making a good try at forgetting him by accepting the attention of the young doctor. I wondered then, and have many times since, why I couldn't have fallen in love with the doctor, who made a fuss over me and proposed marriage . . . Instead I chose a broken-down old miner, sixteen years my senior. The only explanation I can give is that

God directs love and we humans have very little to do with it . . .

Imagine my great satisfaction when, about a week later, up on the hurricane deck of the incoming stage, I recognized the dust covered figure of A.J. Olds. I know that nothing but the eyes of love could have discerned through that crust of red dust and the coming of dark, the figure of the man they loved.

The doctor was sitting on the porch with me when the stage arrived. When I realized that it really was A.J. on top of the stage there never in all my life was such a moment of ecstasy. I forgot all about the doctor sitting there. I jumped up, and like a happy child I clapped my hands with joy and exclaimed, "Oh, there's A.J. Olds."

The doctor arose, tipped his hat, and said, "Good-bye, Miss Thompson, I see the lay of the land, and if I ever call on you again it'll be professionally." Then he was gone.

I sat there in the dark waiting. I had waited only a few minutes when I heard the longed-for footsteps come to my gate. I went to meet him and would have thrown my arms around him, dust covered and dirty as he was, but he would not allow it. He caught me by the arms, and with he on one side of the low fence and I on the other, he delivered a tirade of accusations and abuse. . . .

Then he put his hand on my face, pressing gently and said, "Now, old lady, if you're going to marry me you've got to say so right now, and we'll get married and camp under a tree, for I haven't a damn cent. What d'ya say?"

I had been waiting . . . to . . . say yes. Now I said it.

"Good God, old lady! Do you mean it?" And it didn't take him long to jump that low fence. He didn't even stop to open the gate. Then our arms went around each other in one long embrace.

CARRIE WILLIAMS

Carrie Williams lived in Gold Flat, Nevada County, California, and recorded her thoughts about married life, her child and life in general between 1854 and 1868. Her poignant observations about her husband's private life—nighttimes spent with his musical group, often serenading other women—are offset by her own grueling domestic schedule and constant loneliness. Married life as a matron, she found, was definitely different from the days of her honeymoon.

TUESDAY THE 14TH

Wallace did not come home last night till after 1. He said the band of brass horns went out serenading. I suppose all the bridgets in that neighborhood were beautifull tuted at, from his description . . .

SUNDAY 19TH

I went to hear Mr. Warren preach today. He is up from the Bay awhile, but I am afraid there was more harm done in my going than if I remained quietly at home and never expressed a wish to go anywhere. The reason is, Wallace so hates to take me or go himself. I wish it were otherwise, but I cannot help it. I felt unhappy and discontented all day.

Wallace's mother took charge of Walla [her son] while we were gone. The little fellow seems not to be so well as usual tonight. Dear little toad, he waked up about 4 this morn and kept trying to climb up in bed so that Wallace had to slap him to keep him in the bed. He sobbed and grieved himself to sleep finally . . .

Monday 20ieth

I washed 7 towels, 1 tablecloth and such like. Wallace went with the band to serenade Mrs. Waite. I felt sad to see him go. He wanted me to kiss him before he went away, but I would not. Then he said that perhaps I would never have a chance to again. I felt very miserable all the evening whenever I think of him. O how I wish he would give up going to town so much evenings on one pretext or another and stay with me and I would lay my head in his lap and read to him as I used to do. Those were happy evenings, but soon they passed away, and here I sit alone evening after evening with no companion but my own sad thoughts. . . .

Tuesday the 21st

Today has been dark, cloudy & raining part of the time. Wallace has been working hard most of the day putting in false bottoms in the flume. He came home about 4 oclock, wet and muddy . . . He is now gone to the lodge. His father has been working in the diggings . . . The band went out serenading last night. Mrs. Waite shewed herself on the balcony and made them a graceful acknowledgement, but the fun of the evening was they were standing on the bridge over Deer Creek playing just before starting home. Well out back at one end of the bridge is a house where there is liquor sold. Well the boss of the establishment, thinking himself serenaded, came out and in flattering terms thanked them for the honor and invited them very poitely [sic] in to take something to drink, which invitation they declined, most of them being sons of temperence. I had a good laugh at Wallace about the termination of his serenade.

Saturday the 25th

Well Christmas has come round again . . . Wallace and his father both condescended to be home to supper. His mother had roasted a turkey and chicken. She also had a bread puding that was capital and plum cake not to be beat. You see, she baked 10 loaves of cake last night. Now about Sant [sic] Clauses pranks, I found a bundle of candy tied on the door knob of my room and on opening a drawer in the beaureau [sic] found one of my old ragged stockings containing a beautiful embroidered hand kerchief.

That was the amount of Christmas gifts that fell to my share.

George had his Christmas tree full, and little Walla's stocking was filled to overflowing. The little toad was very much delighted when he saw the varieties of candy that it contained. Strange to say, he did not know enough about candy to know that it was to eat, never having had any before.

Monday 27th

The first of this month I got the last of my year's number of Godey's Magazine, and in the conclusion of Margaret's Home, a beautiful story from the pen of the gifted Alice B. Haven I have spent many a happy evening, following the trials of Margaret the good and patient to their final happy conclusion.

May she be happy the rest of her life . . .

"Home Sweet Home" (Montana Historical Society, Helena)

PART **VII** SEVEN

Banns in

the City

Urban
Victorians

Group of young people sitting in a tree, Las Cruces, New Mexico
(New Mexico State University Library)

> *"We were now home again, and as during my absence Elizabeth had not found a fellow she thought would make a better husband than I, we were married on the 19th of the following month."*
>
> —CARLISLE ABBOTT

CITIES CALLED OUT WITH HAUNTING INVITATION TO footloose young men, too poor or too carefree to marry, without family obligations or a desire to till the soil. Like cowboys, drifters or soldiers, they were judged ineligible by most parents, belonging as they did to the mercurial, rootless world of the dandy. Harriet Levy, a San Francisco girl out strolling with her father on a Saturday evening, spotted the type in a "line of mashers" standing "three deep," who slouched in front of a cigar store on Market Street. They were "dressy men," she wrote, "dandies young and old who stood facing the street, smoking long cigars, or picking their teeth with quill toothpicks." Harriet, a respectable young woman, could only turn her head in disgust.

What gentlewoman would ever make eye contact with a strange man or converse without an introduction? Urban dandies knew this, and took pleasure in teasing prim young schoolgirls, pretending to mistake them for women of the street.

Indeed, urban prostitution had grown so diverse that even a discreet, elegant woman, expensively attired, might receive, or even accept, a proposition—who was to know? Such confusion bred a sense of insecurity—women could no longer rely upon chivalry to remain inviolate. "[I]n this land of equality," wrote French traveler Frederick Marryat in 1835, "it is impossible to know who is who." Genteel women often veered dangerously toward the risqué, wearing shorter skirts, sewn-on bric-a-brac, powder, and rouged cheeks—"the hallmark of the fast woman,"

according to western settler Nannie Alderson. In Nannie's girlhood of the 1870s, the discovery of a "little box of crimson paste" in her mother's bureau had created moral pandemonium. If any type of woman could rouge without recrimination, of what use were social restrictions?

Fashion gave rise to further social commotion when well-bred housewives donned pinchbeck or paste diamonds, handsomely set, purchased openly from cheap stores and available to women of all walks—an unspeakable gaucherie. Unescorted women were nearly as risqué—little wonder that Mary McNair Mathews, who had lost her money while traveling and needed a place to stay, was mistaken for a woman of easy virtue, despite her sober demeanor, modest dress, and air of innocence. When an unsavory Samaritan offered to "see her" to a respectable hotel, she expected chivalry, he expected conquest. "I will pay for your bed if you will share it with me," he began, but stopped short at the sight of her pocket derringer, firmly gripped in a gloved hand, and the hissed epithet, "villain!"

A spirit of audacious democracy stirred up within all classes a sense of vague longings—for success, for wealth and for show, which often translated into a brooding preoccupation with dress. "Smartness," said British critic Isabella Bird of her American peers, "consisted in over-reaching your neighbor in every fashion which is not illegal," and was universally aspired to.

Cities offered tantalizing glimpses into what Americans felt they lacked—namely, worldliness and sophistication. Income and social mobility marked the youth who migrated to the cities, stirring up a gay sense of abandon. Trolley cars and automobiles minimized distance, expediting far-flung courtships, allowing youth once limited to foot or saddle to speed through the countryside, free of parental guidance and eager for the tantalizing privacy of upholstered seats and pull-down shades. Beaches, moving pictures, nickelodeon parlors and restaurants with private booths were suddenly within reach, causing parents deep anxiety as their children motored away, bound for private pursuits—perhaps the theater, the grand opera, or a mandolin club, for music. John Levi, a privileged California youth, recalled that "nearly all" of his friends and their families owned autos by 1910. As a youth growing up in Los Angeles, he drove with supervision by the age of twelve and alone by fourteen—surprising freedom for the day. Despite logistical problems such as vehicle cost, the need to self-store gasoline, and flimsy tires always in need of patching with vulcanized rubber, the automobile turned mobile, motoring youth into a courtship phenomenon to be reckoned with.

To be sophisticated was to be European, specifically French, and countless young urban couples modeled themselves upon what they perceived as glittering, foreign café society, where coffee houses, restaurants and cabarets overflowed, reportedly, with women. They dined *a deaux* on truffles and pâté, frequenting restaurants where they could sample exotic food at any hour amid a maze of mirrors or a flourish of fountains, and where elegantly attired women, "many without bonnets," daintily supped upon orange-flavored ices, cream and strawberries.

Often, prankish couples defied convention by eating oysters, a sophisticated food made more provocative by the belief that it caused cholera—not to mention its aphrodisiac quality. But so far did fashion outweigh fear that, according to the pithy Isabella Bird, the "amount of oysters eaten" in America grew beyond Continental comprehension. Oysters appeared during the Gay Nineties—and earlier—in every part of the country, reigning in the romantic minds of urban and rural sophisticates alike. No party was complete without a shiny tin tub of oysters, fed on cornmeal and salt until plump, then roasted, fried, steamed or eaten raw. Urban couples would scout out the words OYSTER SALOON painted in large letters on a basement signboard and pointing the way to a brightly lit room, filled with happy diners

huddled over tureens of stewed bivalves. A saloon where women could daintily slurp the mollusks rather than alcohol was deemed semi-respectable.

Cities offered glamour, a faster pace of life and opportunities for youth to meet and mingle, whether chaperoned or footloose and free. Love filled the air as young girls hovered around boys at parties, speaking in slang, parroting such mindless phrases as "you are a nonsuch dancer" or "we had the time of our lives," while adults grimaced in annoyance. A girl could "make a mash" by catching the eye of a boy—"mash" being code for boyfriend—but if she were "mashed by" a youth, then it was she who had fallen in love. One energetic flirt made five mashes in quick succession, then was faced with a phalanx of young men eager to escort her to church. What, she wondered, to do?

Often, girls too impatient to wait for mashing struck back by selecting youths with a likely look for "bunching"—the urban equivalent of ganging together. Girls would "bunch" the boys in a group and then join the melee—behavior that exasperated adults in general and congressman's wife Ellen Maury Slayden in particular, she being the hostess in charge of a group of Texas schoolgirls at a tea party. While the girls "bunched" the young men Slayden had enlisted to help at the party, the boys were rendered useless work-wise, while the girls, she noted, simply "stayed bunched."

Fads often held sway over reason, fueled by the surge in novel reading that swept the country. Sentimental "domestic novels," written by women between 1840 and 1880, were eagerly consumed by a "smart" young female audience. These readers pored over the works of authors such as Frederika Bremer, a Swede whose sensational text portrayed the frayed edges of domesticity in startling new detail, citing adultery, divorce, jealousy and revenge. Novels titillated and tempted, pitting male against female, locking protagonists in mock encounters, and provoking both sexual tension and subtly disguised gender hatred.

Pulp plots seemed so gripping they caused women to swoon—but no wonder. "Fainting," according to diarist Katherine Fougera, "became the latest craze" among Victorian women testing the extremes of their femininity. Those too stalwart to collapse were losers in the "frailty matches" that often broke out, with women voicing ever more astonishing claims to helplessness. One was unable to hem a handkerchief for fainting; another blanched simply to think of the vileness of the world. Rivalry revolved even around foot size, with women wearing kid shoes in delicate pastel shades upon which mud and dust made constant havoc, to display the daintiness of shape and size. Ellen Maury Slayden wrote wryly of her meeting with a young woman in Washington, D.C., who "seemed challenged" by Ellen's tiny, size 6 shoe, and immediately "kicked up" her own feet to compare. Fashion also upheld the "Carmen" look—a mysterious draping of veils about the face to create deep black "points" of enticing shadow. One socialite, irritated at the murky tableau, likened the shading to a disfiguring harelip. "I hope not to dream of it," she wrote, "when I seize my pillow and go to sleep." The "wan" look was also all the mode, creating its own level of anxious competition among women who ingested arsenic to induce a pallor and then dusted themselves with lead-based powder. Hair, too, had its own arena, as formal coiffure could veer straight up from the head or angle off into architectural splendor, folded over wires and pads before being frizzed, greased and bedecked with feathers or jewels. Fashion emphasis played upon insecurities, driving women into fierce competition with one another, yet in direct opposition to the Christian values of the day: to support, share, encourage and show a mild spirit to one another.

Technology and chemistry offered beauty benefits never before contemplated. Hefty women could trim away the fleshiness that occurred after the "climactertic," or change of life, drink

Couple in doorway
(The Bancroft Library, University of California at Berkeley)

iodine to shrink unwieldy bustlines or, in a flourish of experimentation, don Dr. Scott's electric corset, which would, according to the promotional brochure, "flood the vital organs" with unidentifiable entities known as steel magnetoids, while "preserving the symmetry and lightness" so useful in a good corset.

Men also embraced medical chicanery, dosing themselves with phosphorous for revitalization, or taking electrically charged baths to spark up a dilatory system. Every fad stirred up a flurry of followers, who would converge for urban soirees such as a phosphene party, during which a group of hand-holding thrill-seekers would receive a shock of electricity from an electrostatic generator. Due to the circle's human conductivity, the shared voltage would stimulate the brain to unleash colorful phosphene "light shows"—a marvel to all.

Another odd "couples" event was noted by emigrant Christian Koch in 1831, on a trip to Baltimore. "I saw here a place where people could get gas," he wrote, "and they became crazy from it. They had the gas in a bottle and he who took it stood in a cage where everyone could look at him. When they had enough they began to roll their eyes & clench their fists. Most of them wanted to fight and struck on the cage with their might. But some were very happy and laughed and started dancing. I tried it myself, but it had no effect on me whatsoever." Apparently, laughing gas, or nitrous oxide, offered a quick path to euphoria by inducing visions—another fad of the day.

Fashion turned dress into costume, and vice versa, while trapping women helplessly in a welter of hooped skirts, nipped waists and endless social rounds. Women of the middle class were increasingly viewed by men as "leisured" and "decorative," and often, to break free from monotony, would model themselves after those popular pulp heroines whose diminutive forms, tiny waists, milky complexions and submissive spirits were idealized in popular periodicals of the day, such as *Godey's Lady's Book*.

Such magazines drew thousands of feminine subscribers from across the country, and presaged the enormous power that advertising would play in upcoming decades. Called "foppery and nonsense" by the sober-minded, pulp romances and advice-filled magazines flourished among a restless population whose high moral tone seemed to be gently sliding downhill. To counteract the trend toward pulp novels, religious journals proliferated, increasing from merely 10 in 1800 to 850 in 1840.

On the other hand, women began to consider what they might have to relinquish in order to marry. "There seems to be such a conflicting of desires," wrote Harriet Johnson in her diary concerning the prospect of marriage. "I cannot forgo all the proud hopes that have buoyed my spirit from my youth up."

While women brooded, men settled into dull providership or were caught up in the social whirl of the city, a sparkling milieu in which affluent bankers, merchants and lawyers flitted from dinner to dance with hair trimmed, boots brushed and, as observed by Ellen Maury Slayden in the dress of a Virginia congressman, often bedecked in long, colored "four-in-hand" ties that nearly obscured the front of a pressed evening shirt. Bachelors often adopted foppish or flirtatious behavior, infusing even the most casual of mixed meetings with a lively current of coquetry. To ready himself for a social evening, one young dandy, Theo Cockrell, "donned black coat and waistcoat, and nice clean cuff . . . trousers, collar, tie and white shirt," as handsome, he imagined, as the Prince of Wales.

Not so, British critics would counter. The social consequences of democracy, so different from the more repressed public system of Britain, bred American men both gross and expeditious, who cultivated, according to one critic, the "disgusting custom" of chewing tobacco. American men, like "ruminating animals," ate with their hats on, balanced peas on a knife and read newspapers behind propped feet, in the presence of ladies. Their very idiom

Miss Lockhart (The Bancroft Library, University of California at Berkeley)

was disgraceful, laced with such colloquialisms as "feeling mighty weak," or "leetle."

Such failings aside, European Victorianism promoted a formality so extreme as to render women helpless and men immobile, unless they used lavish social aids, such as embossed calling cards or gold-topped canes. Like the Puritan "spirituals" of the past, woman should be "pious, pure, submissive, and domestic," look girlish, not venture opinions and blush often—the mark of the virginal soul. A gentleman, in turn, would behave ethically and refrain from hasty attempts upon her virtue unless he was the gentleman-hunter type, who stalked his lady love with flowers and poetry, then withdrew after a flurry of amorous onslaughts and recriminations. Caution dictated that both men and women learn the difference between "love at first sight" and "distinctly keen interest."

A woman could freely refuse any suitor, but she might soften the blow by citing her Christian faith and promising to "remember him in prayer." She thus created a small, emotional adventure for them both, in which truth, pain, expectations and Christian forbearance combined in one exalted, enabling moment. "Chemistry is two-thirds waiting," Freud wrote to his fiancée, identifying the languid, playful courtships that had become a kind of pastime for men and women of the day.

Not all was so lighthearted. Part of the exquisite agony of Victorian love was self-induced drama by partners who enjoyed the emotionality of false partings, suicidal gloom, remorse and the uplift of a poignant reunion. Suppressed passion nearly always turned irrational, sparking countless odd new behaviors as couples completed their nervous vacillation from chaste to brash and back again. Habits of courtship were unstable predictors of marital behavior to follow, given the subtle pulls of Puritanism, Victorian stuffiness, frontier self-determination and courtly love. Chaos in courtship often reflected the country's confusion between old and new; American technology cut an economic swath into the future, yet society seemed mired in the past, its courting couples still caught up in a tangle of clumsy nuance and veiled intent.

Language also grew increasingly unclear. America of the 1830s and 1840s was so awash with weak words and self-conscious prudery it was dubbed the "Golden Age of Euphemism" by critic H. L. Mencken. Romance was worshiped from afar, nothing was called by its proper name and language was deeply masked in symbolism. "I am engaged," "My love for you has doubled," "No!" and "You have broken my heart" were spelled out by stamps glued upside down, side by side, center bottom and center top—assuming that affections had not changed before the arrival of the mail. Historian Linda Lipsett cites another eloquent means of communication—the linen handkerchief, drawn through a young girl's hands, twirled, traded from hand to hand or drawn across the cheek to inform a beau, in twenty-two different ways, of the love or "good riddance" she could not bear to utter. Ivy leaves represented the lasting bond of matrimony, roses placed alongside a plate meant marital happiness, and tortured emotions were obscured by ordinary household references; nutmeg meant "Meet me unexpectedly," while an apple cried out, "You are my present preference!" One man, a Union soldier, spent his days copying letters to his sweetheart in a mirror, backward, so that she could read them only with a looking glass—the ultimate obfuscation.

Every aspect of life teemed with subliminal intent; in a society so rigidly antisexual that books were sorted on the shelves by gender, a chivalrous man would never say "piano leg" in a woman's presence, nor would a woman consume a sausage publicly. In society at its most polite and sensitive, neither sex felt comfortable unless piano legs, with their sensual, human configuration, were hidden behind a modest skirt. Even the term "chicken

Two couples seated by the river
(Lillybridge Collection, Colorado Historical Society)

breast" was fraught with danger, safely discussed only as "white meat" or "chicken parts." Chicken legs, equally scandalous in conversation, became "first joints," the uncouth thighs were "second joints," and the appellation "cock" was discreetly changed to "rooster." That most egregious of terms, "sex," became "cover," "flourish," "leap," "roger" and "thrum," and was usually enjoyed only by fallen women, also known as "bunters," "doxies," "mothers," "nuns" or "sewing women." To be pregnant was to "get caught" or "be unwell." Even a person's features, according to historian Barbara Clark Smith, were thought to reflect inner values. A small mouth bespoke the lack of strong passion, while narrow shoulders were deemed unfit for leadership.

Such verbal inhibitions led to humorous connections, such as one particularly laughable situation observed by the sprightly Mollie Dorsey Sanford, whose suitor of the day, a "black-eyed lawyer from Nebraska City," had encountered a rattlesnake on his way to pay a call. Agitated, yet still too modest to name the snake's most vulgar parts, he blurted out the adventure in detail, describing the snake right down to its "t-a-i-l."

Equally indirect were Victorian love letters—flirty and provocative, sometimes inspired, often insipid, but always imbued with an odd brand of honesty as correspondents teased, taunted and occasionally rebuked one another by mail, without fear of confrontation. James Alvin Bell ventured in writing what he surely would never confide in person to his fiancée, Augusta Anna Hallock Ellicott, or "Gusta." Musing about other women while stationed in the army in Illinois, 1855, he complained: "There is no girls here and you know I CANT get along without them."

When his luck turned, Gusta was the first to be informed that two "fine [girls]" had paid him a visit. "OH DEAR how I carried on," he chortled in one of his hundred-odd letters to his sweetheart. "I think I shall return the[ir] call tomorrow night."

Nor was he alone in his cavalier attitude. Love letters often spoke of "making love" in kittenish, playful terms divorced from sexual content. "Those . . . summer EYES when by our favorite stream we stood," sighed James Alvin Bell to Gusta, signing the letter "your little deer," in oddly-penned missives written in the trenches during the Civil War. Those seeking emotional breakthroughs employed pure, Victorian bathos, charging each sentiment with the tense emotions of a Greek tragedy. "Oh! How often & deeply have I lacerated & torn afresh the wounds in his heart," lamented Lorena Hays, regretting her treatment of her fiancé, Clement.

Couples also turned to literature, quoting Emerson, Longfellow and James Russell Lowell, often cadging favorite verses to pass off as their own. The ability to select, memorize and recite

Officers' quarters, Fort Bridger, Wyoming
(Wyoming State Museum)

popular poetry was the height of sophistication; to claim authorship was a gaucherie, but only if discovered. Tiny booklets were even sold especially for cribbing, causing British traveler Isabella Bird to scorn the "mosaic of unacknowledged quotations" found in love letters in general, and specifically, in the plagiarized ramblings of a young man she met in Colorado, whose "long pieces of published poetry," she complained, were "twenty lines copied from 'Paradise Lost.'"

Victorians had the ability to spin away hours in idle gaming, playing "balancing coins" or "Mansion of Happiness"—trying to attain ultimate virtue through a maze of vices such as audacity, cruelty, immodesty or ingratitude. The losers would forfeit freedom but would win, if all went well, a kiss.

"We encourage no such thing as 'tongue sandwiches,'" wrote young Flora McCune in 1875, as she mused about propriety and intimacy during part of a self-composed and, presumably, self-imposed list of "Rules and Bylaws" of courtship she composed with her best friend. On paper, the two young women staunchly rejected "hugging, kissing or *any* other *nonsense.*" Like most Victorians, they either endorsed or invented rules to govern nearly all of life's events, from tennis to courtship, which created a rigid, obedient and dramatically repressed society.

Such repression, in fact, was best reflected in courtship patterns and wedding prohibitions that had accrued during the mid-years of American urbanization, from around 1860. The frontier practice of marrying quickly, marrying young and marrying without permission gave way to stricter prohibitions. Chaperones were sought; formal courtship periods included courtship letters, which served as a bellwether for serious suitors, determined to wait a year or more before marriage or until they knew one another's hearts.

Like a knight errant, the Victorian suitor, with gleaming mustaches, padded shoulders and hat in hand, was swept up in a mania of "calling" on marriageable girls at a rate that could occupy every day of the week. A hopeful family would announce its address and visiting time, only to find the porch filled with unknown young men, gloves and calling cards in hand, ready to be fed and fussed over under the guise of meeting a marriageable young woman. In reality, such calls were a bachelor's mealtime, in which a day's worth of dining was enjoyed without obligation as he sampled their way from door to door. The custom began to change by the 1880s; hungry young men were no longer as welcome. According to popular social manuals, men were expected to "retain gloves upon the hand during the call" in honor of the fifteen-minute time limit. Also, a well-bred man would *never* dispose of his hat on a chair, but hold it in hand at all times—a sign of readiness and control. After all, if a man could not tend his own hat for an evening, how would he manage a wife?

Further, there loomed the question of engagement. At times this commitment between Victorian youth seemed oddly playful—a promise made lightly and often broken—particularly if the match was not publicized by banns, sealed with a ring or broadcast by wedding invitations. A ring could mean "forever" or could be as casually taken as a lark.

Likewise, when the flirtatious and popular Martha Farnsworth finally agreed to wed a persistent suitor, no one was shocked—they knew her fickle ways and fully understood her statement of intent: "I'll just tell him alright, it is a go," she decided. "It will be easy enough to get out of it again."

Those interested in permanency, or in slowing down the process, would post wedding banns—official announcements that were "published" for "three weeks or three public days," according to an early directive, so that the community could observe and approve before a final commitment. In the South, the list of applicants for marriage licenses hung next to the criminal court cases on the county clerk's door, sparking daily neighborhood speculation upon whose fate would be happier, and whose worse.

Scrutiny was demanded, since a woman's reputation hung in the balance and her future also rested upon her husband's success. Few wished to find themselves in the position of Lorena Hays, who, by her account, became "married, rather unexpectedly, in church, owing to some misunderstanding taking place between self and Husband."

Those unwilling or unable to wed might turn to cohabitation—scandalous behavior for the times. Harriet Levy, a young Jewish girl in San Francisco, described the shock with which her mother heard the request of an unwed couple for bed and board. "But they aren't married!" the matron cried, eventually relenting because the pair were actors, members of the Tivoli opera house and part of a theatrical population so morally delinquent that behavioral expectations simply could not be applied.

Intimate behavior foundered continually upon the shoals of respectability, polite society or not. Nineteenth-century Americans were endlessly caught up in moral vagaries as they tried to cut a reasonable course through life, which included the difficult, nearly unmentionable area of sexuality, in which a question lingered: Would a lady enjoy sexual congress? And if she did, was she still a lady?

Physician William Acton thought not. "The majority of women are not much troubled with sexual feeling of any kind," he maintained, although his opinion was soundly refuted by numbers of middle-class women who had never before confided their deepest thoughts, but who responded with surprising candor in the Mosher Report, one of the most extraordinary studies to come out of the nineteenth century. Conducted by a female medical student, Celia Mosher, the study revealed the true thoughts of a select group of married middle-class women on sexuality as well as their intimate relationships with their husbands.

The 650 pages of "spidery handwritten questionnaires" present an interesting dichotomy. Gently reared Victorian women who blushed furiously at the least sexual innuendo, who were so repressed that "female" ailments were mentioned to a male physician only by means of a rag doll, confessed feelings of deep longing and desire for their husbands, as well as confessing to the terrible hardships imposed upon them by life and marriage. To draw parallels of family perspective, health, and marital happiness, they were asked to describe their mothers and grandmothers. One woman's grandmother was remembered as "Hysterical in early life. Good since," while another saw both herself and her mother "flying into 40,000 pieces in a minute." Most poignant were descriptions of married intimacy.

Q: "Do you sleep with your husband?"

A: "Yes," said one woman, "I know of no reason for not doing so, and prefer company at night."

A: "Yes, when he is at home. I sleep much better and feel altogether more comfortable. The first year in [our marriage] I had a separate bed, believing that was the right thing: but I abandoned it entirely before the end of the year."

A: "Yes, because of companionship and not wanting to be separated."

The Mosher Report revealed that within marriage, women had begun to question the imperative to bear children, understood there were contraceptives other than luck, abstinence, withdrawal or prolonged nursing, and had a sophisticated awareness of the range of choices available.

American women married young, and their additional years of childbearing contributed to a burgeoning population whose numbers multiplied quickly, compared with the European population. As families grew, women sought methods to prevent pregnancy, knowing the dangers to health and family stability that lay in excess childbearing. By 1870, books on family limitation had been widely circulated, with one, Dr. Frederick Hollick's *The Marriage Guide*, reprinted three hundred times in twenty-five years. In 1800, a married couple might have borne seven children; in 1825, six; and by 1850, with northern women leading the decline, the average was five, according to historian Daniel Scott Smith. Across the land, economic and educational considerations were beginning to pare down family size, utilizing a number of preventatives, from folk to science. A minister visited Denver in 1869 and was utterly shocked to find contraceptives advertised in every newspaper. Called "unnatural resolutions," such preparations included water douching, the use of mysterious "syringes,"

pastille suppositories, cocoa butter and cold water rinses or warm water and borax.

Contraceptives were sought by women of all ranks—some who wished to avoid bearing children because it would mar their figures, or others, more socially inclined, who wished to avoid committing a "crime against future children" because they were unwilling, thus unfit, parents. To control family size was to master destiny. To help the woman in such management were a host of publications, among which the *Ladies Magazine* was an instant success. Initially written by teachers, it referred to men as "the grosser sex," to be managed only with luck, pluck, and constant vigilance.

Prolonged nursing was the first, and simplest contraceptive choice; Dr. A. M. Mauriceau, a professor of diseases of women, recommended "half an ounce of a strong decoction of red oak bark . . . thrown into the vagina by means of a female syringe, two or three times a day." Others purchased unnamed nostrums sold commercially, whose discreet label, "Do not drink in the event of pregnancy," actually meant "Take in order to miscarry." For those who rejected flax seed injections, cooling cathartics, milk diets and cold baths, or the habit of swallowing gunpowder, port wine or balsam, there were the ubiquitous "rubber goods," oiled silk shields and the mysterious "French Preventatives" for men, while women applied sponges, a diaphragm called "The Wife's Protector" or syringes filled with alum or sulfates of zinc or iron, only rudimentary protection. Women also used pessaries, or "pissers," which, according to historian John d'Emelio, were considered both female preventatives and supports; they were technologically sound, lightweight and expandable wood or waxed linen interior devices that lent inner support to the womb, solving that entity's persistent habit of "falling" in upon itself. Inner protection, it was believed, would also solve exterior problems.

Until the passage of the Comstock Act of 1873, which forbade indecent advertising, women could turn to "confidential" mail-order medical pamphlets concerning their "many interesting complaints," found in the popular book *Psychological View of Marriage,* by a Dr. LaCroix, 1885.

Others, of a more practical nature, followed the earthy advice of Rose Williams imparted to her pregnant friend, Lettie Mosher: "Well plague take it," Williams remonstrated. "You . . . sleep in one bed and your Man in another." Failing that, Rose must "ask for a female preventative," as they only cost a dollar and came with directions.

Failing such measures, abortions still took place on a regular basis, facilitated by abortifacients such as tansy, fresh roots, hot baths or even the arcane application of rusty-nail water or a silver probe. The specter of the female abortionist, so defamed in newspapers in the east, was in a country setting a reassuring fixture—usually a "healing" woman whose skills turned to midwifery with ease. Rural women would often gather at sewing bees or quilting parties and, in veiled terms, discuss the efficacy of one method over another. "I am so glad no more children for me," confided forty-five-year-old Emily French, a day laborer in Colorado, whose friend was sick in bed after "an operation to rid her of a 2 month fetus." Such candor is rare in diaries and journals, yet is often alluded to in books, periodicals and newspapers of the day. As women spun and carded, knitted, stitched and canned, part of the lore traded back and forth came from the knowledge that, from one house to the next, motherless children and early graves were all-too-frequent reminders that childbirth was often synonymous with maternal death.

Yet despite suffocating controls, the nineteenth century flourished as a period of intense romantic love, in which poetry, dress and popular literature were touched by artistry and passion, as well as the usual repression. Weddings were steeped in romantic

Nuptial celebration
(California Museum of Photography, Keystone-Mast Collection)

excess. Cakes were baked in pans lined with geranium leaves and topped with a miniature bride and groom, accompanied by another, more private pastry, the bride's cake, filled with trinkets and favors representing the sweetness of matrimony—to be cut and served only to the bridesmaids. As noted by writer Jacki Whitford, the white wedding cake was unknown until after the Civil War, when fine white flour, baking soda and powder were more easily obtained.

Bride's Loaves

Nine cupfuls of butter, five pints of sugar, four quarts of flour, five dozen eggs, seven pounds of currants, three and a half of citron, four of shelled almonds, seven of raisins, one and a half pints of brandy, two ounces of mace. Bake in a moderate oven for two hours or more. This will make eight loaves, which will keep for years.

—MARIA PAROLA, NEW COOK BOOK, 1880

Wedding Cake of 1850

20 pounds butter	20 nutmegs
20 pounds sugar	1 ounce mace
20 pounds flour	4 ounces cinnamon
20 pounds raisins	20 glasses brandy
40 pounds currants	10 eggs to the pound
10 pounds citron	

Add cloves to your taste. If you wish it richer, add 2 pounds of currants and 1 pound of raisins to each pound of flour.

—THE CAROLINA HOUSEWIFE, CHARLESTON, 1850

Bride
(Library of Congress)

JOHN THORNBURN

On a visit to Scotland, John Thornburn fell in love with and married the beautiful Isabella Marshall, after which the couple settled in St. Louis. Writing in 1889, he described his high-born in-laws, viewing their request that he draw up a marriage license as quaintly un-American—although he acceded. The following account is Thornburn's view of the wedding ceremony.

Well, the time came. Minister on hand, Brides maides 3 of them and Grooms also 3 of them—all ready. The call was for Ladies to come down to Parlour. Now comes the climax—I walked the floor to the end of the room with my 3 Aid de Comps . . .

I followed behind my [bride] [whose] long blond lace veil [hung] over her head just so much that I could catch a glimpse of those deep black eyes, that cut me once to the Quick.

What . . . was my feelings as this Critical Moment to be ready to Answer to the Questions Put by the Minister?

Why, I just put my Eyes on a Figure of the Brussells Carpet on the Floor as he went on with his Questions Just pictureing in my mind how many Movements the Shuttle that Wove the Carpet made.

[I] finish the Figure in the carpet.

[Then] the awfull sound came—Join hands.

The Grooms Man grasped my hand to get first glove off as a Bet was made between the Ladies Maid and my Man Maid.

And then—I pronounce you Man & Wife.

Oh—Just to think what next came for me to do, was to give a Good Kiss to my Bride

Lord what a Kiss it was
Such a kiss.

In the effort I drew Such a Breath, it busted my Waiste Coat in the effort, and the Bride's cheeck became of such a rosy red hugh that I thought I had bit her . . .

So all over. Went and sit down on sofa—our two dear selves were so elated in our Happy Feelings that we . . . just filled the sofa. Our dear hearts . . . expanded so wide we *filled the Sofa*. Me thought to myself—I was [like] a Noble Turkey, as they strut and swell out their Breast, as proud as Proud Could be . . .

Stranger, go and follow me [in marriage] & you then can feel for your self.

But it must be True Love, or you cant swell out as I did.

Well, [the] Company came up. Ladies wishing all the Joy possible and a kiss. Next came the Gents, my Uncle kissed my [bride], but says this [is] the 1st and the last.

Miss Mildred Hadley, Evanston, Illinois
(State Historical Society of North Dakota)

FRANK CUSHING

Frank Cushing, a recently married man, wrote to his good friend George Vernon about the bliss of the wedded state. Cushing's candor concerning newlywed life was in keeping with the habits of the "romanticized" new male—one who could pen love lyrics with little ado and still be viewed as manly by his peers.

HOME. 2 O'CLOCK IN THE MORNING—
Sena is away and I am alone in the house. She went to Medina last Monday and I shall join her there in about two weeks. It is needless to say that I am horribly lonely. I believe I told you in my last letter that I was ready for any inquiries as to the success of my marriage experiment. Other men may have had as sweet, attractive and loveable wives as mine but [it] cannot seem possible.

I have been married now almost a year and I have not only been as happy as I expected but happy beyond all my expectations. I never knew or imagined before how much a loving woman could add to one's life. I used to think that perhaps in the wear and tear of everyday existence the freshness of romance would be rubbed off, and that it would come to be a sort of commonplace, matter-of-course thing. But I underestimated the power of one woman—well as I thought I knew her—to charm and fascinate me. After the lapse of a year her love is as sweet and thrilling to me as it was on the day of our wedding and my love for her has only grown in depth and intensity as the months have passed.

Nothing has occurred and not a word has been spoken by either of us since our wedding, which I can look back at with the faintest regret or which I would wish to have been otherwise.

She has always been what I always supposed her to be—a loving, generous, noble girl, patient with my moods, quick with intelligent sympathy, perfectly unselfish and full of charming, half laughing, teasing ways, which give spice to companionship but which at the same time, veil a world of deeper tenderness. I have never for a moment tired of her and I don't know how I ever can. Even now, after a year of almost unbroken companionship, I cannot take her in my arms without a faster beating of the heart —without a quick, passionate impulse to hold her close to me and smother her with impetuous kisses.

She is attractive to me in every way. Not only does she, by her character, command my deepest respect, and by her womanly dependence upon me awaken all the latent tenderness of my nature, but she wins from me by her sweet personal attractiveness the most ardent and passionate love of which I am capable. She responds with quick, loving comprehension to my every mood.

I have known women who were more beautiful than she in the beauty of regular features, more brilliant in natural intellectual endowments, more learned in the learning which consists in the acquisition of facts, but never one who ignites so much passion and depth of feeling and warm, loving tenderness as she does.

Her character appeals to and quickens all that is best in my nature while her womanly beauty has a physical charm and fascination which makes her simple presence a delight, and which I can only describe to you by saying it constantly impels me to touch her, to take her in my arms and to hold her more and more closely to me in the sensuous enjoyment (in the good sense of the word) of her personal attractiveness.

I wouldn't write in this way to you, my boy, if I didn't *know* that you would feel as I do the half sacredness of a man's earnest love for a pure and loving woman. Neither would I dare to write you so if I had not been married long enough to be reasonably sure of what I say.

Unidentified couple ("Cities" Collection, National Archives)

In the honeymoon, it is natural that a man should be ardently in love with his wife and he is expected to think her only a little lower than an angel. But the illusion rarely outlasts the first six months. At the end of a year, at any rate, I think a man generally has a very settled and well-grounded conviction with regard to the results of his matrimonial venture.

I have talked with you a good deal about love and marriage and that must be my excuse for giving you at such length the history of my own matrimonial experience. It may all be summed up perhaps by saying that I love my wife, body and soul, more tenderly, ardently and passionately now than I did when I first held her in my arms as my wife, eleven months ago.

EMILY FRENCH

Emily French eloped with her first husband, Marsena H. French, when she was fifteen years old. After six children and a marriage of thirty-one years, the two were divorced, and references to him in Emily's journal turn to phrases such as "awful mean old fellow" and "old rascal." Marsena married a younger woman and Emily— stooped, graying and bone-tired from "working out" as a domestic—teetered between despondency and a deep craving for love. Divorce had freed her from human oppression but created a new, financial burden that was eased only with help from her women friends.

Although she finally married one of three bachelors who "came calling," this segment of her diary, postdating that marriage, serves as a useful bridge between her old life and the new.

MARCH, THURSDAY 6, 1890
I am decided to go to work . . . selling books. I must do something to earn my liveing, that old rascal has robbed us both of nearly all, and I am in such poor health.

MARCH, SUNDAY 9, 1890
Got up, had a good break—then cleaned up to go to hear a sermon by Rev. Self. He is a well meaning man if he is a Presbeterian . . .

MARCH, MONDAY 10, 1890
I carried my two sets of teeth to the express office, sent to Dr.

Drury to mend. I have such luck with under teeth, I dont see what I will do with them.

APRIL, THURSDAY 17, 1890
We love him because he 1st loved us

Mrs. Boston . . . lives next door, had her baby in her arms—little does she know that he [her husband] is so unfaithful to her—I saw her when she was first married. She has had twin boys and lost them since then.

APRIL, FRIDAY 18, 1890
I went & got a powder box & puff for baby, cost $1.50—I have so little money but I am always giveing. . . . I took good care of Anna, the baby is a little treasure.

APRIL, THURSDAY 24, 1890
The Lord is good to all! and his tender mercies are over all his creatures.

Mr. Currier came home, he cannot work, it is snowing, so he has a chance to buy a house fo $40.00.

APRIL, FRIDAY 25, 1890
I came home to find Mr. Tomlinson there, he is very attentive for some reason . . .

MAY, SATURDAY 3, 1890
Wayne Tomlinson came, staid till 12, we had fun playing old maid.

MAY, MONDAY 5, 1890
The heart grows weary when want stares us in the face, so little to get breakfast, what will I do, nothing to encourage me in my work, all wrong, up late, cooked some potatoes, made milk, gravy & old tea.

MAY, FRIDAY 9, 1890
Went to Mrs. Shirell to clean, now I can begin to pay my honest debts again. I worked all day hard, I got a lunch at 11, cider, bread, cheese, blackberries . . . Ida got supper, greens, roast pork, tea, potatoes mashed, rye bread, jelle cake, Doughnuts, so good. I can work better when I have something to eat . . .

MAY, SUNDAY 11, 1890
Wayne [another suitor] here at 9, he likes to come here for some reason . . .

MAY, THURSDAY 15, 1890
I eat my breakfast with Mrs. Bulan, she suffers so from the drunkeness of the men, nothing does them but beer all the while.

JUNE, MONDAY 9, 1890
Will the man I hold dear come soon, I wate with hope & fear both intermingled. God knows I am waiting, he has not come, what can be wrong, perhaps all for the best.

JUNE, TUESDAY 10, 1890
I washed the Star quilt that Annis gave me for a gift on my 45th birthday . . . I am waiting, *will he come,* yes, this night ever to be a remembrance in my poor life, yes, I am his promised wife, he shall be a husband chosen, I am happy.

JUNE, WEDNESDAY 11, 1890
Behold I make all things new
And I can scarcely contain the thought, am I realy loved for the first time in my life—I so craved it now it is mine pure and true. I do try not to be foolish, I am in a new life.

JUNE, THURSDAY 12, 1890
Being dead to sin, we put on the new.

He came again to night, *why*. Can I be contended (sic) with *him, yes*. I sat waiting for the 1 of all to me, Mr. John Lawson came, we were so happy for three hours but we must part, he to go to his mines, I to Annis.

JUNE, TUESDAY 17, 1890
John . . . has the key to my house & to my heart, how I seem to care for him, will he be true, I seem to trust him since the 10 of June—I love as I never thought I should . . .

JULY, WEDNESDAY 9, 1890
A letter from John at last, not one word of love or anything to seem he cares for me. He signs his name yours verry truy. I must, I will see what this means as sure as I shall live.

JULY, THURSDAY 17, 1890
Went down . . . to see if I cannot get a place in Denver to go out to work, tried every thing, 7 places, then the Employ offices . . . A Mr. Jamieson there from Buffalo Park hired me as Cook $35.00 month, can I stand it?

JULY, FRIDAY 18, 1890
She hath done what she could

I washed out my cloths, I am bad in my periods these days . . . Such a strange life is mine. I got my buggy greased at the mountain nook, a nice place among the pines. Got Fanny shod at Evergreen, another Mountain town by Bear Creek, a nice Church where god shall be housed.

JULY, FRIDAY 25, 1890
Thou wilt show me the path of life

As I was working Oh so hard, here come My John—Why do I love him so much? I see something is not right, he wants to see me, I shall now be careful, I *must*. Can it be someone else has a claim on him? I can give him up but *oh dear*. Had Mrs. Netherly tell my fortune, she told it true, said I was to have trouble with a dark haired woman, yes . . . Here is John.

JULY, SATURDAY 26, 1890
There is a way that seemeth right to a man

Mr. Netherly over in town trying to have his wife give up to live with him. She declares she will not unless he will stay sober. He is bound to try, so they made it up, the children so pleased.

JULY, TUESDAY 29, 1890
I should like to see John but he seems to act so queer

AUGUST, WEDNESDAY 6, 1890
God will supply all our needs

A man, Joe Mayer, brought 3 shirts this morning for me to wash. I cut my finger, will I get enough to do? I feel lonely to night, will this be so long, I do so crave love . . . I did dream of John last night, he met me on the stairs. I cannot, must not forget this dream, how I talked & planned on the stairs.

AUGUST, THURSDAY 7, 1890
What think ye of Christ

I wrote to dear John, will I hear soon? Oh how lonely is my life to me, I deserve better things.

AUGUST, TUESDAY 12, 1890
I got up early at Kelleys to wash for her . . . Dr. Bradley & wife in their buggy from Buena Vista Col, she has just lost her baby, 5 weeks old.

OCTOBER, TUESDAY 14, 1890

Mrs. Rodgers made no change in her supper, she dont care what or who. How I do wish I had a little of what she wastes.

OCTOBER, WEDNESDAY 29, 1890

Fried some apples. Mrs. Bertha Mauck . . . called me an adventuress, I could not reason [why] one bit.

NOVEMBER, SUNDAY 9, 1890

I never combed my hair or sat down all day. I lay, for I am not feeling well enough to get up, yet I must. I come unwell last night, I am verry bad of late, my age, must be. I am so glad no more babies for me . . .

DECEMBER, THURSDAY 4, 1890

Sorted old letters, Dannie saw so many of his fathers dear expressions it will last him all the rest of his life, such lying & dissembling, has been all his mean life since I ever knew him . . .

John is not mentioned again in her diary.

MARY ACKLEY

Mary Medley Ackley crossed the plains in April 1852, arriving in Sacramento disconsolate from the death of her mother, who was stricken by typhoid along the trail and buried there, among a cluster of wild roses. Mary resumed school at the age of ten and married at the age of fifteen, typical of many young girls. Her observations about gold-boom humanity include the following event, showing a wife's unspoken dependence upon her husband.

An Irish woman and two daughters lived just across the street from us. Her husband had been killed . . . in a quarrel. She was respectable and good-hearted, but a great, high-tempered woman without any judgment.

Wide West street was just a gulch, and when it rained the water came roaring down the gulch in a ditch back of the woman's house. The ditch was clogged up and the first rain afterward cut a ditch in front of her house.

She insisted that the town authorities should have it attended to, but as it was not done she became angry and said she would turn the water into the street. She got some Indians to help her and they dammed the ditch in front of her house, causing the water to flow into the street. She worked like a trooper and was very much excited. A big pile of rock was on our property. She sent an Indian to get some rocks, but my husband refused to allow the Indian to take any, which enraged her so she wanted to go right over and whip him; but she said she had too much respect for his wife and, anyway, he was too little.

A young man was sent up from downtown to stop her from

turning the water into the street. She hit him with a shovel and he left. I knew she was getting herself into trouble, so I went over to her and said, "You have shown them what you can do, but you have gone far enough. I would be sorry to see you arrested, and I could not prevent it." She commenced to cry, said her husband was dead, and she had no one to advise her.

She stopped at once, and the street was not injured. Had she spent the same energy in cleaning out the ditch behind her house, all would have been well.

Working girl
(University of Washington Library, Seattle)

ELLEN COILE GRAVES

"My punishment I think has paid for my indiscretion..."
—ELLEN COILE GRAVES

Ellen was one of the "new" women of the nineteenth century who believed that love should both precede and preside in marriage—her lukewarm feelings toward her husband finally driving her to desertion. She fled to Philadelphia and opened a "variety and trimmings" store while he sued for divorce. His belief that she would grow to love him was finally conceded to her greater need for freedom and romance.

NOVEMBER 16TH, 1841
COPY OF THE MARRIAGE CERTIFICATE:

To all persons whom it concerns that on this day above written in the City of Philadelphia and Commonwealth of Pennsylvania, Henry B. Graves of the one part, and Ellen Coyle [throughout official documents she is listed as "Coyle" yet signs her own name as "Coile"] of the other having agreed and consented to live together as Man and Wife, and having plighted the solemn vow of Duty and Appreciation, were by me united in the honourable and sacred bonds of Lawful Marriage.

Signed,
JOHN B. HUGANY
PASTOR OF ST. GEORGE,
M.E. CHURCH OF PHILADELPHIA

Nov. 1, 1844
To the Hon: Thomas J. Bell,
President Judge of the Court of Common Pleas
of the County of Chester,

THE LIBEL OF HENRY B. GRAVES . . .
[who was] . . . married to a certain Ellen Coyle (now Ellen G. Graves) and from that time until the fifteenth day of September A.D. 1842 lived and cohabited with the said Ellen as her husband . . . yet so it is that the said Ellen hath wilfully and maliciously deserted and absented herself from the habitation of this libellant without any just or reasonable cause and such desertion hath persisted for the term of two years and upwards and yet doth continue to absent herself from the said libellant—Wherefore your libellant . . . prays your honor . . . to summon the said Ellen C. Graves to appear in this said honourable court . . . to answer the complaint aforesaid, and also that . . . this honourable court may be moved to divorcing her . . . from the . . . fellowship and company of this libellant in all time to come and this libellant from the marriage bond aforesaid as if he had never been married or as if the said Ellen were naturally dead.

And he will be
HENRY B. GRAVES

The divorce proceeds . . .

HENRY B. GRAVES V. ELLEN C. GRAVES
Interrogations to be administered to witnesses who may be . . . affirmed and examined on the part of the Libellant:

Three witnesses are summoned by the Respondent, Henry Graves, to testify if they know the divorcing parties, were present at the marriage, had knowledge of the divorcing couple's marriage and cohabitation, and can offer an opinion upon Ellen's desertion. Thus queried were Ellen's fifteen-year-old sister, Mary Jane, her employer at the variety store, and an employee of Henry Graves.

NOVEMBER 1ST, 1844
Sarah Jane Coile, a witness produced on the part of the Libellant being sworn in due form:
I am the sister of the Respondent. I have known her as long as I can remember anybody. I just became acquainted with Libellant when he was visiting my sister, previous to their marriage, in the City of Philadelphia & I afterwards resided for sometime in his family in . . . Chester County . . .

I was present at the marriage of Libellant and Respondent. They were married at my mother's house . . . by the Rev. John B. Hageny . . . They lived and cohabited together as man and wife from the time they were married until the period of their separation. The next morning after their marriage they moved to Phoenixville in Chester County where he was engaged in business and immediately went to housekeeping . . .

About a month after their marriage I went out to Phoenixville and stayed . . . in their family for a period of about ten weeks. I then returned to the city & remained there for some time & afterwards visited their house again at Phoenixville where I remained about four weeks. Respondent then deserted the house of the Libellant and in company with me went to our mother's house in the city. At the time of her desertion . . . she declared that she never would live with Libellant again Respondent left the Libellant at his own habitation when she went away without any one to keep house for him or in any way to attend to his domestic concerns.

I know of no reasonable cause for her leaving the house of her husband. She said she thought that she could not live happily with him—that was the reason she gave for leaving him. I know of no bad usage on his part towards her—the complaints [were] only that she had no affection for him . . .

Several times since her desertion [he] tried to persuade the Respondent to live . . . with him again. The first time he called for that purpose was on the 1st day of January 1843 . . . [She] stated that she would never live with him again . . .

He has called . . . several times since her desertion to endeavor to persuade the Respondent to live and cohabit with him again. The first time he called for that purpose was on the 1st day of January 1843. In response . . . she said that no, never would she live with him again and then gave him in substance the same answer in every interview afterwards. The last time he called upon her to get her to come & live with him again was five or six months ago . . . She still persisted in her refusal in as strong terms as ever to live with him again. I saw a letter which the Respondent received from Libellant . . . in which he offers to receive her again & strongly urged upon her to come & live with him—he stated that he had commenced proceedings for a divorce but that he would be glad to drop them if she would accede to his request.

On the Sunday following she wrote in reply this letter:

PHILADELPHIA. OCT. 13, 1844
Henry,
I received your letter and in compliance with your request I send you this answer stating my feelings toward yourself   I thought that you was fully acquainted with me to know that you had no cause to imagine that I had for a moment entertained a thought of returning to you   it would be impossible for us to live peaceble together after what has occured and in connection with my feelings towards yourself which is that of perfect coldness   I do not and could not love you   I am not one of those lukewarm creatures who can bestow their affections upon all alike where they please   my affections spring spontaneously   I cannot compel myself to love where there is no congeniality of feeling   I did wrong very wrong in marrying you without feeling or sincere attachment but I believed you was capable of attaching me to you by kind and affectionate treatment   you encouraged me in this belief for you was not deceived in this respect when I married you it was with the full determination of loving you which I beleived to be An easy task   I was mistaken I tried for three months as ardently as ever woman tried but each day devolved something calculated to turn me from you rather than win me to you   I gave up the task for I found it impossible my punishment I think has paid for my indiscretion

I am sorry that you still love me and I trust that this letter will prove effectual in removing your unfortunate attachment   for beleive me that by me it can never be returned and now let me remove every false hope by solemnly assuring you that you and I parted forever in this World it is better that I should speak thus plainly than that you should encourage hopes that will only bring you disappointment   I wish you well sincerely from the bottom of my Heart I should be glad to hear that you was Happyly Married and successful in your Bussiness mother sends her Love to you and the Family   give my love to them likewise and

Beleive me I am you Frend
Ellen Coile

Sarah Ann Hummelwright:

I have known the Respondent about four years. . . . A few weeks before the Respondent let the Libellant she wrote me a letter in which she expressed a determination to leave her husband. She accordingly left him and [then] . . . set up a variety and trimming store. She abandoned this business after being engaged in it for sometime & entered the store of a Mr. Friar as a saleswoman in the City of Philadelphia. During the months that she lived in

West Chester she was in my employ as a Milliner. While she was in my employ I heard her say frequently that she would never live with Libellant again . . .

I reside in this place and keep a fancy store. I am about twenty four years of age.

NOVEMBER 6TH 1844

Job Taylor:

I am a witness produced on the part of the Libellant . . . In September 1842 I lived in [their] family. I worked for Libellant who was then engaged in the manufacture of soap and candles. I boarded with him from August 1842 until the following Spring when I . . . set up business for myself. The respondent left the house of the Libellant on the 15th of September 1842 . . . The day before she left I heard [her say] that she would never come back again & that he need not expect her to come back . . . Libellant asked her if she would be willing to live with him any other place if he would remove from Phoenixville—she said she did not know but that she never would live with him in Phoenixville. [He] . . . asked [her] if she would not come back again to see her friends. I think she replied that she wished to see them . . . but she did not know if she would come back again. He asked her if she would not write to him when she got to the City & let him know how she was getting along . . . she said she didn't know that she should—that she didn't care about writing to him & didn't care how he was getting along . . .

The last conversation I had with the Respondent was in the fall of 1842 when she departed the habitation of her husband & left for Philadelphia . . .

MAIMIE PINZER

"I was honest and asserted myself and refused to fawn . . ."
—MAIMIE PINZER

Maimie Pinzer, born in 1885, lived off and on in Philadelphia and corresponded with a mentor, Mrs. Fanny Quincy Howe, over a twelve-year period. In her letters, she reveals a troubled childhood, years of self-support as a prostitute, a failed marriage to Albert, who lived unsuspectingly on her "ugly" earnings yet lied to her about his own income. In overcoming the loss of an eye, possibly from syphilis, and a strong addiction to morphine, Maimie achieved a brutal honesty uncharacteristic of women of her time. She thrived on "differences of opinion," freely alienated relatives, yet was swayed instantly into lavish charity at the least sign of oppression or need. In 1915 she divorced Albert to remarry, and founded the Montreal Mission, a house of rehabilitation and security for young prostitutes.

WALNUT STREET, PHILADELPHIA
MAY OR JUNE, 1911 . . .

Albert went to Atlantic City to procure work, and was successful; and I have been here alone for two weeks. Saturday night he came home . . . and I don't know what possessed me—the "Old Nick" or what—but I came out in the open with him; and instead of keeping up this silly subterfuge . . . I was open and aboveboard. He heard the truth for the first time in five years—and it sent him packing. [She informed him that the money they have lived on has come from prostitution.] I am a "widow-woman" now, and

Women playing billiards (Library of Congress)

the aspect does not seem so alarming. Why should I persist in living with him? When I married him, I knew exactly what for—it was as a sort of anchor. I was living more or less uncleanly; I had lost my eye, and weighed ninety-six pounds, which at that time I seemed to think was the end of all my attractiveness; I was mentally very low, and I reasoned it all out as one would a business proposition. I saw that he was not blessed with much gray matter and that he was in awe of me, and I intended to always keep him that way. I didn't imagine there was much chance of marrying the sort of a man I could love, for with the loss of my eye, I thought I had lost everything—which I found a mistake, for since I have been married, I could have married, had I been single, one of three men who have proposed to me, not knowing I was married, and any one of them were gentlemen born, and all with considerable money. Prior to Albert's proposal, I had never had a man ask to marry me. Of course, I was only nineteen years past when I went to the hospital; and all of three years I was sick; and then prior to going to the hospital, I lived almost four years with one man . . . When . . . I began to see that I was still attractive to men, I began to use what charms I might Possess to make it possible to have a few of the luxuries which had become necessities . . . To [Albert] I explained that things cost less, and that Brother sent me this, and Sister sent me that, and Uncle the other things. And when I wanted to go on a trip, I'd concoct some fairy tale about a position in another city . . .

Outside of using him as a cloak, I had absolutely no reason to live with him whatever. He doesn't utter over ten words a day . . . and they are generally about: where is such and such a thing? If you ask him to do anything, it is as good as done . . . so I also benefited by having a sort of general servant. Then, may I speak of something else? I will try to make you understand: As for any relation that might exist because of the fact that we were man and wife, he did not interest me at all; so whenever it was necessary, I went almost frantic, although he never knew it.

When Mr. Welsh started to interest himself in me [Mr. Welsh was the social worker who helped Maimie leave the life of prostitution] I wrote him just what Albert had meant to me, and when I ceased living immorally I could see no use in living further with Albert. [Paragraphing added]

I must say, I did never think if I left him, that he would care much, for he was such a phlegmatic person that he would accept it . . . and he would go on as he [had]. For really I wasn't with him more than four months in the year, for on some pretext or other, I'd get away. I'd have gone mad if I had to live with him as most wives do with their husbands. . . .

Later, through not knowing just what better to do, I submitted to Albert's suggestion that he come to Phila., which he did while I was in the hospital. While I worked, things were bearable in a measure. But when I had nothing to do, and work for Albert was as hard to be found as the proverbial needle in a haystack, it was agony indescribable to live with him. Of course the fact that I was living decently kept me home with him all the time, and I can't understand how I stood it the entire winter.

So when I went to Atlantic City to work, I caught him at that miserable trick [hoarding his earnings]—and then when he got home that Saturday, his manner was so arrogant and aggressive; and he has spent money which we could ill afford on things which he would not tell me about; and altogether I was thoroughly disgusted, until I ordered him out . . .

Then here I am—and that is all. I haven't looked ahead, and in truth haven't any idea as to what is next, except that I feel like a person who has been ridded of an enormous white elephant that has been sitting astride of my chest. I even breathe more freely. I know you are thinking "What next?"—but there isn't the remotest idea in my mind of the "next," as yet.

PART **VIII** EIGHT

American

Ethnics

THE WEST SEETHED AND ROILED WITH SO MANY TRADI-
tions that at times a carnival sense prevailed. Courtship customs differed dramatically, depending upon race, religion
and region. While Overlanders shouted "Chivaree!" and
rocked a Conestoga wagon back and forth to heckle the newlyweds within, a Cheyenne brave would would lie in wait for his
intended and rush out with a blanket to "kidnap" her briefly for a
quick cuddle. Such "heathen friskiness" was condemned by
Anglo Americans, who were quick to decry Native American
polygamy and bride prices, while overlooking their own tradition
of dowry and, at least with the Mormons, plural wives. A Chinese couple would wed to the tune of ritualized flute music,
changing clothes half a dozen times during the ceremony, appearing as lavish as nobility in their briefly rented gowns.

The Japanese often wed by proxy, with "picture brides" arriving by the boatload to greet the stranger-husbands they had wed
by arrangement, on the basis of letters, photographs and family
urging. The brides were often voiceless in the family-finalized
process of *omai-kekkon,* and could only hope that honesty had
prompted the new spouse to use his own photo, not that of a
more dashing man. "For a woman who was going to a strange
society and relying upon an unknown husband whom she had
married through photographs, my heart had to be as beautiful as
Mount Fuji," wrote one young wife. Just as the bride feared
duplicity and disappointment, Japanese American men feared
spending their lives alone and unmarried, as so many Chinese
workers before them. "To fail in marriage is to fail in life" was a
national motto, and a man without a home and family was without success.

Chinese, Japanese and Native Americans remained culturally
isolated from Caucasian customs, unless Christianized or assimi-
lated by "free union" marriage—as with female Anglo women
who married their Indian captors, or frontier men who shared

common-law lives with Indian or Mexican wives. Also victims of
sexual imperialism: African Americans, held tight in the bosom
of southern plantation life, already eponymized by an owner's
surname, dressed in the owner's castoff clothes, and, in some
cases, married to mates preselected by a profit-minded planter,
who had little choice but to wed in approximate European style,
without benefit of clergy. In a ragged caricature of an Anglo ceremony, they would "jump the broom" to tie the knot, using a
backward hop over a parallel broom to seal the union. Slaves preferred the offices of clergy to a broom, and after emancipation
many who had "jumped" hastened to find a preacher. One ex-
slave, elegantly dressed in white lawn and knit cotton, was officially wed to her long-time spouse with their nine children to
witness. "We sure had a fine time," recalled her daughter. Weddings were part of a cycle of ceremonies that included Sunday
worship, prayer meetings, revivals, Christmas, baptisms, and
funerals—events that helped African Americans to assert the dignity and meaning of their lives beyond the sufferings of slavery.

Hispanic courtship customs were shaped by a Spanish-Indian
culture that remained aloof from Anglo influence, whose customs
dimmed back into time, their origins lost or obscured. One such
was the serenade, a soulful outburst of angelic song that launched
the beginning of tender passion. But the suit was *sin permiso*
unless a delegation of the groom's friends paid a visit to the girl's
family, seeking official approval of the courtship-to-come. The
final stage was the *peticion de la mano,* or asking of the girl's hand,
which took place when the boy's male relatives ritually pleaded
and argued with the girl's male relatives. The reason? To win
family consent to the couple's four-year engagement. Marriages
were matriarchal; to soften the impact of the wife's last name
superseding that of her husband's, names were linked with *de* or
of—the bride was *of* or *from* her mate. Despite the flowery bandi-
age by both sexes, seemingly insincere as it rose and swelled to a

crescendo of mutual praise, Spanish courtliness offered countless opportunities for social blunder. Beneath the puffery lay a rigid framework of expected behavior; suitors knew to quickly stem the chatter when a sweetheart was accompanied by a father or older brother, then to praise emphatically when mothers were near. For the bride's mama, double portions of flattery were an expected courtesy. At times, the air rang with compliments, each more lavish than the last, traded laughingly back and forth until the verbiage became a colorful folk pastime, artful as a song.

For the Hispanic wedding, gifts were lavished by the groom, whose family status and income was mirrored in the shimmer of the fine satins and jewels bestowed upon his bride. These became her wedding raiment, where, deep in veils and hoods, she knelt to receive the lazlo—a rope of wax beads that symbolically bound her to her mate. To sweeten this captive image, she gave the groom a token box of gold-colored coins, or *arras*. Even if "captive" to one another, the coins signified that both would live in comfort, lacking for nothing. Rice, thrown and scattered by ebullient guests, predicted a future rich with income and nourishment and invoked a universal blessing on the newlyweds.

Stories of minorities in the west were tales of suffering and misuse, occasionally—and happily—interrupted by the gentler rituals of love and union.

Sioux Indian portrait (National Archives)

Native Americans

Mogko (Oraibi Pueblo, Arizona)
in traditional Hopi bridal garments, and reed
container for clothing woven by men of
bridegroom's family, 1901 (Photo by
Carl N. Werntz. Museum of New Mexico)

A S WESTBOUND SETTLERS FORGED THROUGH THE grassy plains and mountain sites of early America, members of the 250 or so remaining tribes were routed and ruined, scattered and forced onto bleak reservations to live in life-long alienation and hostile dependency. Feathered spears and tanned hides gave way to an onslaught of powder and steel— symbols of a culture clash so ruthless as to rend apart an entire continent, decimating the buffalo, and depleting a native popula-tion, at least on the West Coast between the years 1848 and 1910, to a mere twenty thousand. Explorer Zeb Pike mused about the "darke and confused" outlook of the Osage, yet seldom did he or others of the Anglo-European world attempt to understand the complex social and spiritual aspects of Native American life, par-ticularly those having to do with courtship, love and marriage.

In many tribes, a dichotomy existed between the inherent strength of Indian women and the belittling terms by which men described them. A Dakota Indian, He-Who-Walks-Galloping-On, told missionary Stephen Riggs of his problem accepting Christianity, as the Church was weak and "made up of women." He added: "If you had gotten [the men] in first, it would have amounted to something. But now there are only women. Who would follow after women?" Such disparagement stopped short within the confines of conjugal privacy, where mutual respect reigned. What husband would alienate the wife in whose hands rested great domestic power, who controlled food preparation and distribution and owned the tent as well? So deep was a husband's private respect that he feared to utter her name. "Life would be short if I call my wife by her name," a Kiowa man said.

Many women with ambition, wit, skill and will qualified as tribal leaders—their hegemony varying within a specific tradi-tion, but who ascended to authority as elders, leaders, shamans and warriors. "One splendid woman," described by Paiute Sarah Winnemucca, "went into the battlefield after her uncle was killed

. . . and took [his] place, as brave as any man." Mohawks recount the bravery of a woman who brought them victory by hurling boiling maple sap into the faces of attacking Algonquins. Iro-quois women became leaders, Navajo and Apache women joined war societies, Menomini women performed the War Dance and joined the Mete-wan, or medicine lodge, while Southern Paiute women occasionally sang in the men's Circle Dance. Often Native American women were wealthy, and like the Navajo could refuse to share their wealth with a spouse. The talents of Pueblo women in architecture proved startling to early Spanish explorers, who found that they not only constructed and plastered their own dwellings, but owned them as well. Fray Alonso de Benavides, visiting New Mexico in 1626, was stunned by architecture both "sumptuous and beautiful," built by "women and boys and girls." By early Spanish standards, Native American women were considered important economic and social entities.

As such, their marriage arrangements were often resolved by the age of fourteen, the courtship centering around mutual appreciation, clan compatibility and the ceremony of gift giving. Without attraction, a couple might plunge into an unlucky or indifferent marriage; without clan compatibility, the marriage might not take place at all; but without selflessness and generos-ity, the entire social framework of tribal life would be threatened. The etiquette of sharing was the cornerstone of an effective and satisfying society, where to bestow was to be esteemed—the opposite of greed and avarice. Generosity linked back through a couple's antecedents, with status determined by how much their parents had given away during their lives. "A man seeking to be a son-in-law is bound to cater . . . or make presents to the family," wrote journalist Stephen Powers in 1870, observing the habits of California coastal tribes. Wordlessly, a suitor would sling a deer or a "brace of hare or a ham of grizzly-bear meat" at the door of his intended's tepee. Daily, he would heap more gifts at the doorway, his courtship encouraged as his gifts were accepted. If refused, each present would be politely returned by a replacement gift of like quality. In some tribes, the courtship period turned into a well-mannered frenzy of liberality as suitors came and went, offerings were piled high and goods in kind returned. The bridal price of feathers, furs or livestock allowed a man the right to mate, dwell and pursue a livelihood with a woman, but not to mistreat her. If a couple wed without proper gifts in advance, the children, at least among some coastal tribes, would be seen as bastards. Steep Modoc bridal prices completely realigned normal marriage patterns, as young women married only older men who could afford them. A "poor young man without fifty horses"—or three to ten strings of shell money, worth from fifteen to fifty dollars at nineteenth-century currency rates—would marry an older woman. Across native America, young men labored, hunted, scrounged and borrowed to collect a bridal tariff in whelk shell loops, woodpecker scalp headbands, livestock, blankets, obsidian and other valuables. With the Karok, marriage was illegal without prepayment, although certain concessions could be made. A spouse with only half the shell-money bridal price could pay half the sum and be "half married." And if he were also half satisfied, a simple complaint would have the money returned. Among the Comanche, the last stage of the wedding ceremony appeared, to explorer Captain Marryat, "almost sublime." When the lovers crossed hands, the groom asked, "Faithful to the lodge, faithful to the father, faithful to his children?" And the bride replied, "Faithful, ever faithful, in joy and in sorrow, in life and in death."

A husband gained status and respect if he was a good hunter, able to provide fresh venison and other game. His wife routinely performed heavy labor—tilling the soil, digging roots and tanning hides, duties that were burdensome but of great value.

Arranged marriages might throw together two incompatible people, creating a frigid union in the name of tribal alliance, while an elopement carried out the wishes of a lovestruck pair, affecting a marriage that often proved successful. Yet carelessness or fate led to a third alternative: romantic unions so taboo that the resulting sexual thralldom or infatuation could spring only from "love magic," an obsessive behavior that defied group harmony. In tribal society, moderation was prized, while strong feelings, like a rushing river, should be dammed and diverted throughout the entire group, not channeled selfishly toward a single object. To violate this code was so counter to tribal interests that only witchcraft could be at play. Why else would a person's interest roam? "It really isn't love," explained a Mojave man to an interviewer, trying to explain the mysterious transference of power in which a victim would "do anything [for the beloved] . . . even dying." Untangling love's mysteries was the pursuit of the shaman, and "love magic" spells could employ up to three shamans, each working in specific areas to bring the victim back to spouse, family and friends. "I do my part," said a Mojave shaman, Harav He:ya, speaking of the technique of healing, "and then, if the patient is still sick, I send him to another shaman who will cure the remaining sickness."

In a society marked by rituals and celebrations, in which no detail escaped notice and no secret was long held, all feared and guarded against the most onerous of taboos: the marrying of a blood relative. Such an accident would violate a careful system of kinship and clan that went back to each tribe's Ancient Ones, the wellspring of shamanistic power, whose myths dictated who could wed and who could socialize throughout all time, in the majority of the continental tribes. "Potato Clan people I respect and never marry," pointed out a Wolf Clan Cherokee, while Wolf Clan people he could "joke with" but not marry.

Sanctions adhered to, youth still met and mingled at festivities, where opportunities to eye one another or steal a secret conversation were plentiful. Blessings were given and received, food enjoyed and hours passed in chanting and dancing the ceremonies of friendship, anniversary or thanksgiving. Clad ornately in fur robes, feathered headbands and swinging strings of shells, they danced, each cadence turning on the beat of a drum, each dance a renewal of tradition. Princess Isadora, a coastal Indian interviewed by historian Hubert Bancroft, recalled the "pretty dances" of the youth, when "men danced with men and women with women." Apikuni, an adopted Blackfoot whose original name was James Schultz, described "great camps" at which "a thousand Indians, men and women" would pass the night "drinking, chatting, singing, dancing around their evening fires and quarreling not at all." Northern tribes based their huge festivities around the first tapping of maple syrup, known as a Maple Thanksgiving, in which the rising sap was both a tribute to fertility, a "sign of the Creator's renewed covenant" and also, perhaps, a metaphor for youth's own burgeoning love. Other feasts—usually the strawberry, green bean or green corn—also hearkened to the spirit of celebration and thanks.

Of the three hundred recorded tribes remaining by 1900, some were monogamous, some polygamous, and in some tribes, young girls would routinely cohabit with their suitors before marriage, reverting to monogamy after marriage. "I belonged to Solano before I married him," Isador Filomena Solano told an interpreter, remembering how her husband, traveling through the region of her tribe, the Chiructos, had fallen in love with her and stolen her away.

Where polygamy flourished, honors were bestowed upon the first wife, who was foremost in a strict hierarchy of affection. Among the Blackfoot, she was the "sits-beside-him" wife, superior to any additional brides that came into the family as "gifts"— usually younger sisters, who were married by the husband as a courtesy to his first wife. Among the Fox, a young sister was chosen to sleep curled at the head of the nuptial bench, directly

Indian bride (Curtis photo. Southwest Museum)

Sioux Indian portrait ("Indian" Collection, National Archives)

above the heads of the couple, where she remained until she was old enough to become the second wife of her sister's husband.

In matrilineal tribes, women had their pick of husbands, trying out one after another until finally settling down. When a Pueblo Native American man gave his intended "two, three, or four blankets" for her house, he could live with her for "three or four . . . moons" to test their fertility, awaiting the child that would seal their union. If none resulted, the man would leave, and the woman would pluck a flower to adorn her hair, a signal that she was again ready to wed.

Such tales inspired accusations of moral laxity from settlers unable to fathom different traditions or interpret sexual standards as diverse and varied as the tribes themselves.

Each nation had its own strict standards, many of which related to chastity and fidelity. Cheyenne women lived under such iron-handed sexual restraint that virgins routinely wore chastity belts made of leather, to ensure continued celibacy. Apache women faced a severe penalty for adultery—the cutting off of the nose and often ears, along with tribal censure. Nor could a married woman from the California coastal tribes even walk alone with a man not her husband. "We are taught to love everybody," Sarah Winnemucca wrote of her Paiute tribe members—although excessive closeness between brothers and sisters was strictly prohibited. A sibling relationship was one of restraint and formality, with the older brother given the responsibility of "bossing" his younger sister and approving her behavior, for if she turned out "wild," then his reputation would suffer. Brotherly authority, never disrespectful, was always absolute. "[If] my son . . . sees you running around at night, he can shoot you," one Kiowa-Apache father warned his daughter, knowing that her marriage would not take place without the approval of her brother.

Men and women who languished from love might pine and

mourn for months to come, since forbidden love, and the ensuing stealthy liaisons that resulted, often led to dramatic and forced separation, angst, depression and even, in some cases, suicide. A botanist named Pursh, at the Onondoga village in 1807, observed a number of Native Americans using a plant called *cicuta maculata* "to poison themselves when they have an inclination of going out of the world." In 1838, a traveler named Dearborn was told by a Tonawanda Indian that skunk cabbage, the "fatal root," although sweet to the taste, caused violent spasms and death and was eaten in order to die. "[L]ove unrequited," he understood, "was a common cause for suicide."

Infidelity stirred up intense despair for all parties, and the punishment meted out to faithless women could be expulsion or maiming. Among the Choctaw, historian John Terrell reports, a wayward wife would be taken to the center of the village and offered to any man who found her handsome, while her husband was free to destroy the property of her lover without tribal sanction. Punishment also fell upon adulterous men, with restitution ranging from physical injury to heavy fines.

Sanctions were brushed aside in cases of wife sharing, which was considered a simple courtesy and, particularly among the Pueblo culture, an expected result of the mass sexual interaction during religious rites. Captive women were routinely offered as second wives to men of the conquering tribe, yet wife stealing between men of the same tribe was considered an egregious offense. A Blackfoot named Apikuni recalled a tug-of-war held over Crow Woman, who was tanning a buffalo hide when a drunken Cree came along, "picked her up, and started off with her." Apikuni interceded and subdued the Cree, but only after a second Blackfoot had joined in.

Bachelors and spinsters were rare in most Native American cultures, since to forgo children was to reap pity, for only with offspring could a woman be fulfilled or a man gain influence.

Childless, a man was invisible, a "nobody" in the Kiowa-Apache culture, as in others. War often produced a surplus of widowed women, and they, too, were quickly redistributed as second wives in order to save them from loneliness.

An individual who remained unwed was the berdache, a dress-wearing male who performed women's work and was often homosexual, yet in many native settings was simply accepted as a member of a "third gender." Typical was We'wha, a tall, statuesque Zuni with hair sausage-rolled into traditional motif and dressed in woman's clothing, who listed his occupation as "Farmer, Weaver, Potter, Housekeeper." As pointed out by historian Will Roscoe, the first two were male occupations, the second two, female.

Transvestism and homosexuality were tribally recognized among many Native Americans as special conditions, identified early through the power of an adolescent dream that could identify gender. "Third gender" males were often attracted to female regalia and occupations, in some cases dreaming frequently of women's tools—often their metates. If the dreamer then went on to become a shaman, his power would be greater than that of a heterosexual.

No influence was greater upon Native American courtship and marriage practices than the clash of cultures affected by Anglo-Americans, who found in Native American men and women popular figures of derision, whose perceived "lowly status" and "beast-like routines," they believed, subjected them, like chattel, to marital servitude. This also served as a rationale for decades of sexual exploitation by Spanish explorers, trappers, traders, military men and forty-niners. The debauching of Indian women was the result of years of mistreatment, in which women were bought, sold, traded and raped by white men, whose carnal mayhem caused enormous shifts in Native American marital and sexual behavior.

LAURA BLACK
BEAR MILES

**Born March 20, 1904, near Red Moon, Oklahoma,
Laura Black Bear was the great-granddaughter of Red Moon,
a noted Cheyenne chief. She was born at the turn of the century,
and the courtship and wedding rites of her girlhood were analogous
to those of women throughout Cheyenne history.**

I was born in 1904 along the river not far from the trading post, where there were not railroad tracks or roads of any sort. There was a camp there, where we lived, until we moved west, to an area still along the river [and] not far from the trading post. My mother built a house there, where I stayed until [she] passed away . . .

My maiden name was Black Bear, which came from my grandfather on my father's side. My father's name was Joe White Bird, and he had gone to the Carlisle Indian School . . .

In the old days, courtship went like this.

During the daytime the young men [would never] speak or congregate with the young ladies. The way of courtship was that after dark the young man, if he liked a certain young lady, would go and wait patiently behind her tipi. In those days they wore red and blue blankets, which the men still use today, and some of the young men even wore white sheets. Then they would wait for an opportunity. If the young lady happened to have to go out for something, then he would just come up behind her and then wrap her in his blankets.

It was common to see after dark a couple wrapped in a blanket. That was courtship. In that time the young ladies were afraid to step outside. The only time they ever went out was when it was absolutely necessary.

The way a young man asked for a hand in marriage was like this; if a young lady had a brother, he was given the greatest respect by his sister, and if someone liked the young lady, he would take some kind of gift over to the brother, and if the brother accepted the gift, then the sister was promised to the young man who presented the gift . . . even if the young lady had never talked, or so much as looked, at him.

If her brother accepted the gift, then that's the way it was. It was final, and the parents were not even involved.

The brothers and sisters hardly spoke to each other, because of the deep respect they held for one another. There was no joking around . . . Brothers would never kid their sisters. If someone said something [funny] about a sister or brother . . . [they] would have to leave the room in order not to show disrespect.

That respect is also true between father-in-law and daughter-in-law. A father-in-law never speaks to his daughter-in-law unless absolutely necessary. Son-in-law to mother-in-law is the same thing.

After the [bridal] transaction is made, the bride is dressed in the finest buckskins, and goes home with the groom. The groom's relations get together these blankets, bedding materials, and many household items. On the bride's side they . . . give tipis, moccasins, tents and also food, and gather on the bride's side and make a big feast.

On the groom's side they come over with all these quilts and dry goods so all the bride's relations—usually ladies—sort out the various gifts. When they get through, the groom's side of the family—usually men—go over and eat this food that is prepared, and then go and take down the tents and the moccasins, and so forth, that's theirs to take. But of all these gifts, the bride and groom get the best of what is there—the best tipi, the most comfortable bedding, pots and pans and what they're going to need.

All are prepared to give the best. Prestige is distinguished not by how much you have, but by how much you give away. If you give away something very fine, then you are a very prestigious person. Everyone gives their finest. That's the way it is consummated. And so when all the gift giving is over . . . the bride goes home with the groom and they go and pitch their tents.

That's the way I was brought up.

And I was married traditionally.

I didn't have any brothers at the time, but someone presented my aunts with a whole half a beef and wanted to marry me. But I didn't want to marry him! In the meantime, the women had already cut the beef up and they were already cooking it over the fire, and then, we'd already eaten it. "You might as well enjoy this," I said, "but I'm not going to marry him."

This was my first proposal.

My aunt, whom I call "mother," never got married and never had children, though she raised children. But later on in life, [a man] came over and wanted to marry her. She didn't have any brothers, and I only had one son, but my [aunt] thought the world of [this boy.] So [the suitor] came over one day and gave his sister money. In turn she went to my son and presented it to him. My son, he was just a young boy at the time, so he really didn't know what was taking place. At the time, [the suitor] must have been around sixty or so. Since my son had accepted the money, my aunt was sort of [caught]. All she could say was, "well, [my nephew] has already taken the money."

And so they got together.

Unidentified ("Indian" Collection, National Archives)

THREE BEARS

Told By Hugh Monroe, as related to Zebulon Pike

Hugh Monroe, an adopted Indian known as Mahkwi Ipwoatsin,
or Rising Wolf, left the Hudson Bay Company in 1858
to become a "free trapper" and roam with his wife's people,
the Pikunis. Among them he met Three Bears, a "well-built young
man...[with] a firm face and big, honest, eager eyes." Rising Wolf
had been captured by Crows as a youth and raised as a slave, then he
fell in love with a "sacred" Crow woman. Their love, courtship and
attempts at elopement reveal the power of sacred dreams and the
parents' strict guardianship of their young daughter.

Three Bears took great liking for me, and I, for him. So . . . one day, he said to me: " . . . [W]e men are very close-mouthed about women. But I must tell you about one, for you are different. I know that you will not laugh at me."

"Tell it. I will not laugh," I answered.

" . . . I go back to the Crow camp not only to kill . . . Long Elk but also to try to get a girl he wants. A girl who loves me and hates him . . .

"This girl, Mink Woman, and I are of the same winters. She is tall, slender, and round. Has beautiful face; big, kind eyes; hair braids almost touching the grounds as she walks. Her father, Old Bull, when she was little, had a vision. His sacred helper came to him as he slept and said: 'Keep your daughter ever close to you as she grows up, do not let her marry, for I have a certain use for her.'

"Old Bull obeyed his vision. Refused to give the girl to any one of the many who wanted to marry her. Long Elk offered him twenty horses for her, but the father refused. Then Long Elk, watching for the chance, said to the girl one day as she was going for water: 'Run off with me. We will go to our relatives, the Minnetarees, and live with them.'

Answered the girl: 'Run off with you? Long Elk, I hate you. Go away. Never speak to me again.' . . .

"Mink Woman ran to her father about it, and he was very angry at Long Elk; so were many of the people. She was a sacred woman. All men must keep away from her, they said.

"Always, when by ourselves we met, Mink Woman smiled, and her eyes were kind as she looked at me. I loved her, but she, so sacred, could not love me, I thought. So I was surprised . . . when, meeting her one day, she said to me: 'Three Bears, why don't you ask me to run off with you? Go with you to you Pikuni people? . . . I have always loved you, just you, no other,' she said. [J]ust then came her mother to overtake her on the water trail. I hurried to my mother about it, and said she: 'A good girl, that Old Bull's daughter. When we go, she goes with us. She will be a good wife to you. And how that will make to burn that Long Elk's insides.'

"Well, now that I was going, [I] could wait no longer for Long Elk to return, I would take Mink Woman with me, I decided. We had talked about it, and she had said that she would be ready in any night that I would come and awaken her. All that day I tried to have secret talk with her, and she tried for it, too, but always people were near . . .

"Anyhow, I knew where Mink Woman slept; her couch was the second one from the doorway on the south side of the lodge. I had twice been in it and seen her sitting there. Night came. Long I sat waiting for what I was to do, sitting close to the two horses that I had saddled for us to ride. At last the fire in her lodge died out, but still I waited until I felt sure that all within it slept. Then

I crept to her side of the lodge; noiselessly pulled out two lodge-skin pins; reached in under the loosened lodge-skin; softly, lightly felt for her; touched her rounded, robe-covered hip. It would not do to prod her there, else, startled, frightened, she would cry out. I felt for her farther up; touched her hair; found her face and put my hand firmly upon her mouth to hold her quiet and whisper that I had come for her. *Ha!* It was not hers but her mother's mouth that I held, and jerking away she yelled: 'Enemies are here! One seized me! Help! Help me! ' . . . . Old Bull yelled: 'It is that Pikuni youth after our daughter. I will kill him!'

"As I sprang up and ran, the awakened people in the other lodges began yelling. The men ran out from them with ready guns, one of them shouting: 'Enemies have come! Here are two saddled horses that they have tied.'

As I ran for the near timber instead of for the horses, several shots were fired at me, but I got safely into it and kept on in it all the rest of the night. And so going, traveling by night and in the daytime lying hidden, at last I came to you all. But this I tell you—to you alone: I shall soon go back, do my utmost to kill my enemy and get my girl."

Unidentified couple ("Indian" Collection, National Archives)

Black Americans and "Jumping the Broom"

Reverend and Mrs. Thomas Towns, settled with Frémont's army near San Jose, California (Oakland Public Library)

IN THE TRADITIONAL WORLD OF THE SLAVE, MARRIAGE and birth were cause for celebration, allowing men and women to forget, for a moment, the heavy burden of their interminable work. Slaves were encouraged to wed and procreate by slaveholders, who were quick to impose an image of the lusty, seductive "Eve" upon black women, thus justifying the countless sexual unions they inflicted upon the women.

Marriage, either before or after such seductions, was demanded, although any union could be disrupted at any time and either mate forcibly removed. "I saw a husband and wife bidding each other farewell," ex-slave William Robbins recalled, describing the agony of parting that took place daily at traders' pens throughout the south. Matrimony was managed and cohabitation enforced to produce as many children as possible, as Robbins discovered when he was thrust upon a disfigured fourteen-year-old octoroon enslaved on the same property. The girl had been burned with hot tongs for dawdling while working. "I'll have the preacher come over and marry you," the owner instructed Johnson, already anticipating the offspring they would produce. For those who objected, a "whipping bee" was held every Monday morning to convince them of their error; so routine was the flogging that some were punished simply for going to church on Sundays, others for attending a frolic or a get-together, others for sidling away after work hours to visit a far-distant spouse. There was "perfect pandemonium around that community all the time," said Robbins, who later escaped, became a minister, and often reminisced from the pulpit about a plantation heritage so cruel as to rend the fabric of America's history.

But slaves persevered in maintaining their love alliances. Those without permission to visit would slip out after dark to see a spouse, or attend secretly held frolics or religious meetings in the woods, to dance and sway to the music of a medley of instruments, usually "tambourine, banjo and bones." Often, the slave compounds would ring out with music. One man recalled the lilt of Jew's harps and mouth organs, guitars, fiddles, banjos and other common musical instruments; an enterprising entertainer on one plantation was noted for blowing his harmonica through his nose.

The frolic would take on a wild aspect, the scene lit by conch-shell lamps fueled by the smoky grease from raccoons or possums. "After work was done, the people would smoke, sing, tell ghost stories and tales, have dances, music, play home-made fiddles," described one participant. According to another, "at nights the slaves would go from one cabin to the other, talk, dance or play the fiddle or sing." Even prayer meetings were held secretly, with men and women often praising God and singing into upturned kettles to muffle the tumult of worship.

Stripped of homeland and much of their heritage, enslaved Africans still found some solace within their ranks, and preserved old ways of marrying. Forbidden to celebrate a Christian wedding, or, for many decades, to even practice the religion of their masters, slaves adopted the African custom of broom-jumping—perhaps the equivalent of carrying a bride over the threshold. "Broom" weddings were sometimes blessed by the owner, sometimes not. As cited by historian Harriet Cole, the following sheet music, dated 1900, describes the ceremony: "De broomstick's jumped, de world not wide. She's now yo' own. Salute yo' bride!"

Often, without further ceremony or license, the couple simply walked over the broom together. When ex-slave Annie Morgan was married by broom, in the "old" way, "all the colored folks in the neighborhood come," she reminisced. "We—my husband and me—jumped over the broomstick and we have been married, ever since. Most colored folks married that way." Another version: leaping backward, with the one who landed first to "be boss" of the household. "I sailed right over dat broomstick, same as a cricket," said Tempie Durham, cited by Harriet Cole, which

Two men and two women, standing with bicycles (Lillybridge Collection, Colorado Historical Society)

popular lecturer. Their correspondence reveals a mutual affection while documenting the distances that kept them apart. In one letter, she informed him that there was no money, she had to take in wash. His reply urged that she watch the stock market—one of his bonds might begin to rise. "I hope I will be able to give you something nice for your birthday," he wrote. His daughters also despaired of his return; "Please kiss the cat's foot," they wrote—a good-luck invocation and a wish to see their father again.

In 1870, the Fifteenth Amendment granted the vote to all citizens—race, color, and previous condition of servitude notwithstanding. "Today each can say, I am an American citizen," wrote Sanderson. "The constitution of my country recognizes me. The flag and executive arm *protect* me!" Slavery, the greatest stumbling block to political accord, had been removed.

As the status of blacks improved, so, too, did that of black women. Some made their way to the vaudeville stage, performed as artists and worked for women's rights. Enjoying a newfound freedom, black women joined their white sisters in the battle for temperance and higher education. Black men and women struggled to learn, teaching themselves to read by cutting letters from newspapers, laying them side by side and puzzling out the words. "We had, by stratagem, learned the alphabet while in slavery," recalled Wendell Phillips, "but not the writing characters. . . . We concluded to give our whole minds to the work."

The assimilation of blacks into European-American culture had a powerful effect upon black marriages. There was a strong movement within the black community toward what were seen as ideal marriages. Some upwardly mobile women, highly motivated toward "better English, good housekeeping, and the social graces," joined women's clubs, finding in groups such as the Female Emancipation Society and the Ladies Commercial Club a means of community support. Others plunged into church work, while a few, such as Mary Ellen Pleasant, became activists. Pleas-ant, a quick-witted girl whose owner had sent her to Boston to be educated, married a wealthy black Bostonian, and swore vengeance upon the system which had once enslaved her.

If a marriage flagged or failed, women were often held responsible. In one black-owned community newspaper, wives were advised that a good woman could bring a footloose husband home. "Manage your husbands," owner L. W. Warren touted, "and see results." He frequently editorialized on the duties and obligations of wives, pointing out the failings of "worthless girls who have the giggling and spending vices reduced to a frazzle." His next theory: 98 percent of the divorces were the wife's fault, 1 percent the husband's and the rest due to the absence of love. In tightly knit, deeply religious black communities of the late nineteenth century, divorce was anathema, and any woman so inclined drew harsh invective from the pulpit and was excluded from popular social clubs. Families were enjoined by society and the church to stay together—no matter what.

Men who first left slavery, or chased opportunity west, outnumbered women by more than two to one in 1860, according to historian Douglas Daniels. For years, urban sites were havens for shifting numbers of young males who, if they married, faced such economic struggle that they survived only with difficulty, often migrating to outlying areas to raise children by working in agriculture. Single black men, in some towns, were suspect. "Bachelors are a Detriment to Langston," clamored a literary society in one small settlement, alarmed by the growing number of single black men streaming into town.

Blacks who stayed in western sites were particularly committed to advancement, creating families and seeking refinement. Their lives had begun to change, some approaching financial comfort. Courting couples appeared on city streets, dressed elegantly in black broadcloth, white vests, silks and satins, gaily attending social events and trading small talk and social favors.

Increasingly, weddings were noted in newspapers, as urban black culture took on the aspect of "society." One, cited by Douglas Daniels, was that of William H. Hall, who returned to New York to marry his sweetheart, flush with earnings from the California gold mines and eager to host a wedding unequaled in the history of "colored society in New York." Again cited by Daniels was the sophisticated 1867 San Francisco ceremony of Wellington C. Patrick and Mrs. Sarah Anderson, who wed in a billowing tent to the strains of music by the Black Pacific Brass Band, while white passersby wondered at a "colored" event being "so refined."

Honeymoons generally took place at home or nearby, as blacks were reluctant to travel for pleasure in a distinctly unpleasant and discriminatory environment. But some safe harbors did exist throughout the country, where blacks could enjoy a nuptial retreat—one was a thriving black community that sprang up in 1889 in Coconut Grove, Florida, while another, Highland Beach, Maryland, was founded in 1893 as a respite site for blacks. Couples also traveled along the southern coast or to Harpers Ferry, Virginia, the home of Hampton University, a popular destination for privileged blacks.

In the burgeoning middle class of self-made black preachers, teachers, attorneys and shopkeepers, a fascinating documentary, a correspondence found in the collection of black minister Jeremiah Sanderson, reveals in the romantic lives of African-Americans in San Francisco their similarity to white Victorian courtship of the day. Postmarked 1870, the letters were anonymously written to Mr. DeSouzer, the fiancé of Sanderson's daughter, Florence, "tak[ing] the liberty" to inform him that Florence "acts very indifferently for one being engaged." In fact, the author continued, "she flirts desperately . . . with at least a half dozen young men." Finishing his mischief, the author signed himself: "from a friend and well-wisher of your happiness . . . There is no need of

answer." Incensed, Florence wrote to Mr. DeSouzer, who did not reply. To her father she fumed: "I shall give him back his freedom," and signed herself, in the letter to her father, "your loving and perhaps misguided daughter." On April 14, 1871, she admitted to trying to please her parents in her choice of husband. "I may have loved him then," she wrote, "but to be candid I am sure I did not."

Two girls dressed for church (Library of Congress)

PAULINE LYONS WILLIAMSON

**Pauline Lyons Williamson, a middle-class black widow
who emigrated to California, experienced the typical, pervasive
attitude of the times regarding her marital status: as a minority and
a woman, she was expected to accept an offer quickly, suitable or not.
The following exchange shows the matchmaking complexity;
all parties had a deep concern for propriety—so much so that
Pauline finally abandoned the project in disgust. The rest of her
stay in California was equally misbegotten—although trained as a
nurse, she was unable to find work while trying to educate
herself further and support her young son.**

OAKLAND, NOV. 10TH, 1885

My dear May,

Now my dear . . . it seems that before I came to California a friend of Mrs. Thomas [her aunt]—a gentleman, saw my picture and being desirous of getting a wife questioned Ms. T concerning me, the gentleman being a West Indian by birth is very wealthy, but has refrained from marrying because he could not meet any lady who came up to his ideas of what a wife ought to be.

The gentleman, who was a perfect stranger to me but a friend of Ms. T agreed with Ms. T that I was the one suited to be a good wife. The name of the West Indian gentleman I do not know so I will call him Mr. H. Ms. T's accomplice in the business I shall call Mr. B.

Mrs. T & Mr. B put their heads together to make me marry Mr. H, they both saw Mr. H [and] set forth my charms, and they agreed that it would be all right as soon as I came, so Mr. H said he would marry me.

Mrs. T told him the only obstacle in the way [was] the child but he promised her that he would fix that all right, he would send the child away to boarding school, so it was settled. Ms. T was to receive a diamond ring for her trouble and Mr. B was to receive a diamond scarf [a reward] for his trouble from Mr. H as soon as the marriage took place.

October was the time fixed for it so as to give him time to arrange for his going into business for himself. He opened a perfumery store in Panama during the holiday week, [and] we were to sail immediately for Panama which was to be my future home.

Behold the sequel: neither party told me anything of what was going on [when] I came. Mr. B was the first one to broach the subject to me, then he did not tell me about Mr. H, but simply hoped I would like California and he knew I would become so much attached that I never would want to leave, and finally, I would marry some one here.

I told him I did not care to marry, but he assured me I would marry out here, [since] every one that came to make a living ended by marrying, and in a few days he would show me some thing that would bind me forever to California. But still I did not suspect anything because I thought he was only showing off. But he kept it up so much that I finally told [him] I did not see why people worried so about my getting married. I came to earn a living and not to hunt a husband, and I intended to remain single. [Still] not a word about Mr. H did [my aunt] say.

So one day in talking I told [her] I had a friend in New York that I thought I would marry if he did what I wanted him to do, [which] was to come out to California. And if he came I would marry him.

So whenever the California gentlemen were mentioned I would bring up New York gentlemen, and in fun on my part, lauded them up to the skies, my own in particular being lord over all.

Now in the mean time Uncle comes home, and we are invited to take tea at Mr. B's. That was the time fixed for me to meet Mr. H for the first time, but before the day arrived Uncle, Mr. B, Mrs. T and myself were in Frisco and it seems Mr. H passed us on the street, and she steps up to him and tells him the game is all up, I am engaged to be married. He says he is very sorry and thanks her kindly for the interest she has shown, and refuses to be introduced to me, as he does not wish to place himself in any ones way and unless he can have the lady to himself. He will not even call on her or be introduced.

I remember that she stopped in the street and spoke to some one, but as I was ignorant of all this, I did not pay any attention to what went on, but walked along with Mr. B . . .

Mr. H would not come to the party as he felt much disappointed at the way the affair had turned out. Mr. B has told me since that if I had only said I would marry that he would have gone right after Mr. H and in ten minutes time it would have been all fixed.

A little while after I received a letter from my friend in New York saying he had changed his mind and would [not come] to California, so I told [Ms. T]. Well, then the storm broke over my head, and she was furious. For it seems she had been around telling people I was engaged to be married, [and] that the gentleman was a coming out from New York. Then she up and told me about Mr. H, and what she had planned for me, and that since I would have my own way she was done with me. And she did not care what happened, and a whole lot of stuff.

She had even gone so far as to make out who she intended to send cake [to]. She intended to make New York and Brooklyn jealous of my good fortune, and all was to be done at her expense cake and all. Then as soon as I was safely in Panama, she was going to arrange her affairs and come to Panama and pay me a visit, but sure as I preferred a New York nigger I was served just right.

She would love to set my ass in a butter firkin and I would have had servants to wait on me and plenty of money, but I would not, so then she thought I had better go home, that I was not happy, and she didn't want anyone around who was not contented.

I was always fretting because I was not at work, and she did not see why I was in such a hurry to work. Then I said, I missed father and mother so much, I had better go back to them. When Uncle came home he would pay my fare back home, that is why she wrote as she did, for she was dreadfully put out on account of my not fulfilling her wishes, when she had bragged and boasted of me to him.

Well, I can't repeat all that was said, but finally I told her if Mr. H would come and see me I would accept his attentions, so she said she would see Mr. B and see what could be done.

Mr. B came to see us and the matter was talked over, he said he was afraid it was too late now to do anything as Mr. H had gone to Panama, so he wrote to him, and two weeks ago he received an answer saying Mr. H would think the matter over and would let him know in a short time what he would do.

So there the matter rests. There will be a steamer in from Panama about the 1st of this month, and then I suppose he will send his answers. He is a Roman Catholic but I don't think he will come back as he is very high tone.

You may rest assured I will never consent to have my boy sent away from me for any man, and I think the whole transaction was crazy to go so far without my knowledge . . .

Spanish Americans

Three girls near Hispanic church ("West" Collection, National Archives)

ONE OF THE FORCES GOVERNING MARRIAGE AND courtship practices in Hispanic California, Texas and New Mexico was the expectation that no person could live alone; in fact, to live was to marry, and vice versa, neither condition relevant without the other. Marriage was the cornerstone of community balance and personal satisfaction, endorsed by need, tradition and the Catholic church—the foundation of every interaction, from ritual and religion to celebration, day of penance or fiesta. In its acceptance of celebration, the Church differed from straight-laced Protestant sects; yet at times, a fiesta could go too far. Fray Pedro Font, a member of de Anza's expedition, was affronted by the constant mirth and revelry of his Spanish brethren. "I remained alone," he wrote. "I did not think it best to go to the fandango, lest by my presence I should sanction this worldly merrymaking." Instead, he tried to encourage "singing the Mass of the Most Holy Trinity" as an alternate means of rejoicing.

Font's reluctance turned lordly when it came to governing the young Indian girls at the missions. His diary records efforts to restrict the "converted girls, whom they call nuns" under lock and key at night, to prevent their fleeing to the hills to tryst with young Indian men, or worse, with soldiers. "They . . . do so very nicely," he wrote of their escapades, "as if they were little Spaniards." Font scarcely knew how to protect the women, as their "affable and friendly" behavior was continually misinterpreted by the soldiers, who, he admitted, "were disorderly" with the women of many tribes. During the mission years, a disastrous precedent was being established: Indian women were seen as the sexual conquests of Spanish men, despite the vigilance of the mission priests, who were already convinced that women—any women—were provocative in the extreme. Such prejudice was evident in the guidebook of the Misión Concepción in San Antonio, advising the priest to "always select a man for the job" of cook, as "the employment of women could lead to disorder with single men in the kitchen." No amount of supervision could prevent debauchery, always a threat, or a population of mestizo half-breeds—always a reality.

In 1645 more than 300,000 Indians had been baptized in the American southwest and Mexico—an attempt to establish Catholic dominion over a rough and unconverted culture that, however, housed huge numbers of Indians within mission walls, within reach of Spanish soldiers.

Two hundred years later, commerce and trade drew white explorers, trappers and traders down the Santa Fe trail—twelve hundred miles from St. Louis, Missouri, to Santa Fe, then farther afield toward the final trading destination of Chihuahua, Mexico—with some wagons being charged by the government of Mexico as much as five hundred dollars just to reach the coast. Feasting on smoky goat meat and pinto beans, captivated by elusive, black-shawled women, the American travelers pushed along the dusty Santa Fe Trail, their path brightened by geraniums cascading from dark doorways, while all about lay the remnants of Spanish hegemony and conquest—the baked-clay world of the Mexican mestizo, whose nature had been so forcibly shaped.

Travel journals are filled with poignant observations of Spanish life and courtship practices; men were charmed and dazzled by the commingling of Spanish, Indian, mestizo and Anglo; their descriptions are filled with the "laughing, dancing, singing and love-making" experienced along the way. Captain Frederick Marrayat, traveling to Monterey, California, found a place so "sweet, the dogs are polite" and "what was more strange, the Americans . . . almost honest." Furthermore, he was captivated by the warm-hearted hospitality of "pretty girls, with flashing dark eyes and long tapered fingers," who eagerly swarmed about him when he dismounted to undo his leggings and pry off his spurs. Armed with a sack of doubloons and a desire to dance, he soon found

Fiesta at Casa de Adobe (Southwest Museum)

what countless other travelers had often written about: the spirited hospitality of the California Spanish. Like others who glimpsed their leisurely frivolity, day after day he hoped to keep the site secret. Eastern settlers, he feared, would stifle the fandangos with "the coal fires and raw beef-steak" of New England; they would reform this "fairy" spot, and "render it stiff and gloomy" as any Yankee enclave.

While the Catholic church blustered about vice and love and reconciled the population with prayers and "light penances," the citizens of Mexico living in Alto California continued to court, flirt, dine, drink and generally amuse themselves in the spirit of what appeared, to many Americans, the utmost indolence and unproductivity. The Castilian landowners never ceased to socialize, with festivities that rotated from one rancho to another, while half-breeds and Indians formed a mute vanguard of laborers, servants and menials with their own secret celebrations.

One fiesta, described by Texas political prisoner George Kendall, taken captive by Mexicans in 1856, took place between female hospital workers and inmates. There seemed to be no health or criminal restrictions when it came to fiesta; everyone was set free to mingle and dance at will. "A set of [one or more couples] would take the floor . . . Some of the dancers upon crutches, and almost all . . . lame or disabled. The music would strike up . . . accompanied by singing. . . . True feelings of merriment were there."

What dazzled Captain Marryat, and so many others, was the rich attire and "admirable taste" of unmarried girls, dressed in white satin and long lacy white mantillas, which they would flounce and swirl at the least provocation. In a girl's hair would perch a tortoiseshell comb, with gold ribbons swirled about to keep the comb in place.

Even the matrons were garnished with a frill of gaudy colors topped by huge tortoiseshell combs, so unlike the conservative-dress of married matrons in the continental states. From where came such celebratory spirit? Perhaps, some decided, from the deep Spanish sense of security afforded women in Mexico by the nearly blind protection of Spanish law, often to the detriment of their husbands. Whether disgruntled, dissolute or genuinely mistreated, women could always depend upon civil and ecclesiastical authority for support or redress, which cast certain restraints upon male behavior. A Spanish husband could not undertake a major journey without his wife's consent; and if he overstayed his agreed-upon time, a judge would immediately order his return, no matter whether from Chile or California. In return, women were expected to comply with sexual demands, and weather the rages and jealousies imposed by overbearing husbands.

Protected domestically and legally, Spanish women wielded great influence within the family setting; they spent their lives within large, close-knit groups of relatives that increased with every wedding. Rather than uproot a woman from her family, marriage increased the number of family members available to her. A marriage would endure, due to the religious constraints of Catholicism, which forbade divorce, and its binding social and economic aspects.

Bloodlines were a careful consideration in the tight-knit fraternity of Spanish landholders, or Californios, with hospitality given to those of true Castilian, or "white," stock, which would often include light-skinned European or American passersby. The Spanish patricians turned out for births, deaths and weddings, the latter of which called for extended celebration.

Californio girls were betrothed before the age of twelve and often married by sixteen. In the oligarch families, the daughter quietly accepted the match made by her parents, happy to count the items of her hope chest that piled up about her in the year before marriage. Fine laces, silk *rebozos* from Spain, tortoiseshell combs as heavy and ornate as a crown filled her wedding chest, while congratulations filled her head with happy anticipation. Despite parental planning, the Californio youth were not without spunk and recourse. Courtship still occurred, betrothal or not, often with young Spanish gentry gathering at a rancho for an "egg frolic," where empty eggshells were filled with gold dust or perfume, sealed with wax, then splintered over the head of a likely love interest. When interest in eggs paled, the crowd might slap one another with wet napkins, or heave pitchers of water back and forth. As cited by author Norine Dresser, women were also selected by a man's stepping behind them as they danced and dropping a hat over their head—somewhat in the spirit of playing horseshoes. A girl thus singled out could either continue to wear the hat, cantered down over her eyes, or let it fall to the ground as a sign of rejection.

A groom's dowry price might be a roll of gold coins; the explorer Mariano Vallejo placed thirteen gold coins and three gold rings in a collection plate as a bride price. The rings, blessed by the priest, sealed the ceremony, after which Vallejo offered the dowry to his bride—a symbol of the lifetime of earnings he would lay at her feet. (In this, the Spanish government concurred: military officers were legally obliged to give up two-thirds of their pay to maintain their wives.) As a final gesture, the woman spilled the coins on the altar, to show that love was more important than money, or else by way of donating the money to the church. Then, they were lightly bound together around the shoulders with a silken cord—their togetherness symbolized by the tying of the knot.

Where once bloodlines had been pure, with the arrival of more travelers, soldiers and miners from the States, weddings became increasingly interracial, assuming an important role in the social assimilation of Mexican-American society, continuing a tradition that began when the Spanish conquistadors routinely married Indian women, and whose offspring were the Spanish-speaking

New Mexico wedding, ca. 1900 (Southwest Museum)

mulattoes of the southwest. At the time of American conquest in 1846, there were 75,000 Spanish in the southwest, and the outflow of mixed marriages muted ethnic hostility. Eloise McLoughlin, writing in 1840, described one of many mixed blood weddings near San Francisco, celebrated by "bullfights in the day and dancing at night . . . and a great deal of sweet wine especially."

The few hundred Anglos who penetrated California during the 1820s and 1830s were entirely Hispanicized, marrying daughters of the California Spanish elite, joining the Catholic church, revising their names into matrilineal order and accepting Mexican citizenship. In New Mexico, the wealthy Jaramillio family, leaders of the established Spanish ruling class, tied itself to the intruding westerners through the marriage of two daughters to Charles Bent and Kit Carson—important marriages, socially.

When a Chinese laundryman married a Spanish woman in Silver City, Nevada, in 1889, no one knew if it was miscegenation or social outreach, but one thing was certain: the tide of mixed marriages could not be stemmed. In Santa Fe in 1870, 63 percent of Anglo men had founded mixed families. Anglo men would adopt the sweeping, ornate Spanish capes, and dance energetically with vivacious Spanish women; social equals, they met at the same *bailes,* dined together at noon at the open ranchero tables, the scent of bougainvillea mingling with the call of the Angelus bell. Their social harmony and proximity were one step removed from wedlock—the ingredients of the cross-cultural west were in place.

The American military engineered other marriage-line crossovers. U.S. Army soldiers stationed in small, dusty towns throughout Arizona and New Mexico could find solace at the *bailes:* "The Mexican gals are very gay" wrote one soldier. By the standards of Dr. J. D. Stillman, the military men consorting with Spanish women in California seemed to "vegetate"; many drank, yet "some seem[ed] happy with their Mexican wives." Official Hispanic law demanded formal marriages, but along the racial borders, folk practice often solemnized the informal union of the military men who casually "wed" the laundresses attached to their roving military camps. Only married women could be employed as laundresses, according to a Civil War order. Thus the laundresses would draw up written contracts with soldiers agreeing to live with them conjugally, but without legal marriage. After being discharged, a soldier would leave both contract and wife behind.

Both cultures were bemused by one another. Just as Anglo men were entranced by Spanish women—who seldom went out alone, even on household errands; who were watched, hawklike, by mothers, particularly after puberty—so Spanish men marveled at the Anglo women, who, according to traveler Domingo Sarmiento, were as "free as a butterfly," able to travel about unescorted, spend "two or three years of flirting" before striking an engagement, "of which the parents are not notified until the very eve." To the Spanish, such cavalier treatment of parents was unthinkable, but, then, so were American manners. No proper Hispanic couple would display conjugal bliss publicly on such a trip as a "honeymoon," wrote Sarmiento, who was particularly aghast at a so-called bridal chamber on a riverboat, in which "pink lamps" glowed wantonly at night.

In the boisterous, brawling colony of Texas, still affianced to Mexico and victim of a violent border element that flowed like an illegal tide into Mexico in the 1830s, another kind of marriage began to take place. Americans fleeing south shook free of husbands, wives and families, to remarry in what were called "Texas weddings." Behind terra-cotta mission walls, statues offered prayerful benediction over growing numbers of whites who celebrated second marriages under the auspices of the Catholic church. Catholic in character, Mexican in jurisdiction, illegal in spirit, such weddings were sealed in the Catholic church between couples already married by a minister in Protestant ceremonies to distant and abandoned partners who would never learn of the bigamous situation. Since couples united outside the Catholic church were judged unmarried in Catholic eyes, they were relatively free to wed again. Adherence to the Catholic, colonial system was encouraged by Stephen F. Austin, who tried to sooth the restless Americans living under Mexican rule while convincing Mexican authorities of the settlers' continued loyalty. What better way than an array of new, "legitimate" Catholic weddings?

No matter who married whom—Catholic to Protestant, Spanish to Anglo—or who was domiciled or subjugated, as with the Indian nations, cross-cultural unions worked their steady, pervasive influence upon western populations, mingling language, bloodlines and heritage to shape a rich history of passion, pillage, sorrow and, at best, love.

JAMES HENRY GLEASON

Born in Plymouth in 1823, Gleason sailed to Monterey, Alta California, in 1845, and quickly was caught up in the languid and gracious life of the Spanish gentility. His correspondence with his sister, Frances, continued until his death in 1861, and sketches a life filled with some financial success and popularity. His view of prosperous and patrician California before the onslaught of the raucous Gold Rush is a valuable study in contrasts. Although "below medium size" and less than healthy, his good humor and enterprise won the hand of Catarina Demetria Watson over another, more prosperous suitor.

MONTEREY
U. STATES OF AMERICA
JULY 25, 1846
MISS FRANCES A. GLEASON
My dear Sister,
[I know] you are very anxious for me to come home . . . but why destroy the fine prospects that are now presented to me by being absent eighteen months . . .

[Here] I am received into the highest society and *respected far more than I would be at home.*

The greater likelihood is that I shall go as a *married* man. I am engaged to the belle of Monterey! Miss Kate Watson. They are fine people all of them and my Kate is beyond compare. Her father James Watson is a great honest hearted man who is a friend to every one. He is quite well off being worth about 60,000$. He

is very hospitable and his house at the rancho near town is the stopping place for all his friends. . . .

in haste your dear Brother James

MONTEREY JANUARY 28, 1847
Dear Sister . . . My last letter to you was by the "Levant" Since then I have purchased three house lots in San Francisco which will in a few years hence be valued at $8000 or $10,000 . . . I have been on this coast now ten months and have acquired a knowledge of the Spanish language and become acquainted with the people and country consequently my chance of *making a fortune* is somewhat more promising than that of thousands now arriving strangers in the country . . . there is a good society here now *far better than in Plymouth* and my beautiful little Spanish wife (that is to be) Catarina will make you happy.

Dearly your brother,
James

PR. U.S. SHIP "PREBBLE"
MONTEREY CALIFORNIA MAY 2, 1847
My dear Sister
I have just finished my fourth business letter to the Sand'ch Islands—lit my cigar—and now I am ready to devote my time to a dear acquaintance. I am not married yet but tomorrow I intend to ask for the hand of Catarina Watson, *we must be united,* she is one of the lovliest—a disposition that an angel might envy, her father is a merchant in this place, worth about 30,000$. I have a rival, [the] sole heir to about 50,000$ these are large numbers. However I have hopes of success Kate tells me that she loves me—that she will wed me and no other—David Spence, my rival, has been her companion from infancy yet my happy disposition and *good looks* has removed from her all the attachments she had

to him, and the charm of *Fifty thousand.* I am received into the family as a favorite . . .

There is not a young man in California with more promising prospects before him than are now presented to me. Mr. Watson is aware of this and this encourages me to hope for success . . . You must excuse me for a few moments my servant has just brought into the office a piece of pie. I wish I could share with you it looks so nice.

15 minutes later

Having ate my pie—smoked a cigar—walked the terrace, blowed my nose, and censured the servant for a blunder I again return to you. I am thinking of a subject to commence upon—here's one at once.

The above ten lines are filled with nonsense I must quit that for I pay 1.50 cts. postage for this letter in advance.

Sister . . . I would that your days were as happy as mine. Nearly every afternoon a pic-nic in the woods with the Senoritas and nearly every night a dance. Our music [is] the guitar and harp and for a partner, a Spanish maiden whose very existence is *Love.* I imagine myself associated with Angels while moving around in a waltz with these lovely beings their very language—the Castillian—is sufficient to warm the coldest heart when they speak of *Love* . . .

MONTEREY 30 MAY 1847
NIGHT 11 O.CLOCK
My Affectionate Sister, . . .
I have *popped the question* for the hand of that lovely girl Catarina Watson her parents wish me to wait for 18 months and then ask for her again as she is too young to marry only 14 years of age. She tells me that she will have me and none other we often speak of you in our *love chats* she wishes you to come to her country—to her home

Wedding feast, New Mexico, ca. 1900
(Southwest Museum)

Her father is worth about 40,000$ I am now enjoying the happiest days of my life nothing but Pic-nic's and dances . . .

CALIFORNIA APRIL 1 1848
Dearly Beloved Sister . . .
The last two years [have] been a continual round of pleasure and joy, it has appeared to me like a dream. I am a particular favourite with the Californians and there is not a house on the Coast [where] I [have not the] freedom of one of the family. a Ball or *Mereanda* cannot pass off *alegre* without [my] presence. Dona Narisa de Osio is now waiting my return to Monterey to give me a splendid Ball . . . I have often wished you could see me at times traveling up and down the coast in my California riding dress,

sometimes camping out in the mountains surrounded by wild indians and bears other times at some rancho luxuriating on a bullock hide stretched out over a few sticks, at other times dressed up in fine broad cloth at the house of a rich family as I am at present while writing this Doña Arcadia and Isadora pursuad[e] me every few moments to [sing] while the latter is running her delicate fingers over the harp strings . . .

I have a good prospect for the future. I . . . hope to acquire a fortune I have a house building in Monterey which ought to be finished now it will cost 1600$ to 1800$. I have besides this in Monterey about 350 yards of land in house lots. I own also in San Francisco a house lot of 50 yards which I have leased and I own in Benecia 3 more house lots . . . I purchased this land very cheap before the Am. flag was hoisted in California the land I have in S. Fran'co cost me 200.$ and I have been offered for it 1400.$

Your very Affectionate Brother
James

MONTEREY NOV'R 15, '49
DONA FRANCESCA GLEASON, PLYMOUTH
My dear sister
Well Fanny I'm married. My bonny Kate is now reclining over my shoulder & anxious to know what I am about to say . . . she understands but few words in English. She saw "My" & "Kate" in the second line and knew what it meant at once but the "bonny" which intervenied was a damper. I told her it was saltfish and she curled her pretty lip . . .

I was married on the 7th of Oct at 3 Oc in the morning. a large dinner party was given by my father at his house in the afternoon and a dance followed in the evening. the expenses must have been nearly $1000 . . . there are thousands now in the country seeking employment & suffering for the want of funds to support themselves with . . .

My wife joins me in love to you all.
Your Affec't Brother James

SAN FRANCISCO MAR 31, 1850
My dear sister
My wife tells me to say that as she cannot write in English. You must excuse her and as a token of her deep affection . . . she will send a pina scarf by Mrs Paty . . . they are valued here at 125.$ each. She will also send her Deguerotype in her bridal dress and reclining on a harp as she was at a moment on the marriage eve, when my attention was called to her.

SAN FRANCISCO JULY 1, 1850
My dear sister Fanny
I have a great desire to go home but it seems that every month I remain here plunges me still deeper in business. . . . I left my wife well at Monterey & should nothing occur to frustrate the workings of nature I shall be a Father in a few months, and then I am going home partly to see my old acquaintences and relations & partly to get clear of a squalling baby. I like babys very much but not untill they arrive at a certain age. . . .

Wedding portrait of Miss Eddie Ross and William Henry Cobb, Albuquerque, New Mexico, September 14, 1891
(Photo by William Henry Cobb. Museum of New Mexico)

Asian
Americans

"If you have a daughter, don't marry her to a Gold Mountain man."
—Anonymous Cantonese
FOLK SONG

Asian bride (Idaho State Historical Society)

THE THRONGS OF CHINESE SOJOURNERS SEEKING GOLD and freedom in the west followed twin paths of hope and sacrifice, one inviting prosperity, the other denying home comforts to thousands of lonely men living away from their wives. Most were unschooled peasants, footloose and penniless in a time of great famine in China, who responded in droves to the lure of "big pay, large houses . . . food and clothing" in "Gold Mountain," or America, where there was "money . . . to spare" and Americans were "very rich."

Thus tempted, the eager sojourners flooded the west coast, dangling personal effects from bamboo poles as they searched for work as houseboys, launderers, gardeners, cooks, miners, or laborers building roads, sifting for gold tailings, harvesting tomatoes or onions or pruning trees. Money eked from their labors was gambled or hoarded or sent home with an energy and conviction that roused great resentment in Americans and increased race antipathy. Reviled on the streets, often stoned and beaten, pig-tailed men stoically accepted brutality as the price to pay to maintain their heritage in a foreign land.

To combat boredom, they gathered in dank, crowded rooms, gambling and smoking opium, their nights enlivened by visits from Chinese prostitutes, or wife-substitutes. Whites considered the Chinese a "depraved class" who had flooded America with "criminal and demoralizing" women. In 1858, laws were enacted to prevent "the landing of each and every Chinese . . . person" but were later declared unconstitutional. Their isolation was extreme, their moral obligation to faraway wives, children and families always pressing. As their numbers grew—increasing from fifty-four recorded in California on February 1, 1849, to four thousand by the end of 1850—their resolve grew stronger to return to China, where even the most modest profits earned in America would support a wife, in-laws and children in China. One man, King Kwong, worked as a houseboy and laundryman,

earning three hundred dollars a year—enough to lavishly ensconce his wife, brother and parents in a four-story home he built in his village, elevating the family status.

Unschooled peasants who normally lacked all prestige could change a family's fate, but it was not so easy for women. Victims of feudal and male-imposed restrictions for centuries, they were also excluded from American residence by strict immigration laws. A peasant family hoping to improve its lot might bind a daughter's feet, ostensibly to prevent wanderlust, but in reality an attempt to attract a prosperous mate. Otherwise, her only choice was to become a courtesan, singsong girl [entertainer], concubine, nanny or nurse; or worse, sink into life at the gambling dens, tea-houses and brothels.

If a woman married well, she would spend her life idle, her arch-broken feet curved backward into three-inch "lily" prongs, her long nails sheathed in holsters of gold and silver, perhaps spangled with tiny bells that tinkled out a patrician disdain for hand labor. At ease with both luxury and subjugation, she would quietly live a life dependent not upon her "pretty face and . . . tiny feet" but upon her ability to bear sons, to submit to her husband's will, to stoically bear chastisement while suffering singing girls and concubines with a smile. There was no possibility of divorce under strict Confucian law. However, less stringent Chinese regulations permitted divorce by mutual consent, with the husband given special grounds if his wife failed to bear sons, acted impiously, failed to serve her in-laws, was jealous, gossipy, seriously ill or of a "thievish nature." Women could not divorce, and often found their only hope was suicide, to return posthumously to bedevil husband, concubines and in-laws, too.

In China, men and women were betrothed at an early age, observing the traditional use of matchmakers and heeding the advice of soothsayers, who tested for a propitious wedding day by the use of *feng shui*, a belief in spiritual alignment.

Such intercession was necessary, as the man and woman could not interact. From childhood, each sex was trained in elaborate Confucian rituals that assigned them to "men's and women's courts," where they maintained a cool distance from one another until adulthood. Even then, a pair stayed safely apart until their wedding night.

So circumspect were married couples that even death brought no outward signs of grief—a reserved behavior that was often judged harshly by foreigners. Chinese, however, were equally shocked at the western notion of a "love match," an indiscretion seldom tolerated in rural China, where such willful behavior often ended by the couple's death by drowning in a giant wicker basket—a community reminder that duty, not desire, formed the framework of Chinese society.

Marriage was also, in many cases, the advent of a polygamous future that plunged women into slavery and men into debt and created a household rife with unrest, revealed in the Chinese characters for "woman." A single woman under a roof signifies "peace"; two signify "quarrel"; and three, "intrigue and disorder." "Polygamy prevails in almost every family," wrote a Presbyterian mission worker, who noticed that often the first wife, with "useless, small feet," would urge her husband to "take a second and even a third [wife] to share her isolation and relieve her of household chores." Missionary Emma Cable reports in 1888 visiting "thirty-six little footed wives . . . and eighteen little footed daughters" who, by their mutilated feet, signaled their social position.

Despite missionary efforts, foot-binding in America persisted. One woman, asked in 1880 why she followed "such a cruel custom," replied that "small feet" would lead her daughter to a good husband. But, she was asked, did not she, herself, have both large feet and a good husband? Yes, the woman answered, but her husband had "make mistake" and she wanted to be sure her daughter's husband did not. One girl, Ah Kew, wrote her first letter in English to one of her favorite teachers, Mrs. Condit, at the Occidental School in San Francisco: "Dear Lady . . . My mamma make my feet small, [I] cannot run all same as Ah Yeng [her brother]." However, other women, more independent, removed the bindings as a symbolic act of affinity with their new country. Miraculously, feet that had been curled back upon themselves for years could be used again.

Most Chinese were equally baffled and often shocked by white behavior, as was Zhang Deyi, a Chinese interpreter who visited New York in 1868 and noted the tableside intimacy of American men and women. He shuddered to see unrelated men and women "sitting together with their shoes touching"—an intimacy almost as shocking as the sight of unbound feminine feet, each "nearly a foot long." Oddly, Zhang still found the American belles graceful despite their awkward extremities, just as some Chinese men began to accept the westernizing of their wives.

A Chinese wedding, brightened by the wail of bamboo reed flutes and the bride's numerous changes of silken gowns, often brought a married woman unexpectedly from life in a rural Chinese village to a life of slavery in America—one of the 85 percent of Chinese women brought to America who were sold by "body contracts" to brothel owners along the Barbary Coast, or in other seaport cities. Such was the traffic in "wives" that by 1860 the number of women increased from the 7 recorded in 1850 to 33,149. The census registered as "prostitutes" more than two thirds of the nearly 40,000 Chinese women in California in the 1870s, and many of those had been tricked into contract sexual labor for periods of four to six years, in order to pay back their passage. Yet seldom were the true causes of prostitution mentioned: exclusionary laws that prevented wives from joining their husbands, and growing demand for Chinese prostitutes by men, both Asian and white.

Kidnapping and trickery were common in the sex trade of the frontier, where the dollar value of a slave was often from $500 to $2,000 each. "Girls are sold in the by-ways of San Francisco for $2,000," wrote Mrs. P. D. Browne, chairman of the Home Headquarters Committee. "We have in our possession a bill of sale for a Chinese girl for $2,000." Although many young Chinese girls were sold as babies, then raised by brokers and merchants in grimy locales, such as San Francisco's Spofford Alley or the Beehive House in Chinatown, others were recruited in even a more heinous fashion—through marriage to a benevolent, older businessman who would appear in their home village in China and sweep them up into an idyllic marriage. In one case, a virtuous young woman, Ah Yung, returned happily with her new spouse to America in 1902, to live happily for some months. One day he announced plans for an upcoming business trip; would she entrust herself to the care of his good friend? Ah Yung trustingly dipped her finger in ink and traced her name to her own bill of sale, still completely unsuspecting. Only when she was forcibly removed to a brothel did she realize what had happened, and her cries mingled with those of the other lifelong victims.

Those who managed to escape brothel life were legendary: China Annie, who fled to marry her lover, Ah Guan, in Boise, where, despite legal charges brought against her for "stealing her own valuable self," she was acquitted. Polly Bemis was another, who began as an auctioned slave, was "won" in a poker game, married and, after years of strife and difficulty, ended up homesteading with her husband, Charlie Bemis, along the Salmon River in Idaho.

Although few descriptions exist of early western Chinese marriages, in Butte County, Montana, in 1880, the census records 42 percent of the Chinese men as married but living without wives. Chinese immigration law shaped early marriage policies, as only a couple's children were allowed to emigrate.

Young Asian couple (Idaho State Historical Society)

By 1900, only 5 percent of the ninety thousand Chinese in the west were women—generally large-footed, lower-class Cantonese women whose weddings, despite their poverty, sparked a rollicking festivity of bells, gongs, drums, or fireworks wrapped in red paper. Tiny shredded drifts of paper littered the streets after the firework explosion. While guests watched the parade, the bride began the ritual of changing her clothes.

In China, astrology would dictate the date and time of the wedding—a union that would be sealed by a day's worth of clashing music by cymbal and snare drum. The bride's dark hair, brushed and braided, shone with a thick layer of oil; her cheeks were patted with vermilion paint until they glowed. She would glide in a chair, obscured behind a red curtain, in a bridal procession preceded by a phalanx of flute and horn players, gaily announcing the unfolding of the ceremony by the ritualized notes of the flute.

The bridal array of dresses was a spectator's wonder, one bright silken gown after another, while the groom, resplendent as a mandarin, would drink and banter with his cohorts in a back room. Savory fried pig marked the beginning of the nuptial feast, followed by crab legs or prawns and a costly soup of thin-stripped chicken and fragile noodles, cooked for hours until soft. A dish of creamy white rice served over a bed of creamy red rice signified yin and yang, or fortune, while hazelnut *linzi* invoked fertility and the promise of "a boy every year."

In America, the wedding finery was rented, and for one night the groom would wear brass buttons rather than buttons of cheaper, looped cloth. Often, American neighbors were invited in to sup from heavily laden tables, awash with sweetmeats, confections, roasted chicken or a succulent roasted pig. Reflecting both East and West, the nuptial dinner would provide two favorite dishes: the Buddhist symbol of marital completeness—two mandarin ducks—and two fish for luck in marriage.

In China, a bride would return home to her mother for tea after three days, or kneel ceremonially to serve tea to her mother-in-law. In the West, lacking female relatives or a supportive female society, she was immediately plunged into a workaday life of housekeeping, washing or cooking. According to the Presbyterian mission women, a new bride would "make button holes in shoes . . . a dollar for a dozen pairs," while a husband might earn four hundred dollars a year in trade. Even in a wealthy family, the wife would sew constantly. Ah Foong, a little-footed wife and one of the first women to have come to the West Coast, "lived in the same rooms that she had as a bride, having crossed the threshold but three times in over thirty years." She was seen by the mission women as "young looking" and "well preserved," despite her lack of fresh air and exercise. She had mothered five children and sewed incessantly, despite well-to-do status. "Why do rich Chinese women sew all the time, and rich American women do not?" she was asked. "What can a China woman do?" she replied. "She not sew, she go crazy."

Most West Coast Chinese couples before 1900 lived in utter poverty, usually in the twelve-block-long Chinese quarters in San Francisco—a jumbled warren of tiny, smoke-blackened rooms where single men slept stacked side by side like winnowed grain, or where families shared a kitchen and bathroom, and where the spicy scent of fried meat mingled with dank human stench.

Women had few social options, other than private visits to one another—a proper lady would never be seen on the streets. Their only approved social activity was the Chinese theater, where a woman could sit in special female galleries, hide discreetly behind a fan and giggle at the brightly lit players on stage turning cartwheels, tumbling and capering. Occasionally, men would join their wives for social calls, giving to friends the gifts of "ginger and tea pots, peacock feather fans, litchi nuts, embroidered scarves and China lilies for good luck."

The mission home workers constantly had to fend off Chinese men seeking a second wife who had been taught and trained at their mission school. One such applicant was emphatically declined. Wasn't polygamy a "flagrant transgression" of American laws? He was asked. His reply: "You [know] Utah? You [know] Salt Lake?" Such defense was reinforced by Bret Harte, who called the Chinese "peaceable citizens," and in comparing them with Mormons, found the "balance of immorality" greater toward the Saints than the Celestials.

As more Chinese women emigrated to the west and weddings became more common, the threat of being surreptitiously "sold off" lessened as Chinese men converted to Christianity, or realized that the women trained in the missionary homes were held in respect by the community, and were thus greater assets. The report of the 13th Annual Meeting of the Women's Foreign Mission of 1903 reported "six weddings during the year—five Chinese and one Japanese." One report, citing the admission of eleven new Chinese women, said "all were brought here by men who wished to marry them."

Not all marriages were slave-based or involuntary. Once in America, some couples managed to shake free of taboos regarding love, slaves and indentured servants, and claim marriage, American-style, for themselves. One couple managed to employ the judicial system in their favor. Deeply in love and recently eloped, they then outwitted the woman's slaveholder by persuading the judge who issued a warrant for their arrest that they were of age and unmarried, so why not? In the face of the judge's favorable ruling, the angry slaveholder had no choice but to relinquish his valuable property, the beautiful Cun Cum. He was sobered to realize that all his lofty status in the Chinese community organization of the Sze Yap Chinese Company meant little in an American court of law. Once free, the happy couple thanked their American friends with an "elegant selection of Chinese can-

dies, cakes and confects" given as gifts to one and all.

Slavery was not limited to young or unmarried girls. Miss A. M. Houseworth of the Occidental Mission in San Francisco reported a young married woman who sought help, as she feared that her elderly husband was about to sell her. One obstacle to such rescues was the innate delicacy of the Chinese temperament—despite cruelty and mistreatment, which were daily occasions, women observed a quiet decorum with men. "In six years visiting I have yet to encounter men or women quarreling in the Chinese quarters," wrote one missionary woman. Nor had she ever observed "an indelicate word or look." Women were subservient to Chinese men, whether they lived in China or on the West Coast. Their quiet cooperation was essential. When remonstrated about beating his wife, one San Francisco Chinese man admitted he punished her for gossiping, and worse, for *talking back*. Chinese women were not like American women, he pointed out. "No read, no write, no sense," he explained. Little wonder, as Chinese children had learned *bai hoi*—or to stand aside—to avoid conflict from their earliest years.

This was a question the mission women sought to answer. They fanned out in numbers to the tumbledown homes of the Chinese women, inspecting each hovel for signs of civilized industry and enlightened, Western thought. Any effort made was a step toward ending slavery.

Japanese women who emigrated to America were often "picture brides," married to young Japanese males by proxy in their native villages. Traveling four thousand miles to greet their new mates, each faced a vital question: Would this be a lifelong mistake or a successful union? And furthermore, had he sent a photograph of himself, or someone else? Most Japanese women were innocent of world affairs, had little education, and were particularly shocked by new American ideas and customs.

MRS. HANAYO INOUYE

**Hanayo Inouye differed from many of the illiterate young
"picture brides" who came to America to meet never-before-seen
husbands. As the daughter of a middle-class farming family, her
childhood had been relatively privileged. After eight years of
school, she felt confident in choosing her husband—
a Japanese man visiting the village from America.
Once wed they traveled to California, where they successfully
managed a ranch in Marysville and raised their family.**

We landed in San Francisco . . . in late September. For some time
I just kept wanting to go back home. I . . . was lonely for my
mother. She made me beautiful kimonos when I became of marriageable age, but I never got to put them on, not even once. She
wanted me to wear them when I became a real bride. . . . She used
to tell me, "When you become a bride, neighbors will look forward to seeing you wear new kimonos every day. . . . You have to
wait until then."

Well, naturally, she was not expecting me to leave home so
quickly. . . .

For quite a long time after I came here, I thought of my
mother almost every moment. In fact, when I cut my finger as I
was picking grapes, I called out "Mother!" quite unconsciously.
However, I think I began to like it here for its vastness of land and
for the fact that a day's work meant a day's wages.

When I arrived . . . my husband said, "We are going to the
country. You'd better not put good clothes on." When we got to
the farm, Mr. Omaye showed me around and said, "Please make

yourself comfortable in here." I couldn't be more surprised! He
motioned to a corner of the barn where there was hay spread in a
square shape with a partition! That was all there was! I certainly
did not feel like taking off my clothes and napping there. I never
felt more distressed in my whole life. My husband should have
told me about such conditions before I left Japan. He had shown
me some pictures of himself in suits and of nothing but the best
scenery. Naturally, I thought I was coming to a really nice place
when I left Japan. I might have taken it differently had I been
raised in a less fortunate family. . . .

When I asked my husband where the toilet was, he pointed
outside. It was out in the field. He then told me to hit the toilet
with a stick before going in . . . [as] there were black spiders living
in it. . . . Many people were bitten by those black spiders, and I
heard someone died of a fever caused by the spider bites. I was
quite scared of the place. I realized, however, that no matter how
much I thought of my mother back in Japan or of anybody, it
wouldn't do any good. I knew then I had to live with it and give it
a try. But I told myself I was going back home as soon as I made
some money here.

HU SHI

**Born in 1891, Shi was too young to experience the
full bitterness of exclusionism; instead, he flourished at Cornell
University, where, over a period of seven years, he earned a
bachelor's degree, academic prizes, and even converted to
Christianity. His final conversion came in the midst of a lecture
tour on marriage practices; his pro-Chinese stance began to
falter as he learned more of women's suffrage and observed a
number of American marriages. Shi, as Nationalist China's
ambassador to the United States from 1937 to 1942, was later
chastised for his "worship-America mentality."**

JANUARY 4, 1914

It suddenly occurred to me that the position of women in our
country is high than that of Western women. We look after a
woman's modesty and chastity, and do not allow her to be burdened with having to arrange her marriage, which is taken care of
by parents. Men and women are both born to make families. Our
women do not need to offer themselves in social intercourse for
the sake of marriage; nor need they labor to find a spouse for
themselves. This gives weight to the dignity of women. But in the
West it is not like this. As soon as a woman grows up she devotes
herself to looking for a spouse . . . Those who are plain and dull
or who do not want to lower themselves to charm men end up as
old spinsters. Thus, lowering women's dignity and making them
offer themselves as bait for men is the flaw in Western freedom of
marriage . . .

JANUARY 27, 1914

. . . Love in Western marriages is self-made; love in Chinese marriages is duty-made. After engagement, a woman has a particular
tenderness toward her betrothed. Therefore when she happens to
hear people mention his name, she blushes and feels shy; when
she hears people talk about his activities, she eavesdrops atten-
tively; when she hears about his misfortunes, she feels sad for
him; when she hears about his successes, she rejoices for him. It is
the same with a man's attitude toward his fiancée. By the time
they get married, husband and wife both know that they have a
duty to love each other, and therefore they can frequently be con-
siderate and caring to one another, in order to find love for one
another. Before marriage this was based on imagination and done
out of a sense of duty; afterwards . . . it can develop into genuine
love.

NOVEMBER 22, 1914

Tonight I went over to the room of my friend Mr. Bogart, who is
a teaching assistant in law . . . and we talked about the problem of
marriage. He had heard me lecture on the Chinese marriage system and approved of it. He also thinks that in the Western marriage system choosing a mate is not an easy matter, but takes time,
effort, and money, that the ideal woman may not be found in the
end [and] after a long time one may have to compromise and settle for second best . . .

JANUARY 4, 1915

I took the train to Niagara Falls to visit Dr. and Mrs. Mortimer J.
Brown, who had taught in China for two years . . .

The Browns get along very well. They have no children and
share the burdens of housework . . . This is a most happy Western family. The wife does the washing and cleaning herself, and,
taking pity on her, the husband found a way to buy her a washing

machine to save her work . . . The kitchen table was very low, Mrs. Brown was rather tall, and out of consideration Mr. Brown himself acted as a carpenter to lengthen the legs for her by a foot. Such little matters are sufficient to show the feelings of shared love and concern of this family. In comparison, what do [such traditional Chinese notions of love and honor as] "respecting each other like guests," "raising the tray to eyebrow level," or "painting eyebrows on one's wife" amount to?

OCTOBER 30, 1915
Since knowing Miss Williams, my lifelong views toward women have changed exactly, as have my views about social relations between the sexes . . . Now I have come to realize that the highest goal of women's education lies in creating a type of woman capable of freedom and independence . . .

Family portrait (Idaho State Historical Society)

Bibliography

Ackley, Mary E. *Crossing the Plains and Early Days in California.* San Francisco: Privately printed for author, 1928.

Adams, James Truslow, ed. *Album of American History: Colonial Period.* Chicago: Consolidated Book Publishers, 1954.

Aikman, Duncan. *Calamity Jane and the Lady Wildcats.* Lincoln: University of Nebraska Press, 1987.

Alderson, Nannie T. and Helena Huntington Smith. *A Bride Goes West.* Lincoln: University of Nebraska Press, 1942.

Altherr, Dr. Thomas L. *Procreation or Pleasure? Sexual Attitudes in American History.* Malabar, FL: Robert E. Krieger Publishing Co., 1983.

Anderson, Antone A. and Clara Anderson McDermott. *The Hinckley Fire.* New York: Comet Press Books, 1954.

Arkush, R. David and Leo O. Lee, eds. *Land Without Ghosts: Chinese Impressions of America from the Mid-Nineteenth Century to the Present.* Berkeley: University of California Press, 1989.

Armitage, Susan and Elizabeth Jameson. *The Women's West.* Norman: University of Oklahoma Press, 1987.

Armstrong, Maurice W., Ph.D., Lefferts A. Loetscher, Ph.D., and Charles A. Anderson, M.A. *The Presbyterian Enterprise.* Philadelphia: The Westminster Press, 1956.

Armstrong, David and Elizabeth Metzger. *The Great American Medicine Show.* New York: Prentice Hall, 1991.

Arrington, Leonard J. and Davis Bitton. *The Mormon Experience: A History of the Latter-day Saints.* New York: Alfred A. Knopf, 1979.

Aurand, A. Monroe. *Bundling.* Harrisburg, Pa.: The Aurand Press, 1928.

Bakanowski, Adolf, O.R. *Polish Circuit Rider: The Texas Memoirs of Adolf Bakanowski.* Cheshire, Conn: Cherry Hill Books, 1971.

Bard, Emile; adapted by H. Twitchell. *Chinese Life in Town and Country.* New York and London: G. P. Putnam's Sons, 1905.

Barsness, Larry. *Gold Camp: Alder Gulch and Virginia City, Montana.* New York: Hastings House, 1962.

Bayless, Dorothy Martin and M. Georgeann Mello. *Marriage Affadavits 1893–1897, Sacramento County, California.* Privately printed, limited edition, 1981.

Beauchamp, Rev. William M. *Iroquois Folk Lore: Gathered from the Six Nations of New York.* Port Washington, N.Y.: Ira J. Friedman, Inc., 1922.

Bell, Ernest A. *Fighting the Traffic in Young Girls.* G. S. Ball, 1910.

Bell, E. J., Jr. *Homesteading in Montana: Life in the Blue Mountain Country, 1911–1923.* Bozeman: Big Sky Books, Montana State University, 1975.

Best, J. J., M.D.; Stuart E Brown, Jr., ed. *Letters from Dakota: or Life and Scenes Among the Indians (Fort Berthold Agency, 1889–1890).* Typescript at North Dakota Heritage Center.

Biddle, Ellen McGowan. *Reminiscences of a Soldier's Wife.* Philadelphia: J. B. Lippincott Co., 1907.

Binder, Pearl. *Muffs and Morals.* New York: William Morrow & Co, 1954.

Bishop, Beverly D. and Deborah W. Bolas, eds. *In Her Own Write: Women's History Resources in the Library and Archives of the Missouri Historical Society.* St. Louis: Missouri Historical Society, 1983.

Blair, Karen J., ed. *Women in Pacific Northwest History, An Anthology.* Seattle and London: University of Washington Press, 1988.

Blegen, Theodore C. and Philip D. Jordan. *With Various Voices.* Saint Paul: Itasca Press, 1949.

Blitsten, Dorothy R. *The World of the Family.* New York: Random House, 1963.

Blynet, Molly Dolan. *Wedded Bliss: A Victorian Bride's Handbook.* New York: Abbeville Press, 1992.

Bolton, Herbert Eugene. *Font's Complete Diary: A Chronicle of the Founding of San Francisco.* Berkeley: University of California Press, 1931.

Booth, Edmund. *Forty Niner: The Life Story of a Deaf Pioneer.* Stockton, Cal.: San Joaquin Pioneer and Historical Society, 1953.

Brady, Cyrus Townsend. *Recollections of a Missionary in the Great West.* New York: Charles Scribner's Sons, 1900.

Breathnach, Sarah Ban. *Victorian Family Celebrations: Previously Published as Mrs. Sharp's Traditions.* New York: Simon & Schuster, 1990.

Breed, Nellie E. Private letter, written June 3, 1865. Wells Fargo History Department Collection, San Francisco, Cal.

Briggs, Dr. Wallace A. "Letter to Mrs. Reith Informing Her of Her Pregnancy," July 23, 1896. From the private collection of the Wells Fargo Bank History Department, San Francisco.

Broadbent, J. L. *Celestial Marriage*. Salt Lake City: Shepard Book Co., 1929.

Burner, David, Robert Marcus and Jori Tilson, eds. *America Through the Looking Glass*, Vol. II. Englewood Cliffs, N.J.: Prentice Hall, 1974

Burt, Elizabeth. *Indians, Infants and Infantry*. Denver: Old West Publishing Co., 1960.

Bushman, Claudia, ed. *Mormon Sisters: Women in Early Utah*. Salt Lake City: Olympus Publishing Co., 1976.

Bynum, Victoria E. *Unruly Women: The Politics of Social and Sexual Control in the Old South*. Chapel Hill: University of North Carolina Press, 1992.

Cable, Mary and the editors of *American Heritage*. *American Manners & Morals*. New York: American Heritage Publishing Co., 1969.

Canfield, Chauncey L. *The Diary of a Forty-Niner*. Boston and New York: Houghton Mifflin Company, 1920.

Clark, Dennis Woodruff. "A Letter from San Francisco." *Quarterly of The Society of California Pioneers*, 5:4 (December 1928).

Clifton, James A. *The Prairie People: Continuity and Change in Potawatomi Indian Culture, 1665–1965*. Lawrence, Kans.: The Regents Press of Kansas, 1977.

Cobb, Bess. Personal letter. North Dakota Heritage Center. Dated July 31, 1907; letter from Cobb to Helen Munson, Viroqua, Wis., concerning homesteading in Leipzig, North Dakota.

Cohen, David Steven. *The Dutch-American Farm*. New York: New York University Press, 1992.

Cohen, Rabbi Harry A. *A Basic Jewish Encyclopedia*. Hartmore, Conn.: Hartmore House, 1965.

Collier, E. T. and Sylvia Bailer, eds. *Interviews with Toni Smith and Maria Copa*. San Rafael, Cal.: Miwok Archaeological Preserve of Marin, 1991.

Conant, Roger. *Mercer's Belles: The Journal of a Reporter*. Seattle: University of Washington Press, 1960.

Connolly, S. J. *Priests and People in Pre-Famine Ireland*. New York: St. Martin's Press, 1982.

Corey, Elizabeth; Philip Gerber, ed. *Bachelor Bess: The Homesteading Letters of Elizabeth Corey, 1909–1919*. Iowa City: University of Iowa Press, 1990.

Crawford, Lucy; Stearns Morse, ed. *Lucy Crawford's History of the White Mountains*. Boston: Appalachian Mountain Club, 1978.

Crockett, David. *A Narrative of the Life of David Crockett*. Lincoln: University of Nebraska Press, 1987.

Custer, Elizabeth B. *Tenting on the Plains*. Williamstown, Mass: Corner House Publishers, 1973.

D'Assailly, Gisele. *Ages of Elegance: Five Thousand Years of Fashion and Frivolity*. Paris: Librairie Hachette and Time-Life, 1968.

Dalziel, Hazel Webb. *Joyful Childhood Memories of a Pioneer Woman*. Published by Jack Dalziel and Kirby Dalziel Brock, 1988.

Marquis de Chastellux. *Travels in North America in the Years 1780, 1781 and 1782*. Chapel Hill: University of North Carolina Press, 1963.

d'Emilio, John and Estelle B. Freedman. *Intimate Matters: A History of Sexuality in America*. New York: Harper & Row, 1988.

De Ville, Winston, translator. *Marriage Contracts of Natchitoches, 1739–1803*. Nashville: Benson Printing Company, 1961.

DeQuille, Dan. *Washoe Rambles*. Los Angeles: Dawson's Book Shop, 1963.

Dell, Ernest F. *Love Letters of Famous Men and Women*. New York: Dodd, Mead & Company, 1941.

Dick, Everett. *The Sod House Frontier, 1854–1890: A Social History of the Northern Plains from the Creation of Kansas & Nebraska to the Admission of the Dakotas*. New York: Appleton-Century Co., 1937.

The Doctrines and Discipline of the Methodist Episcopal Church. Cincinnati: Swormsted & Power, 1850.

Douglas, Ann. *The Feminization of American Culture*. New York: Avon Books, 1978.

Dresser, Norine. "Marriage Customs in Early California." *The Californians*. November/December 1991.

Druey, Clifford Merrill, Ph.D. *Presbyterian Panorama*. Philadelphia: Board of Christian Education of the Presbyterian Church, 1952.

Duberman, Martin. *About Time: Exploring the Gay Past*. New York: Penguin Books, 1991.

Duden, Gottfried. *Report on a Journey to the Western States of North America.* Columbia: The State Historical Society of Missouri and University of Missouri Press, 1980.

Dustin, Daniel. Private letter written from French Corral [Cal.], November 2, 1853. From the E. A. Wiltsee collection, frame 73. San Francisco: Wells Fargo Archives.

Dye, Silvia. *Sandhill Stories: Life on the Prairie, 1875–1925.* Berkeley: Parthenon Publications, 1980.

Dyer, John. *The Snow-Shoe Itinerant.* Cincinnati: Cranston & Stowe, 1890.

Earle, Alice Morse. *Two Centuries of Costume in America 1620–1820,* Volume 1. Rutland, Vt.: Charles E. Tuttle Company, 1971

Eggan, Fred. *Social Anthropology of North American Tribes.* Chicago: University of Chicago Press, 1937.

Ehrenreich, Barbara and Deirdre English. *For Her Own Good: 150 Years of Experts' Advice to Women.* New York: Anchor Books, 1978.

Embry, Jessie L. *Mormon Polygamous Families,* Volume One. Salt Lake City: University of Utah Press, 1987.

Emrich, Duncan, ed. *The Folklore of Weddings and Marriage.* New York: American Heritage Press, 1970.

Erdoes, Richard. *Saloons of the Old West.* New York: Alfred A. Knopf, 1979.

Ewart, Shirley. *Cornish Mining Families of Grass Valley, California.* New York: AMS Press, 1989.

Farquhar, Francis P. *The Ralston-Fry Wedding and the Wedding Journey to Yosemite, May 20, 1858, from the Journal of Miss Sarah Haight.* Berkeley: Friends of the Bancroft Library, 1961.

Fielding, William J. *Strange Customs of Courtship and Marriage.* New York: Garden City, 1942.

Fierman, Floyd S. "The Goldberg Brothers: Arizona Pioneers." *The American Jewish Archives,* Vol. XVIII, No. i (April 1966).

Fishman, Nathaniel. *Married Woman's Bill of Rights.* New York: Liveright Publishing Corporation, 1943.

Fisk, Elizabeth Chester; Rex C. Myers, ed. *Lizzie: The Letters of Elizabeth Chester Fisk, 1864–1893.* Helena, Mont.: Mountain Press Publishing Company, 1989.

Foote, Mary Hallock; Rodman W. Paul, ed. *A Victorian Gentlewoman in the Far West.* San Marino, Cal: The Huntington Library, 1972.

Fougera, Katherine Gibson. *With Custer's Cavalry.* Lincoln: University of Nebraska Press, 1968.

French, Emily; Janet Lecompte, ed. *The Diary of a Hard-Worked Woman.* Lincoln: University of Nebraska Press, 1987.

Garvin, Kristina. *The Message of Marriage.* El Paso: Weatherford Publications, 1989.

Gay, Peter. *The Tender Passion: The Bourgeois Experience, Victoria to Freud.* New York: Oxford University Press, 1986.

Gentry, Curt. *The Madams of San Francisco.* Sausalito, Cal: Comstock Editions, Inc., 1964.

Gibbens, Byrd, ed. *This Is a Strange Country. Letters of a Westering Family, 1880–1906.* Albuquerque: University of New Mexico Press, 1988.

Glanz, Dr. Rudolph. *The Jews of California.* New York: Waldon Press, Inc., 1960.

Gleason, James Henry. *Beloved Sister: The Letters of James Henry Gleason, 1841–1859.* Glendale: The Arthur H. Clark Co., 1978.

Goering, Violet and Orlando J. "Jewish Farmers in South Dakota—the Am Olam." *South Dakota History,* Vol. 12, Number 4, Winter 1982.

Goldman, Marion S. *Gold Diggers & Silver Miners: Prostitution and Social Life on the Comstock Lode.* Ann Arbor: University of Michigan Press, 1981.

Goodson, Stephanie Smith. "Plural Wives," *Mormon Sisters,* ed. Claudia L. Bushman. Salt Lake City: Olympus Publishing Co., 1926.

Gould, Stephen. *Chinese in Tustin.* Yorba Linda, Cal.: Shumway Family History Services, 1989.

Grittner, Frederick K. *White Slavery: Myth, Ideology, and American Law.* New York: Garland Publishing, Inc., 1990.

Guerin, Mrs. E. J., *Mountain Charley, or the Adventures of Mrs. E. J. Guerin, Who Was Thirteen Years in Male Attire.* Norman: University of Oklahoma Press, 1968.

Harte, Bret. *Bret Harte's California: Letters to the Springfield Repubican and Christian Register, 1866–76.* Albuquerque: University of New Mexico Press, 1990.

Hawke, David Freeman. *Everyday Life in Early America*. New York: Harper & Row, 1988.

Hayes, Lorena L; Jeanne Hamilton Watson, ed. *To the Land of God and Wickedness: The 1848–59 Diary of Lorena L. Hayes*. St. Louis, Mo.: The Patrice Press, 1988.

Haywood, C. Robert. *Victorian West: Class and Culture in Kansas Cattle Towns*. Lawrence, Kans.: University Press, 1991.

Heiset, Craig N. *The Country Bride Quilt*. Intercourse, Pa.: Good Books, 1988.

Heizer, Robert F., and Alan F. Almquist. *The Other Californians*. Berkeley, Los Angeles: University of California Press, 1971.

Hewes, Claire (Hofer). "Reminiscences." 1898. Ms. in typescript, Special Collections Department, University of Nevada Library, Reno.

Himmelfarb, Gertrude. *Marriage and Morals Among the Victorians*. New York: Alfred A. Knopf, 1986.

Hine, Robert V. *The American West: An Interpretive History*. Boston: Little, Brown and Company, 1973.

Holder, Preston. *The Hoe and the Horse on the Plains*. Lincoln: University of Nebraska Press, 1970.

Hom, Gloria Sun. *Chinese Argonauts: An Anthology of the Chinese Contributions to the Historical Development of Santa Clara County*. San Mateo: Foothill Community College, 1971.

Howard, George Elliott, Ph.D. *A History of Chicago*. Chicago: University of Chicago Press, 1904.

Hudnall, Mary Prowers. "Early History of Bent County." *The Colorado Magazine*. Denver: The State Historical Society of Colorado, Vol. xxii, no. 6, November 1945.

Irvin, Helen Dreiss. *Women in Kentucky*. Lexington, Ky.: University Press of Kentucky, 1979.

Ito, Kazuo. *Issei: A History of Japanese Immigrants in North America*. Seattle: Executive Committee for Publication, 1973.

Jensen, Joan M. and Darlis A. Miler. *New Mexico Women: Intercultural Perspectives*. Albuquerque: University of New Mexico Press, 1986.

Jones, Evan. "The Lore of the Wedding Cake." *Bon Appetit,* June 1991, p. 12.

Jones-Eddy, Julie. *Homesteading Women: An Oral History of Colorado, 1890–1905*. New York: Twayne Publishers, 1992.

Kaganoff, Nathan M., Librarian. *Preliminary Survey of the Manuscript Collections Found in the American Jewish Historical Society Library*. New York: American Jewish Historical Society, 1967.

Kaplan, Marion A. *The Marriage Bargain: Women and Doweries in European History*. New York: The Haworth Press, 1985.

Kasper, Shirl. "Annie Oakley: The Magical Year in London." *Montana*, Vol. 42:2, Spring 1992.

Kendall, George Wilkins. *Narrative of the Texan Santa Fe Expedition*, Vol II. Austin: The Steck Company, 1935.

Kennedy, Michael Stephen. *The Assiniboines: From the Accounts of the Old Ones Told to First Boy (James Larpenteur Long)*. Norman: University of Oklahoma Press, 1961.

Kephart, Horace. *Our Southern Highlanders*. New York: Outing Publishing Company, 1913.

King, Charles. *Campaigning with Crook*. Norman: University of Oklahoma Press, 1978.

Koch, Christian, ed. (Peter Koch Lutken). *Diary, 1831–1836*. Private collection.

Kohl, Edith Eudora. *Land of the Burnt Thigh*. New York: Funk & Wagnalls Company, 1938.

Koren, Elisabeth. *The Diary of Elisabeth Koren* Northfield, Minn.: North Central Publishing Co., 1955.

Kraemer, David. *The Jewish Family: Metaphor and Memory*. New York: Oxford University Press, 1989.

Lampe, Philip E. *Adultery in the United States*. Buffalo: Prometheus Books, 1987.

Lanier, Doris. "The Early Chautauqua in Georgia." *Journal of American Culture*. Vol. II: 3, Fall 1988.

Larkin, James Ross. *Reluctant Frontiersman: James Ross Larkin on the Santa Fe Trail 1856–1857*. Albuquerque: University of New Mexico Press, 1990.

Laverick, Elizabeth. *With This Ring*. London: Elm Tree Books, 1979.

Lederer, Richard M., Jr. *Colonial American English*. Essex, Conn.: Verbatim, 1985.

Levinson, Alice Gerstle. *Family Reminiscences: An Interview Conducted by Ruth Teiser*. Berkeley: University of California Regional Oral History Office, Bancroft Library, Berkeley, 1967 .

Levi, John Newmark, Sr. "This Is the Way We Used to Live." *Western States Jewish Historical Quarterly*, Vol. IV, Nos. 1–4.

Levorsen, Barbara. *The Quiet Conquest: A History of the Lives and Times of the First Settlers of Central North Dakota*. Hawley, Minn: *The Hawley Herald*, 1974.

Lewis, Jan. *The Pursuit of Happiness: Family and Values in Jefferson's Virginia*. London: Cambridge University Press, 1983.

Lieber, Constance L., and John Sillito, eds. *Letters from Exile: The Correspondence of Martha Hughes Cannon and Angus M. Cannon 1886–1888*. Salt Lake City: Signature Books, 1989.

Lipsett, Linda Otto. *To Love and to Cherish: Brides Remembered*. San Francisco: Quilt Digest Press, 1989.

Lohmolder, Jo, Lois Young and Laura Z. Clavio. "Ideas for an Herbal Wedding: Special Touches in Decor, Gifts and Food." *The Herb Companion,* June/July 1990, pp. 22–31.

Lord, Eliot. *The Italians in America*. New York: B.F. Buck & Co., 1906.

Lowe, Blanche Beal. "Growing Up in Kansas." *Kansas History,* Vol. 12:2, Summer 1989.

Luchetti, Cathy. *Home on the Range: A Culinary History of the American West*. New York: Villard, 1993.

Luchetti, Cathy. *Under God's Spell: Frontier Evangelists 1772–1915*. San Diego: Harcourt Brace, 1989.

Luchetti, Cathy, in collaboration with Carol Olwell. *Women of the West*. New York: Orion Books, 1992.

Lundwall, N. B. *Marrying Out of the Faith*. Dugway, Utah: Pioneer Press, 1968.

Lystra, Karen. *Searching the Heart: Women, Men and Romantic Love in Nineteenth-Century America*. New York: Oxford University Press, 1989.

McCunn, Ruthanne Lum. *Chinese American Portraits: Personal Histories 1828–1988*. San Francisco: Chronicle Books, 1988.

McDaniel, George W. *Hearth and Home: Preserving a People's Culture*. Philadelphia: Temple University Press, 1982.

Mackey, Margaret Gilbert. *Early California Costumes, 1796–1850*. Stanford: Stanford University Press, 1932.

McLeod, Alexander. *Pigtails and Gold Dust*. Caldwell, Idaho: The Caxton Printers, 1967.

McWhorter, L. V. *Hear Me, My Chiefs! Nez Perce History and Legend*. Caldwell, Idaho: The Caxton Printers, 1983.

Marryat, Captain Frederick. *Narrative of the Travels and Adventures of Monsieur Violet*. New York: Harper & Brothers, 1843.

Marshall, Rosalind K. *Virgins and Viragos: A History of Women in Scotland from 1080 to 1980*. Chicago: Academy Chicago Ltd., 1983.

Mathews, Mary McNair. *Ten Years in Nevada or Life on the Pacific Coast*. Originally published: Buffalo: Baker, Jones, 1880. Reissued: Lincoln: University of Nevada Press, 1985.

Matlins, Antoinette, Antonio Bonano, and Jane Crystal. *Engagement & Wedding Rings. The Definitive Buying Guide for People in Love*. South Woodstock, Vt.: Gemstone Press, 1990.

Mauriceau, Dr. A. M. *The Married Woman's Private Medical Companion*. New York: privately printed, 1849.

May, Elaine T. *Great Expectations: Marriage and Divorce in Post-Victorian America*. Chicago: University of Chicago Press, 1981.

Meilleur, Helen. *A Pour of Rain: Stories from a West Coast Fort*. Victoria, B.C.: Sono Nis Press, 1980.

Merriam, Florence A. *My Summer in a Mormon Village*. Boston and New York: Houghton, Mifflin and Company, 1894.

Minkema, Kenneth P. "Hannah and Her Sisters: Sisterhood, Courtship and Marriage in the Edwards Family in the Early Eighteenth Century." January 1991 (V. Turner, citation).

Mitchell, Edwin Valentine. *It's an Old New England Custom*. New York: Bonanza Books, Inc., 1955.

Moore, Arthur K. *The Frontier Mind*. New York: McGraw-Hill, 1963.

Montgomery, James W. *Liberated Woman: A Life of May Arkwright Hutton*. Spokane: Gingko House Publishers, 1974.

Mosher, Celia Duel. *The Mosher Survey: Sexual Attitudes of 45 Victorian Women*. New York: Arno Press, 1980.

Motz, Marilyn Ferris. *True Sisterhood: Michigan Women and Their Kin, 1820–1920*. Albany: State University of New York Press, 1983.

Moynihan, Ruth B., Susan Armitage and Christine Fischer Dichamp, eds. *So Much to Be Done: Women Settlers on the Mining and Ranching Frontier.* Lincoln: University of Nebraska Press, 1990.

Nevins, Allan, ed. *America Through British Eyes.* New York: Oxford University Press, 1948.

Newmark, Rosa. "A Letter from Mother to Daughter: Los Angeles to New York, 1867." *Western States Jewish Historical Quarterly.* 5:1, October 1972.

Nicholson, Shirley. *A Victorian Household: Based on the Diaries of Marion Sambourne.* London: Barrie & Jenkins, 1988.

Noall, Claire. *Guardians of the Hearth: Utah's Pioneer Midwives and Women Doctors.* Bountiful, Utah: Horizon Publishers, 1974.

Osterud, Nancy Grey. *Bonds of Community: The Lives of Farm Women in Nineteenth-Century New York.* Ithaca: Cornell University Press, 1991.

Pachter, Marc, ed. *Abroad in America: Visitors to the New Nation 1776–1914.* Reading, Mass: Addison-Wesley Publishing Company in Association with the National Portrait Gallery, Smithsonian Institution, 1976.

Patterson-Black, Sheryll. "Women Homesteaders on the Great Plains Frontier," *Frontiers* 1 (Spring 1976).

Perkin, J. *Women and Marriage in Nineteenth-Century England.* London: Routledge, 1989.

Phillips, Roderick. *Putting Asunder: A History of Divorce in Western Society.* Cambridge: Cambridge University Press, 1988.

Pierce, Josiah Jr. *Letters to Laura: Letters from Josiah Pierce, Jr., to Laura Dunham, 1884–1889.* Boston: The Godine Press, 1974.

Poling-Kempes, Lesley. *The Harvey Girls: Women Who Opened the West.* New York: Paragon House, 1991.

Powers, Stephen. *Tribes of California.* Berkeley: University of California Press, 1976.

Mary Prag Papers: "Reminiscences of Her Days with the Mormons." Judah Magnes Memorial Museum.

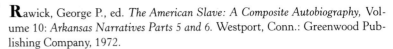

Rawick, George P., ed. *The American Slave: A Composite Autobiography,* Volume 10: *Arkansas Narratives Parts 5 and 6.* Westport, Conn.: Greenwood Publishing Company, 1972.

Rawick, George P., ed. *The American Slave: A Composite Autobiography, Volume 16: Kansas, Kentucky, Maryland, Ohio, Virginia, and Tennessee Narratives.* Westport, Conn.: Greenwood Publishing Company, 1972.

Redmond, Elizabeth. "The Codman Collection of Pictures." *Old Time New England: The Bulletin of The Society for the Preservation of New England Antiquities,* Vol. LXXI. Cambridge, 1981, pp. 103–113.

Reese, Linda W. "Dear Oklahoma Lady." *Chronicles of Oklahoma* 68:3, Fall 1988.

Reichlin, Ellie. "Reading Family Photographs: A Contextual Analysis of the Codman Family Photographic Collection." *Old Time New England: The Bulletin of The Society for the Preservation of New England Antiquities,* Vol. LXXI. Cambridge, 1981, pp. 115–149.

Richards, Clarice E. *A Tenderfoot Bride.* New York: Fleming H. Revell Company, 1920.

Riley, Glenda. *The Female Frontier: A Comparative View of Women on the Prairie and the Plains.* Lawrence: University of Kansas Press, 1988.

Riley, Glenda. *Frontierswomen: The Iowa Experience.* Ames: Iowa State University Press, 1981.

Riley, Glenda, ed. "Proving Up: The Memoir of Girl Homesteader Martha Stoecker Norby." *South Dakota History,* 16:1, Spring 1986.

Riley, Glenda. "Torn Asunder: Divorce in Early Oklahoma Territory." *Chronicles of Oklahoma,* 68:4, Winter 1989–90.

Rohrlich, Ruby and Elaine Hoffman Baruch. *Women in Search of Utopia: Mavericks and Mythmakers.* New York: Schocken Books, 1984.

Root, Riley. *Journal of Travels from St. Joseph to Oregon.* Oakland: Biobooks, 1955.

Roscoe, Will. *The Zuni Man-Woman.* Albuquerque: University of New Mexico Press, 1991.

Rosen, Ruth. *The Lost Sisterhood: Prostitution in America, 1900–1918.* Baltimore: Johns Hopkins University Press, 1982.

Rosen, Ruth, ed. *The Maimie Papers.* New York: The Feminist Press in Cooperation with the Schlesinger Library of Radcliffe College, 1977.

Rosenbaum, Fred. *Free to Choose: The Making of a Jewish Community in the American West.* Berkeley: The Judah L. Magnes Memorial Museum, 1976.

Ross, Nancy Wilson. *Westward the Women.* New York: Alfred A. Knopf, 1944.

Ross, Pat. *With Thanks & Appreciation: The Sweet Nellie Book of Thoughts, Sentiments, Tokens and Traditions of the Past.* New York: Viking Studio Books, 1989.

Rothman, Ellen K. *Hands and Hearts: A History of Courtship in America.* New York: Basic Books, 1984.

Ruether, Rosemary and Rosemary Skinner Keller. *Women and Religion in America,* Volume 3: *1900–1968.* San Francisco: Harper & Row, 1986.

Russell, Marian. *Land of Enchantment: Memoirs of Marian Russell Along the Santa Fe Trail.* Evanston, Ill.: The Branding Iron Press, 1954.

Salamon, Sonya. *From Prairie Patrimony: Family, Farming and Community in the Midwest.* Chapel Hill: University of North Carolina Press, 1992.

Sanford, Mollie Dorsey. *Mollie: The Journal of Mollie Dorsey Sanford in Nebraska and Colorado Territories 1857–1866.* Lincoln: University of Nebraska Press, 1959.

Sarasohn, Eileen Sunada. *The Issei: Portrait of a Pioneer, an Oral History.* Palo Alto, Cal.: Pacific Books, 1983.

Savager, W. Sherman. *Blacks in the West.* Westport, CT: Greenwood Publishing Company, 1976.

Scandinavian Jubilee Album. Salt Lake City: Press of the Deseret News, 1900.

Scheuerman, Richard D. and Clifford E. Trafzer. *The Volga Germans.* Moscow: University Press of Idaho, 1980.

Schill, Loula Blair. "Some Memories of Loula Blair Schill, 1876–1966." Manuscript, private collection of David Brownell.

Schlissel, Lillian. *Women's Diaries of the Westward Journey.* New York: Schocken Books, 1982, 1992.

Schlissel, Lillian, and Byrd Gibbens and Elizabeth Hampsten. *Far from Home.* New York: Schocken Books, 1989.

Siu, Bobby. *Women of China: Imperialism and Women's Resistance 1900–1949.* London: Zed Press, 1982.

Slayden, Ellen Maury. *Washington Wife: Journal of Ellen Maury Slayden.* New York and Evanston: Harper and Row, 1962.

Sloane, Eric. *The Seasons of America Past.* New York: Promontory Press, 1987.

Smith, Barbara Clark and Kathy Peiss. *Men and Women: A History of Costume, Gender and Power.* Washington: The Smithsonian, 1989.

Smith, Merril D. *Breaking the Bonds: Marital Discord in Pennsylvania, 1730-1830.* New York: New York University Press, 1991.

Soderlund, Jean. "Women's Authority in Pennsylvania and New Jersey Quaker Meetings, 1680–1760." *William & Mary Quarterly,* 44, October 1987.

Solano, Isadora. Bancroft Interview. MSS transcript. Bancroft Library, University of California.

Spence, Jonathan D. *The Death of Woman Wang.* New York: Viking Press, 1978.

Stapley, Sophia Parker. *Together Again: An Autobiographical History.* Oakland, Cal: Third Party Associates, Inc., 1976.

Stiles, Henry Reed. *Bundling: Its Origin, Progress and Decline in America.* Cambridge, Miss: Applewood Books, n.d. (reprint from 1800s).

Strahorn, Carrie Adell. *Fifteen Thousand Miles by Stage.* New York: G. P. Putnam's Sons, 1911.

Stratton, Joanna L. *Pioneer Women: Voices from the Kansas Frontier.* New York: Simon and Schuster, 1981.

Summerhays, Martha. Milton Quaife, ed. *Vanished Arizona: Recollections of My Army Life.* Chicago: The Lakeside Press, 1939.

Sweet, William Warren. *Religion on the American Frontier: The Baptists, 1783–1830.* New York: Cooper Square Publishers, 1964.

Tally, Frances. "American Folk Customs of Courtship and Marriage: The Bedroom." *Forms Upon the Frontier.* Utah State University Monograph Series, Vol. XVI, No. 2, April 1968.

Taves, Ann. *Religion and Domestic Violence in Early New England: The Memoirs of Abigail Abbot Bailey.* Bloomington: Indiana University Press, 1989.

Taylor, Joyce L. "A Profile of Three American Women 1888–1983." Paper presented at San Diego State University, 1983.

Terrell, John Upton and Donna M. *Indian Women of the Western Morning: Their Life in Early America.* Garden City, N.Y.: Anchor Books, 1976.

Time-Life Books, eds. Text by Joan Swallow. *The Women.* Alexandria, Va.: Time-Life Books, 1978.

Timmons, William. *Twilight on the Range: Recollections of a Latterday Cowboy.* Austin: University of Texas Press, 1962.

Toor, Frances. *A Treasury of Mexican Folkways*. New York: Crown Publishers, 1947.

Tullock, James Francis. Compiled and edited by Gordon Keith. *The James Francis Tullock Diary 1875–1910*. Portland, Ore.: Binford & Mort, 1978.

Twitchell, H. *Chinese Life in Town and Country: Adapted from the French of Emie Bard*. New York and London: G. P. Putnam's Sons, 1905.

Ubbelohde, Carl, Maxine Benson, Duane A. Smith, eds. *A Colorado Reader*. Denver: Pruett Publishing Company,

Unruh, John D. *The Plains Across: The Overland Emigrants and the Trans-Mississippi West, 1840–60*. Urbana: University of Illinois Press, 1982.

Van Kirk, Sylvia. "The Role of Native Women in the Creation of Fur Trade Society in Western Canada, 1670–1830." *The Women's West*. Norman: University of Oklahoma Press, 1987.

Vorspan, Max and Lloyd P. Gartner. *History of the Jews of Los Angeles*. San Marino: The Huntington Library, 1970.

Waltz, Anna Langhorne. "West River Pioneer: A Woman's Story, 1911–1915." *South Dakota History*, Vol. 17:2, Summer 1987.

Ward, Harriet Sherril. *Prairie Schooner Lady: The Journal of Harriet Sherril Ward, 1853*. Los Angeles: Westernlore Press, 1959.

Waters, Lydia Milner. "Account of a Trip Across the Plains in 1855." *Quarterly of The Society of California Pioneers*, 6:2, June 1929.

Watters, T. *Stories of Everyday Life in Modern China: Told by Chinese and Done into English*. London: David Nutt, Stand, 1896.

Wells, E. Hazard. *Magnificence and Misery: A Firsthand Account of the 1897 Klondike Gold Rush*. New York: Doubleday & Company, 1984.

The Western Writers of America. *The Women Who Made the West*. New York: Doubleday & Company, 1980.

Williams, George III. *Rosa May: A Search for a Mining Camp Legend*. Dayton, Nev: Tree by the River Publishing Company, 1979.

Willis, Ann Bassett. "Queen Ann of Brown's Park." *The Colorado Magazine*, 29:82, (April 1952), 93–96.

Woloch, Nancy. *Women and the American Experience*. New York: Alfred A. Knopf, 1984.

Wood, Edward J. *The Wedding Day in All Ages and Countries*. New York: Harper and Bros, 1869.

Wunder, John R. *At Home on the Range: Essays on the History of Western Social and Domestic Life*. Westport, Conn.: Greenwood Press, 1985.

Young, Brigham. *The Diary of Brigham Young, 1857*. Salt Lake City: Tanner Trust Fund, University of Utah Library, 1980.

Zanjini, Sally, "Hang Me If You Will: Violence in the Last Western Mining Boomtown," *Montana*, Vol 42:2, Spring 1992.

Caroline Lockhart
(American Heritage Center, University of Wyoming)

Sources and Acknowledgments

Carlisle Abbott's story is taken from his book *Recollections of a California Pioneer* (New York: The Neale Publishing Company, 1917).

Mary E. Ackley's story is taken from *Crossing the Plains and Early Days in California: Memories of Girlhood in California's Golden Age*, privately printed for the author, 1928.

A segment reprinted from *A Bride Goes West*, by Nannie T. Alderson and Helena Huntington Smith, copyright © 1942 by Farrar and Rinehart, Inc. renewed is used with permission of the University of Nebraska Press.

Excerpts of the journal of Harriet Ames are taken from the typescript copy at Library of Congress.

Permission to use a portion of *Tomboy Bride*, by Harriet Fish Backus, is granted by Pruett Publishing, Boulder, Colorado.

Abigail Bailey's reminiscences, reprinted here with the permission of the Indiana University Press, are from *Religion and Domestic Violence in Early New England: The Memoirs of Abigail Abbot Bailey* by Ann Taves.

The writings of Cyrus Townsend Brady are found in *Recollections of a Missionary in the Great West* (New York: Charles Scribner's Sons, 1900).

Permission to publish an excerpt from the typescript memoir of Sarah Elizabeth Canfield is granted by the State Historical Society of North Dakota.

Permission to quote from the writings of Tommie Clack's book, with Mollie Clack, *Pioneer Days . . . Two Views* (Texas: Reporter Publishing Company, 1979), has been given by the author and the Reporter Publishing Company.

Permission has been granted by the University of Washington Press to use a portion of select material from Roger Conant's *Mercer's Belles* (Seattle: University of Washington Press, 1960).

The story of John Connell is taken from the book *From River Clyde to Tymochtee and Col. William Crawford* by Grace U. Emahiser, 1964.

David Crockett's story comes from an early 1834 edition published by E. L. Carey and A. Hart, Philadelphia, titled *A Narrative of the Life of David Crockett*, reprinted by the University of Nebraska Press, 1987, with an introduction by Paul Andrew Hutton.

The story of Hannah Crosby comes from *Sketch of the Life of Hannah A. Crosby*, taken from the Historical Records Survey and the Federal Writers Project of the Utah Works Administration, 1935–1939.

Permission to publish the letter of Frank Cushing has been granted by the Southwest Museum.

Harriet Newell Jones Dodd's account from the William B. Dodd and Family Papers is published with the permission of the Minnesota Historical Society.

The stories of Peggy and Lorenzo Dow are taken from Dow's autobiography, *The Dealings of God, Man and the Devil* (St. Louis, 1849).

Permission to publish a segment of the writings of *The Life of an Ordinary Woman* by Anne Ellis has been granted by Houghton Mifflin Company.

Emily French's *Diary of a Hard-Worked Woman* is quoted by permission of University of Nebraska.

Permission to publish excerpts of Katherine Gibson Fougera's reminiscences from *With Custer's Cavalry* have been granted by the author's heir, Margaret G. Lewis.

Permission to excerpt from Andrew Garcia's *Tough Trip Through Paradise*, edited and introduced by Bennett H. Stein, has been granted by Houghton Mifflin Company.

Permission to use a portion of *Beloved Sister: The Letters of James Henry Gleason, 1841 to 1859* has been granted by the Arthur H. Clark Co.

The divorce materials of Ellen Coile Graves come from the divorce record of *Graves* vs. *Graves*, and are published by permission of the Chester County Archives, West Chester, Pennsylvania.

The life of Mountain Charley is exerpted from her memoirs, *Mountain Charley, or the Adventures of Mrs. E. J. Guerin, Who Was Thirteen Years in Male Attire*, reprinted by the University of Oklahoma Press, 1968.

Ann Hafen's reminiscences are taken from "Grandmother Hafen's Life Story," by Ann Hafen, Bunkerville, Nevada, and privately printed for her descendants in Denver, Colorado, 1938, in the book *Memories of a Handcart Pioneer*.

Mary Jane Hayden's memoir is from her book *Pioneer Days* (San Jose, Cal: Murgotten's, 1915).

The story of Hanayo Inouye is published with the permission of the Issei Oral History Project, Inc., and was taken from *The Issei*, ed. Eileen Sunada Sarasohn (Palo Alto, Cal.: Pacific Books, 1983).

Malinda Jenkins's story comes from *The Gambler's Wife: The Life of Malinda Jenkins* (Boston: Houghton Mifflin Company, 1933).

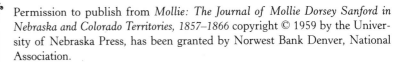

Permission to publish a portion of Harriet Levy's *920 O'Farrell Street* has been granted by Doubleday & Co.

Excerpts are taken from Mary McNair Matthews's *Ten Years in Nevada, or, Life on the Pacific Coast,* published by Baker, Jones & Co., 1880.

The reminiscences of Florence A. Merriam are taken from *My Summer in a Mormon Village* (Boston and New York: Houghton, Mifflin and Company, 1894).

Permission to quote from the oral history of Laura Black Bear Miles is granted by her grandson, Victor Orange.

Permission to publish an excerpt from the life of Anna Brewster Morgan is granted by Simon & Schuster, publisher of *Pioneer Women,* copyright © 1981 by Joanna L. Stratton.

The material for Anna Cora Mowatt's story is drawn for *Autobiography of an Actress* (Boston: Ticknor, Reed & Fields, 1853).

The University of Nevada Press has granted permission to use material from Sarah E. Olds's *Twenty Miles from a Match: Homesteading in Western Nevada.*

Bethenia Owens-Adair's memoirs come from her autobiography, *Dr. Owens-Adair, Some of Her Life Experiences,* published in 1906 by Mann and Beach, Portland, Oregon.

Permission to publish a segment of the diary of Keturah Penton is granted by Bonnie Belknap and Arthur Bayley.

Permission to quote from the reminiscences of Maimie Pinzer has been granted by the Schlesinger Library. The excerpt is taken from *The Maimie Papers,* edited by Ruth Rosen (New York: The Feminist Press in cooperation with the Schlesinger Library of Radcliffe College, 1977).

Permission to use an excerpt from *A Tenderfoot Bride* by Clarice E. Richards (New York, 1920) has been granted by the Fleming H. Revell Company.

Permission to cite an excerpt from the George Riley diary, from the book *Bonds of Community: The Lives of Farm Women in Nineteenth Century New York,* by Nancy Grey Osterud, is granted by Cornell University Press, 1991.

Jessie Hill Rowland's story in *Pioneer Women* by Joanna Stratton is quoted by permission of Simon & Schuster.

Portions of Marian Sloan Russell's memoirs, *The Land of Enchantment: Memoirs of Marian Russell Along the Santa Fe Trail,* have been included; her story is published by the University of New Mexico Press.

Permission to publish from *Mollie: The Journal of Mollie Dorsey Sanford in Nebraska and Colorado Territories, 1857–1866* copyright © 1959 by the University of Nebraska Press, has been granted by Norwest Bank Denver, National Association.

Hu Shi's impressions come from Hu Shi, "Meiguo de furen" (American women), in *Hu Shi wencun* (Essays of Hu Shi) (Shanghai: Yadong, 1921, first published in *Xin gingnian* 5[3] [September 15, 1918], 213–14.

Portions from the letters of Elinore Pruitt Stewart were reprinted from *Letters on an Elk Hunt* (Lincoln: University of Nebraska Press, 1979); permission to reprint an excerpt from one letter has been granted by the Houghton Mifflin Company; the material is drawn from *Letters of a Woman Homesteader,* copyright ©1913 and 1914 by *The Atlantic Monthly;* 1914 and 1942 by Elinore Pruitt Stewart.

Martha Summerhayes' *Vanished Arizona: Recollections of My Army Life* was printed in Philadelphia by J. B. Lippincott Co., 1908.

John Thornburn's story comes from the John Thornburn Reminiscence, a handwritten autobiography, 1864, published here with the permission of the Montana Historical Society.

Excerpts from *Twilight on the Range: Recollections of a Latterday Cowboy* by William Timmons, copyright © 1962, are used by permission of the University of Texas Press.

Carrie Williams's reminiscence is drawn from the letters of Carrie Williams and published with the permission of the Beinecke Rare Book and Manuscript Library, Yale University, New Haven, Connecticut.

An excerpt from the letters of Pauline Lyons Williamson is published with the permission of the New York Public Library, New York.

Index